P9-DEW-786

Math in Focus®

Singapore Math®
by Marshall Cavendish

Consultant and Author
Dr. Fong Ho Kheong

Authors
Chelvi Ramakrishnan and Gan Kee Soon

U.S. Consultants
Dr. Richard Bisk
Andy Clark
Patsy F. Kanter

U.S. Distributor

Published by Marshall Cavendish Education
An imprint of Marshall Cavendish Education Private Limited
Times Centre, 1 New Industrial Road, Singapore 536196
Customer Service Hotline: (65) 6213 9444
U.S. Office Tel: (1-914) 332 8888 Fax: (1-914) 332 8882
E-mail: tmesales@mceducation.com
Website: www.mceducation.com

Distributed by
Houghton Mifflin Harcourt
222 Berkeley Street
Boston, MA 02116
Tel: 617-351-5000
Website: www.hmheducation.com/mathinfocus

First published 2015

Math in Focus® Student Book 5A
ISBN 978-0-544-19363-5

Printed in the United States of America

1 2 3 4 5 6 7 8 1401 20 19 18 17 16 15
4500463700 A B C D E

Contents

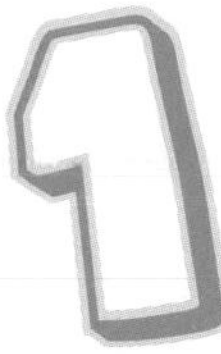

Whole Numbers

Chapter Opener 1

Recall Prior Knowledge 2

• Writing numbers in word form, standard form, and expanded form • Identifying the value of each digit in a number • Comparing numbers • Rounding to the nearest hundred • Using rounding and front-end estimation to estimate sums and differences

Quick Check

1 Numbers to 10,000,000 5

Learn Count by ten thousands • Write numbers in standard form and word form • Read numbers to 1,000,000 by periods • Count by hundred thousands • Write numbers in standard form and word form • Read numbers to 10,000,000 by periods

Hands-On Activity Search for quantities that occur in the millions on the Internet

Let's Explore Explore negative numbers in context

2 Place Value 16

Learn Each digit of a number has a value and a place • Numbers to 1,000,000 can be written in expanded form • Each digit of a number has a value and a place • Numbers to 10,000,000 can be written in expanded form

Look for **Practice and Problem Solving**

Student Book A and Student Book B	Workbook A and Workbook B
• **Let's Practice** in every lesson • **Put on Your Thinking Cap!** in every chapter	• **Independent Practice** for every lesson • **Put on Your Thinking Cap!** in every chapter

3 Comparing Numbers to 10,000,000 20

Learn Compare numbers by using a place-value chart • Compare numbers greater than 1,000,000 • Find rules to complete number patterns

4 Rounding and Estimating 25

Learn Round numbers to the greater thousand • Round numbers to the thousand that is less • Use rounding to estimate sums and differences • Use front-end estimation with adjustment to estimate sums • Use front-end estimation with adjustment to estimate differences • Use rounding to estimate products • Use compatible numbers to estimate quotients

Put on Your Thinking Cap! Problem Solving 35

Chapter Wrap-Up 36

Chapter Review/Test 38

Hundred Thousands	Ten Thousands	Thousands	Hundreds	Tens	Ones
2	3	7	9	8	1
5	0	0	6	0	0

Look for **Assessment Opportunities**

Student Book A and Student Book B	Workbook A and Workbook B
• **Quick Check** at the beginning of every chapter to assess chapter readiness • **Guided Learning** after every example or two to assess readiness to continue lesson • **Chapter Review/Test** in every chapter to review or test chapter material	• **Cumulative Reviews** six times during the year • **Mid-Year and End-of-Year Reviews** to assess test readiness

Whole Number Multiplication and Division

Chapter Opener 41

Recall Prior Knowledge Writing numbers in expanded form and word form • Using bar models to show the four operations • Rounding to the nearest thousand • Estimating products by rounding • Estimating products by using front-end estimation • Estimating quotients by using related multiplication facts 42

Quick Check

1 Using a Calculator 47

Learn Get to know your calculator • Use your calculator to add • Use your calculator to subtract • Use your calculator to multiply • Use your calculator to divide

Hands-On Activities Practice entering numbers into the calculator • Find sums and differences using a calculator • Find products and quotients using a calculator

2 Multiplying by Tens, Hundreds, or Thousands 51

Learn Look for a pattern in the products when 10 is a factor • Break apart a number to help you multiply by tens • Look for a pattern in the products when 100 or 1,000 is a factor • Break apart a number to help you multiply by hundreds or thousands • Round factors to the nearest ten or hundred to estimate products • Round factors to the nearest ten or thousand to estimate products

Hands-On Activities Use place value to find a rule for multiplying a whole number by 10 • Break apart factors that are multiples of 10 (Associative Property) • Use place value to find a rule for multiplying a whole number by 100 or 1,000 • Break apart factors that are multiples of 100 or 1,000 (Associative Property)

3 **Multiplying by Powers of Ten** 64

Learn Look for a pattern in products when 10^2 is a factor • Look for a pattern in products when 10^3 is a factor • Use exponents to solve problems

4 **Multiplying by 2-Digit Numbers** 68

Learn Multiply a 2-digit number by tens • Multiply a 2-digit number by a 2-digit number • Multiply a 3-digit number by tens • Multiply a 3-digit number by a 2-digit number • Multiply a 4-digit number by tens • Multiply a 4-digit number by a 2-digit number

5 **Dividing by Tens, Hundreds, or Thousands** 74

Learn Look for patterns when dividing by 10 • Break apart a number to help you divide by tens • Look for patterns when dividing by 100 or 1,000 • Break apart a number to help you divide by hundreds or thousands • Round numbers to estimate quotients
Hands-On Activities Use place value to find a rule for dividing a whole number by 10 • Break apart divisors that are multiples of 10 (Associative Property) • Use place value to find rules for dividing a multiple of 100 or 1,000 by 100 or 1,000 • Break apart divisors that are multiples of 100 or 1,000 (Associative Property) • Find divisors of given whole numbers that are multiples of tens, hundreds or thousands
Let's Explore Use a place-value table to divide whole numbers that are not multiples of 10 or 100 by 10 or 100

6 **Dividing by 2-Digit Numbers** 86

Learn Use different methods to divide by tens • Divide a 2-digit number by a 2-digit number • Divide a 3-digit number by a 2-digit number • Divide the tens before dividing the ones • Divide a 4-digit number by a 2-digit number • Divide the hundreds, then the tens, and then the ones
Math Journal Reading and Writing Math

7 Order of Operations 94

Learn Work from left to right when a numeric expression uses only addition and subtraction • Work from left to right when a numeric expression uses only multiplication and division • Always work from left to right. Multiply and divide first. Then add and subtract • Carry out any operations in parentheses first • Order of operations • Carry out operations in parentheses before operations in brackets • Order of operations

Hands-On Activity Form numeric expressions with two or more operations and then simplify them

Let's Explore Explore the meaning of 'left to right' in the order of operations

8 Real-World Problems: Multiplication and Division 102

Learn The remainder can be part of an answer • Increase the quotient when it includes the remainder • Some problems require two steps to solve • Some problems require more than two steps to solve • Read a table to find information • Solve problems by drawing bar models • Some problems can be solved using other strategies

Put on Your Thinking Cap! Problem Solving 115

Chapter Wrap-Up 116

Chapter Review/Test 118

	Ten Thousands	Thousands	Hundreds	Tens	Ones
900			●●●●●●●●●		
900 ÷ 100					●●●●●●●●●
14,000	●	●●●●			
14,000 ÷ 1000				●	●●●●

3 Fractions and Mixed Numbers

Chapter Opener 120

Recall Prior Knowledge Like fractions have the same denominator • Unlike fractions have different denominators • A mixed number consists of a whole number and a fraction • Finding equivalent fractions• Expressing fractions in simplest form • Representing fractions on a number line • Identifying prime and composite numbers • Expressing improper fractions as mixed numbers • Adding and subtracting like fractions • Adding and subtracting unlike fractions • Reading and writing tenths and hundredths in decimal and fractional forms • Expressing fractions as decimals 121

Quick Check

1 Adding Unlike Fractions 128

Learn Find common denominators to add unlike fractions • Use benchmarks to estimate sums of fractions

Hands-On Activity Use a computer drawing tool to model adding unlike fractions. Then find the sums.

Let's Explore Explore the relationship between the values of fractions and their sums

Math Journal Reading and Writing Math

2 Subtracting Unlike Fractions 133

Learn Find the common denominators to subtract unlike fractions • Use benchmarks to estimate differences between fractions

Hands-On Activity Use a computer drawing tool to model subtracting unlike fractions. Then find the differences.

Let's Explore Explore the relationship between the values of fractions and their differences

3 Fractions, Mixed Numbers, and Division Expressions 137

Learn Rewrite division expressions as fractions • Rewrite division expressions as mixed numbers

Hands-On Activities Write division expressions and fractions for a paper-strip model • Write division expressions, improper fractions, and mixed numbers for a paper-strip model

4 Expressing Fractions, Division Expressions, and Mixed Numbers as Decimals 143

Learn Express a fraction as a decimal by finding an equivalent fraction • Express division expressions as decimals • Express mixed numbers as decimals

5 Adding Mixed Numbers 146

Learn Add mixed numbers without renaming • Add mixed numbers with renaming • Use benchmarks to estimate sums of mixed numbers

Let's Explore Explore the relationship between the values of mixed numbers and their sums

6 Subtracting Mixed Numbers 151

Learn Subtract mixed numbers without renaming • Subtract mixed numbers with renaming • Use benchmarks to estimate differences between mixed numbers

7 Real-World Problems: Fractions and Mixed Numbers 156

Learn Write division expressions as fractions and mixed numbers • Draw a model to solve a one-step problem • Draw a model to solve a two-step problem

Math Journal Reading and Writing Math 160

Put on Your Thinking Cap! Problem Solving 161

Chapter Wrap-Up 162

Chapter Review/Test 164

4 Multiplying and Dividing Fractions and Mixed Numbers

Chapter Opener 167

Recall Prior Knowledge Finding equivalent fractions • Simplifying fractions • Adding and subtracting fractions • Expressing improper fractions as mixed numbers and mixed numbers as improper fractions • Expressing fractions as decimals • Multiplying fractions by a whole number • Finding the number of units to solve a problem • Drawing a model to show what is stated • Using the order of operations to simplify expressions 168

Quick Check

1 Multiplying Proper Fractions 172

Learn Use models to multiply fractions • Multiply fractions without models

Hands-On Activity Make area models to multiply two fractions (Commutative Property)

Let's Explore Explore the difference between multiplying two whole numbers and multiplying two proper fractions

2 Real-World Problems: Multiplying with Proper Fractions 176

Learn Multiply fractions to solve real-world problems • Give the answer as a fractional remainder

3 Multiplying Improper Fractions by Fractions 182

Learn Multiply improper fractions by proper fractions

4 Multiplying Mixed Numbers and Whole Numbers 184

Learn Multiply mixed numbers by whole numbers

Hands-On Activity Make an area model to multiply a mixed number and a whole number and compare the product with the factors

Let's Explore Break apart a mixed number into a product of yet another mixed number and a whole number

5 Real-World Problems: Multiplying with Mixed Numbers 189

Learn Multiply mixed numbers by whole numbers to solve real-world problems • Express the product of a mixed number and a whole number as a decimal • Solve two-step problems involving multiplication with mixed numbers

6 Dividing Fractions and Whole Numbers 193

Learn Divide a fraction by a whole number • Divide a whole number by a unit fraction

Hands-On Activity Make an area model to divide a fraction by a whole number

7 Real-World Problems: Multiplying and Dividing with Fractions 200

Learn Find parts of a whole to solve real-world problems • Find fractional parts of a whole and the remainder • Find fractional parts and wholes given one fractional part • Find fractional parts of a remainder when given wholes • Divide a whole number by a unit fraction to solve real-world problems

Math Journal Reading and Writing Math 210

Put on Your Thinking Cap! Problem Solving 211

Chapter Wrap-Up 212

Chapter Review/Test 214

Algebra

Chapter Opener 216

Recall Prior Knowledge Comparing numbers with symbols • Multiplication is the same as repeated addition • Number properties • Inverse operations • Order of operations 217

Quick Check

1 Number Patterns and Relationships 220

Learn Identify and extend a number pattern • Identify the relationship between two sets of numbers

Hands-On Activity Generate number patterns using given rules

2 Using Letters as Numbers 224

Learn Write a numerical expression to show how numbers in a situation are related • Use variables to represent unknown numbers and form expressions involving addition and subtraction • A variable can be used in place of a number in an algebraic expression • Algebraic expressions can be evaluated for given values of the variable • Use variables to form expressions involving multiplication • Use variables to form expressions involving division

Hands-On Activity Form different types of algebraic expressions using letter and number cards

Let's Explore Explore different ways of evaluating and writing equivalent division expressions

Math Journal Reading and Writing Math

3 Simplifying Algebraic Expressions 235

Learn Algebraic expressions can be simplified • Like terms can be added • A variable subtracted from itself results in zero • Like terms can be subtracted • Use the order of operations to simplify algebraic expressions • Collect like terms to simplify algebraic expressions

Hands-On Activity Make closed figures using craftsticks to write algebraic expressions in context

4 Inequalities and Equations 242

Learn Algebraic expressions can be used in inequalities and equations
• Algebraic expressions can be compared by evaluating them for a given value of the variable • Equality properties • Solve equations with variables on one side of the equal sign • Solve equations with variables on both sides of the equal sign

5 Real-World Problems: Algebra 252

Learn Write an addition or subtraction expression for a real-world problem and evaluate it • Write a multiplication or division expression for a real-world problem and evaluate it • Use algebraic expressions to compare quantities and solve equations

Math Journal Reading and Writing Math 257

Put on Your Thinking Cap! Problem Solving 257

Chapter Wrap-Up 258

Chapter Review/Test 260

Area

Chapter Opener 262

Recall Prior Knowledge Forming angles • Classifying angles • Identifying perpendicular line segments • Area is the amount of surface covered • Finding area by counting square units • Finding area by using formulas 263

Quick Check

1 Finding the Area of a Rectangle with Fractional Side Lengths 267

Learn Find the area of a rectangle with fractional side lengths • Find the area of a rectangle whose side lengths are mixed numbers

2 Base and Height of a Triangle 271

Learn A triangle has three vertices, three sides and three angles • Any one side of a triangle can be its base • A triangle is measured by its base and its height • Sometimes the height is not part of the triangle

Hands-On Activity Verify whether the height of a triangle is always perpendicular to the base

3 Finding the Area of a Triangle 276

Learn The area of a triangle is half the area of a rectangle with the same 'base' and 'height' or half its base times height • Find the area of a triangle using the 'area of a triangle' formula

Hands-On Activities Verify that the area of a non right triangle is half its base times its height • Verify that all possible pairs of base and height measurements in a triangle will give the same area

Let's Explore Explore the relationship among the areas of different triangles with equal bases and heights

Put on Your Thinking Cap! Problem Solving 282

Chapter Wrap-Up 283

Chapter Review/Test 284

Ratio

Chapter Opener 286

Recall Prior Knowledge Comparing numbers using subtraction • Understanding fractions • Writing fractions in simplest form • Using models to solve problems 287

Quick Check

1 Finding Ratio 289

Learn Use a ratio to compare two numbers or quantities by division • A ratio may not give the actual quantities compared • Use a part-whole model to show a ratio

2 Equivalent Ratios 296

Learn Equivalent ratios show the same comparisons of numbers or quantities • Use the greatest common factor to write ratios in simplest form • Use multiplication to find missing terms in equivalent ratios • Use division to find missing terms in equivalent ratios

Hands-On Activity Model equivalent ratios using equal sets of colored cubes

3 Real-World Problems: Ratios 303

Learn Find simplest-form ratios to compare quantities in real-world problems • Use the whole to find the missing part in a ratio • Find the new ratio after one term changes • Use models to find a ratio • Find the other term given the ratio and one term

Math Journal Reading and Writing Math

4 Ratios in Fraction Form 310

Learn Ratios can also be written in fraction form • Write ratios in fraction form to find how many times one number or quantity is as large as another • Draw a model to represent a ratio given in fraction form

Let's Explore Explore the relationship between a ratio written in ratio form and fraction form

Math Journal Reading and Writing Math

5 Comparing Three Quantities 316

Learn Use ratios to compare three quantities • Use multiplication to find missing terms in equivalent ratios • Use division to find missing terms in equivalent ratios

Hands-On Activity Model and simplify three-term ratios using sets of colored counters and ten frames

6 Real-World Problems: More Ratios 322

Learn Find simplest-form ratios to compare quantities in real-world problems • Find equivalent ratios or use models to solve real-world problems • Draw models to solve problems involving ratios in fraction form • Draw models to solve real-world problems

Let's Explore Form as many sets of equivalent ratios possible from a given set of numbers

Math Journal Reading and Writing Math

Put on Your Thinking Cap! Problem Solving 332

Chapter Wrap-Up 333

Chapter Review/Test 334

Glossary 336

Index 354

Photo Credits 373

Common Core State Standards Correlations C1–C8

Welcome to

Math in Focus®

This exciting math program comes to you all the way from the country of Singapore. We are sure you will enjoy learning math with the interesting lessons you'll find in these books.

What makes *Math in Focus*® different?

- **Two books** You don't write in the in this textbook. This book has a matching **Workbook**. When you see the pencil icon ON YOUR OWN, you will write in the **Workbook**.
- **Longer lessons** Some lessons may last more than a day, so you can really understand the math.
- **Math will make sense** Learn to use bar models to solve word problems with ease.

In this book, look for

Learn
This means you will learn something new.

Guided Learning
Your teacher will help you try some sample problems.

Let's Practice
You practice what you've learned to solve more problems. You can make sure you really understand.

Now you get to practice with lots of different problems in your own **Workbook**.

Also look forward to *Games, Hands-On Activities, Math Journals, Let's Explore,* and *Put on Your Thinking Cap!*
You will combine logical thinking with math skills and concepts to meet new problem-solving challenges. You will be talking math, thinking math, doing math, and even writing about doing math.

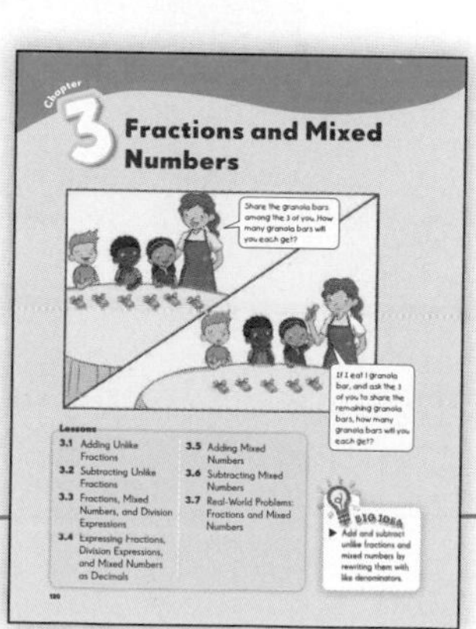

What's in the Workbook?

Math in Focus® will give you time to learn important new concepts and skills and check your understanding. Then you will use the practice pages in the **Workbook** to try:

- Solving different problems to practice the new math concept you are learning. In the textbook, keep an eye open for this symbol ON YOUR OWN. That will tell you which pages to use for practice.
- *Put on Your Thinking Cap!*

  Challenging Practice problems invite you to think in new ways to solve harder problems.

  Problem Solving challenges you to use different strategies to solve problems.
- Math Journal activities ask you to think about thinking, and then write about that!

Students in Singapore have been using this kind of math program for many years.
Now you can too — are you ready?

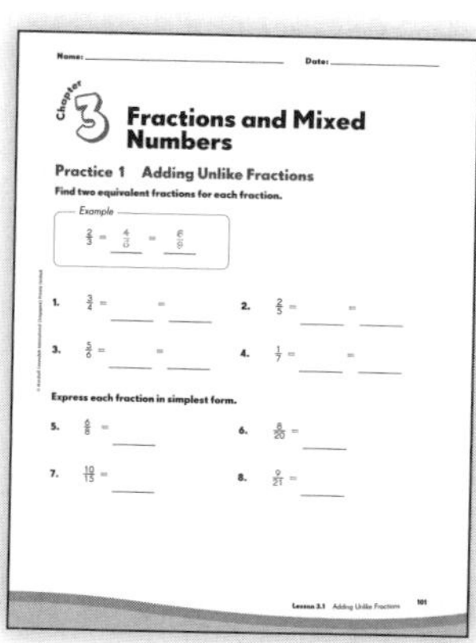

Name: ______ Date: ______

Chapter 3 **Fractions and Mixed Numbers**

Practice 1 Adding Unlike Fractions

Find two equivalent fractions for each fraction.

Example

$\frac{2}{3} = \frac{4}{6} = \frac{6}{9}$

1. $\frac{3}{4}$ = ______ = ______
2. $\frac{2}{5}$ = ______ = ______
3. $\frac{5}{6}$ = ______ = ______
4. $\frac{1}{7}$ = ______ = ______

Express each fraction in simplest form.

5. $\frac{6}{8}$ = ______
6. $\frac{8}{20}$ = ______
7. $\frac{10}{15}$ = ______
8. $\frac{9}{21}$ = ______

Lesson 3.1 Adding Unlike Fractions 101

Chapter 1

Whole Numbers

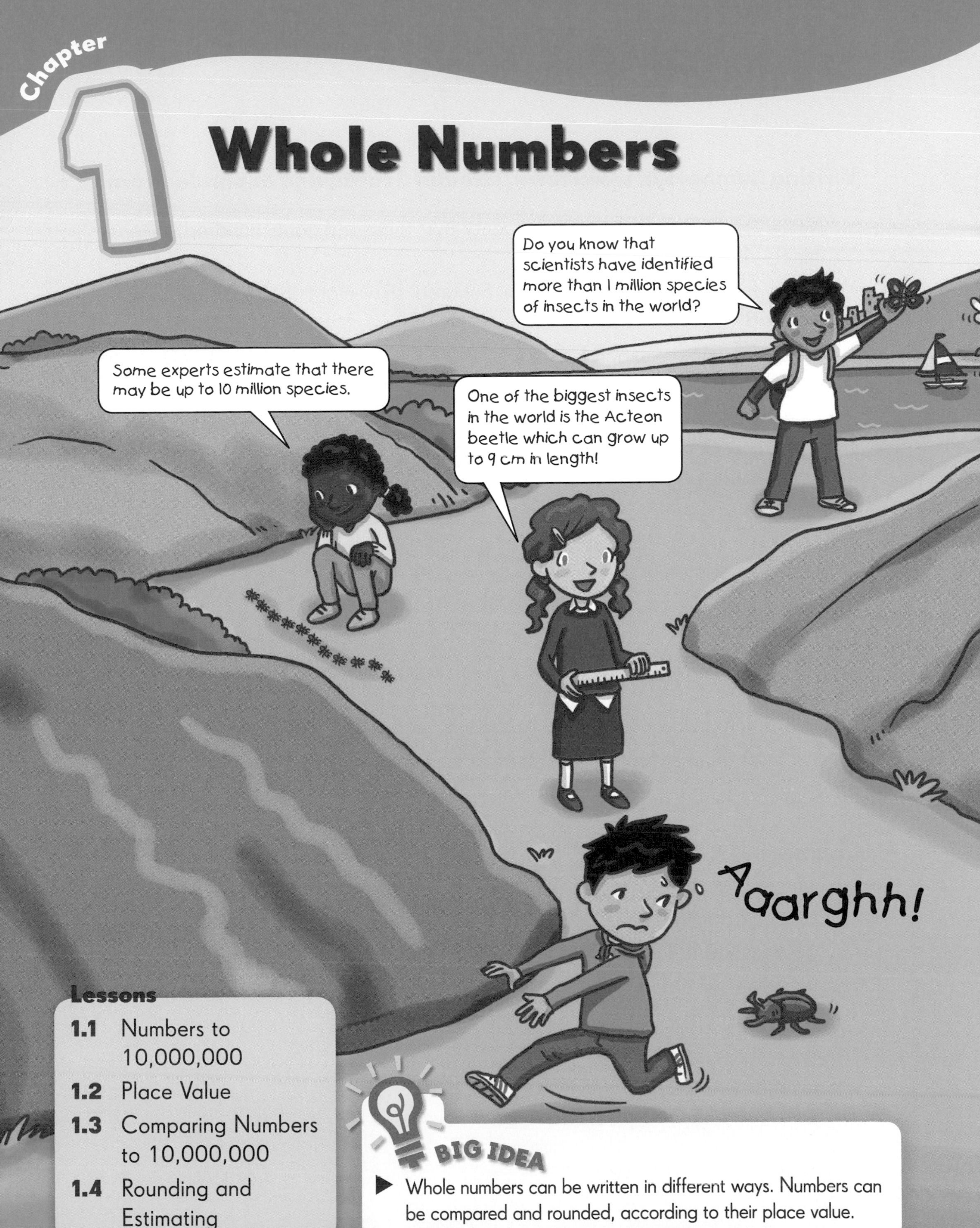

Do you know that scientists have identified more than 1 million species of insects in the world?
Some experts estimate that there may be up to 10 million species.
One of the biggest insects in the world is the Acteon beetle which can grow up to 9 cm in length!
Aaarghh!

Lessons

1.1 Numbers to 10,000,000

1.2 Place Value

1.3 Comparing Numbers to 10,000,000

1.4 Rounding and Estimating

BIG IDEA

▶ Whole numbers can be written in different ways. Numbers can be compared and rounded, according to their place value.

Recall Prior Knowledge

Writing numbers in word form, standard form, and expanded form

- Write 25,193 in word form: twenty-five thousand, one hundred ninety-three
- Write forty-seven thousand, two hundred sixty-eight in standard form: 47,268
- Write 32,146 in expanded form: 30,000 + 2,000 + 100 + 40 + 6

Identifying the value of each digit in a number

Ten Thousands	Thousands	Hundreds	Tens	Ones
●	●	●	●	●
1	1	1	1	1

1 one
1 ten = 10 ones
1 hundred = 10 tens
1 thousand = 10 hundreds
1 ten thousand = 10 thousands

Comparing numbers

Ten Thousands	Thousands	Hundreds	Tens	Ones
1	0	2	3	4
	9	4	2	3

10,234 is greater than 9,423 because 1 ten thousand (10,000) is greater than 9 thousands (9,000).

Rounding to the nearest hundred

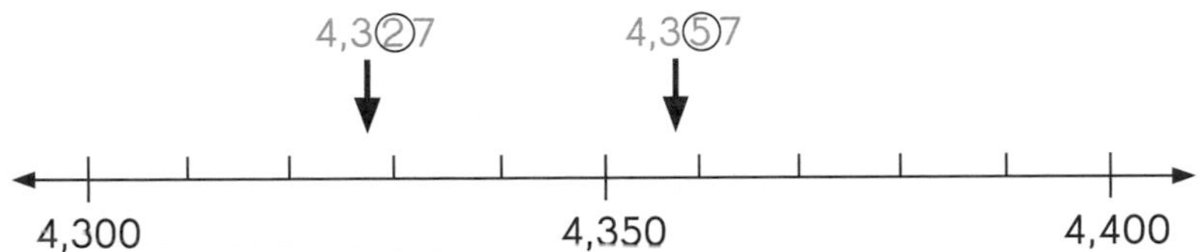

When the tens digit is 0, 1, 2, 3, or 4, round the number to the lesser hundred.

4,3②7 rounded to the nearest hundred is 4,300.

When the tens digit is 5, 6, 7, 8, or 9, round the number to the greater hundred.

4,3⑤7 rounded to the nearest hundred is 4,400.

Using rounding and front-end estimation to estimate sums and differences

Estimate the sum of 287 and 805.

Using rounding:

287 rounded to the nearest hundred is 300.
805 rounded to the nearest hundred is 800.

300 + 800 = 1,100

The estimated sum is 1,100.

Using front-end estimation:

Add the values of the leading digits.

287 → **2**00
805 → **8**00

200 + 800 = 1,000

The estimated sum is 1,000.

Estimate the difference between 686 and 417.

Using rounding:

686 rounded to the nearest hundred is 700.
417 rounded to the nearest hundred is 400.

700 – 400 = 300

The estimated difference is 300.

Using front-end estimation:

Subtract the values of the leading digits.

686 → **6**00
417 → **4**00

600 – 400 = 200

The estimated difference is 200.

Complete.

1. Write 95,718 in word form.
2. Write seventy-eight thousand, two hundred thirteen in standard form.
3. Write 31,485 in expanded form.
4. 2 tens = ___ ones
5. 3 hundreds = ___ tens
6. 5 thousands = ___ hundreds
7. 7 ten thousands = ___ thousands

Compare.

8. Which is greater, 20,345 or 21,345?
9. Which is less, 10,001 or 9,991?

Round each number to the nearest hundred.

10. 880
11. 1,249
12. 2,901
13. 8,997

Estimate by rounding to the nearest hundred.

14. 936 + 465
15. 853 – 217

Estimate by using front-end estimation.

16. 519 + 472
17. 758 – 329

Lesson

1.1 Numbers to 10,000,000

Lesson Objectives

- Count by ten thousands and hundred thousands to 10,000,000.
- Use place-value charts to show numbers to 10,000,000.
- Read and write numbers to 10,000,000 in standard form and in word form.

Vocabulary

hundred thousand

standard form

word form

periods

million

Learn

Count by ten thousands.

1 ten thousand (10,000), 2 ten thousands (20,000), 3 ten thousands (30,000), 4 ten thousands (40,000), 5 ten thousands (50,000), 6 ten thousands (60,000), 7 ten thousands (70,000), 8 ten thousands (80,000), 9 ten thousands (90,000), 10 ten thousands (100,000)

Add 1 ten thousand to 9 ten thousands to get 10 ten thousands.

10 ten thousands is the same as 1 hundred thousand. You write 1 hundred thousand as 100,000.

10 ten thousands = 1 **hundred thousand**

Hundred Thousands	Ten Thousands	Thousands	Hundreds	Tens	Ones
	●●●●● ●●●●●				

↓

Hundred Thousands	Ten Thousands	Thousands	Hundreds	Tens	Ones
●					
1	0	0	0	0	0
stands for 1 hundred thousand or 100,000	stands for 0 ten thousands or 0	stands for 0 thousands or 0	stands for 0 hundreds or 0	stands for 0 tens or 0	stands for 0 ones or 0

Guided Learning

Count by hundred thousands.

1 One hundred thousand 100,000
Two hundred thousand 200,000
Three hundred thousand 300,000
Four hundred thousand ____
Five hundred thousand ____
____ 600,000
____ 700,000
Eight hundred thousand ____
____ 900,000

A comma between the thousands digit and the hundreds digit helps you to read the number more easily.
100,000

Learn Write numbers in standard form and word form.

What is the number in standard form and word form?

Hundred Thousands	Ten Thousands	Thousands	Hundreds	Tens	Ones
●●● ●●●	●●● ●●	●●●	●		●● ●●
stands for 6 hundred thousands	stands for 5 ten thousands	stands for 3 thousands	stands for 1 hundred	stands for 0 tens	stands for 4 ones

	Standard Form	Word Form
6 hundred thousands	600,000	six hundred thousand
5 ten thousands	50,000	fifty thousand
3 thousands	3,000	three thousand
1 hundred	100	one hundred
0 tens	0	
4 ones	4	four

Number in standard form: 653,104
Number in word form: six hundred fifty-three thousand, one hundred four

Guided Learning

Write the number shown in the place-value chart in standard form and word form.

2

Hundred Thousands	Ten Thousands	Thousands	Hundreds	Tens	Ones
●●●●●	●●●●●	●●●●●●●	●●●●●●	●●●●●●●	●●●●●●
stands for 5 hundred thousands	stands for 5 ten thousands	stands for 7 thousands	stands for 6 hundreds	stands for 7 tens	stands for 6 ones

	Standard Form	Word Form
☐ hundred thousands	☐	☐
☐ ten thousands	☐	☐
☐ thousands	☐	☐
☐ hundreds	☐	☐
☐ tens	☐	☐
☐ ones	☐	☐

Number in standard form : ☐

Number in word form : ☐

Hundred Thousands	Ten Thousands	Thousands	Hundreds	Tens	Ones
●●●●●●	●●●●●●●●	●●●●●●		●●●●	●●●●

Number in standard form : ☐

Number in word form : ☐

Learn Read numbers to 1,000,000 by periods.

Groups of three places are called periods. You can read numbers to 1,000,000 by grouping them into periods.

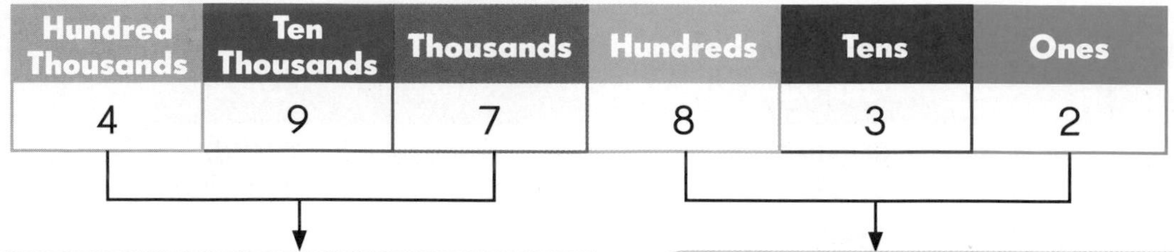

Hundred Thousands	Ten Thousands	Thousands	Hundreds	Tens	Ones
4	9	7	8	3	2

First read the thousands period:
four hundred ninety-seven thousand

Then read the remaining period:
eight hundred thirty-two

497,832 is read as four hundred ninety-seven thousand, eight hundred thirty-two.

767,707

767,707 is read as seven hundred sixty-seven thousand, seven hundred seven.

Guided Learning

Write in word form.

4. 325,176

5. 438,834

6. 906,096

7. 680,806

8. 700,007

9. 999,999

Learn Count by hundred thousands.

1 hundred thousand (100,000), 2 hundred thousands (200,000),
3 hundred thousands (300,000), 4 hundred thousands (400,000),
5 hundred thousands (500,000), 6 hundred thousands (600,000),
7 hundred thousands (700,000), 8 hundred thousands (800,000),
9 hundred thousands (900,000), 10 hundred thousands (1,000,000)

Add 1 hundred thousand to 9 hundred thousands to get 10 hundred thousands.

10 hundred thousands is the same as 1 million. You write 1 million as 1,000,000.

10 hundred thousands = 1 **million**

Millions	Hundred Thousands	Ten Thousands	Thousands	Hundreds	Tens	Ones
	○○○○○ ○○○○○					

Millions	Hundred Thousands	Ten Thousands	Thousands	Hundreds	Tens	Ones
●						
1	0	0	0	0	0	0
stands for 1 million or 1,000,000	stands for 0 hundred thousands or 0	stands for 0 ten thousands or 0	stands for 0 thousands or 0	stands for 0 hundreds or 0	stands for 0 tens or 0	stands for 0 ones or 0

Guided Learning

Count by millions.

10

One million	1,000,000
Two million	2,000,000
Three million	3,000,000
	4,000,000
Five million	5,000,000
Six million	6,000,000
Seven million	7,000,000
	8,000,000
Nine million	
Ten million	10,000,000

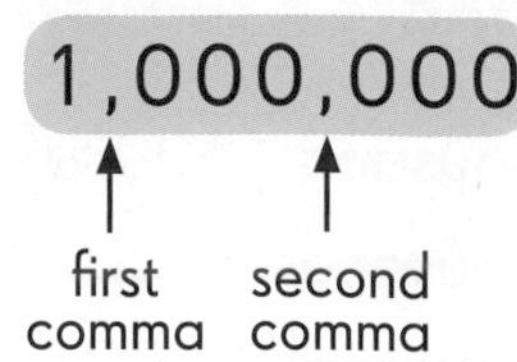

Use two commas to separate the periods. The first comma indicates the millions period. The second comma indicates the thousands period.

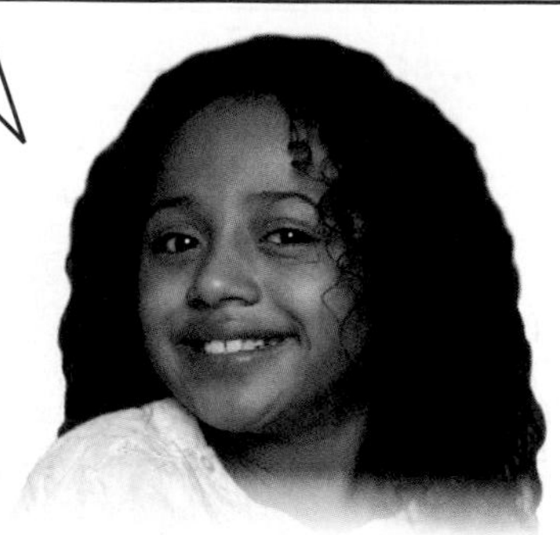

Learn Write numbers in standard form and word form.

What is the number in standard form and word form?

Millions	Hundred Thousands	Ten Thousands	Thousands	Hundreds	Tens	Ones
●●●	●●●●●	●●●●●●	●●●●●●●		●●●●	●●●●●
stands for 3 millions	stands for 5 hundred thousands	stands for 6 ten thousands	stands for 7 thousands	stands for 0 hundreds	stands for 4 tens	stands for 5 ones

	Standard Form	Word Form
3 millions	3,000,000	three million
5 hundred thousands	500,000	five hundred thousand
6 ten thousands	60,000	sixty thousand
7 thousands	7,000	seven thousand
0 hundreds	0	
4 tens	40	forty
5 ones	5	five

Number in standard form: 3,567,045

Number in word form: three million, five hundred sixty-seven thousand, forty-five

Hands-On Activity

Work in groups of four or five.
Search for quantities that occur in the millions on the Internet.
Search for at least five such quantities.
Print the search results your group finds.
Present your findings to the rest of your class.

The population of Virginia is one quantity that is reported in the millions.

According to the U.S. annual population estimate by state, the population of Virginia in 2007 was about 7,700,000.

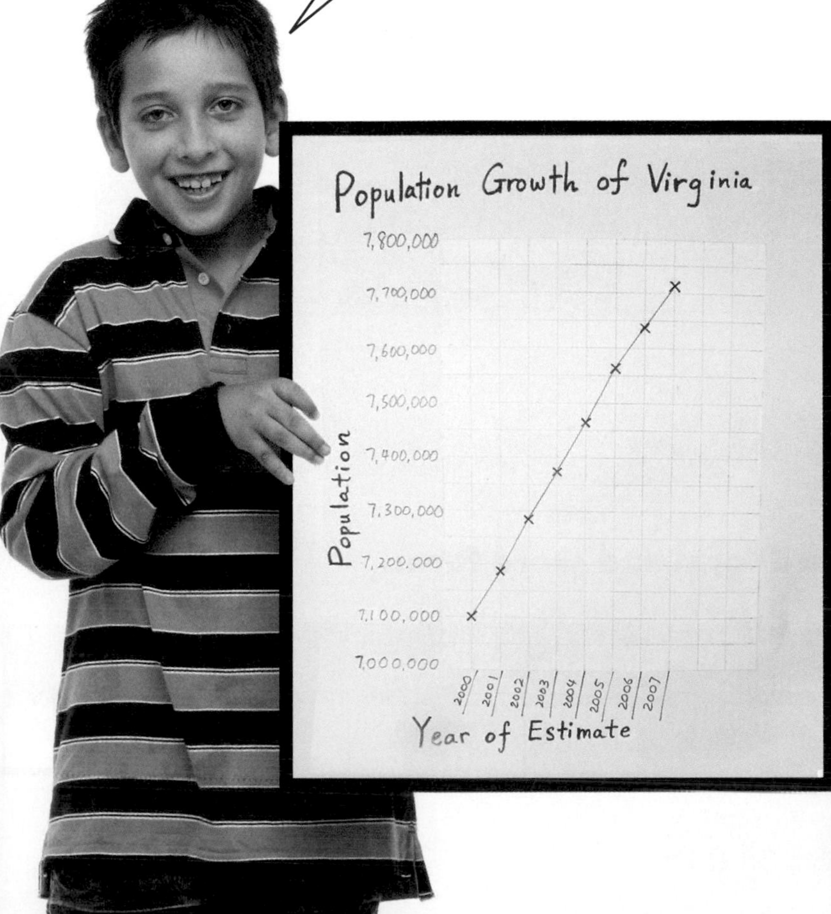

Guided Learning

Write the number shown in the place-value chart in standard form and word form.

11

Millions	Hundred Thousands	Ten Thousands	Thousands	Hundreds	Tens	Ones
●●●●	●●●●●●		●●●●●	●●●	●●●●●●●	●●●●●●●●●
stands for 4 millions	stands for 6 hundred thousands	stands for 0 ten thousands	stands for 5 thousands	stands for 3 hundreds	stands for 7 tens	stands for 9 ones

	Standard Form	Word Form
☐ millions	☐	☐
☐ hundred thousands	☐	☐
☐ ten thousands	☐	☐
☐ thousands	☐	☐
☐ hundreds	☐	☐
☐ tens	☐	☐
☐ ones	☐	☐

Number in standard form : ☐

Number in word form : ☐

Write the number in standard form and word form.

12

Millions	Hundred Thousands	Ten Thousands	Thousands	Hundreds	Tens	Ones
●●●●●●	●●●	●●●●		●●●●●	●●●●●●●●	●

Number in standard form : ☐

Number in word form : ☐

Learn Read numbers to 10,000,000 by periods.

You can also read numbers to 10,000,000 by grouping them into periods.

Millions	Hundred Thousands	Ten Thousands	Thousands	Hundreds	Tens	Ones
5	8	2	4	4	2	8

First read the millions period: five million

Then read the thousands period: eight hundred twenty-four thousand

Finally, read the remaining period: four hundred twenty-eight

5,824,428 is read as five million, eight hundred twenty-four thousand, four hundred twenty-eight.

6,035,350

6,035,350 is read as six million, thirty-five thousand, three hundred fifty.

Guided Learning

Write in word form.

13 1,234,567

14 2,653,356

15 4,404,044

16 8,888,888

17 5,090,909

18 7,006,060

Let's Practice

Write in standard form.

1. Two hundred thousand, one hundred six
2. Nine million, five hundred twenty
3. Five million, two thousand, twelve

Write in word form.

4. 215,905
5. 819,002
6. 6,430,000
7. 5,009,300

ON YOUR OWN

Go to Workbook A: Practice 1 and 2, pages 1–6

Let's Explore!

Can there be numbers less than zero?

1. The table shows the minimum temperature on each day of a week in Chicago.

Day	Mon.	Tue.	Wed.	Thu.	Fri.	Sat.	Sun.
Temperature	–4°C	–14°C	–16°C	–17°C	–5°C	2°C	6°C

A temperature of 2°C means 2 degrees Celsius **above** zero.
A temperature of –4°C means 4 degrees Celsius **below** zero.

–4, –5, –14, –16, and –17 are **negative numbers**. They are used here to show temperatures below 0°C.

2, and 6 are **positive numbers**. They are used here to show temperatures above 0°C.

Positive numbers can be written with a '+' sign in front of them. For example, 2, and 6 can also be written as +2, and +6 respectively. The '+' sign helps to distinguish them from negative numbers.

2 The table shows the heights of four places in relation to sea level.

Place	New Orleans, Louisiana	Death Valley, California	Dead Sea, Israel	Marianas Trench, Pacific Ocean
Height	–6 feet	–282 feet	–1,378 feet	–35,797 feet

The negative heights mean that the places are below sea level.

How many feet below sea level is each place?

Can you think of other examples where negative numbers are used?

Use the Internet to search for more uses of negative numbers.

3 Negative numbers can be shown on a number line in each of these ways.

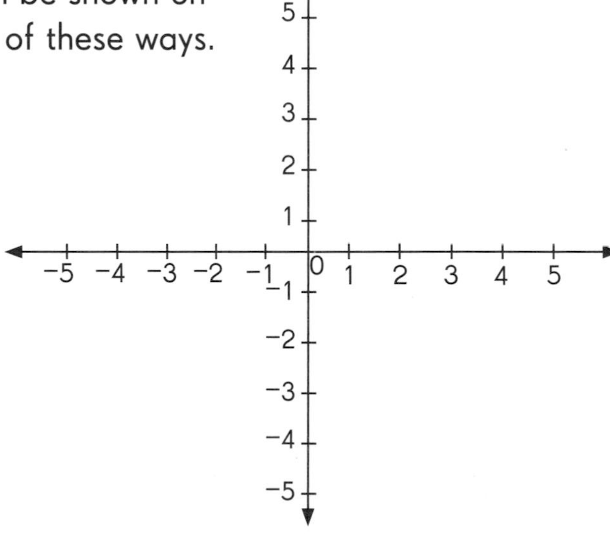

Notice that for every positive number, there is an opposite negative number. For example, 4 and –4 are opposites.

Write the opposite negative number for each positive number.

a 8 **b** 50 **c** 173 **d** 2,469

Lesson 1.2 Place Value

Vocabulary
place
value
expanded form

Lesson Objectives

- Identify the place value of any digit in numbers to 10,000,000.
- Read and write numbers to 10,000,000 in expanded form.

Learn — Each digit of a number has a value and a place.

Hundred Thousands	Ten Thousands	Thousands	Hundreds	Tens	Ones
8	6	1	2	5	7

In 861,257:
the digit 8 stands for 800,000.
the value of the digit 8 is 800,000.

the digit 6 stands for 60,000.
the value of the digit 6 is 60,000.

the digit 1 stands for 1,000.
the value of the digit 1 is 1,000.

the digit 8 is in the hundred thousands place.
the digit 6 is in the ten thousands place.
the digit 1 is in the thousands place.

Guided Learning

Complete.

1. In 670,932, the value of the digit 6 is ____.
2. In 937,016, the digit ____ is in the hundreds place.
3. In 124,573, the digit in the hundred thousands place is ____.
4. In 971,465, the digit 6 is in the ____ place.
5. In 289,219, the digit 8 is in the ____ place.

Guided Learning

State the value of the digit 2 in each number.

6. 81**2**,679 ___
7. **2**60,153 ___
8. 8**2**7,917 ___

For each number, state the place the digit 2 is in.

9. 18**2**,679 ___
10. **2**60,153 ___
11. 8**2**7,917 ___

Learn Numbers to 1,000,000 can be written in expanded form.

Look at the values of the digits in 381,492. For example, the value of the digit 3 is 300,000. You can add the values of the digits to get the number.

381,492 = 300,000 + 80,000 + 1,000 + 400 + 90 + 2

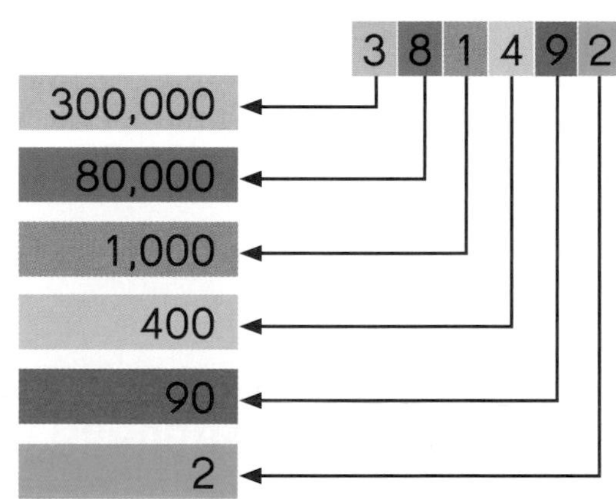

381,492 in expanded form: 300,000 + 80,000 + 1,000 + 400 + 90 + 2

Guided Learning

Complete to express each number in expanded form.

12. 761,902 = 700,000 + ___ + 1,000 + 900 + 2
13. 124,003 = ___ + 20,000 + 4,000 + 3
14. 900,356 = 900,000 + 300 + ___ + 6

Learn Each digit of a number has a value and a place.

Millions	Hundred Thousands	Ten Thousands	Thousands	Hundreds	Tens	Ones
1	6	4	9	0	0	0

In 1,649,000:
the digit 1 stands for 1,000,000.
the value of the digit 1 is 1,000,000.

the digit 1 is in the millions place.
the digit 4 is in the ten thousands place.
the digit 9 is in the thousands place.

Guided Learning

Complete.

15. In 7,296,000:
   a. the digit ______ is in the millions place.
   b. the digit 2 stands for ______.
   c. the digit 9 is in the ______ place.

Learn Numbers to 10,000,000 can be written in expanded form.

5,649,000 = 5,000,000 + 600,000 + 40,000 + 9,000

5,000,000 ← 5
600,000 ← 6
40,000 ← 4
9,000 ← 9

Complete to express each number in expanded form.

16. 7,200,000 = 7,000,000 + ______

17. 6,235,000 = ______ + 200,000 + 30,000 + 5,000

18. 2,459,000 = 2,000,000 + 400,000 + ______ + 9,000

Let's Practice

State the value of the digit 5 in each number.

1. 64,0**5**1 ____
2. 783,**5**62 ____
3. 1**5**7,300 ____
4. **5**91,368 ____

Complete.

5. In 493,128, the digit ____ is in the ten thousands place.
6. 638,215 = ____ + 30,000 + 8,000 + 200 + 10 + 5
7. In 357,921, the value of the digit 3 is ____ and the digit 7 is in the ____ place.
8. 829,359 = 800,000 + ____ + 9,000 + 300 + 50 + 9

State the value of the digit 6 in each number.

9. **6**,390,000 ____
10. 8,100,**6**00 ____
11. 7,**6**20,548 ____
12. 9,0**6**0,001 ____

Complete.

13. In 7,005,000, the digit ____ is in the millions place.
14. In 2,321,654, the digit in the hundred thousands place is ____.
15. 9,197,328 = 9,000,000 + 100,000 + 90,000 + 7,000 + ____ + 20 + 8
16. 2,403,800 = ____ + 400,000 + 3,000 + 800

ON YOUR OWN

Go to Workbook A: Practice 3, pages 7–10

Lesson 1.3 Comparing Numbers to 10,000,000

Lesson Objectives

- Compare and order numbers to 10,000,000.
- Identify and complete a number pattern.
- Find a rule for a number pattern.

Vocabulary
greater than (>)
less than (<)

Learn Compare numbers by using a place-value chart.

Which number is less, 237,981 or 500,600?

When comparing numbers, look at the value of each digit from left to right. Remember, '>' means '**greater than**' and '<' means '**less than**'.

Hundred Thousands	Ten Thousands	Thousands	Hundreds	Tens	Ones
2	3	7	9	8	1
5	0	0	6	0	0

Compare the values of the digits starting from the left.
2 hundred thousands is less than 5 hundred thousands.
So, 237,981 is less than 500,600.

237,981 < 500,600

Learn Compare numbers greater than 1,000,000.

Which number is less, 3,506,017 or 5,306,007?

Millions	Hundred Thousands	Ten Thousands	Thousands	Hundreds	Tens	Ones
3	5	0	6	0	1	7
5	3	0	6	0	0	7

Compare the values of the digits starting from the left.
3 millions is less than 5 millions.
So, 3,506,017 is less than 5,306,007.

3,506,017 < 5,306,007

Guided Learning

Complete. Use the place-value chart to help you.

1. Which number is greater, 712,935 or 712,846?

Hundred Thousands	Ten Thousands	Thousands	Hundreds	Tens	Ones
7	1	2	**9**	3	5
7	1	2	**8**	4	6

Compare the values of the digits starting from the left. If they are the same, compare the next digits. Continue until the values of the digits are not the same.

Here, the values of the digits in the hundreds place are different.

Compare the values of the digits in the hundreds place.

___ hundreds is greater than ___ hundreds.

So, 712,935 is ___ than 712,846.

712,935 ◯ 712,846

Complete.

2. Which number is greater, 4,730,589 or 4,703,985?
4,7**3**0,589
4,7**0**3,985

Compare the values of the digits starting from the left. If they are the same, compare the next digits. Continue until the values of the digits are not the same.

Here, the values of the digits in the ten thousands place are different.

Compare the values of the digits in the ten thousands place.

___ ten thousands is greater than ___ ten thousands.

So, ___ is greater than ___.

___ > ___.

Compare the numbers. Use < or >.

3. 345,932 ◯ 435,990

4. 100,400 ◯ 99,900

5. 5,245,721 ◯ 524,572

6. 3,143,820 ◯ 4,134,820

Order the numbers from least to greatest.

7. 324,688 32,468 3,246,880

8. 1,600,456 1,604,654 1,064,645

Learn Find rules to complete number patterns.

What is the next number in each pattern?

a. 231,590 331,590 431,590 531,590 ...

To get the next number in the pattern, add 100,000 to the previous number.

231,590 331,590 431,590 531,590 631,590

+100,000 +100,000 +100,000 +100,000

331,590 is 100,000 more than **2**31,590.

431,590 is 100,000 more than **3**31,590.

531,590 is 100,000 more than **4**31,590.

100,000 more than **5**31,590 is **6**31,590.

The next number is 631,590.

b. 755,482 705,482 655,482 605,482 ...

705,482 is 50,000 less than **75**5,482.

655,482 is 50,000 less than **70**5,482.

605,482 is 50,000 less than **65**5,482.

50,000 less than **60**5,482 is **55**5,482.

The next number is 555,482.

Guided Learning

Find the missing numbers.

9. 1,345,024   3,345,024   5,345,024 ...
   3,345,024 is ___ more than 1,345,024.
   5,345,024 is ___ more than 3,345,024.
   ___ more than 5,345,024 is ___.
   The next number is ___.

10. 820,346   810,346   800,346 ...
   810,346 is ___ less than 820,346.
   800,346 is ___ less than 810,346.
   ___ less than 800,346 is ___.
   The next number is ___.

Let's Practice

Answer each question.

1. Which is greater, 568,912 or 568,921? ___
2. Which is less, 71,690 or 100,345? ___
3. Which is the greatest, 81,630, 81,603 or 816,300? ___
4. Which is the least, 125,000, 12,500 or 25,000? ___

Order the numbers from least to greatest.

5. 901,736   714,800   199,981 ___
6. 645,321   654,987   645,231 ___

Order the numbers from greatest to least.

7. 36,925 925,360 360,925 ____

8. 445,976 474,089 474,108 ____

Find the missing numbers.

9. 580,356 600,356 620,356 640,356 ...

600,356 is ____ more than 580,356.

620,356 is ____ more than 600,356.

640,356 is ____ more than 620,356.

____ more than 640,356 is ____.

10. 4,030,875 3,830,875 3,630,875 3,430,875 ...

3,830,875 is ____ less than 4,030,875.

3,630,875 is ____ less than 3,830,875.

3,430,875 is ____ less than 3,630,875.

____ less than 3,430,875 is ____.

Find the rule. Then complete the number pattern.

11. 325,410 ____ 305,410 295,410 ____ 275,410

12. 2,390,000 3,400,000 4,410,000 ____ 6,430,000

ON YOUR OWN

Go to Workbook A: Practice 4, pages 11–14

Lesson 1.4 Rounding and Estimating

Lesson Objectives

- Round numbers to the nearest thousand.
- Locate numbers on a number line.
- Use rounding to estimate or check sums, differences, and products.
- Use related multiplication facts to estimate quotients.

Vocabulary
round
estimate
front-end estimation with adjustment
compatible numbers

Learn **Round numbers to the greater thousand.**

What is 6,541 rounded to the nearest thousand?

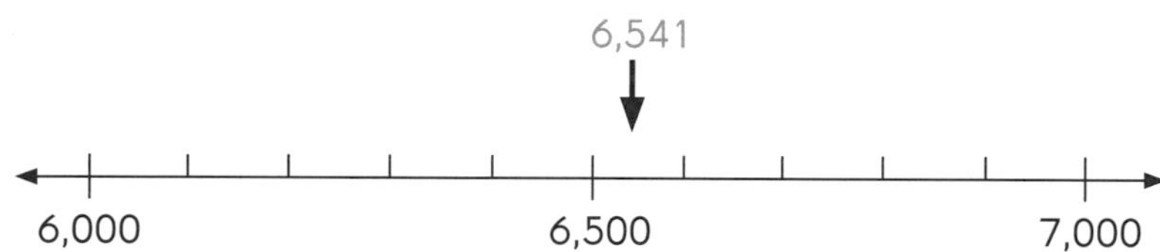

6,541 is between 6,000 and 7,000.
6,541 is nearer to 7,000 than to 6,000.
6,541 rounded to the nearest thousand is 7,000.

Guided Learning

Complete. Use the number line to help you.

1

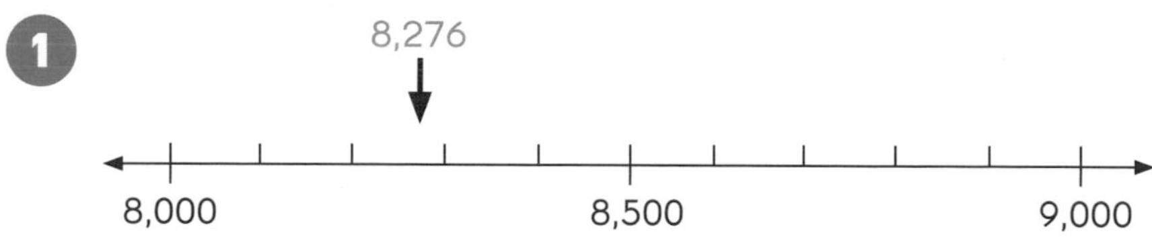

8,276 is between 8,000 and ___.

8,276 is nearer to ___ than to ___.

8,276 rounded to the nearest thousand is ___.

Learn Round numbers to the greater thousand.

What is 9,500 rounded to the nearest thousand?

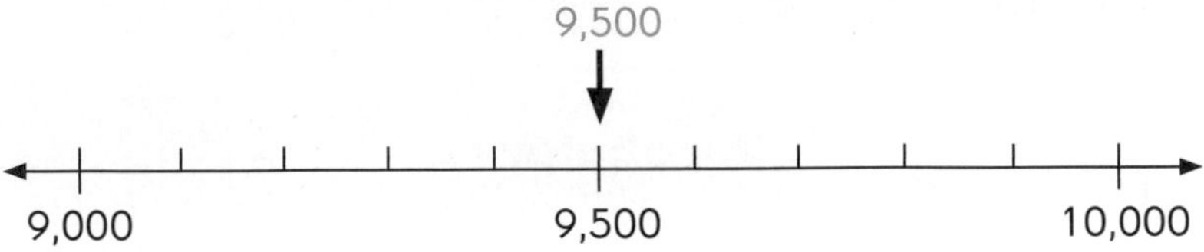

9,500 is exactly halfway between 9,000 and 10,000.
9,500 rounded to the nearest thousand is 10,000.

Guided Learning

Answer each question. Use the number line to help you.

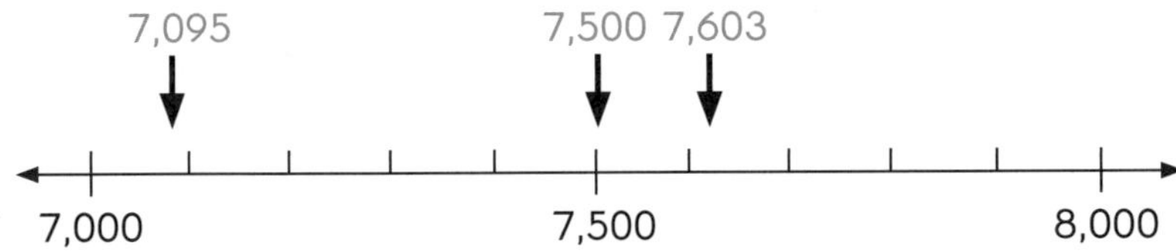

2. What is 7,095 rounded to the nearest thousand? ▭

3. What is 7,500 rounded to the nearest thousand? ▭

4. What is 7,603 rounded to the nearest thousand? ▭

Learn Round numbers to the thousand that is less.

What is 85,210 rounded to the nearest thousand?

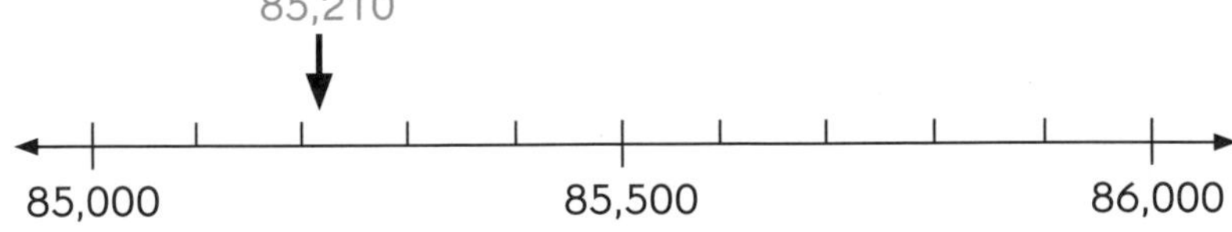

85,210 is between 85,000 and 86,000.
85,210 is nearer to 85,000 than to 86,000.
85,210 rounded to the nearest thousand is 85,000.

Guided Learning

Copy the number line. Use an ✗ to mark the position of 125,231 and 125,780. Then round each number to the nearest thousand.

5

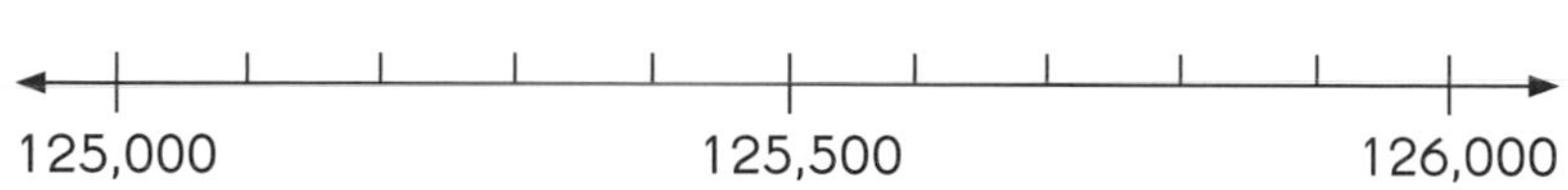

Round each number to the nearest thousand.

6 6,321 ___ 7 9,873 ___ 8 6,995 ___ 9 12,051 ___

10 65,500 ___ 11 89,773 ___ 12 325,699 ___ 13 600,039 ___

Answer each question. Draw a number line to help you.

14 Rounding to the nearest thousand, what is the least number that rounds to

a 4,000? ___ b 80,000? ___

15 Rounding to the nearest thousand, what is the greatest number that rounds to

a 7,000? ___ b 50,000? ___

Learn Use rounding to estimate sums and differences.

Round the numbers 6,521 and 5,079 to the nearest thousand.

6,521 rounds to 7,000.
5,079 rounds to 5,000.

Then estimate: a 6,521 + 5,079 b 6,521 − 5,079

a 6,521 + 5,079 rounds to 7,000 + 5,000 = 12,000

b 6,521 − 5,079 rounds to 7,000 − 5,000 = 2,000

Guided Learning

Round each number to the nearest thousand. Then estimate the sum or difference.

16 7,192 + 1,642 ___

17 5,701 − 3,214 ___

18 6,290 + 5,500 + 3,719 ___

19 9,810 − 1,600 − 7,391 ___

Learn Use **front-end estimation with adjustment** to estimate sums.

Estimate the sum of 4,615, 2,537, and 1,828.

Add the values of the leading digits.

4,615 → **4**,000
2,537 → **2**,000
1,828 → **1**,000

4,000 + 2,000 + 1,000 = 7,000

Then, estimate the sum of what is left over to the nearest thousand.

615 + 537 + 828 → 600 + 500 + 800 = 1,900

1,900 rounded to the nearest thousand is 2,000.

Adjust the estimate.

7,000 + 2,000 = 9,000

The estimated sum is 9,000.

Adjusting the estimate gives you a closer estimate than using only the leading digits.

Guided Learning

Use front-end estimation with adjustment to estimate each sum.

20. 4,261 + 7,879 + 6,175

Add the values of the leading digits.

4,261 → ____

7,879 → ____

____ → ____

____ + ____ + ____ = ____

Then, estimate the sum of what is left over to the nearest thousand.

261 + ____ + ____ → ____ + ____ + ____ = ____

____ rounded to the nearest thousand is ____.

Adjust the estimate.

____ + ____ = ____

The estimated sum is ____.

21. 2,619 + 7,391 + 4,738 ____

22. 5,559 + 6,041 + 8,244 ____

23. 3,497 + 7,198 + 8,253 ____

24. 1,864 + 5,907 + 9,541 ____

Learn Use front-end estimation with adjustment to estimate differences.

Estimate the difference between 4,837 and 2,152.

Subtract the values of the leading digits.

4,837 ⟶ **4**,000
2,152 ⟶ **2**,000

4,000 – 2,000 = 2,000

Then, estimate the difference of what is left over to the nearest thousand.

837 – 152 ⟶ 800 – 100 = 700

700 rounded to the nearest thousand is 1,000.

Adjust the estimate.

2,000 + 1,000 = 3,000

The estimated difference is 3,000.

Estimate the difference between 5,134 and 2,918.

Subtract the values of the leading digits.

5,134 ⟶ **5**,000
2,918 ⟶ **2**,000

5,000 – 2,000 = 3,000

Then, estimate the difference of what is left over to the nearest thousand.

918 – 134 ⟶ 900 – 100 = 800

800 rounded to the nearest thousand is 1,000.

Adjust the estimate.

3,000 – 1,000 = 2,000

The estimated difference is 2,000.

Guided Learning

Use front-end estimation with adjustment to estimate each difference.

25 9,872 – 2,215

Subtract the values of the leading digits.

9,872 → ___

___ → ___

___ – ___ = ___

Then, estimate the difference of what is left over to the nearest thousand.

872 – ___ → ___ – ___ = ___

___ rounded to the nearest thousand is ___.

Adjust the estimate.

___ + ___ = ___

The estimated difference is ___.

26 3,842 – 1,206 ___

27 5,770 – 2,216 ___

28 8,671 – 4,329 ___

29 6,983 – 3,507 ___

30 7,966 – 2,643 ___

Guided Learning

Use front-end estimation with adjustment to estimate each difference.

31. 8,275 − 3,860

Subtract the values of the leading digits.

8,275 → ___

___ → ___

___ − ___ = ___

Then, estimate the difference of what is left over to the nearest thousand.

860 – ___ → ___ − ___ = ___

___ rounded to the nearest thousand is ___.

Adjust the estimate.

___ − ___ = ___

The estimated difference is ___.

32. 5,016 − 2,770 ___

33. 6,392 − 2,931 ___

34. 7,210 − 4,932 ___

35. 9,550 − 1,697 ___

Learn **Use rounding to estimate products.**

Estimate the value of 7,120 × 5.

First, round 7,120 to the nearest thousand.

7,120 rounds to 7,000.

7,000 × 5 = 35,000

7,120 × 5 is about 35,000.

Guided Learning

Estimate the value of 6,327 × 7.

Round the 4-digit number to the nearest thousand first.

 36 6,327 rounds to ___.

___ × 7 = ___

6,327 × 7 is about ___.

Estimate each product.

37 2,145 × 7 ___

 38 8,756 × 6 ___

Learn Use compatible numbers to estimate quotients.

Compatible numbers are numbers that are easy to add, subtract, multiply, or divide. They can be used to estimate sums, differences, products, or quotients.

In division, compatible numbers are number pairs that are easy to divide.
Such number pairs are obtained from basic facts for division.
You can use compatible numbers to estimate quotients.

Estimate the value of 3,465 ÷ 6.

Look for compatible numbers close to 3,465 and 6.

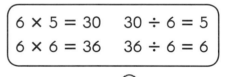

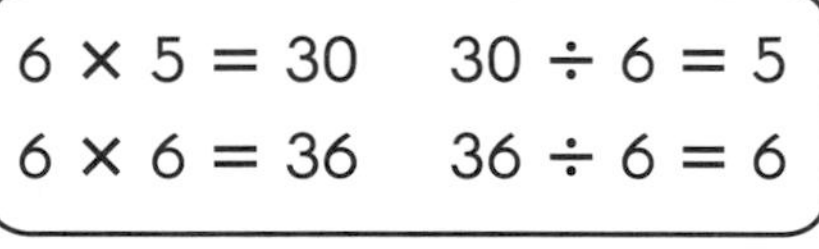

3,000 ÷ **6** = **5**00

3,600 ÷ **6** = **6**00

Compatible number pairs are:

3,000 and 6 or 3,600 and 6

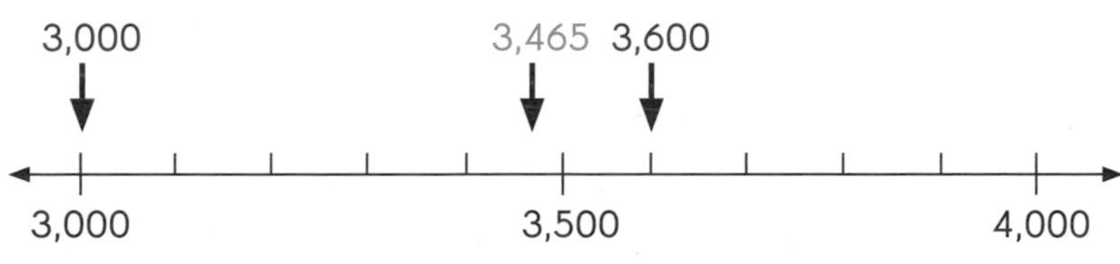

3,465 is nearer to 3,600 than to 3,000.

Choose 3,600 to make this estimate.

3,600 ÷ 6 = 600

3,465 ÷ 6 is about 600.

Guided Learning

Estimate the value of 6,742 ÷ 8.

39

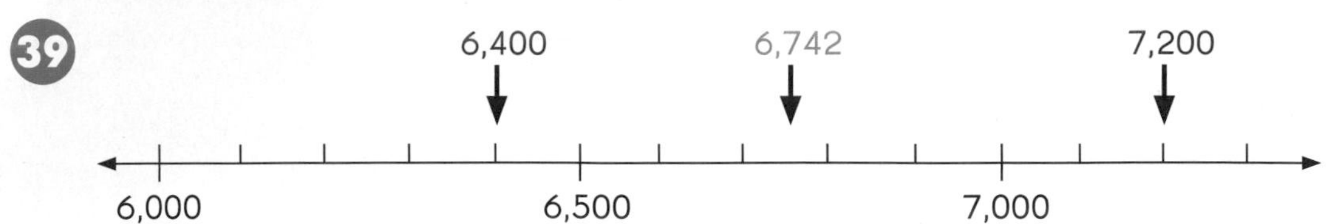

Choose ___ to make the estimate.

___ ÷ 8 = ___

6,742 ÷ 8 is about ___.

Look for compatible numbers.

6,742 ÷ 8 → 6,400 ÷ 8
6,742 ÷ 8 → 7,200 ÷ 8

6,742 is nearer to ___ than to ___.

Estimate each quotient.

40 1,745 ÷ 3 ___

41 4,467 ÷ 6 ___

Let's Practice

Round each number to the nearest thousand.

1 80,295 ___

2 229,078 ___

3 549,947 ___

Answer the question. Draw number lines to help you.

4 Rounding to the nearest thousand, what is

a the least number that rounds to 8,000? ___

b the greatest number that rounds to 60,000? ___

Round each number to the nearest thousand. Then estimate the sum or difference.

5 3,670 − 2,189 ___

6 3,638 + 7,917 + 6,148 ___

Use front-end estimation with adjustment to estimate each sum or difference.

7. 7,958 + 5,233 + 4,068

8. 3,725 + 1,882 + 6,536

9. 9,978 − 4,209

10. 8,134 − 4,917

Estimate each product.

11. 3,322 × 8

12. 9,245 × 5

Estimate each quotient.

13. 6,581 ÷ 7

14. 8,502 ÷ 9

ON YOUR OWN
Go to Workbook A:
Practice 5, page 15–24

CRITICAL THINKING SKILLS

Put On Your Thinking Cap!

PROBLEM SOLVING

1. Three cards have different whole numbers on them.
Each number, when rounded to the nearest ten, is 30.
What can the three numbers be?

2. Without adding the 99s, use a quicker way to find the value of:

   a. 99 + 99

   b. 99 + 99 + 99 + 99 + 99 + 99

   c. What is the value of the digit in the ones place in each case?

   d. What is the least number of 99s which must be added to get a 1 in the ones place?

ON YOUR OWN
Go to Workbook A:
Put on Your Thinking Cap!
pages 25–26

Chapter Wrap Up

Study Guide

You have learned...

Numbers to 10,000,000

Write

Standard form:
6,245,781

Word form:
six million, two hundred forty-five thousand, seven hundred eighty-one

Expanded form:
6,245,781 =
6,000,000 +
200,000 + 40,000 +
5,000 +700 + 80 + 1

Compare

Greater than:
9,195,079 > 8,753,426

Less than:
5,187,326 < 7,946,704

Using rounding

Addition:
2,381 + 4,502 rounds to
2,000 + 5,000 = 7,000

Subtraction:
7,185 − 2,738 rounds to
7,000 − 3,000 = 4,000

Multiplication:
3,856 × 7 rounds to
4,000 × 7 = 28,000

Show

Millions	Hundred Thousands	Ten Thousands	Thousands	Hundreds	Tens	Ones
●●●●●●	○○	●●●●	●●●●●	○○○○○○○	●●●●●●●●	●
6	2	4	5	7	8	1

▶ Whole numbers can be written in different ways. Numbers can be compared and rounded, according to their place value.

Find patterns

505,347   605,347   705,347 ...
605,347 is 100,000 more than 505,347.
705,347 is 100,000 more than 605,347.
Rule: Add 100,000 to a number in the pattern to get the next number.

Estimate

Using compatible numbers

Division:
5,456 ÷ 6

4,800 ÷ 6 = 800
5,400 ÷ 6 = 900

5,456 ÷ 6
→ 5,400 ÷ 6 = 900

Using front-end estimation with adjustment

Sum:
5,174 + 1,546 + 7,301
→ 5,000 + 1,000 + 7,000 = 13,000
174 + 546 + 301
→ 100 + 500 + 300 = 900
→ 1,000
13,000 + 1,000 = 14,000

Difference:
5,915 − 3,250
→ 5,000 − 3,000 = 2,000
915 – 250 → 900 − 200 = 700
→ 1,000
2,000 + 1,000 = 3,000

Chapter Review/Test

Vocabulary

Fill in the blanks.

hundred thousand
standard form
word form
periods
million
place-value
expanded form
greater than (>)
less than (<)
round
estimate
front-end estimation with adjustment
compatible numbers

1. You can read numbers up to 10,000,000 by grouping them into ___ which are groups of three places.

2. The number 2,002,002 in ___ is two ___, two thousand, two.

3. The method shown for estimating 3,924 + 7,806 is called ___.

   3,924 → 3,000
   7,806 → 7,000
   3,000 + 7,000 = 10,000 ← Add the values of the leading digits.

   924 + 806
   → 900 + 800 = 1,700
   → 2,000 ← Estimate the sum of what is left over to the nearest thousand.

   10,000 + 2,000 = 12,000 ← Adjust the estimate.

4. Numbers that are easy to add, subtract, multiply or divide are called ___. In division, they are number pairs that are easy to divide.

Concepts and Skills

Look at the place-value chart. Then complete the sentences.

Millions	Hundred Thousands	Ten Thousands	Thousands	Hundreds	Tens	Ones
●●●●●	○○○○○○○○	●●●●●●●●●	●●●●●●	○○○○	●	○○○

5. Number in standard form: ___

6. Number in word form: ___

7. Number in expanded form: ___

Complete.

Millions	Hundred Thousands	Ten Thousands	Thousands	Hundreds	Tens	Ones
2	9	3	7	0	4	5

In 2,937,045:

8 The digit 9 stands for ______.

9 The value of the digit 2 is ______.

10 The digit 3 is in the ______ place.

Compare the numbers. Fill each ◯ with > or <.

11 8,417,855 ◯ 8,045,762

12 604,259 ◯ 1,105,873

Find the rule. Then complete the number pattern.

13 8,584,671 8,084,671 7,584,671 ______ ______

14 300,534 1,400,534 2,500,534 ______ ______

Round each number to the nearest thousand.

15 1,939 ______

16 527,138 ______

Estimate each sum or difference.

17 8,068 + 2,643 ______

18 5,632 + 2,165 + 7,464 ______

19 3,815 − 1,113 ______

20 5,325 − 1,689 ______

Estimate each product.

21 9,301 × 5 ______

22 3,876 × 6 ______

Estimate each quotient.

23. 6,783 ÷ 8

24. 4,463 ÷ 5

Problem Solving

Use the table to answer each question.

The land areas of some countries are shown below.

Country	Land area (square miles)
Canada	3,851,808
France	211,209
Hong Kong	426
Singapore	268
Thailand	198,456
United States	3,717,811

25. Write the land area of Canada in word form.

26. Order the countries from greatest to least land area.

27. Which countries have a land area greater than 1,000,000 square miles?

28. Which countries have a land area of 200,000 square miles when their land areas are rounded to the nearest hundred thousand square miles?

Whole Number Multiplication and Division

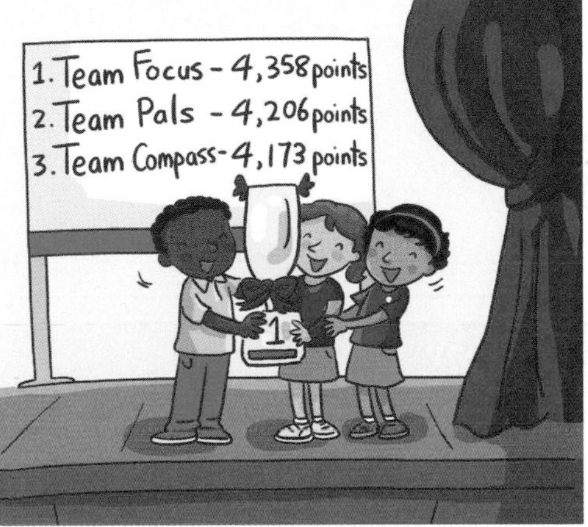

Lessons

2.1 Using a Calculator
2.2 Multiplying by Tens, Hundreds, or Thousands
2.3 Multiplying by Powers of Ten
2.4 Multiplying by 2-Digit Numbers
2.5 Dividing by Tens, Hundreds, or Thousands
2.6 Dividing by 2-Digit Numbers
2.7 Order of Operations
2.8 Real-World Problems: Multiplication and Division

- Patterns can be used to help you multiply and divide numbers.
- Numeric expressions can be simplified using the order of operations.
- Multiplication and division can be used to solve real-world problems.

Recall Prior Knowledge

Writing numbers in expanded form and word form

Write 4,937,512 in expanded form and word form.

Expanded form:
4,000,000 + 900,000 + 30,000 + 7,000 + 500 + 10 + 2

Word form:
Four million, nine hundred thirty-seven thousand, five hundred twelve

Using bar models to show the four operations

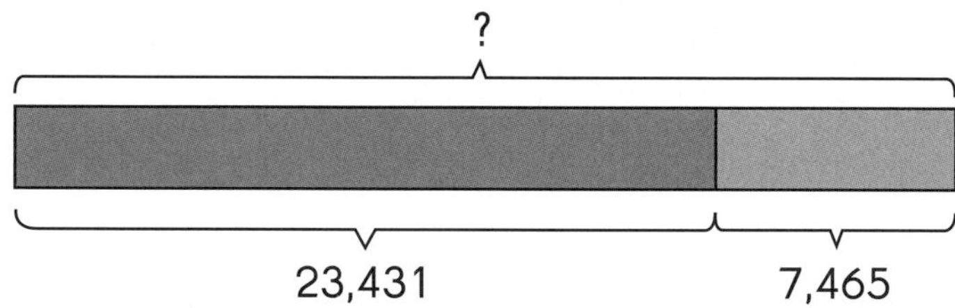

? = 23,431 + 7,465
= 30,896

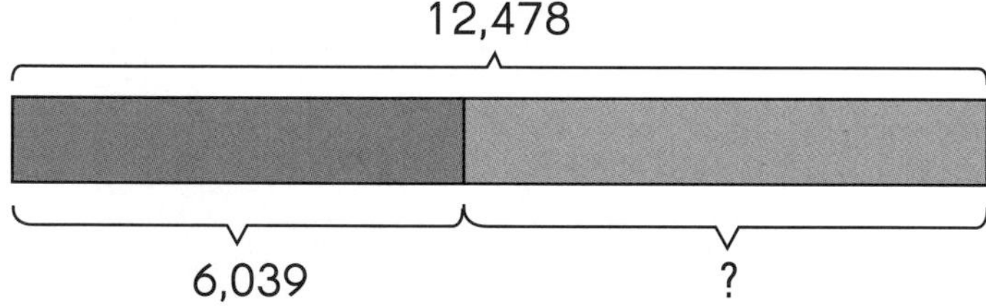

? = 12,478 − 6,039
= 6,439

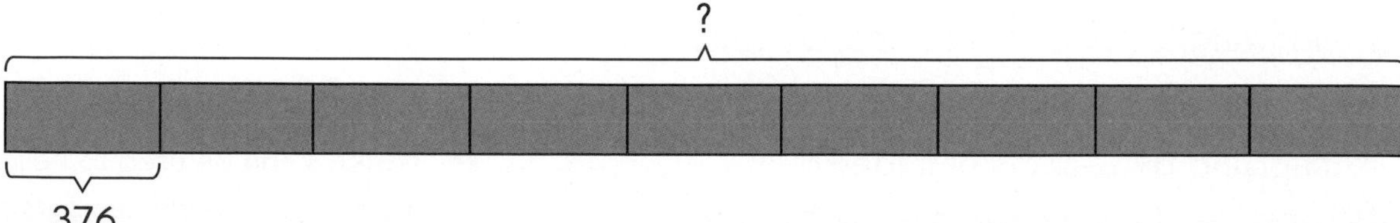

? = 9 × 376
= 3,384

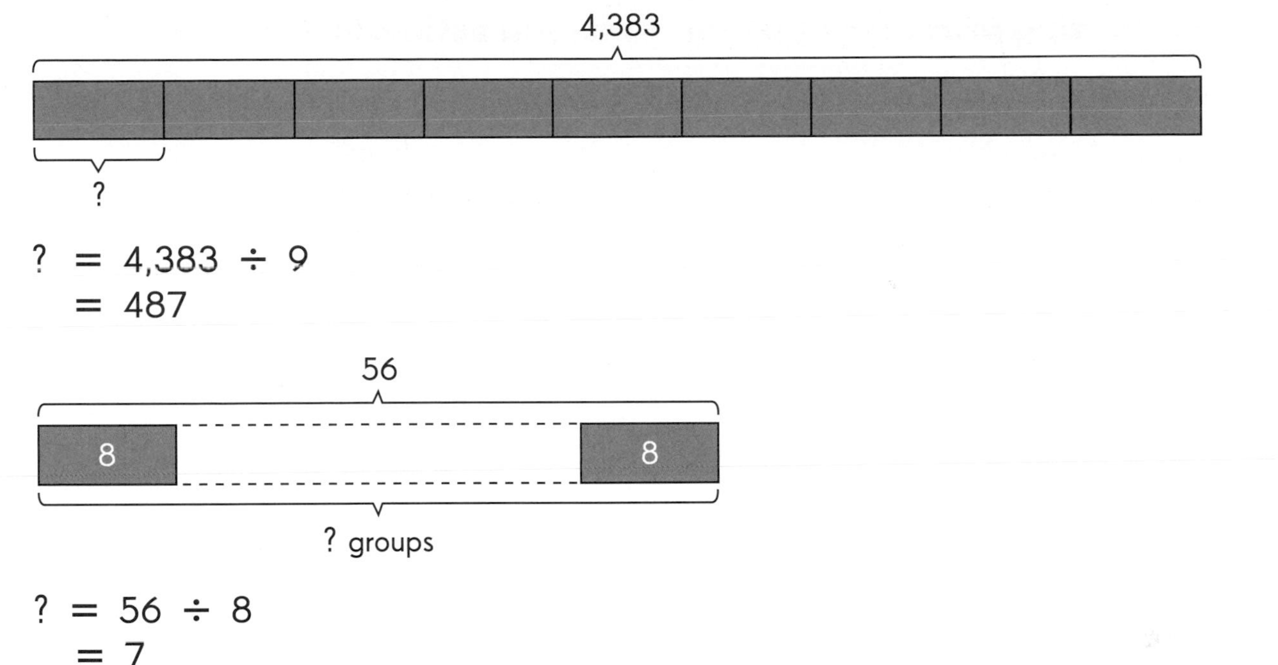

$? = 4{,}383 \div 9$
$\;\;= 487$

$? = 56 \div 8$
$\;\;= 7$

Rounding to the nearest thousand

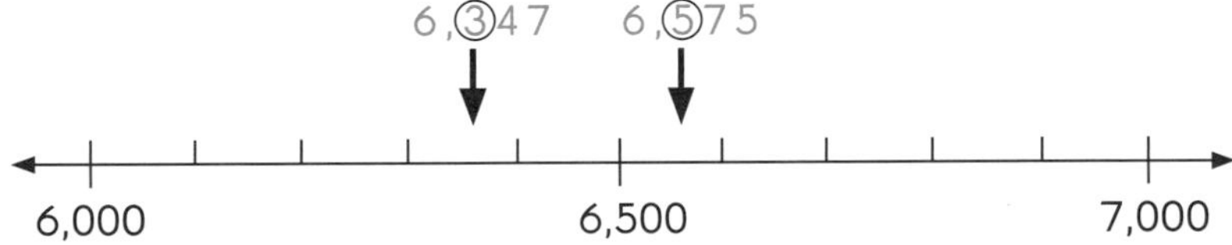

When the hundreds digit is 0, 1, 2, 3, or 4, round the number to the lesser thousand.

6,③47 rounded to the nearest thousand is 6,000.

When the hundreds digit is 5, 6, 7, 8, or 9, round the number to the greater thousand.

6,⑤75 rounded to the nearest thousand is 7,000.

Estimating products by rounding

Estimate the value of 684×9.

684 rounded to the nearest hundred is 700.

$700 \times 9 = 6{,}300$

684×9 is about 6,300.

Estimating products by using front-end estimation

Estimate the value of 563×7.

$563 \longrightarrow 500$
$500 \times 7 = 3{,}500$

563×7 is about 3,500.

Estimating quotients by using related multiplication facts

Estimate the value of $156 \div 4$.

Look for compatible numbers close to 156 and 4.

$4 \times 30 = 120$
$4 \times 40 = 160$

156 is nearer to 160 than to 120.

Choose 160 to make this estimate.

$160 \div 4 = 40$

$156 \div 4$ is about 40.

✔ Quick Check

Write the numbers in expanded form and in word form.

1. 8,753,924

   Expanded form: ___ + ___ + ___ + ___ + ___ + ___ + ___

   Word form: ___

2. 5,905,478

   Expanded form: ___ + ___ + ___ + ___ + ___ + ___

   Word form: ___

Find each missing number.

3

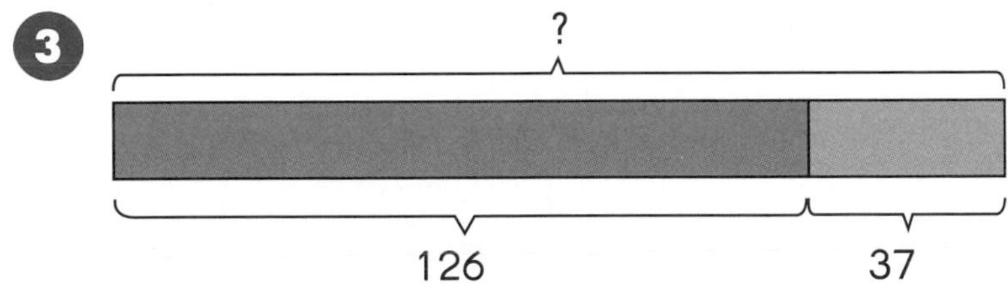

? = 126 ◯ 37

= ☐

4

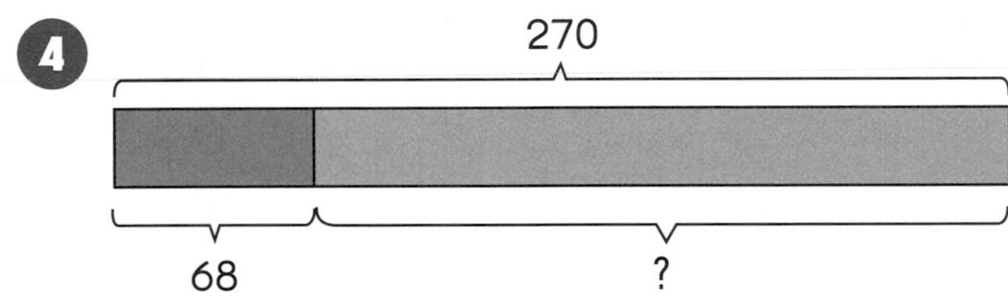

? = 270 ◯ 68

= ☐

5

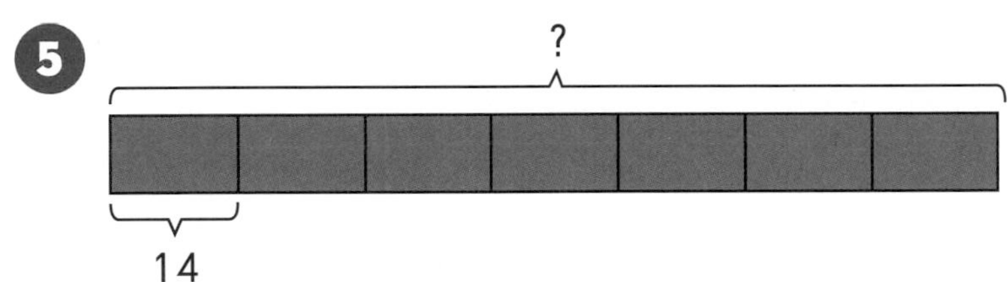

? = 7 ◯ 14

= ☐

6

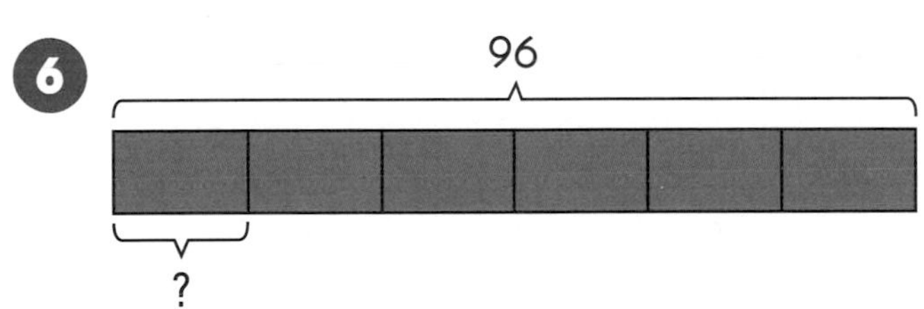

? = 96 ◯ 6

= ☐

7

135

5 5

? groups

? = 135 ◯ 5

= ☐

Round to the nearest thousand.

8. 750 ☐

9. 10,497 ☐

10. 14,568 ☐

Estimate each product by rounding.

11. 203×6 ☐

12. 792×4 ☐

13. 857×3 ☐

Estimate each product by using front-end estimation.

14. 142×9 ☐

15. 967×5 ☐

16. 374×6 ☐

Estimate each quotient by using related multiplication facts.

17. $178 \div 3$ ☐

18. $265 \div 5$ ☐

19. $532 \div 6$ ☐

Lesson 2.1 Using a Calculator

Lesson Objective

- Use a calculator to add, subtract, multiply, and divide whole numbers.

Learn Get to know your calculator.

Turn on your calculator.

Follow the steps to enter numbers on your calculator.

To enter 12,345, press: [1] [2] [3] [4] [5]

To clear the display on your calculator, press: [C]

Display

0

12345

0

Hands-On Activity

WORK IN PAIRS

Enter these numbers on your calculator. Clear the display on your calculator before entering the next number.

1. 735
2. 9,038
3. 23,104
4. 505,602

Check each number on your calculator with your partner's number. Do both calculators show the same number on the display screen?

Learn Use your calculator to add.

Add 417 and 9,086.

Press	Display
C	0
4 1 7	417
+ 9 0 8 6	9086
=	9503

The sum is 9,503.

Find the sum of $1,275 and $876.

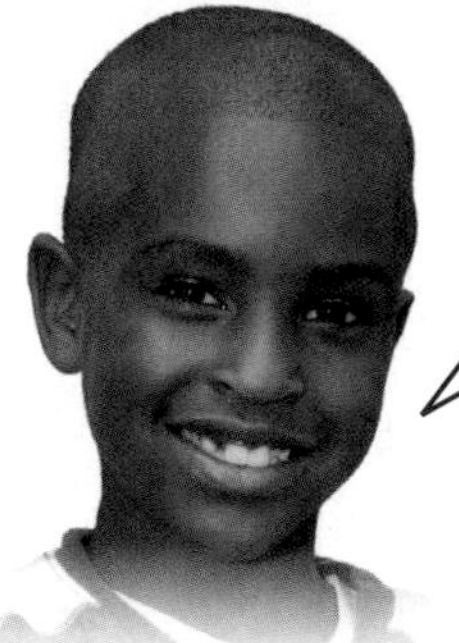

Remember to write the correct unit in your answer.

Press	Display
C	0
1 2 7 5	1275
+ 8 7 6	876
=	2151

The sum of $1,275 and $876 is $2,151.

Learn Use your calculator to subtract.

Subtract 6,959 from 17,358.

Press	Display
C	0
1 7 3 5 8	17358
− 6 9 5 9	6959
=	10399

The difference is 10,399.

Find the difference between 1,005 pounds and 248 pounds.

Remember to write pounds in your answer.

Press	Display
C	0
1 0 0 5	1005
− 2 4 8	248
=	757

The difference between 1,005 pounds and 248 pounds is 757 pounds.

Hands-On Activity

Find the sum or difference.

1. 7,064 + 2,378
2. 3,675 − 1,976
3. 734 km + 9,868 km
4. \$3,250 − \$1,865

Think of one addition and one subtraction problem.
Ask your partner to find the sum or difference using a calculator.
Check your partner's answers with a calculator.

Learn Use your calculator to multiply.

Multiply 253 by 127.

Press	Display
C	0
2 5 3	253
× 1 2 7	127
=	32131

The product is 32,131.

Find the area of a rectangle with length 36 meters and width 24 meters.

Press	Display
C	0
3 6	36
× 2 4	24
=	864

Area = length × width
Remember that the unit for area is square meters, square inches, and so on.

The area of the rectangle is 864 square meters.

Learn Use your calculator to divide.

Divide 4,572 by 36.

Press	Display
C	0
4 5 7 2	4572
÷ 3 6	36
=	127

The quotient is 127.

Find 168 quarts divided by 16.

Press	Display
C	0
1 6 8	168
÷ 1 6	16
=	10.5

168 quarts divided by 16 is 10.5 quarts.

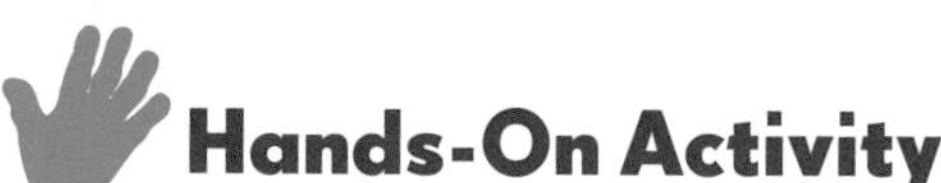

Hands-On Activity

WORK IN PAIRS

Remember to press C before you begin each problem.

Find the product or quotient.

1. 1,065 × 97
2. 13,674 × 7
3. 1,075 ÷ 25
4. 10,840 ÷ 40
5. 25 m × 48 m
6. 406 oz ÷ 28

Think of one multiplication and one division problem. Ask your partner to find the product or quotient using a calculator. Check your partner's answers with a calculator.

ON YOUR OWN

Go to Workbook A: Practice 1, pages 27–28

Lesson 2.2 Multiplying by Tens, Hundreds, or Thousands

Lesson Objectives

- Multiply numbers by 10, 100, or 1,000 using patterns.
- Multiply numbers up to 4 digits by multiples of 10, 100, or 1,000.
- Use rounding to estimate products.

Vocabulary
product
factor

Learn Look for a pattern in the products when 10 is a factor.

10	10	10	10	10	10	10

$7 \times 10 = 70$

10	10	10	10	10	10	10	10	10

$9 \times 10 = 90$

10	10	10	10	10	10	10	10	10	10

$10 \times 10 = 100$

10	10	10	10	10	10	10	10	10	10	10	10

$12 \times 10 = 120$

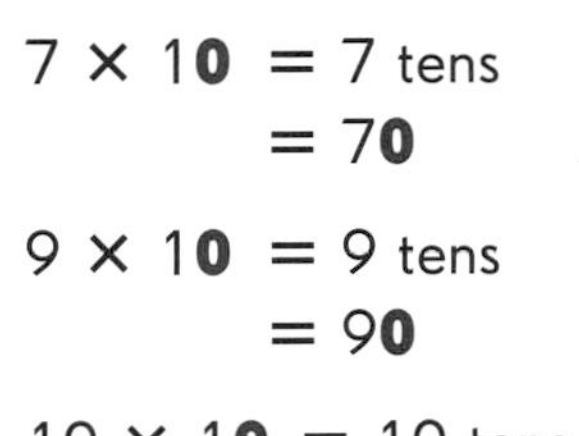

7×10 = 7 tens
= 70

9×10 = 9 tens
= 90

10×10 = 10 tens
= 100

12×10 = 12 tens
= 120

Continued on next page

Look at the place-value chart.

	Hundreds	Tens	Ones
7			
7 × 10			
9			
9 × 10			
10			
10 × 10			
12			
12 × 10			

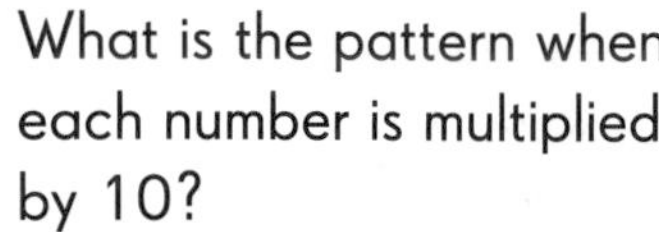

What is the pattern when each number is multiplied by 10?

	Hundreds	Tens	Ones
7			7
7 × 10		7	0
9			9
9 × 10		9	0
10		1	0
10 × 10	1	0	0
12		1	2
12 × 10	1	2	0

Each digit moves one place to the left when the number is multiplied by 10.

Hands-On Activity

Copy and complete the table.

	Hundred Thousands	Ten Thousands	Thousands	Hundreds	Tens	Ones
231				2	3	1
231 × 10			2	3	1	0
2,345			2	3	4	5
2,345 × 10						
4,108			4	1	0	8
4,108 × 10						

Write the products.

1. 231 × 10
2. 2,345 × 10
3. 4,108 × 10

What rule can you use when you multiply a whole number by 10?

Guided Learning

Multiply.

1. 60 × 10
2. 135 × 10
3. 503 × 10
4. 2,876 × 10
5. 6,082 × 10
6. 6,010 × 10

Find the missing factors.

7. $8 \times \square = 80$

8. $22 \times \square = 220$

9. $\square \times 10 = 5{,}280$

10. $\square \times 10 = 74{,}600$

Learn Break apart a number to help you multiply by tens.

6 × 20

20		20		20		20		20		20	
10	10	10	10	10	10	10	10	10	10	10	10

$$\begin{aligned} 6 \times 20 &= 6 \times 2 \text{ tens} \\ &= (6 \times 2) \times 10 \\ &= 12 \times 10 \\ &= 120 \end{aligned}$$

$$\begin{aligned} 27 \times 30 &= 27 \times 3 \text{ tens} \\ &= (27 \times 3) \times 10 \\ &= 81 \times 10 \\ &= 810 \end{aligned}$$

Multiplying a number by 20 is the same as multiplying it by 2 and then by 10.

Multiplying a number by 30 is the same as multiplying it by 3 and then by 10.

Hands-On Activity

Copy and complete the table by multiplying each number by 6 and by 60. An example is shown.

	× 6	× 60
42	252	2,520
65		
861		

Look at the answers in the table. Find the missing numbers.

1. 42 × 60 = (42 × 6) × ___
2. 65 × 60 = (65 × ___) × ___
3. 861 × 60 = (861 × ___) × ___

Guided Learning

Find the missing numbers.

11. 62 × 40 = (62 × 4) × 10
 = ___ × 10
 = ___

12. 307 × 80 = (307 × ___) × 10
 = ___ × 10
 = ___

Multiply.

13 274 × 50

14 1,970 × 90

15 8,145 × 40

Learn Look for a pattern in the products when 100 or 1,000 is a factor.

100	100	100	100	100

5 × 1**00** = 5**00**

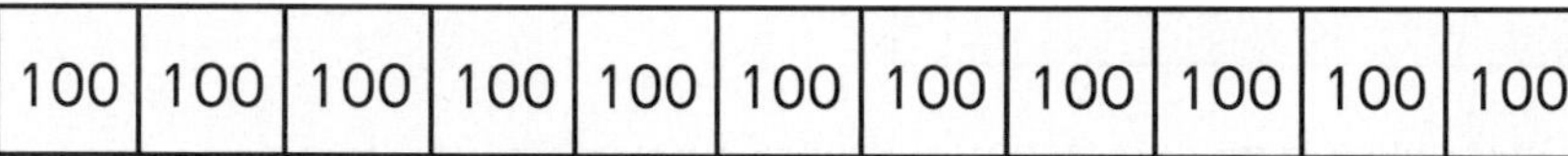

11 × 1**00** = 1,1**00**

5 × 1**00** = 5 hundreds
= 5**00**

11 × 1**00** = 11 hundreds
= 1,1**00**

1,000	1,000	1,000	1,000	1,000

5 × 1,**000** = 5,**000**

5 × 1,**000** = 5 thousands
= 5,**000**

11 × 1,**000** = 11 thousands
= 11,**000**

1,000	1,000	1,000	1,000	1,000	1,000	1,000	1,000	1,000	1,000	1,000

11 × 1,**000** = 11,**000**

Look at the place-value chart.

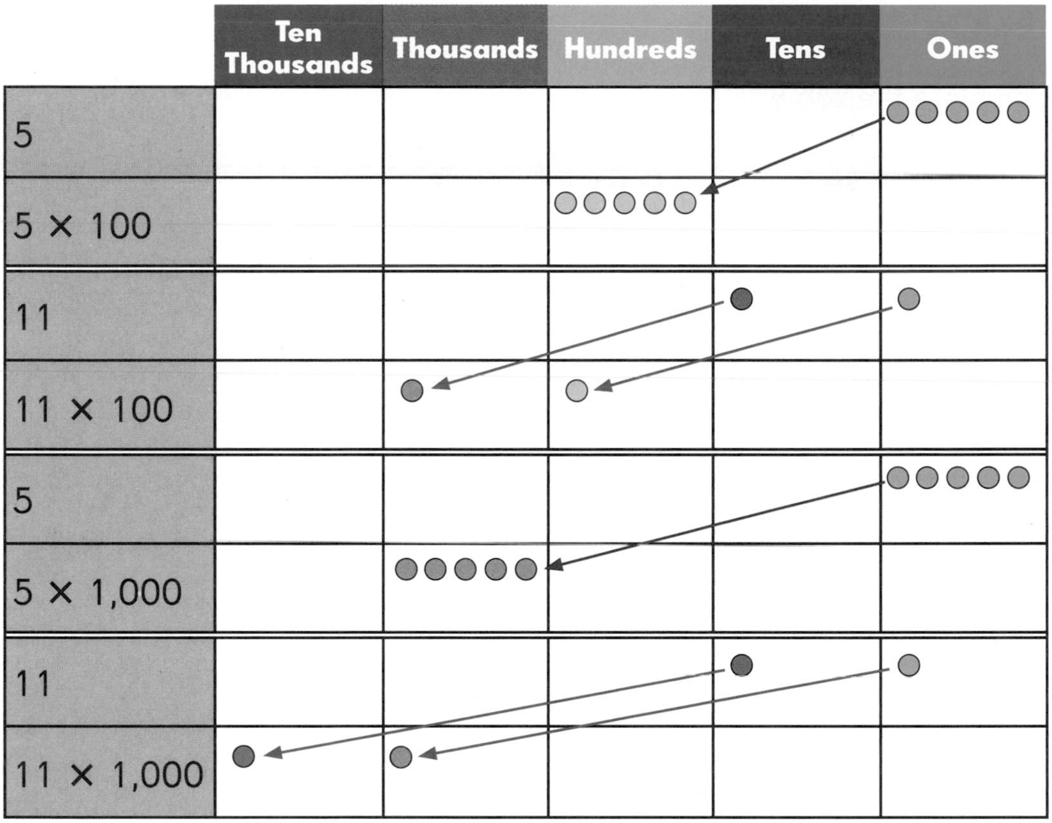

	Ten Thousands	Thousands	Hundreds	Tens	Ones
5					●●●●●
5 × 100			●●●●●		
11				●	●
11 × 100		●	●		
5					●●●●●
5 × 1,000		●●●●●			
11				●	●
11 × 1,000	●	●			

	Ten Thousands	Thousands	Hundreds	Tens	Ones
5					5
5 × 100			5	0	0
11				1	1
11 × 100		1	1	0	0
5					5
5 × 1,000		5	0	0	0
11				1	1
11 × 1,000	1	1	0	0	0

Each digit moves two places to the left when the number is multiplied by 100.
Each digit moves three places to the left when the number is multiplied by 1,000.

Hands-On Activity

Copy and complete the table.

	Millions	Hundred Thousands	Ten Thousands	Thousands	Hundreds	Tens	Ones
174					1	7	4
174 × 100			1	7	4	0	0
174 × 1,000		1	7	4	0	0	0
3,298				3	2	9	8
3,298 × 100							
3,298 × 1,000							

Write the products.

1. 174 × 100
2. 174 × 1,000
3. 3,298 × 100
4. 3,298 × 1,000

What rule can you use when you multiply a whole number by 100?

What rule can you use when you multiply a whole number by 1,000?

Guided Learning

Multiply.

16 27×100 ___ 17 615×100 ___ 18 $9{,}670 \times 100$ ___

19 $18 \times 1{,}000$ ___ 20 $487 \times 1{,}000$ ___ 21 $5{,}346 \times 1{,}000$ ___

Find the missing factors.

22 $26 \times$ ___ $= 2{,}600$ 23 $195 \times$ ___ $= 195{,}000$

24 ___ $\times 100 = 49{,}000$ 25 ___ $\times 1{,}000 = 168{,}000$

Learn **Break apart a number to help you multiply by hundreds or thousands.**

7×200

200		200		200		200		200		200		200	
100	100	100	100	100	100	100	100	100	100	100	100	100	100

$7 \times 200 = 7 \times 2$ hundreds
$= (7 \times 2) \times 100$
$= 14 \times 100$
$= 1{,}400$

$67 \times 5{,}000 = 67 \times 5$ thousands
$= (67 \times 5) \times 1{,}000$
$= 335 \times 1{,}000$
$= 335{,}000$

Multiplying a number by 200 is the same as multiplying it by 2 and then by 100.

Multiplying a number by 5,000 is the same as multiplying it by 5 and then by 1,000.

Hands-On Activity

Copy and complete the table by multiplying each number by 7, 700, and 7,000. An example is shown.

	× 7	× 700	× 7,000
78	546	54,600	546,000
113			
251			

Look at the answers in the table. Find the missing numbers.

1. 78 × 700 = (78 × 7) × ▢
2. 113 × 700 = (113 × ▢) × ▢
3. 251 × 700 = (251 × ▢) × ▢
4. 78 × 7,000 = (78 × 7) × ▢
5. 113 × 7,000 = (113 × ▢) × ▢
6. 251 × 7,000 = (251 × ▢) × ▢

Guided Learning

Find the missing numbers.

26. 72 × 400 = (72 × 4) × 100
 = ▢ × 100
 = ▢

27. 123 × 700 = (123 × ▢) × ▢
 = ▢ × 100
 = ▢

Find the missing numbers.

28 $6 \times 5{,}000 = (6 \times 5) \times 1{,}000$
$= \square \times 1{,}000$
$= \square$

29 $18 \times 6{,}000 = (18 \times \square) \times \square$
$= \square \times 1{,}000$
$= \square$

Multiply.

30 81×500 $\square$

31 932×800 $\square$

32 $6{,}455 \times 900$ $\square$

33 $6{,}007 \times 800$ $\square$

34 $73 \times 4{,}000$ $\square$

35 $905 \times 8{,}000$ $\square$

36 $654 \times 3{,}000$ $\square$

37 $807 \times 9{,}000$ $\square$

Learn **Round factors to the nearest ten or hundred to estimate products.**

Estimate the product of 632 and 26.

Round 632 to the nearest hundred.

Round 26 to the nearest ten.

632 rounds to 600, and 26 rounds to 30.

$600 \times 30 = (600 \times 3) \times 10$
$= 1{,}800 \times 10$
$= 18{,}000$

The product is about 18,000.

The estimate of a product is often farther from the actual answer than other estimates. But it still gives you an idea of the size of the answer.

Guided Learning

Estimate.

38 Estimate the product of 228 and 57.

Round 228 to the nearest hundred.
Round 57 to the nearest ten.
228 rounds to ___, and 57 rounds to 60.

$\_\_\_ \times 60 = (\_\_\_ \times 6) \times 10$
$= \_\_\_ \times 10$
$= \_\_\_$

39 702 × 15 ___ **40** 27 × 364 ___ **41** 38 × 246 ___

42 851 × 19 ___ **43** 511 × 62 ___ **44** 35 × 424 ___

Learn Round factors to the nearest ten or thousand to estimate products.

A museum gift shop sold 1,215 sets of dinosaur models.
There were 26 dinosaur models in each set.
Estimate the total number of dinosaur models the shop sold.

Round 1,215 to the nearest thousand.
Round 26 to the nearest ten.
1,215 rounds to 1,000, and 26 rounds to 30.

$1,000 \times 30 = (1,000 \times 3) \times 10$
$= 3,000 \times 10$
$= 30,000$

The shop sold about 30,000 dinosaur models.

Guided Learning

Estimate.

45 Estimate the product of 1,238 and 56.

Round 1,238 to the nearest thousand.
Round 56 to the nearest ten.
1,238 rounds to 1,000, and 56 rounds to ___.

1,000 × ___ = (1,000 × ___) × ___
= ___ × ___
= ___

46 99 × 38 ___

47 67 × 439 ___

48 9,281 × 32 ___

49 2,065 × 41 ___

Let's Practice

Multiply.

1 412 × 10 ___

2 792 × 100 ___

3 740 × 1,000 ___

4 703 × 60 ___

5 815 × 700 ___

6 169 × 3,000 ___

Estimate each product.

7 3,711 × 9 ___

8 2,087 × 37 ___

9 1,985 × 302 ___

Solve.

10 A factory produces 452 beads in 1 minute.
Estimate the number of beads the factory produces in 56 minutes.

___

ON YOUR OWN

Go to Workbook A: Practice 2, pages 29–36

Lesson

2.3 Multiplying by Powers of Ten

Lesson Objective

- Multiply whole numbers by 10 squared or 10 cubed.

Vocabulary

exponent base

square cube

Learn **Look for a pattern in products when 10^2 is a factor.**

Exponents can be used when you multiply a number by itself.

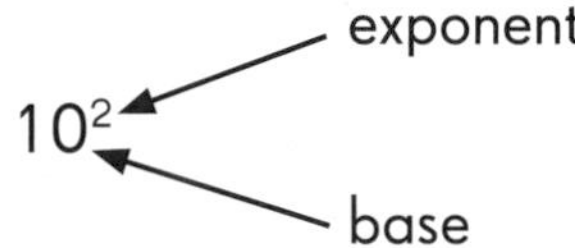

The **base** is the number being multiplied.

The **exponent** tells you how many times to use the base as a factor.

When you multiply 10 by itself, you get 10×10.

10×10 is called the **square** of 10.

You can write 10×10 as 10^2, which is read as "10 squared."

So, $10^2 = 10 \times 10$.

a) Find 23×10^2.

$$\begin{aligned} 23 \times \mathbf{10^2} &= 23 \times (10 \times 10) \\ &= 23 \times 100 \\ &= 2{,}3\mathbf{00} \end{aligned}$$

$$\begin{aligned} 23 \times \mathbf{10^2} &= 23 \text{ hundreds} \\ &= 2{,}3\mathbf{00} \\ 316 \times \mathbf{10^2} &= 316 \text{ hundreds} \\ &= 31{,}6\mathbf{00} \end{aligned}$$

b) Find 316×10^2.

$$\begin{aligned} 316 \times \mathbf{10^2} &= 316 \times (10 \times 10) \\ &= 316 \times 100 \\ &= 31{,}6\mathbf{00} \end{aligned}$$

Guided Learning

Multiply.

1. 35×10^2 ______
2. 93×10^2 ______
3. 140×10^2 ______
4. 256×10^2 ______

Learn **Look for a pattern in products when 10^3 is a factor.**

You can also multiply using an exponent of 3.

$10 \times 10 \times 10$ is called the **cube** of 10.
You can write $10 \times 10 \times 10$ as 10^3, which is read as "10 cubed."

So, $10^3 = 10 \times 10 \times 10$.

a. Find 45×10^3.

$45 \times \mathbf{10^3} = 45 \times (10 \times 10 \times 10)$
$= 45 \times 1{,}000$
$= 45{,}\mathbf{000}$

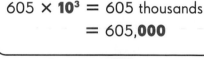

$45 \times \mathbf{10^3} = 45$ thousands
$= 45{,}\mathbf{000}$
$605 \times \mathbf{10^3} = 605$ thousands
$= 605{,}\mathbf{000}$

b. Find 605×10^3.

$605 \times \mathbf{10^3} = 605 \times (10 \times 10 \times 10)$
$= 605 \times 1{,}000$
$= 605{,}\mathbf{000}$

Guided Learning

Multiply.

5 88×10^3 ☐

6 315×10^3 ☐

7 560×10^3 ☐

8 $7,008 \times 10^3$ ☐

Learn Use exponents to solve problems.

Mr. Wang wants to tile the front entryway to his home. The entryway is 36 square feet. Each square foot of tile that he chooses is 10 tiles by 10 tiles. How many tiles does he need to buy?

Area of entryway = 36 square feet

Number of tiles in each square foot = 10^2

Total number of tiles needed = 36×10^2

$= 36 \times (10 \times 10)$

$= 36 \times 100$

$= 3,600$

Mr. Wang needs to buy 3,600 tiles.

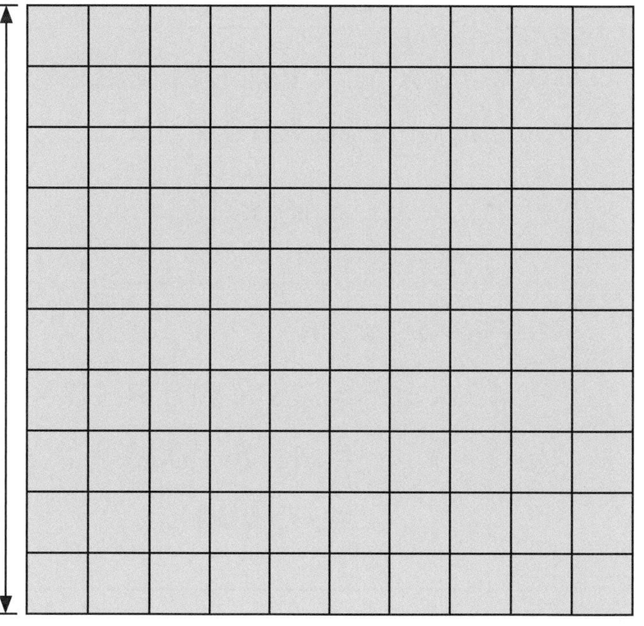

There are 10^3 grams in a kilogram. How many grams are there in 15 kilograms?

Number of grams = 15×10^3

$= 15 \times (10 \times 10 \times 10)$

$= 15 \times 1,000$

$= 15,000$ grams

There are 15,000 grams in 15 kilograms.

Guided Learning

9 Mr. Wang later decides to use the same tile in a hallway that has an area of 48 square feet. How many tiles must he buy for this project?

Total number of tiles = ___ × ___

= ___ × (___ × ___)

= ___ × ___

= ___ tiles

10 There are 10^3 millimeters in a meter. How many millimeters are in 23 meters? ___

Let's Practice

Multiply.

1 27×10^2 ___

2 80×10^2 ___

3 306×10^2 ___

4 145×10^2 ___

5 520×10^2 ___

6 60×10^3 ___

7 48×10^3 ___

8 143×10^3 ___

9 630×10^3 ___

Use the table of metric measures to convert the measurements.

Equivalent Metric Measures		
10^2 centimeters = 1 meter	10^3 millimeters = 1 meter	10^3 meters = 1 kilometer

10 7 meters = ___ centimeters

11 3 meters = ___ millimeters

12 25 meters = ___ centimeters

13 15 meters = ___ millimeters

14 5 kilometers = ___ meters

15 12 kilometers = ___ meters

ON YOUR OWN

Go to Workbook A: Practice 3, pages 37–40

Lesson 2.4 Multiplying by 2-Digit Numbers

Lesson Objective

- Multiply a 2-, 3-, or 4-digit number by a 2-digit number.

Learn: Multiply a 2-digit number by tens.

Multiply 12 by 30.

Method 1

$12 \times 30 = (12 \times 3) \times 10$
$= 36 \times 10$
$= 360$

12 × 30 is the same as 12 × 3 tens.

$12 \times 3 \text{ tens} = 36 \text{ tens}$
$= 36 \times 10$
$= 360$

12 × 3 = 36	36	36	36	36
36	36	36	36	36

Method 2

$$\begin{array}{r} 1\ 2 \\ \times\ \ 3\ \mathbf{0} \\ \hline 3\ 6\ \mathbf{0} \end{array}$$ ← multiply 12 by 3 tens

$$\begin{array}{r} 1\ 2 \\ \times\ \ \ 3 \\ \hline 3\ 6 \end{array}$$ ← multiply 12 by 3

Multiply 60 by 20.

60 × 20 is the same as 60 × 2 tens.

60 × 2 tens = 120 tens
= 120 × 10
= 1,200

Method 1

$$60 \times 20 = (60 \times 2) \times 10$$
$$= 120 \times 10$$
$$= 1,200$$

Method 2

$$\begin{array}{r} 6\,0 \\ \times \quad 2\,\mathbf{0} \\ \hline 1,2\,0\,\mathbf{0} \end{array}$$

$$\begin{array}{r} 6\,0 \\ \times \quad 2 \\ \hline 1\,2\,0 \end{array}$$

Learn Multiply a 2-digit number by a 2-digit number.

Multiply 63 by 28.

$$\begin{array}{r} \overset{2}{6}\,3 \\ \times \quad 2\,8 \\ \hline 5\,0\,4 \\ 1,2\,6\,0 \\ \hline 1,7\,6\,4 \end{array}$$

504 ← multiply 63 by 8 ones
1,260 ← multiply 63 by 2 tens
1,764 ← add

Check!

Estimate the value of 63 × 28.
63 rounds to 60, and 28 rounds to 30.
60 × 30 = 1,800
The estimate shows the answer 1,764 is reasonable.

Guided Learning

Multiply. Show your work.

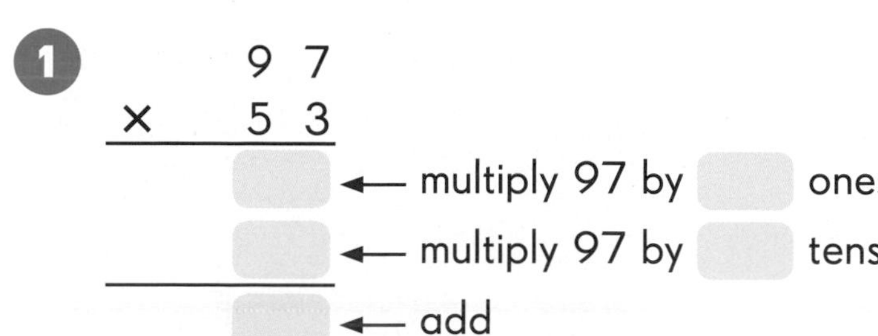

1

$$\begin{array}{r} 9\,7 \\ \times \quad 5\,3 \\ \hline \end{array}$$

___ ← multiply 97 by ___ ones
___ ← multiply 97 by ___ tens
___ ← add

Check!

Estimate the value of 97 × 53.
97 rounds to ___, and
53 rounds to ___.
___ × ___ = ___
The estimate shows the answer ___ is ___.

Multiply. Estimate to check if your answers are reasonable.

2. 72 × 90 ☐
3. 25 × 40 ☐
4. 34 × 70 ☐
5. 19 × 12 ☐
6. 65 × 44 ☐
7. 38 × 72 ☐
8. 99 × 95 ☐
9. 91 × 85 ☐

Learn Multiply a 3-digit number by tens.

Multiply 520 by 30.

Method 1

$$\begin{aligned} 520 \times 30 &= (520 \times 3) \times 10 \\ &= 1{,}560 \times 10 \\ &= 15{,}600 \end{aligned}$$

520 × 30 is the same as 520 × 3 tens.

$$\begin{aligned} 520 \times 3 \text{ tens} &= 1{,}560 \text{ tens} \\ &= 1{,}560 \times 10 \\ &= 15{,}600 \end{aligned}$$

Method 2

$$\begin{array}{r} 5\ 2\ 0 \\ \times \quad 3\ \mathbf{0} \\ \hline 1\ 5,\ 6\ 0\ \mathbf{0} \end{array}$$

$$\begin{array}{r} 5\ 2\ 0 \\ \times \quad 3 \\ \hline 1,\ 5\ 6\ 0 \end{array}$$

Learn Multiply a 3-digit number by a 2-digit number.

Multiply 623 by 32.

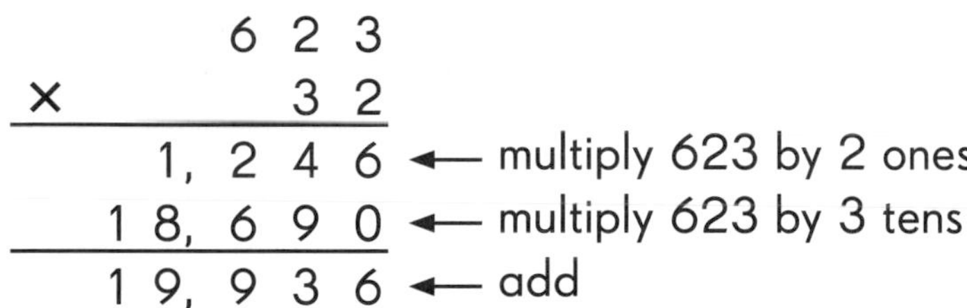

Check!

Estimate the value of 623 × 32.
Using front-end estimation:
623 → 600
32 → 30
600 × 30 = 18,000
The estimate shows the answer 19,936 is reasonable.

When both factors are **rounded down**, the estimate will be **less** than the actual product.

When both factors are **rounded up**, the estimate will be **greater** than the actual product.

What happens when one factor is rounded up and the other is rounded down?

Guided Learning

Multiply. Show your work.

10

$$\begin{array}{r} 514 \\ \times\ 72 \\ \hline \square \\ \square \\ \hline \square \end{array}$$

← multiply 514 by ___ ones
← multiply 514 by ___ tens
← add

Check!

Estimate the value of 514 × 72.
Using front-end estimation:
514 → 500
72 → 70
___ × ___ = ___
The estimate shows the answer ___ is ___.

Multiply. Estimate to check if your answers are reasonable.

11. 681 × 60 ___ 12. 210 × 80 ___ 13. 651 × 70 ___
14. 413 × 12 ___ 15. 516 × 21 ___ 16. 294 × 48 ___

Learn Multiply a 4-digit number by tens.

Multiply 7,360 by 20.

Method 1

7,360 × 20 = (7,360 × 2) × 10
= 14,720 × 10
= 147,200

7,360 × 20 is the same as 7,360 × 2 tens.

7,360 × 2 tens = 14,720 tens
= 14,720 × 10
= 147,200

Method 2

```
      7, 3 6 0
×          2 0
--------------
  1 4 7, 2 0 0
```

```
     1
  7, 3 6 0
×        2
----------
1 4, 7 2 0
```

Learn Multiply a 4-digit number by a 2-digit number.

Multiply 5,362 by 76.

```
       2  4  1
       2  3  1
    5, 3  6  2
×        7   6
--------------
  3 2, 1  7  2 ← multiply 5,362 by 6 ones
3 7 5, 3  4  0 ← multiply 5,362 by 7 tens
--------------
4 0 7, 5  1  2 ← add
```

Check!

Estimate the value of 5,362 × 76.
5,362 rounds to 5,000.
76 rounds to 80.
5,000 × 80 = 400,000
The estimate shows the answer 407,512 is reasonable.

Guided Learning

Multiply. Show your work.

17

$$\begin{array}{r} 9,\ 2\ 0\ 5 \\ \times \quad\quad 2\ 4 \\ \hline \square \\ \square \\ \hline \square \end{array}$$

← multiply 9,205 by ___ ones

← multiply 9,205 by ___ tens

← add

Check!

Estimate the value of 9,205 × 24.
9,205 rounds to ___, and
24 rounds to ___.
___ × ___ = ___
The estimate shows the answer
___ is ___.

Multiply. Estimate to check if your answers are reasonable.

18 1,246 × 50 ___ **19** 5,913 × 60 ___ **20** 3,352 × 14 ___

21 9,540 × 36 ___ **22** 1,598 × 72 ___ **23** 2,535 × 47 ___

Let's Practice

Multiply. Estimate to check if your answers are reasonable.

1 20 × 30 ___ **2** 41 × 70 ___ **3** 300 × 50 ___

4 430 × 80 ___ **5** 413 × 90 ___ **6** 2,000 × 70 ___

7 3,700 × 40 ___ **8** 2,550 × 60 ___ **9** 56 × 32 ___

10 26 × 76 ___ **11** 589 × 77 ___ **12** 817 × 69 ___

13 3,438 × 81 ___ **14** 1,256 × 45 ___ **15** 4,522 × 38 ___

ON YOUR OWN

Go to Workbook A:
Practice 4, pages 41–46

Lesson

2.5 Dividing by Tens, Hundreds, or Thousands

Lesson Objectives

- Divide numbers by 10, 100, or 1,000 using patterns.
- Divide numbers up to 4 digits by multiples of 10, 100, or 1,000.
- Use rounding and related multiplication facts to estimate quotients.

Vocabulary
quotient
dividend
divisor

Learn Look for patterns when dividing by 10.

70

7	7	7	7	7	7	7	7	7	7

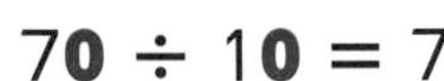

7**0** ÷ 1**0** = 7

7 × 1**0** = 7**0**
So, 7**0** ÷ 1**0** = 7.

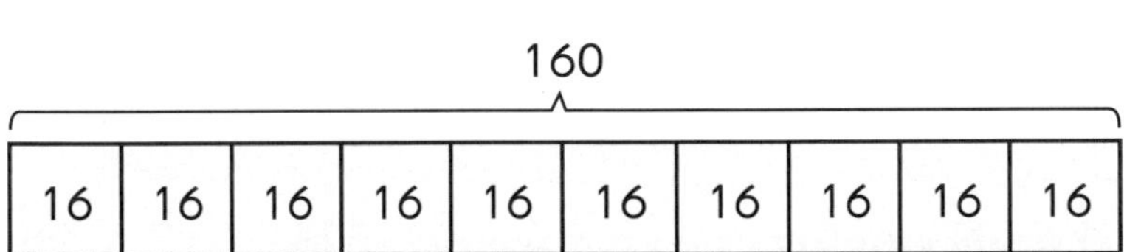

16**0** ÷ 1**0** = 16

16 × 1**0** = 16**0**
So, 16**0** ÷ 1**0** = 16.

1,800

180	180	180	180	180	180	180	180	180	180

1,80**0** ÷ 1**0** = 180

180 × 1**0** = 1,80**0**
So, 1,80**0** ÷ 1**0** = 180.

Look at the place-value chart.

	Thousands	Hundreds	Tens	Ones
70			●●●●●●●	
70 ÷ 10				●●●●●●●
160		●	●●●●●●	
160 ÷ 10			●	●●●●●●
1,800	●	●●●●●●●●		
1,800 ÷ 10		●	●●●●●●●●	

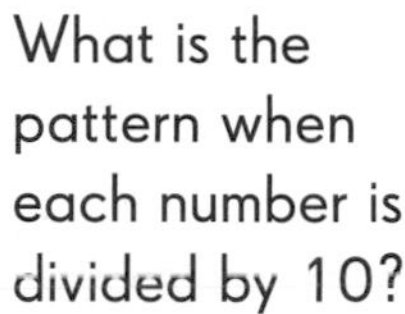

What is the pattern when each number is divided by 10?

	Thousands	Hundreds	Tens	Ones
70			7	0
70 ÷ 10				7
160		1	6	0
160 ÷ 10			1	6
1,800	1	8	0	0
1,800 ÷ 10		1	8	0

Each digit moves one place to the right when the number is divided by 10.

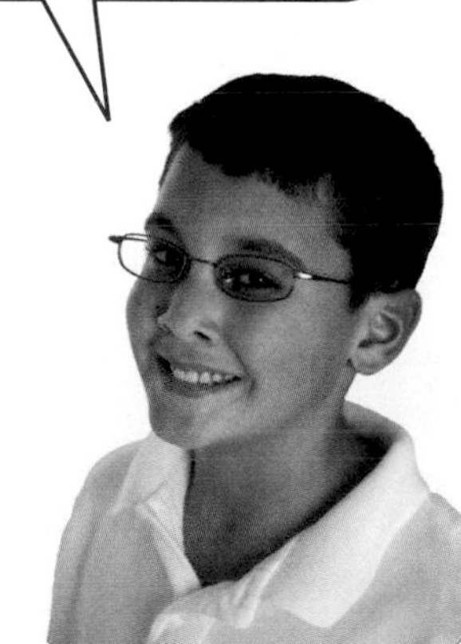

Hands-On Activity

Copy and complete the table.

	Thousands	Hundreds	Tens	Ones
360		3	6	0
360 ÷ 10			3	6
1,580	1	5	8	0
1,580 ÷ 10				

Divide.

1. 360 ÷ 10
2. 1,580 ÷ 10

Guided Learning

To divide a whole number with 0 in the ones place by 10, just drop the zero.
3,74**0** ÷ 1**0** = 374

Divide.

1. 90 ÷ 10 ____
2. 380 ÷ 10 ____
3. 1,900 ÷ 10 ____
4. 43,650 ÷ 10 ____

5. 23,040 ÷ 10 ____
6. 53,600 ÷ 10 ____

Find the missing numbers.

7. 2,600 ÷ ____ = 260
8. 19,500 ÷ ____ = 1,950

9. ____ ÷ 10 = 4,900
10. ____ ÷ 10 = 1,680

Learn Break apart a number to help you divide by tens.

$60 \div 30 = (60 \div 10) \div 3$
$= 6 \div 3$
$= 2$

Dividing a number by 30 is the same as dividing it by 10 and then by 3.

$420 \div 70 = (420 \div 10) \div 7$
$= 42 \div 7$
$= 6$

Hands-On Activity

Copy and complete the table by dividing each number by 9 and by 90. An example is shown.

	÷9	÷90
540	60	6
720		
810		

Look at the answers in the table. Find the missing numbers.

1. $540 \div 90 = (540 \div \square) \div 9$
2. $720 \div 90 = (720 \div \square) \div \square$
3. $810 \div 90 = (810 \div \square) \div \square$

Guided Learning

Find the missing numbers.

11. $850 \div 50 = (850 \div 10) \div 5$

$= \square \div 5$

$= \square$

12. $7{,}200 \div 80 = (7{,}200 \div \square) \div \square$

$= \square \div 8$

$= \square$

Divide.

13. $160 \div 40$ $\square$

14. $700 \div 50$ $\square$

15. $6{,}320 \div 20$ $\square$

16. $8{,}400 \div 60$ $\square$

Learn Look for patterns when dividing by 100 or 1,000.

9 × 1**00** = 9**00**

So, 9**00** ÷ 1**00** = 9.

14 × 1**00** = 1,4**00**

So, 1,4**00** ÷ 1**00** = 14.

---

9 × 1,**000** = 9,**000**

So, 9,**000** ÷ 1,**000** = 9.

14 × 1,**000** = 14,**000**

So, 14,**000** ÷ 1,**000** = 14.

Look at the place-value chart.

	Ten Thousands	Thousands	Hundreds	Tens	Ones
900			○○○○○○○○○		
900 ÷ 100					○○○○○○○○○
1,400		○	○○○○		
1,400 ÷ 100				○	○○○○
9,000		○○○○○○○○○			
9,000 ÷ 1,000					○○○○○○○○○
14,000	○	○○○○			
14,000 ÷ 1,000				○	○○○○

What is the pattern when each number is divided by **100** and by **1,000**?

	Ten Thousands	Thousands	Hundreds	Tens	Ones
900			9	0	0
900 ÷ 100					9
1,400		1	4	0	0
1,400 ÷ 100				1	4
9,000		9	0	0	0
9,000 ÷ 1,000					9
14,000	1	4	0	0	0
14,000 ÷ 1,000				1	4

Each digit moves two places to the right when the number is divided by 100.
Each digit moves three places to the right when the number is divided by 1,000.

Hands-On Activity

Copy and complete the table.

	Ten Thousands	Thousands	Hundreds	Tens	Ones
700			7	0	0
700 ÷ 100					7
3,600		3	6	0	0
3,600 ÷ 100					
8,000		8	0	0	0
8,000 ÷ 1,000					
54,000	5	4	0	0	0
54,000 ÷ 1,000					

Divide.

1. 700 ÷ 100
2. 3,600 ÷ 100
3. 8,000 ÷ 1,000
4. 54,000 ÷ 1,000

What rule can you use when you divide a multiple of 100 by 100?

What rule can you use when you divide a multiple of 1,000 by 1,000?

Guided Learning

Divide.

17. 400 ÷ 100 ▢

18. 1,500 ÷ 100 ▢

19. 20,500 ÷ 100 ▢

20. 10,000 ÷ 1,000 ▢

21. 124,000 ÷ 1,000 ▢

22. 3,230,000 ÷ 1,000 ▢

Learn Break apart a number to help you divide by hundreds or thousands.

$$600 \div 300 = (6\mathbf{00} \div 1\mathbf{00}) \div 3$$
$$= 6 \div 3$$
$$= 2$$

$$6{,}000 \div 2{,}000 = (6{,}\mathbf{000} \div 1{,}\mathbf{000}) \div 2$$
$$= 6 \div 2$$
$$= 3$$

Dividing a number by 300 is the same as dividing it by 100 and then by 3.

Dividing a number by 2,000 is the same as dividing it by 1,000 and then by 2.

Hands-On Activity

Copy and complete the table by dividing each number by 6 and by 600. An example is shown.

	÷ 6	÷ 600
1,200	200	2
4,200		
5,400		

Look at the answers in the table. Find the missing numbers.

1. 1,200 ÷ 600 = (1,200 ÷ ___) ÷ 6
2. 4,200 ÷ 600 = (4,200 ÷ ___) ÷ ___
3. 5,400 ÷ 600 = (5,400 ÷ ___) ÷ ___

Copy and complete the table by dividing each number by 8 and by 8,000. An example is shown.

	÷ 8	÷ 8,000
32,000	4,000	4
48,000		
64,000		

Look at the answers in the table. Find the missing numbers.

1. 32,000 ÷ 8,000 = (32,000 ÷ ___) ÷ 8
2. 48,000 ÷ 8,000 = (48,000 ÷ ___) ÷ ___
3. 64,000 ÷ 8,000 = (64,000 ÷ ___) ÷ ___

Guided Learning

Find the missing numbers.

23 $2,400 \div 400$

$= (2,400 \div 100) \div 4$

$= \square \div 4$

$= \square$

24 $35,000 \div 7,000$

$= (35,000 \div 1,000) \div 7$

$= \square \div 7$

$= \square$

Divide.

25 $800 \div 200$ ☐

26 $5,400 \div 600$ ☐

27 $7,200 \div 900$ ☐

28 $18,000 \div 3,000$ ☐

29 $45,000 \div 5,000$ ☐

30 $102,000 \div 2,000$ ☐

Learn Round numbers to estimate quotients.

Estimate $1,728 \div 38$.

To estimate $1,728 \div 38$, round the divisor 38 to 40, and choose a number close to the dividend 1,728 that can be evenly divided by 40.

divisor → $38\overline{)1,728}$ ← dividend

The number that is being divided is the **dividend**.
The number that the dividend is being divided by is the **divisor**.

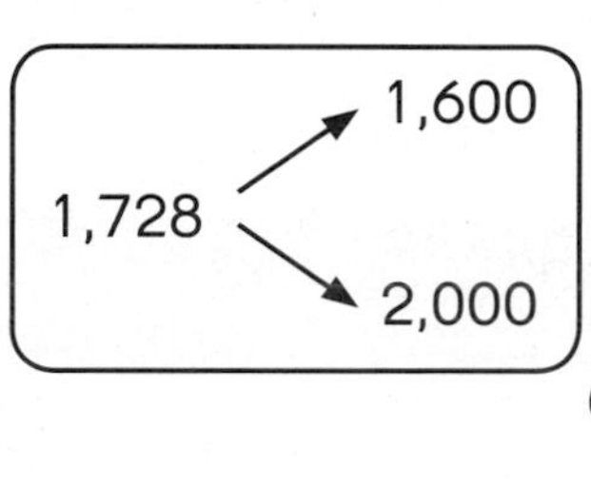

38 rounds to 40.
1,728 is nearer to 1,600 than to 2,000.

$1,600 \div 40 = (1,600 \div 10) \div 4$
$= 160 \div 4$
$= 40$

$1,728 \div 38$ is about 40.

Guided Learning

Estimate.

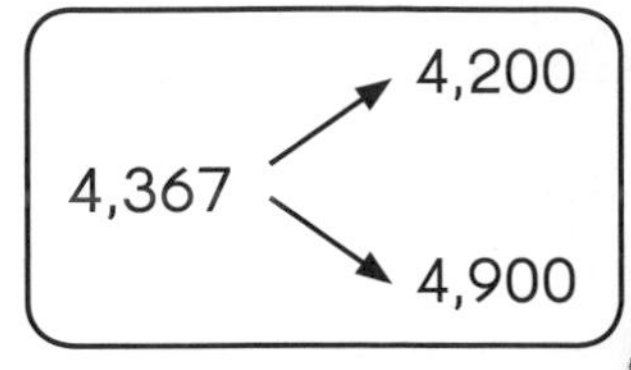

31 Estimate the quotient of 4,367 divided by 670.
670 rounds to 700.
4,367 is nearer to 4,200 than to 4,900.

$\square \div 700 = (\square \div \square) \div 7$
$= \square$

32 $987 \div 17$ $\square$

33 $6,106 \div 28$ $\square$

34 $4,932 \div 96$ $\square$

35 $3,785 \div 379$ $\square$

Hands-On Activity

Find three whole numbers that can evenly divide each number shown. The whole numbers or divisors must be multiples of ten, one hundred, or one thousand. Use different divisors for each number in the list.

4,500 | 420 | 2,000 | 40 | 88,000

An example is shown.

Number	Can be divided by	Answer
4,500	10	$4,500 \div 10 = 450$
4,500	30	$4,500 \div 30 = 150$
4,500	500	$4,500 \div 500 = 9$

Discuss with your partner how you can find these quotients.

1. 43 ÷ 10
2. 735 ÷ 100

Use the following table to help you.

Thousands	Hundreds	Tens	Ones	Tenths	Hundredths

Let's Practice

Divide.

1. 870 ÷ 10
2. 9,000 ÷ 10
3. 7,100 ÷ 100
4. 82,000 ÷ 100
5. 3,000 ÷ 1,000
6. 97,000 ÷ 1,000
7. 500 ÷ 20
8. 7,070 ÷ 70
9. 8,100 ÷ 300
10. 65,600 ÷ 800
11. 6,000 ÷ 3,000
12. 54,000 ÷ 9,000

Estimate.

13. 6,726 ÷ 19
14. 4,008 ÷ 12

ON YOUR OWN

Go to Workbook A: Practice 5, pages 47–52

Lesson 2.6

Dividing by 2-Digit Numbers

Lesson Objective

- Divide a 2-, 3-, or 4-digit number by a 2-digit number.

Vocabulary
remainder

Learn Use different methods to divide by tens.

Divide 180 by 20.

Method 1

$18\not{0} \div 2\not{0} = 9$

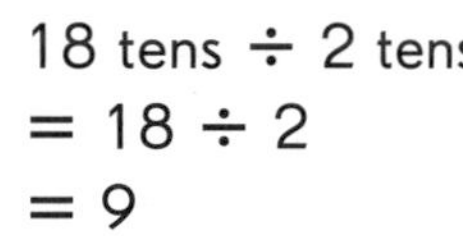

Method 2

```
        9
2 0 ) 1 8 0
      1 8 0  ← 9 × 20
      -----
          0
```

Use Method 2 when the dividend cannot be exactly divided by the divisor.
For 180 ÷ 40, dropping the zeros gives an incorrect **remainder**.

Incorrect

2 is the remainder.
$18\not{0} \div 4\not{0} = 4 \text{ R } 2$

```
      4
4 ) 1 8
    1 6
    ---
      2
```

Correct

20 is the remainder.
180 ÷ 40 = 4 R 20

```
          4
4 0 ) 1 8 0
      1 6 0
      -----
        2 0
```

Guided Learning

Divide.

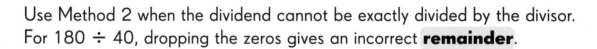

1. 240 ÷ 80 = ____
2. 4,000 ÷ 50 = ____
3. 5,200 ÷ 90 = ____

Learn Divide a 2-digit number by a 2-digit number.

Divide 83 by 15.

15 rounds to 20.

Estimate the quotient.
$4 \times 20 = 80$

$$\begin{array}{r} 4 \\ 20\overline{)83} \end{array}$$

$$\begin{array}{r} 4 \\ 15\overline{)83} \\ 60 \\ \hline 23 \end{array}$$

← This should be less than 15.

The estimated quotient is too small. Try 5.

$$\begin{array}{r} 5 \text{ R } 8 \\ 15\overline{)83} \\ 75 \\ \hline 8 \end{array}$$

The quotient is 5 and the remainder is 8.

Divide 88 by 23.

23 rounds to 20.

Estimate the quotient.
$4 \times 20 = 80$

$$\begin{array}{r} 4 \\ 20\overline{)88} \end{array}$$

$$\begin{array}{r} 4 \\ 23\overline{)88} \\ 92 \\ \hline \end{array}$$

← This should be less than 88.

The estimated quotient is too big. Try 3.

$$\begin{array}{r} 3 \text{ R } 19 \\ 23\overline{)88} \\ 69 \\ \hline 19 \end{array}$$

The quotient is 3 and the remainder is 19.

Guided Learning

4 **Divide 65 by 16.**

16 rounds to ___.
Estimate the quotient.
3 × ___ = ___

$$\begin{array}{r} 3 \\ \_\_\_ \overline{)\,6\;5} \end{array}$$

The estimated quotient is too ___. Try ___.

$$\begin{array}{r} 3 \\ 1\;6 \overline{)\,6\;5} \\ \underline{\_\_\_} \\ \_\_\_ \end{array}$$

$$\begin{array}{r} \_\_\_ \text{ R } \_\_\_ \\ 1\;6 \overline{)\,6\;5} \\ \underline{\_\_\_} \\ \_\_\_ \end{array}$$

The quotient is ___ and the remainder is ___.

5 **Divide 94 by 32.**

32 rounds to ___.
Estimate the quotient.
3 × ___ = ___

$$\begin{array}{r} 3 \\ \_\_\_ \overline{)\,9\;4} \end{array}$$

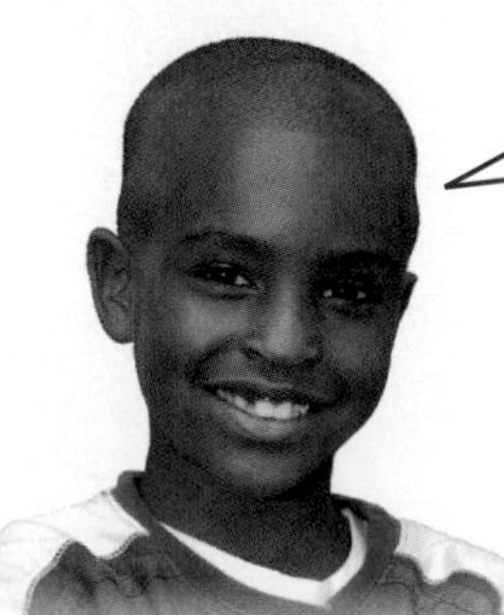

The estimated quotient is too ___. Try ___.

$$\begin{array}{r} 3 \\ 3\;2 \overline{)\,9\;4} \\ \underline{\_\_\_} \end{array}$$

$$\begin{array}{r} \_\_\_ \text{ R } \_\_\_ \\ 3\;2 \overline{)\,9\;4} \\ \underline{\_\_\_} \\ \_\_\_ \end{array}$$

The quotient is ___ and the remainder is ___.

Guided Learning

Divide.

6 $82 \div 16$ ____ 7 $69 \div 17$ ____ 8 $64 \div 12$ ____

Learn: Divide a 3-digit number by a 2-digit number.

Divide 235 by 32.

```
        7 R 11
32 ) 2 3 5
     2 2 4  <— 7 × 32
     -----
       1 1
```

32 rounds to 30.

Estimate the quotient.
$7 \times 30 = 210$
$8 \times 30 = 240$

The quotient is about 7.

The quotient is 7 and the remainder is 11.

Guided Learning

Divide. Show your work.

9
```
          ____ R ____
75 ) 6    1    2
     ____ ____ ____
     --------------
          ____ ____
```

75 rounds to 80.

Estimate the quotient.
$7 \times 80 = 560$
$8 \times 80 = 640$

The quotient is about ____.

The quotient is ____ and the remainder is ____.

Divide.

10 $153 \div 27$ ____ 11 $270 \div 39$ ____

12 $661 \div 74$ ____ 13 $802 \div 92$ ____

Learn Divide the tens before dividing the ones.

Divide 765 by 23.

```
      3 3 R 6
2 3 ) 7 6 5
      6 9      ← 23 × 3 tens
      ---
        7 5
        6 9    ← 23 × 3
      ---
          6
```

7 hundreds 6 tens = 76 tens
76 tens ÷ 23 = 3 tens R 7 tens
7 tens 5 ones = 75 ones
75 ÷ 23 = 3 R 6

The quotient is 33 and the remainder is 6.

Guided Learning

Divide. Show your work.

14

```
          ___ ___ R ___
2 1 )  3   1   7
      ___ ___        ← 21 × ___ tens
      -----------
      ___ ___ ___
      ___ ___ ___    ← 21 × ___
      -----------
              ___
```

The quotient is ___ and the remainder is ___.

Divide.

15 153 ÷ 11 ___

16 271 ÷ 14 ___

17 837 ÷ 67 ___

18 963 ÷ 27 ___

Learn Divide a 4-digit number by a 2-digit number.

Divide 6,118 by 75.

```
        8 1 R 43
75 ) 6,1 1 8
     6 0 0   ←— 75 × 8 tens
     -----
       1 1 8
         7 5 ←— 75 × 1
     -----
         4 3
```

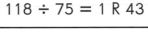

6 thousands 1 hundred 1 ten = 611 tens
611 tens ÷ 75 = 8 tens R 11 tens
11 tens 8 ones = 118 ones
118 ÷ 75 = 1 R 43

The quotient is 81 and the remainder is 43.

Guided Learning

Divide. Show your work.

19

```
          ___ ___ R ___
56 ) 5,  1   4   9
     ___ ___ ___      ←— 56 × ___ tens
     ---------------
         ___ ___ ___
             ___ ___  ←— 56 × ___
     ---------------
             ___ ___
```

The quotient is ___ and the remainder is ___.

Divide.

20 4,531 ÷ 50 ___

21 2,304 ÷ 29 ___

22 3,650 ÷ 82 ___

23 8,432 ÷ 96 ___

Learn Divide the hundreds, then the tens, and then the ones.

Divide 5,213 by 15.

```
      3 4 7 R 8
1 5 ) 5 , 2 1 3
      4 5         ← 15 × 3 hundreds
      -----
        7 1
        6 0       ← 15 × 4 tens
      -----
        1 1 3
        1 0 5     ← 15 × 7
      -------
            8
```

5 thousands 2 hundreds = 52 hundreds
52 hundreds ÷ 15 = 3 hundreds R 7 hundreds

7 hundreds 1 ten = 71 tens
71 tens ÷ 15 = 4 tens R 11 tens

11 tens 3 ones = 113 ones
113 ÷ 15 = 7 R 8

The quotient is 347 and the remainder is 8.

Guided Learning

Divide. Show your work.

24

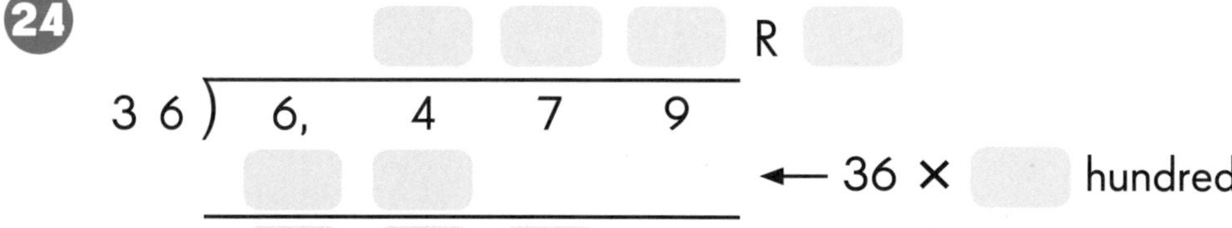

```
        ? ? ? R ?
3 6 ) 6, 4 7 9
      ? ?          ← 36 × ? hundred
      -------
      ? ? ?
      ? ? ?        ← 36 × ? tens
      -------
        ? ? ?
        ? ? ?      ← 36 × ?
        -----
          ? ?
```

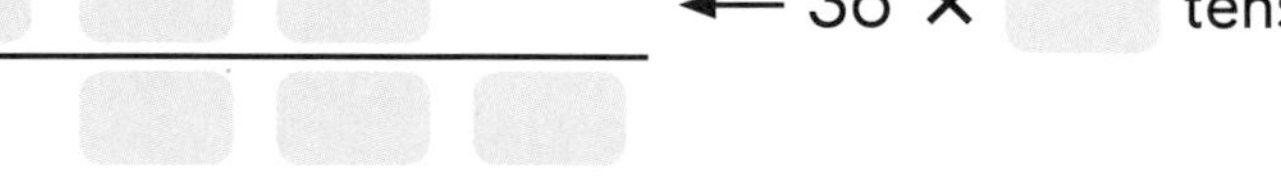

The quotient is ___ and the remainder is ___.

Divide.

25 6,025 ÷ 18 ___

26 1,822 ÷ 11 ___

27 5,283 ÷ 37 ___

28 9,532 ÷ 81 ___

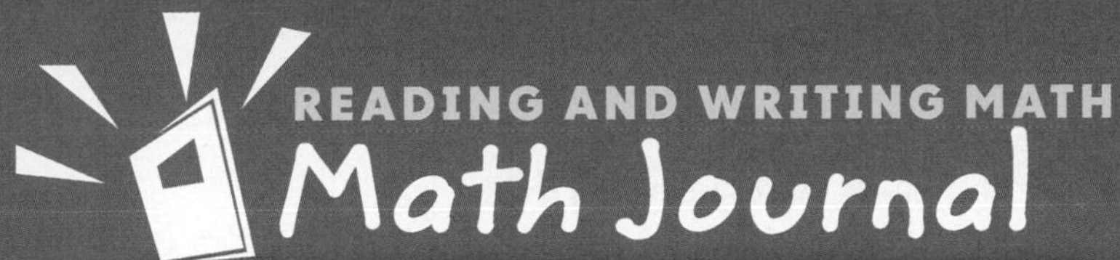

Angela wants to work out the division below:

$187 \div 32$

The first step of her work is as shown:

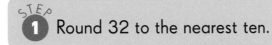

Round 32 to the nearest ten.

How should she continue from here? Show the rest of the steps.

Let's Practice

Divide.

1. $90 \div 30$
2. $60 \div 40$
3. $56 \div 34$
4. $270 \div 20$
5. $720 \div 90$
6. $981 \div 90$
7. $105 \div 12$
8. $600 \div 73$
9. $6{,}300 \div 70$
10. $3{,}541 \div 20$
11. $6{,}400 \div 51$
12. $5{,}283 \div 36$
13. $5{,}340 \div 15$
14. $8{,}206 \div 24$
15. $3{,}722 \div 45$

ON YOUR OWN

Go to Workbook A: Practice 6, pages 53–58

Lesson 2.7 Order of Operations

Lesson Objective

- Use order of operations to simplify a numeric expression
- Evaluate numerical expressions with parentheses, brackets, and braces.

Vocabulary
numeric expression
order of operations

Learn Work from left to right when a numeric expression uses only addition and subtraction.

96 commuters are on a train. At the next station, 26 commuters get off and 48 commuters get on. How many commuters are on the train now?

First expression $\mathbf{96} - \mathbf{26} + 48$ ← Work from left to right.

Second expression $\mathbf{70} + 48$

118

96 − 26 + 48 is a numeric expression.
A numeric expression contains only numbers and operation symbols. There is no equal sign.

Now there are 118 commuters on the train.

Guided Learning

Simplify.

1. 37 + 8 − 25 ___
2. 67 − 21 + 20 ___
3. 32 − 12 + 26 − 15 ___
4. 50 + 27 − 19 − 35 ___

Learn **Work from left to right when a numeric expression uses only multiplication and division.**

Rogers & Co. orders 40 cartons of paper towels from Diego's paper store. Each carton contains 24 rolls of paper towels. The paper store delivers 60 rolls of paper towels each day. How many days will it take for the paper store to deliver all the paper towels?

First expression $\mathbf{40 \times 24} \div 60$ ← Work from left to right.

Second expression $\mathbf{960} \div 60$

16

It will take 16 days for the paper store to deliver all the paper towels.

Guided Learning

Simplify.

5. $12 \times 20 \div 6$ ▭

6. $63 \div 9 \times 12$ ▭

7. $28 \times 5 \div 10 \div 7$ ▭

8. $48 \div 8 \times 60 \div 3$ ▭

Learn **Always work from left to right. Multiply and divide first. Then add and subtract.**

There are 28 children and 56 men at a park. The number of men is 4 times the number of women. How many children and women are at the park?

First expression $28 + \mathbf{56 \div 4}$ ← Divide first.

Second expression $\mathbf{28 + 14}$ ← Then add.

42

$56 \div 4 = 14$
There are 14 women.

There are 42 children and women at the park.

Continued on next page

Sarah has 900 stamps in her collection. She arranges 25 stamps on each page of a stamp album. The album has 30 pages. How many stamps are left?

30 × 25 = 750
Sarah puts 750 stamps into the album.

First expression 900 − **30 × 25** ← Multiply first.

Second expression 900 − **750** ← Then subtract.

150

There are 150 stamps left.

Guided Learning

Simplify.

9 13 + 20 × 7 ___

10 70 − 75 ÷ 5 ___

11 15 + 18 × 5 ÷ 9 ___

12 80 − 54 ÷ 9 × 11 ___

13 48 − 6 × 6 + 34 ___

14 33 + 210 ÷ 30 − 25 ___

Learn

Carry out any operations in parentheses first.

There are 670 boys and 530 girls at a track and field event. Each student participates in one event. Each event has 40 students participating. How many events are there?

First expression **(670 + 530)** ÷ 40 ← Perform all operations in the parentheses first.

Second expression **1,200** ÷ 40 ← Then divide.

30

There are 30 events.

Guided Learning

Simplify.

15 $17 - (38 - 29)$ ___

16 $690 \div (15 \times 2)$ ___

17 $(44 - 33) \times 7$ ___

18 $80 \div (40 - 32)$ ___

Learn

Order of operations

STEP 1 Work inside the parentheses.

STEP 2 Multiply and divide from left to right.

STEP 3 Add and subtract from left to right.

Jimmy has 60 ounces of pecans and 64 ounces of macadamia nuts. He mixes and packs them into 9-ounce packets. He packs 8 packets. How many ounces of nuts does he have left?

First expression $(60 + 64) - 8 \times 9$ ← Perform all operations in the parentheses first.

Second expression $124 - 8 \times 9$ ← Then multiply.

Third expression $124 - 72$ ← Finally, subtract.

52

He has 52 ounces of nuts left.

Guided Learning

Simplify.

19 $107 + (44 - 33) \times 7$ ___

20 $80 \times (40 \div 5) \div 10$ ___

21 $(64 + 32) \div 8 - 3$ ___

22 $98 - (34 - 26) \times 7$ ___

Learn Carry out operations in parentheses before operations in brackets.

A hardware store employee must sort a box containing different kinds of screws. Of the 960 screws, 218 are brass, 94 are steel, and the rest are zinc. She needs to pack the zinc screws into packages of 12. How many packages of zinc screws will she make?

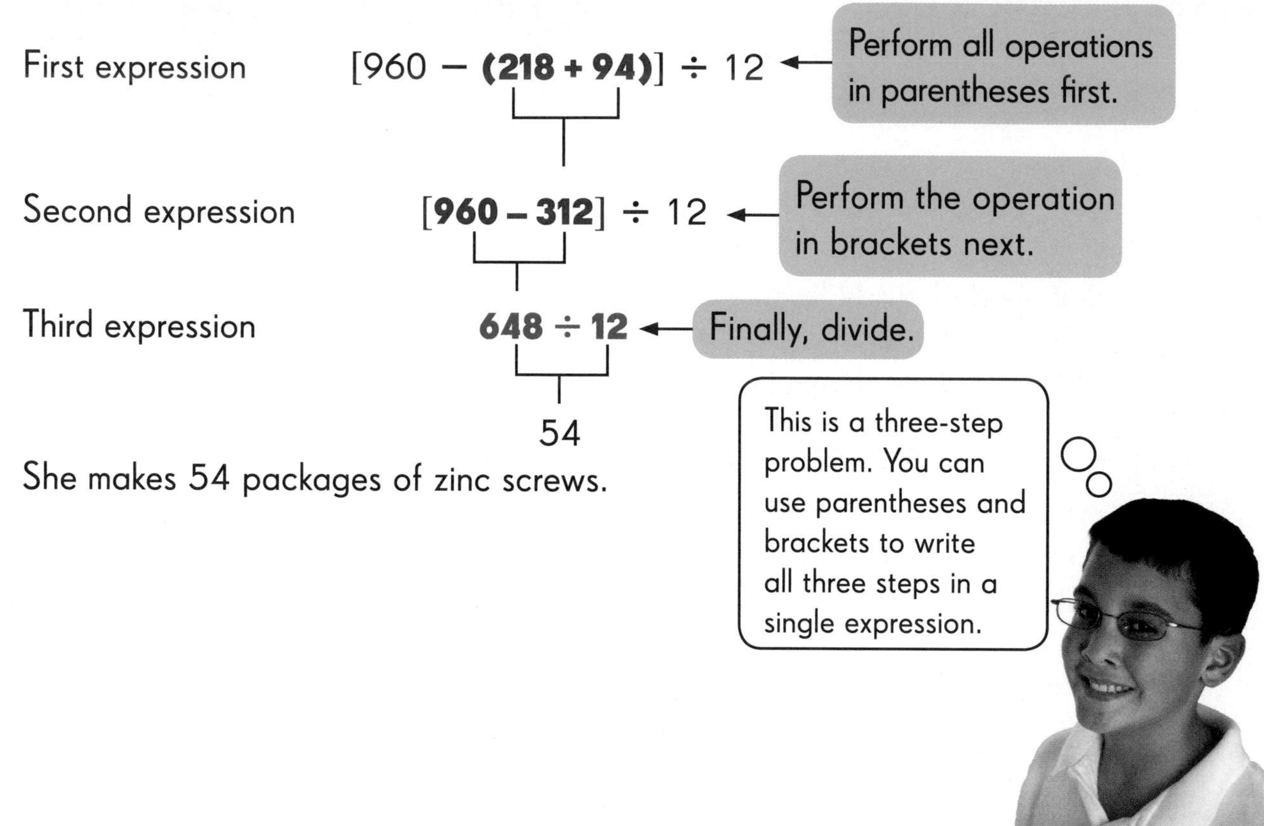

First expression
[960 − (218 + 94)] ÷ 12
Perform all operations in parentheses first.
Second expression
[960 − 312] ÷ 12
Perform the operation in brackets next.
Third expression
648 ÷ 12
Finally, divide.
54
This is a three-step problem. You can use parentheses and brackets to write all three steps in a single expression.

She makes 54 packages of zinc screws.

Guided Learning

Evaluate.

23 [447 − (48 + 127)] ÷ 8

24 [598 − (164 − 36)] ÷ 5

25 [275 − (76 + 28)] × 7

26 [211 − (254 − 87)] × 16

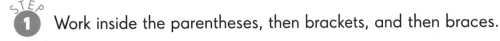

Learn Order of operations

STEP 1 Work inside the parentheses, then brackets, and then braces.

STEP 2 Multiply and divide from left to right.

STEP 3 Add and subtract from left to right.

Simplify $72 \div \{36 \div [(4 + 2) \times 3]\}$.

Step 1 $72 \div \{36 \div [\mathbf{(4 + 2)} \times 3]\}$ ← Perform operations in parentheses first.

Step 2 $72 \div \{36 \div \mathbf{[6 \times 3]}\}$ ← Next, perform operations in brackets.

Step 3 $72 \div \mathbf{\{36 \div 18\}}$ ← Then perform operations in braces.

Step 4 $72 \div 2$ ← Finally, divide.

36

So, $72 \div \{36 \div [(4 + 2) \times 3]\} = 36$.

Guided Learning

Evaluate.

27. $108 \div \{36 \div [12 \div (3 \times 2)]\}$ ☐

28. $420 \div \{[15 - (8 - 3)] \times 2\}$ ☐

29. $\{60 \div [7 + (2 \times 4)]\} \times 22$ ☐

30. $95 - \{48 + [36 \div (2 \times 3)]\}$ ☐

Hands-On Activity

WORK IN PAIRS

Use copies of the cards to form a numeric expression with two or more operations.

0 1 2 3 4 5 6 7 8 9

+ − × ÷ ( ) [ ]

Example

3 2 8 × 5 4 ÷ 3 6

Simplify the expression and compare your answer with your partner's.

Let's Explore!

1. To find the value of $12 \times 20 \div 4$, find 12×20 first. Then, divide the result by 4.
   Next, find $20 \div 4$ first. Then, multiply the result by 12.
   What do you notice?
   Try this activity with other numbers and operations.

2 

WORK IN PAIRS

Look at the five expressions in the table below.
The first partner is to simplify each expression from left to right.
The second partner is to simplify the expression using the order of operations.
Use a copy of this table and record your answers. Discuss your results.

Number Sentence	Partner A's Answers	Partner B's Answers
9 + 6 − 5		
48 ÷ 4 × 2		
36 ÷ 6 − 3		
14 + 4 × 2		
50 − 8 ÷ 2		

Let's Practice

Simplify.

1. 96 − 50 + 64
2. 175 + 25 − 95
3. 6 × 40 ÷ 3
4. 250 ÷ 5 × 53
5. 79 + 27 × 2
6. 280 − 72 ÷ 8
7. 35 × (560 ÷ 70)
8. 540 ÷ (293 − 203)
9. [267 − (37 + 54)] × 14
10. 420 ÷ {[15 − (8 − 3)] × 2}
11. 108 ÷ {36 ÷ [12 ÷ (3 × 2)]}
12. 179 + [618 − (241 − 55)] ÷ 12

ON YOUR OWN

Go to Workbook A: Practice 7, pages 59–68

Lesson 2.8 Real-World Problems: Multiplication and Division

Lesson Objectives

- Use efficient strategies to solve multi-step problems involving multiplication and division.
- Express and interpret the product or quotient appropriately.

Learn **The remainder can be part of an answer.**

Rena has a roll of ribbon 250 centimeters long. She cuts it into a number of pieces that measure 20 centimeters each. How many pieces does she cut?
What is the length of the remaining ribbon?

Length of ribbon = 250 cm
Length of each piece = 20 cm
Number of pieces = 250 ÷ 20
= 12 R 10

$$\begin{array}{r} 12 \text{ R } 10 \\ 20\overline{)250} \\ \underline{20} \\ 50 \\ \underline{40} \\ 10 \end{array}$$

Rena cuts the ribbon into 12 pieces.
The length of the remaining ribbon is 10 centimeters.

Guided Learning

Solve. Show your work.

1 A bin of potatoes weighs 100 pounds. The potatoes are packed into bags weighing 15 pounds each. How many bags of potatoes are there? How many pounds are left?

Weight of potatoes = 100 lb
Weight of each bag = 15 lb
Number of bags = ___ ÷ ___
= ___

There are ___ bags of potatoes. ___ pounds of potatoes are left.

Learn Increase the quotient when it includes the remainder.

A school has 120 fifth-graders who are going by bus on a field trip. Each bus holds 35 students. What is the number of buses needed?

Number of fifth-graders = 120

Number of fifth-graders in 1 bus = 35

Number of buses = 120 ÷ 35

= 3 R 15

```
      3 R 15
35 ) 120
     105
     ---
      15
```

The 15 remaining fifth-graders would need 1 more bus.

Add 1 more to the quotient: 3 + 1 = 4

The number of buses needed is 4.

Guided Learning

2 Julie has 172 stamps. She wants to put them in an album. Each page of the album holds 25 stamps. How many pages of the album will Julie need to hold all her stamps?

Number of stamps = ___

Number of stamps on 1 page = ___

Number of pages = ___ ÷ ___

= ___ R ___

To divide by 25, recall the multiples of 25.
4 × 25 = 100
5 × 25 = 125
6 × 25 = 150
7 × 25 = 175
So 172 ÷ 25 = 6 with a remainder of 22.

Julie will need ___ more page to hold the remaining ___ stamps.

Add ___ more to the quotient: ___ + ___ = ___

The number of pages Julie will need is ___.

Learn: Some problems require two steps to solve.

The Fairfield Elementary School library is in the shape of a rectangle. It measures 36 yards by 21 yards. The school's principal, Mr. Jefferson, wants to carpet the library floor. Find the cost of carpeting the library fully if a 1-square-yard carpet tile costs \$16.

First, find the floor area of the library.

Area = length × width
= 36 × 21
= 756 yd^2

Estimate the answer.
36 rounds to 40.
21 rounds to 20.
40 × 20 = 800
756 is a reasonable answer.

The floor area of the library is 756 square yards.

Then, find the cost of carpeting.

Cost of carpeting
= area × cost of 1 yd^2
= 756 × \$16
= \$12,096

Estimate to check if the answer is reasonable.

It will cost \$12,096 to carpet the library fully.

Guided Learning

Solve. Show your work.

3. Mr. McGuiness fills 250-gallon fuel tanks at \$3 per gallon at a gas station. How much money does he need to pay for filling 9 such tanks?

Total amount of fuel = 9 × 250 = ____

Cost of fuel = ____ × \$3 = \$____

He needs to pay \$____.

Learn Some problems require more than two steps to solve.

A group of volunteers buys 32 cartons of 40 apples. The volunteers pack the apples into bags of 5 each and sell each bag for $4 to raise funds for a charity. How much do they collect after selling all the apples?

First, find the total number of apples.

Total number of apples = number of cartons × number of apples in a carton
= 32 × 40
= 1,280

There are 1,280 apples.

Next, find the number of bags.

Number of bags = total number of apples ÷ number of apples in a bag
= 1,280 ÷ 5
= 256

There are 256 bags of apples.

Number of bags:
(32 × 40) ÷ 5
= 256

Then, find how much money they collected.

Amount collected = number of bags × price of a bag
= 256 × $4
= $1,024

The volunteers collected $1,024.

Guided Learning

Solve. Show your work.

  Ms. Hernandez buys a car and pays for it in equal payments of $478. After 45 payments, she still owes $3,090. How much would each payment be if she pays for the car in 60 equal payments?

First, find the total amount paid in equal payments.

Amount paid = number of payments × amount for each payment
= 45 × $478
= $____

Then, find the cost of the car.

Cost of car = total amount paid + amount she still has to pay
= $____ + $3,090
= $____

Cost of the car:
(45 × $478) + $3,090
= $____

Which operation will you use to find how much she would pay for each of the 60 payments?

$____ ◯ ____ = $____

She would pay $____ for each of the 60 equal payments.

Learn Read a table to find information.

The table shows the wages of workers in a plumbing company.
Ms. Jensen works Tuesday through Sunday. How much is she paid?

Weekdays	\$170 per day
Saturdays and Sundays	\$315 per day

First, find the number of weekdays and the number of Saturdays and Sundays she worked.

Number of weekdays worked = 4 days

Number of Saturdays and Sundays worked = 2 days

Ms. Jensen's wages for 4 weekdays = 4 × \$170
= \$680

Her wages for Saturday and Sunday = 2 × \$315
= \$630

Total wages = \$680 + \$630
= \$1,310

Ms. Jensen is paid \$1,310.

Total wages:
(4 × \$170) + (2 × \$315)
= \$1,310

Guided Learning

Solve. Show your work.

5 The table shows the charges at a parking garage.

First Hour	Second Hour	After the Second Hour
\$7	\$5	\$3 per hour

Mr. Lee parked his car here from 9 A.M. to 2 P.M. one day. How much did he pay?

Total number of hours = ____ h

Parking fee for the first hour = \$____

Parking fee for the second hour = \$____

Parking fee from 11 A.M. to 2 P.M. = ____ × \$____ = \$____

Total parking fee = \$____ + \$____ + \$____ = \$____

Mr. Lee paid \$____.

Let's Practice

Solve. Show your work.

1. A water tank contains 1,250 gallons of water. The water is used to fill some 30-gallon barrels. How many barrels can be filled completely? How much water will be left?

2. Some students in a stamp club collected a total of 6,707 stamps. They gave away 569 of the stamps. Then the students put equal numbers of the remaining stamps into 18 albums. How many stamps were in each album?

3. A grocer had 49 boxes of strawberries. Each box contained 75 strawberries. The strawberries were repacked into small boxes with 15 strawberries. How many small boxes of strawberries were there?

4. Mr. Tan paid $2 for each package of 12 granola bars. He sold each granola bar for $0.50. In a week, he sold a total of 4,385 granola bars.
   a. What is the least number of packages of granola bars?
   b. How much did he pay for this number of packages of granola bars?
   c. How much money did he make after he sold 4,385 granola bars?

5. A restaurant owner bought 245 cartons of canned corn. Each carton held 28 cans of corn. There were 2,198 cans of yellow corn and the rest were white corn. All the cans of white corn were used equally over 42 months. How many cans of white corn did the restaurant owner use each month?

6. The table shows the cost of beads by weight at a store. Chyna and Desmond bought some beads from the store.

Weight	Cost
First 2 ounces	70¢
Each additional ounce	30¢

   a. Chyna bought beads weighing 5 ounces in all. Find the cost of the beads.
   b. Desmond paid $6.10 for his beads. Find the total weight of the beads that he bought.

ON YOUR OWN

Go to Workbook A: Practice 8, pages 69–74

Learn Solve problems by drawing bar models.

Hector, Teddy, and Jim scored a total of 4,670 points playing a video game. Teddy scored 316 points less than Hector. Teddy scored 3 times as many points as Jim. How many points did Teddy score?

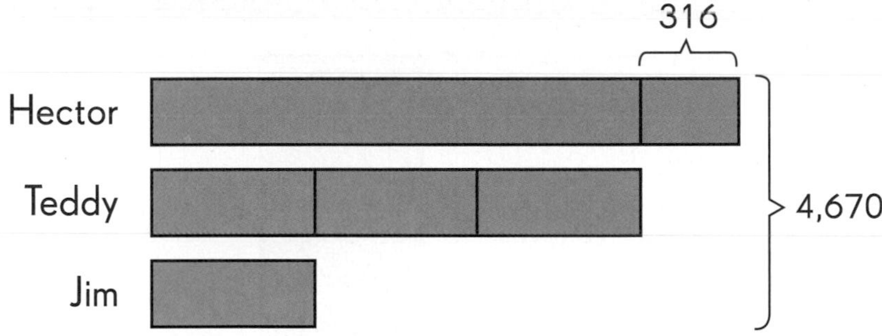

First, subtract 316 points from Hector's score so that he will have the same number of points as Teddy.

This also means subtracting 316 points from the total number of points.

4,670 − 316 = 4,354

The drawing shows there are 7 equal units after subtracting the 316 points. Divide the remaining points by 7 to find the number of points that represent one unit.

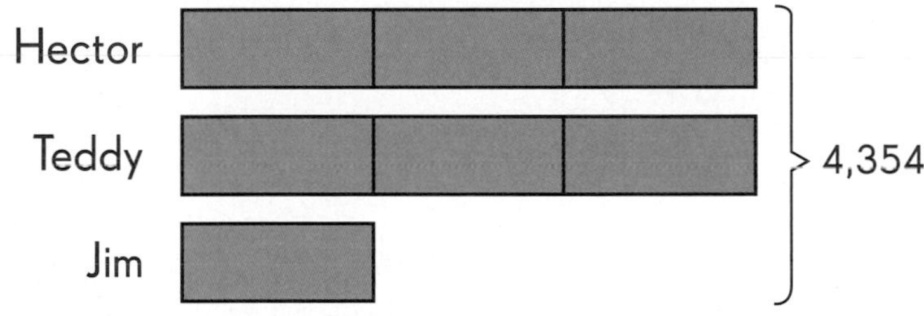

7 units → 4,354 points

1 unit → 4,354 ÷ 7 = 622 points

3 units → 3 × 622 = 1,866 points

Teddy scored 1,866 points.

Guided Learning

Solve. Show your work.

  The cost of 4 belts and 5 ties is \$247. Each tie costs 3 times as much as a belt. What is the total cost of a tie and a belt?

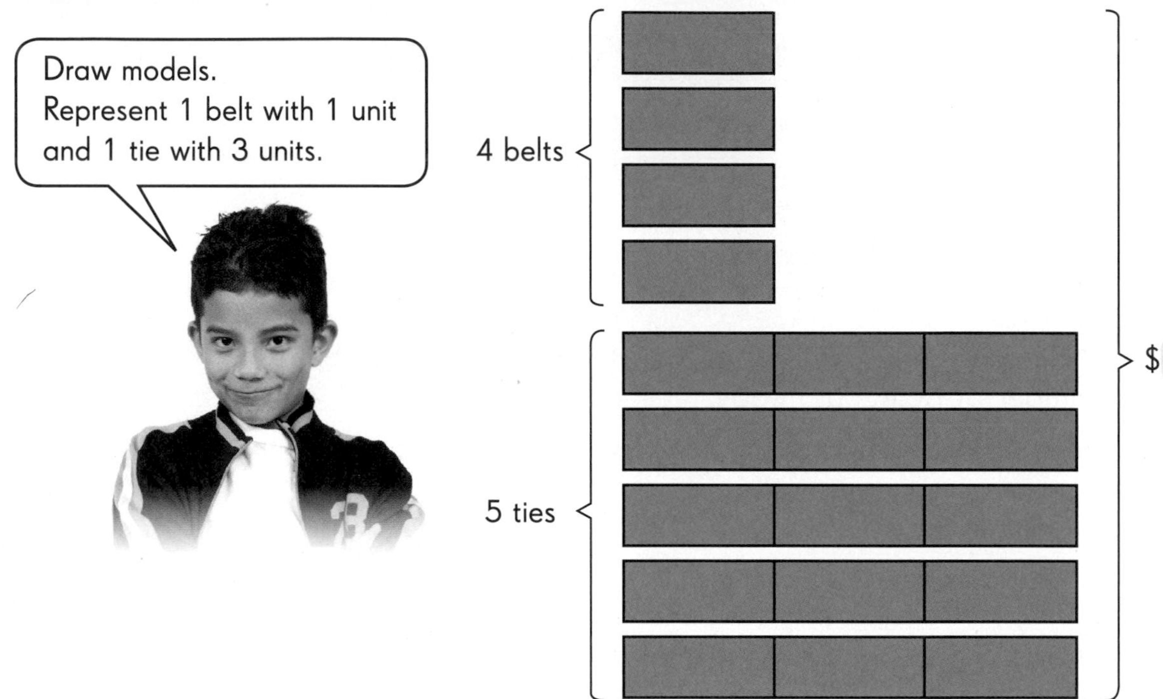

Draw models.
Represent 1 belt with 1 unit and 1 tie with 3 units.
4 belts
5 ties
$

___ units → \$247

1 unit → \$247 ÷ ___ = \$___

Each belt costs \$___.

3 units → 3 × \$___ = \$39

Each tie costs \$___.

\$___ + \$___ = \$___

The total cost of a belt and a tie is \$___.

7 A florist had an equal number of red and yellow tulips. She sold 624 red tulips. Then she had 4 times as many yellow tulips as red tulips. How many tulips did she have at first?

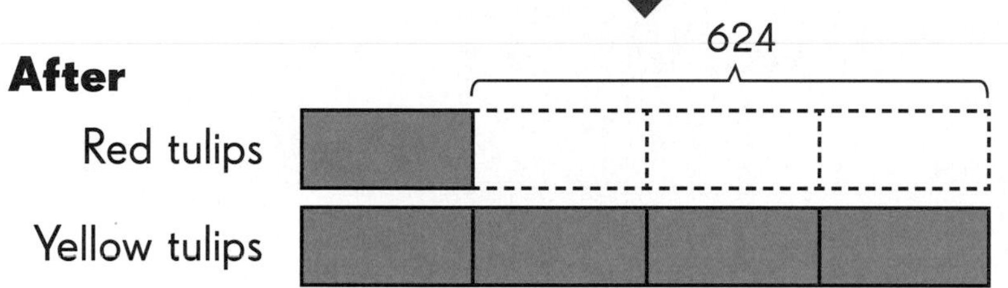

1 unit represents the number of red tulips left and 4 units represent the number of yellow tulips.

3 units → 624 tulips

1 unit → 624 ÷ 3 = 208 tulips

8 units → 8 × ___ = ___ tulips

She had ___ tulips at first.

8 Ella and Michelle had $1,250. Ella and Surya had $830. Michelle had 4 times as much as Surya. How much did Ella have?

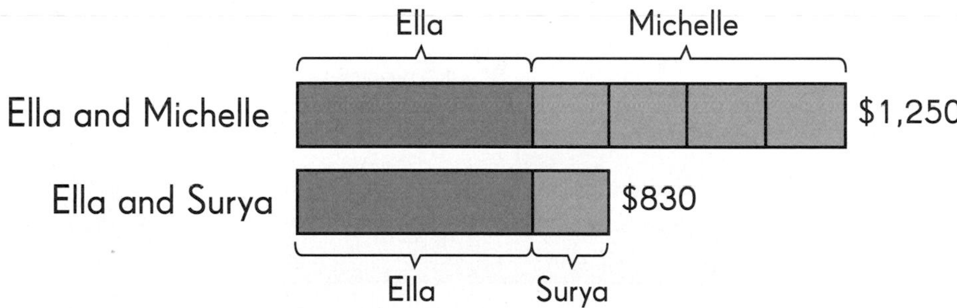

$1,250 – $830 = $420

The difference between the amount Michelle and Surya had was $420.

3 units → $420

1 unit → $420 ÷ 3 = $___

Surya had $___.

$830 – $___ = $___

Ella had $___.

Learn Some problems can be solved using other strategies.

Mandy is 12 years old and Nacha is 15 years older. In how many years will Nacha be twice as old as Mandy?

Method 1

$12 + 15 = 27$

Nacha is 27 years old now.

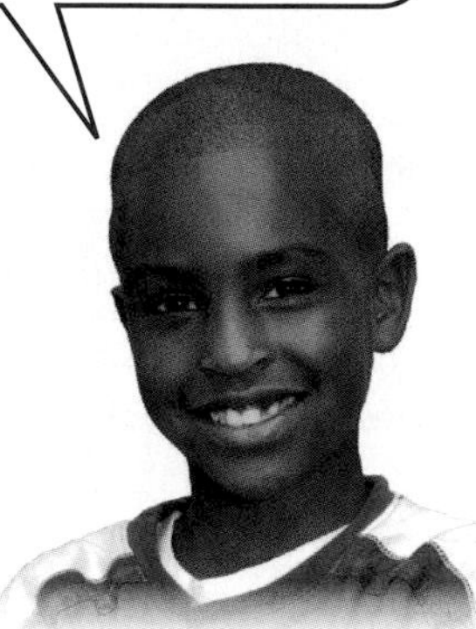

Mandy's Age	Nacha's Age	Is it twice?
12 (now)	27 (now)	No
13	28	No
14	29	No
15	30	Yes

Nacha will be twice Mandy's age in 3 years' time.

Method 2

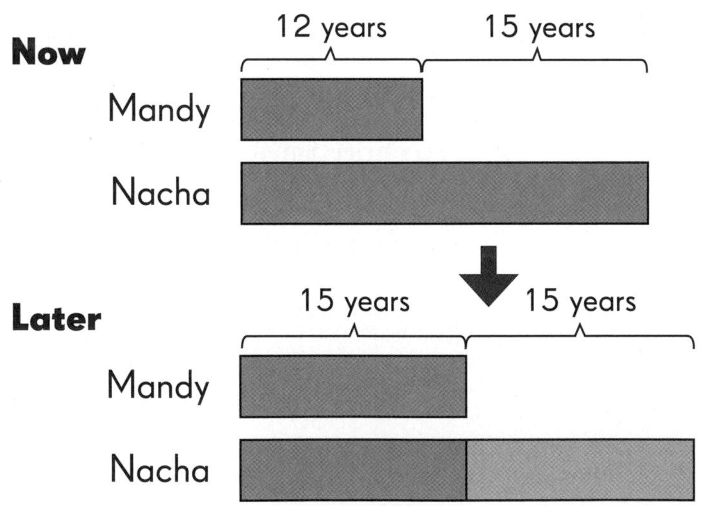

1 unit → 15 years

$15 - 12 = 3$

Nacha will be twice Mandy's age in 3 years' time.

Guided Learning

Solve. Show your work.

9 There are 20 cars and motorcycles altogether in a parking lot. The total number of wheels is 50. How many motorcycles are there?

Use the data — number of vehicles and number of wheels — to make an organized list.
Remember, the number of cars and motorcycles must always add up to 20.

Number of Cars	Number of Motorcycles	Number of Wheels	Are there 50 Wheels?
10	10	40 + 20 = 60	No (too many)
9	11	36 + ___ = 58	No (too many)
___	12	32 + 24 = 56	No (too many)
5	15	20 + 30 = 50	___

There are ___ motorcycles.

Let's Practice

Solve. Show your work.

1 Mrs. Atkins pays $1,800 for a new refrigerator, washer, and dryer. The refrigerator costs $250 more than the washer. The dryer costs half as much as the washer. How much does the washer cost? ___

2. Apples are sold at 3 for $2 at Busy Mart. At Big Foods, the same apples are sold at 5 for $2. Kassim buys 15 apples from Big Foods instead of Busy Mart. How much does he save?

3. Margaret paid $87 for a skirt and a blouse. The skirt costs twice as much as the blouse. What was the cost of the skirt?

4. A shopkeeper sold a total of 15 boxes of pencils on Monday and Tuesday. She sold 3 more boxes on Monday than on Tuesday. There were 12 pencils in each box. How many pencils did she sell on Monday?

5. Jane had $7 and her sister had $2. Their parents gave each of them an equal amount of money. Then, Jane had twice as much money as her sister. How much money did their parents give each of them?

6. On a farm, there are some cows and some chickens. If the animals have a total of 40 heads and 112 legs, how many cows are there?

7. Naomi, Macy, and Sebastian have 234 stamps in all. Naomi gives 16 stamps to Macy and 24 stamps to Sebastian. Naomi then has 3 times as many stamps as Macy, and Macy has twice as many stamps as Sebastian. How many stamps does Naomi have at first?

8. A group of people pays $720 for admission tickets to an amusement park. The price of an adult ticket is $15, and a child ticket is $8. There are 25 more adults than children. How many children are in the group?

9. A tank and a pail contain a total of 5,136 milliliters of water. Jacob pours 314 milliliters of water from the pail into the tank. The amount of water in the tank is now 7 times what is left in the pail. How much water was in the pail at first?

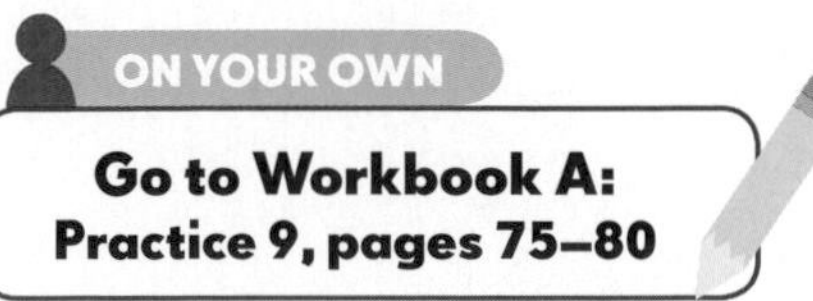

Go to Workbook A: Practice 9, pages 75–80

CRITICAL THINKING SKILLS

Put On Your Thinking Cap!

PROBLEM SOLVING

The [9] key on the calculator is not working.

Explain how you can still use the calculator to find 1,234 × 79 in two ways.

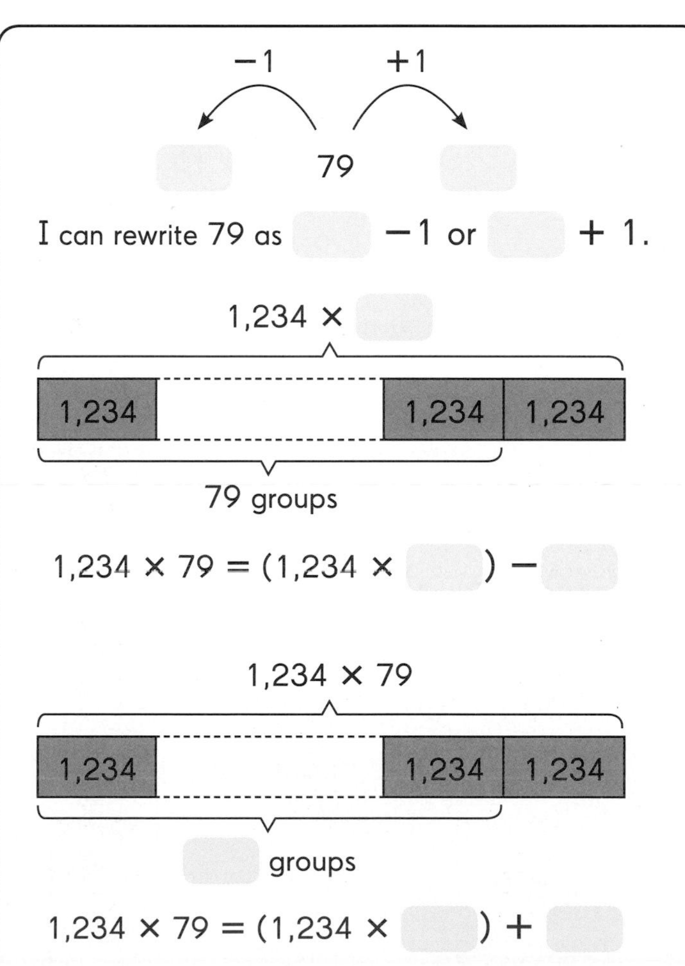

ON YOUR OWN

Go to Workbook A: Put on Your Thinking Cap, pages 81–84

Chapter Wrap Up

Study Guide

You have learned...

Whole Numbers

Using a calculator

- Add
- Subtract
- Multiply
- Divide

Multiplication

Use a rule to multiply a number by 10, 100, or 1,000.

Write one, two, or three zeros after the number to find the product.

1,234 × 1**0** = 12,34**0**
1,234 × 1**00** = 123,4**00**
1,234 × 1,**000** = 1,234,**000**

Use strategies to multiply a 2-digit, 3-digit, or 4-digit number by a 2-digit number.

Estimate a product by rounding or front-end estimation.

By rounding:

4,694 × 58

5,000 × 60 = 300,000

4,694 × 58 is about 300,000.

By front-end estimation:

1,259 × 26

1,000 × 20 = 20,000
1,259 × 26 is about 20,000.

- Patterns can be used to help multiply and divide numbers.
- Numeric expressions can be simplified using the order of operations.
- Multiplication and division can be used to solve real-world problems.

Division

Use a rule to divide a number by 10, 100, or 1,000.

Drop one, two, or three zeros after the number to find the quotient.

5,678,00**0** ÷ 1**0** = 567,800
5,678,0**00** ÷ 1**00** = 56,780
5,678,**000** ÷ 1**000** = 5,678

Use strategies to divide a 2-digit, 3-digit, or 4-digit number by a 2-digit number.

Order of operations

1. Work inside the parentheses, then the brackets, and then the braces.
2. Multiply and divide from left to right.
3. Add and subtract from left to right.

Estimate a quotient by rounding the divisor. Then find the multiple of the divisor that is nearest to the dividend.

3,310 ÷ 42

40 × 80 = 3,200
40 × 90 = 3,600
3,310 is nearer to 3,200 than to 3,600.

3,200 ÷ 40 = 80
So, 3,310 ÷ 42 is about 80.

Use multiplication, division, and order of operations to solve real-world problems.

Chapter Review/Test

Vocabulary

Fill in the blanks.

product
factors
dividend
divisor
quotient
remainder
numeric expressions
order of operations

1. In $5,280 \times 63 = 332,640$,

   5,280 and 63 are the ___ and 332,640 is the ___.

2. In $9,472 \div 15 = 631$ R 7,

   9,472 is the ___, 15 is the ___,

   631 is the ___ and 7 is the ___.

3. $8,167 + 929$, and $1,597 \times 16$ are examples of ___.

4. A numeric expression with more than two operations is simplified using the ___.

Concepts and Skills

Multiply.

5. 17×10 ___
6. 502×100 ___
7. $863 \times 1,000$ ___
8. 548×60 ___
9. 659×300 ___
10. $935 \times 8,000$ ___
11. 17×10^2 ___
12. 19×10^3 ___
13. $7,020 \times 10^2$ ___

Estimate each product.

14. $4,734 \times 28$ ___
15. $7,651 \times 46$ ___
16. $9,470 \times 32$ ___

Multiply. Estimate to check if your answers are reasonable.

17. $2,757 \times 14$ ___
18. $3,648 \times 27$ ___
19. $8,359 \times 55$ ___

Divide.

20 $680 \div 10$

21 $7{,}000 \div 100$

22 $241{,}000 \div 1{,}000$

23 $1{,}200 \div 40$

24 $6{,}900 \div 300$

25 $64{,}000 \div 8{,}000$

Estimate each quotient.

26 $4{,}232 \div 18$

27 $8{,}267 \div 93$

28 $1{,}135 \div 84$

Divide. Give the quotient and remainder.

29 $295 \div 31$

30 $4{,}135 \div 14$

31 $6{,}397 \div 28$

Simplify.

32 $51 - 17 + 37$

33 $81 \div 9 \times 24$

34 $66 - 16 \div 8$

35 $28 \times (69 + 50)$

36 $(24 - 16) \times [48 \div (11 + 5)]$

37 $120 \div \{[48 \div (2 \times 4)] - 2\}$

Problem Solving

Solve.

38 Elena bought 49 packs of red balloons, 66 packs of blue balloons, and 35 packs of yellow balloons. Each pack contained 12 balloons. She mixed them up and gave away some balloons. She then repacked the balance into packs of 25.

a How many balloons were there altogether?

b She gave away 225 balloons. How many large packs of 25 balloons were there?

c She paid $3 for each pack of a dozen balloons. She sold each new pack of 25 balloons for $10. How much money did she make?

Chapter 3

Fractions and Mixed Numbers

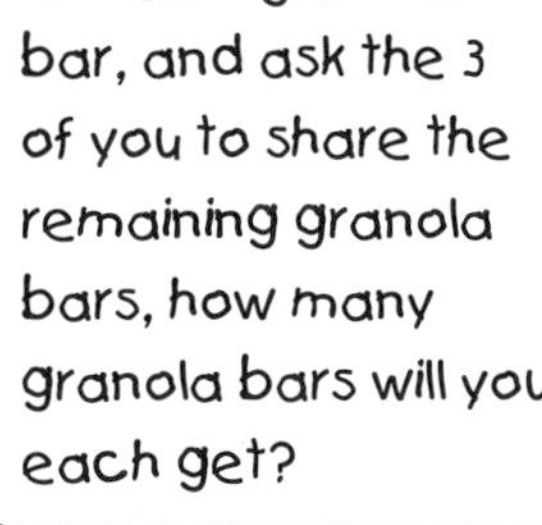

Lessons

3.1 Adding Unlike Fractions

3.2 Subtracting Unlike Fractions

3.3 Fractions, Mixed Numbers, and Division Expressions

3.4 Expressing Fractions, Division Expressions, and Mixed Numbers as Decimals

3.5 Adding Mixed Numbers

3.6 Subtracting Mixed Numbers

3.7 Real-World Problems: Fractions and Mixed Numbers

▶ Add and subtract unlike fractions and mixed numbers by rewriting them with like denominators.

Recall Prior Knowledge

Like fractions have the same denominator.

Liam had $\frac{2}{5}$ of a cracker.

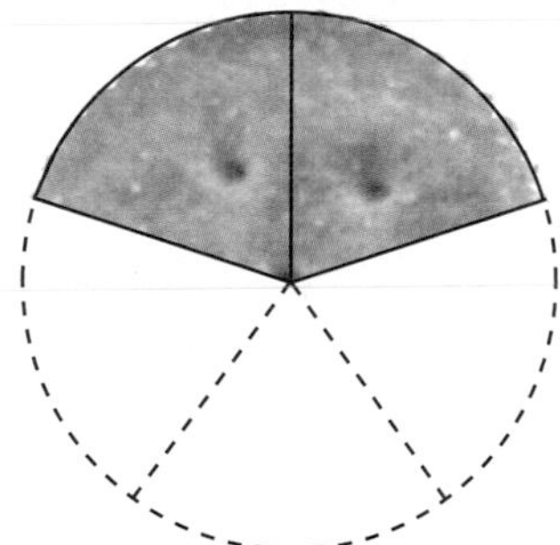

Walt had $\frac{3}{5}$ of a cracker.

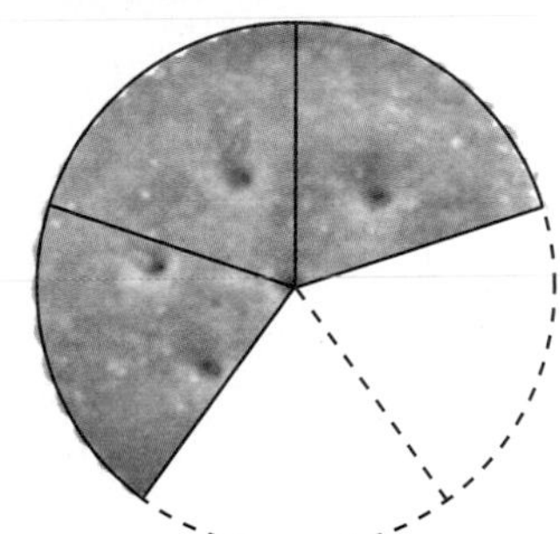

$\frac{2}{5}$ and $\frac{3}{5}$ are like fractions.

They have the same denominator, 5.

Unlike fractions have different denominators.

In one box, $\frac{3}{4}$ of a pizza was left.

In another box, $\frac{2}{5}$ of a pizza was left.

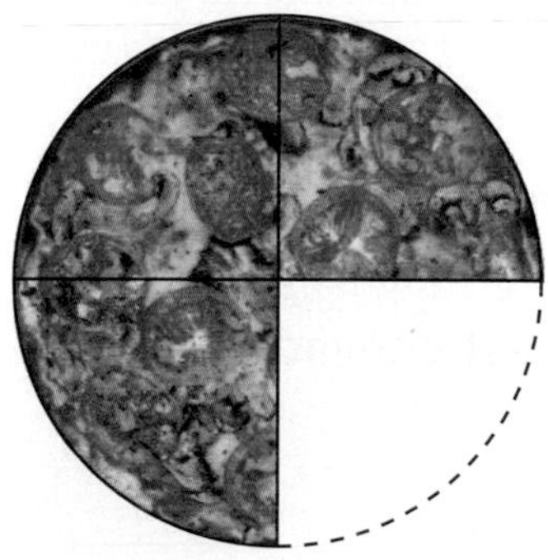

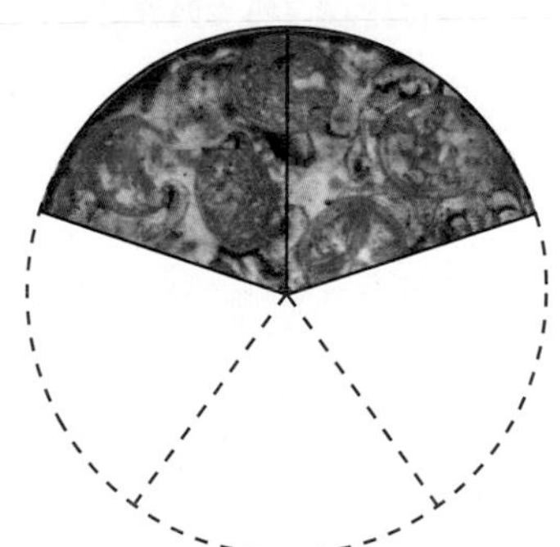

$\frac{3}{4}$ and $\frac{2}{5}$ are unlike fractions.

They have different denominators, 4 and 5.

A mixed number consists of a whole number and a fraction.

1 whole

1 whole

1 half

$$2 + \frac{1}{2} = 2\frac{1}{2}$$

whole number — fraction — mixed number

Finding equivalent fractions

$$\frac{3}{4} = \frac{6}{8}$$ (× 2 for the numerator and × 2 for the denominator)

$$\frac{8}{12} = \frac{4}{6}$$ (÷ 2 for the numerator and ÷ 2 for the denominator)

Expressing fractions in simplest form

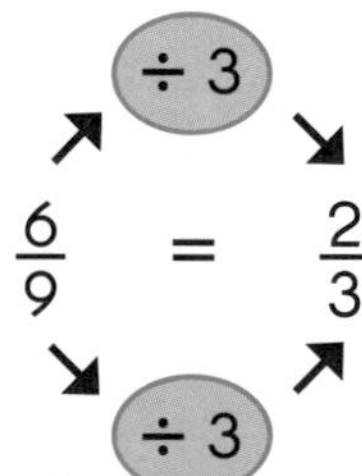

$$\frac{8}{12} = \frac{2}{3}$$ (÷ 4 for the numerator and ÷ 4 for the denominator)

Divide the numerator and denominator by their greatest common factor.

Representing fractions on a number line

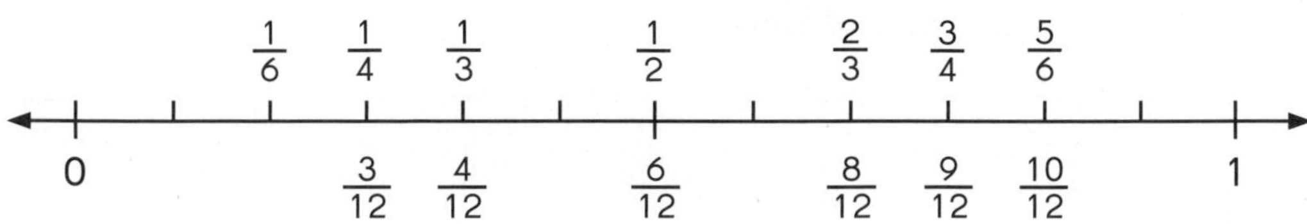

Identifying prime and composite numbers

2 and 5 are prime numbers. They have no factors other than 1 and themselves.

$2 = 2 \times 1$ $\quad\quad$ $5 = 5 \times 1$

8 and 24 are composite numbers. They have factors other than 1 and themselves.

$$\begin{aligned} 8 &= 1 \times 8 \\ &= 2 \times 4 \end{aligned} \qquad \begin{aligned} 24 &= 1 \times 24 \\ &= 2 \times 12 \\ &= 3 \times 8 \\ &= 4 \times 6 \end{aligned}$$

Expressing improper fractions as mixed numbers

Express $\frac{5}{3}$ as a mixed number.

Using models:

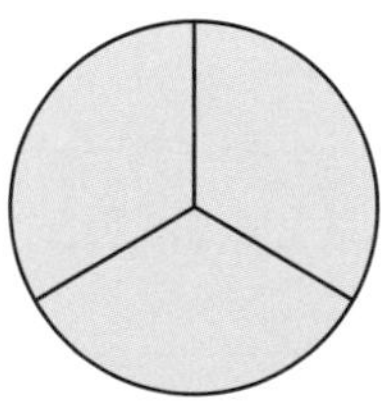

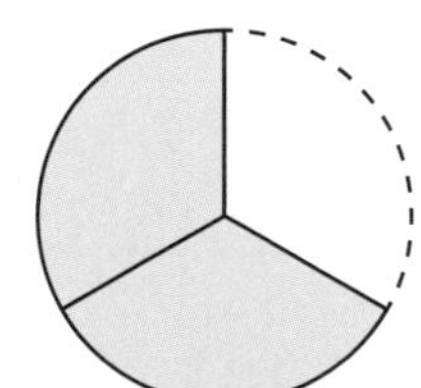

$$\begin{aligned} \frac{5}{3} &= 5 \text{ thirds} \\ &= 3 \text{ thirds} + 2 \text{ thirds} \\ &= \frac{3}{3} + \frac{2}{3} \\ &= 1 + \frac{2}{3} \\ &= 1\frac{2}{3} \end{aligned}$$

Using division:

$\frac{5}{3}$ means 5 divided by 3.

number of wholes → 1

$$\begin{array}{r} 1 \\ 3\overline{)5} \\ 3 \\ \hline 2 \end{array}$$

2 ← number of thirds

Divide the numerator by the denominator.
$5 \div 3 = 1 \text{ R } 2$
This is the division rule.

There is 1 whole and 2 thirds in $\frac{5}{3}$.
$\frac{5}{3} = 1\frac{2}{3}$

Adding and subtracting like fractions

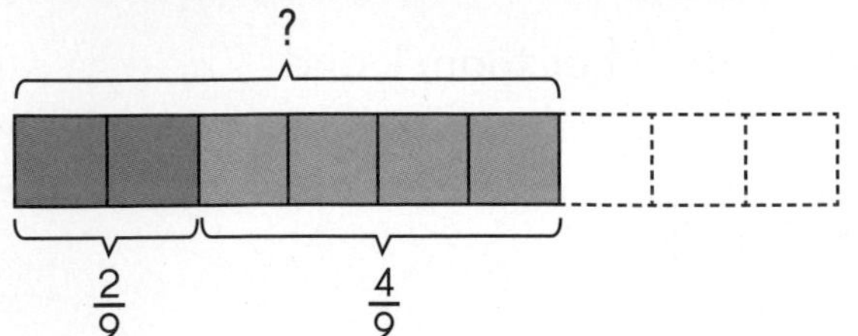

$$\frac{2}{9} + \frac{4}{9} = \frac{6}{9}$$
$$= \frac{2}{3}$$

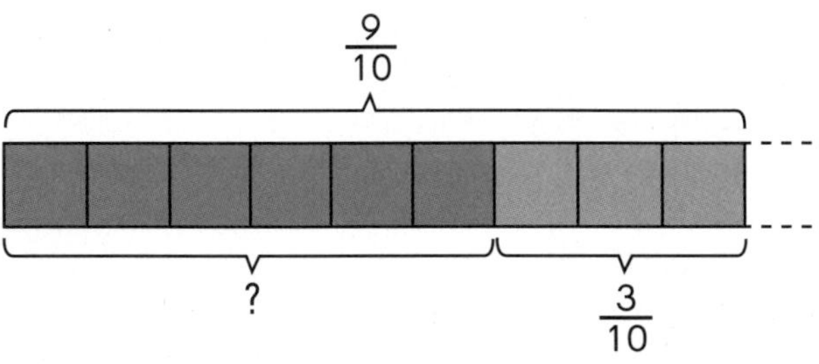

$$\frac{9}{10} - \frac{3}{10} = \frac{6}{10}$$
$$= \frac{3}{5}$$

Adding and subtracting unlike fractions

$$\frac{2}{3} + \frac{1}{6} = \frac{4}{6} + \frac{1}{6}$$
$$= \frac{5}{6}$$

$$\frac{1}{3} + \frac{4}{9} + \frac{2}{3} = \frac{3}{9} + \frac{4}{9} + \frac{6}{9}$$
$$= \frac{13}{9}$$
$$= 1\frac{4}{9}$$

$$\frac{3}{4} - \frac{5}{12} = \frac{9}{12} - \frac{5}{12}$$
$$= \frac{4}{12}$$
$$= \frac{1}{3}$$

$$1 - \frac{2}{9} - \frac{7}{18} = \frac{18}{18} - \frac{4}{18} - \frac{7}{18}$$
$$= \frac{7}{18}$$

$$2 - \frac{4}{5} - \frac{9}{10} = \frac{20}{10} - \frac{8}{10} - \frac{9}{10}$$
$$= \frac{3}{10}$$

Reading and writing tenths and hundredths in decimal and fractional forms

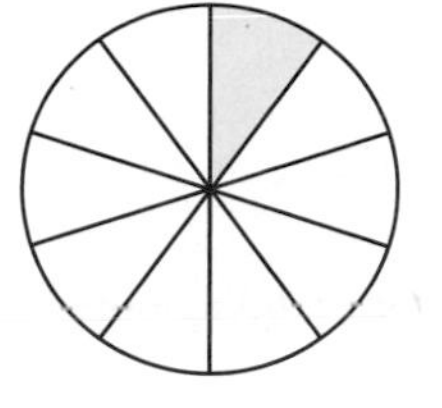

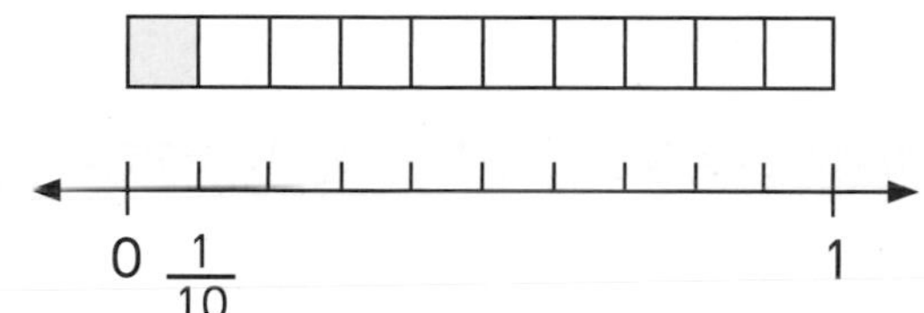

$\frac{1}{10}$ (one tenth) is 0.1 in decimal form. You read 0.1 as one tenth.

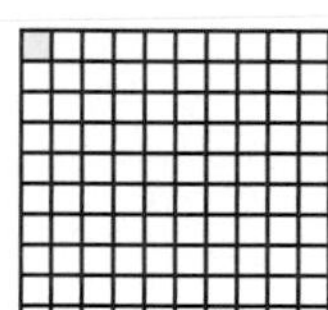

$\frac{1}{100}$

0 0.1 0.2 0.3 0.4 0.5 0.6 0.7 0.8 0.9 1

$\frac{1}{100}$ (one hundredth) is 0.01 in decimal form. You read 0.01 as one hundredth.

Expressing fractions as decimals

Express $\frac{9}{10}$ as a decimal.

$\frac{1}{10}$ = 1 tenth

= 0.1

$\frac{9}{10}$ = 9 tenths

= 0.9

Express $\frac{17}{100}$ as a decimal.

10 hundredths = 1 tenth

$\frac{17}{100}$ = 17 hundredths

1 tenth 7 hundredths

$\frac{17}{100}$ = 1 tenth 7 hundredths

= 0.17

✔ Quick Check

Find the like fractions in each set.

1 $\frac{3}{4}$, $\frac{1}{2}$, $\frac{2}{5}$, $\frac{1}{4}$

2 $\frac{5}{6}$, $\frac{5}{9}$, $\frac{9}{10}$, $\frac{7}{9}$

Find the unlike fractions in each set.

3. $\frac{1}{8}$, $\frac{2}{7}$, $\frac{3}{8}$, $\frac{1}{2}$

4. $\frac{5}{9}$, $\frac{5}{12}$, $\frac{1}{10}$, $\frac{7}{9}$

Find the number of wholes and parts that are shaded. Then write the mixed number.

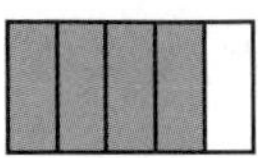

5. ___ wholes ___ parts = ___ $\frac{\square}{\square}$

Complete to show the equivalent fractions.

6. $\frac{3}{5} = \frac{\square}{10}$

7. $\frac{15}{20} = \frac{\square}{4}$

Express each fraction in simplest form.

8. $\frac{8}{10} = \square$

9. $\frac{12}{16} = \square$

Find the equivalent fractions which are missing from the number line. Give your answers in simplest form.

10.

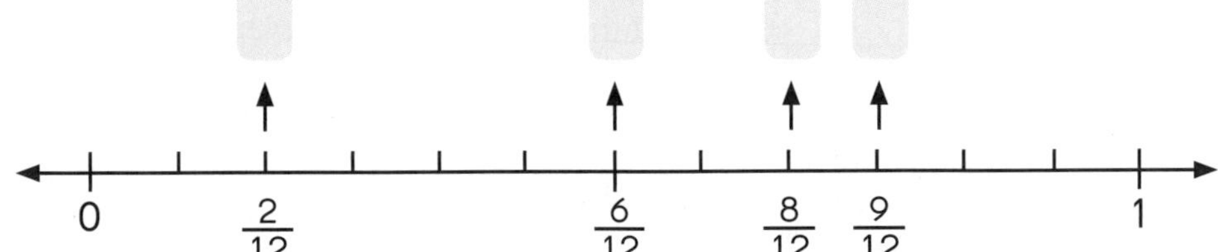

Find the prime numbers.

11. 12, 2, 8, 3, 7, 15

Find the composite numbers.

12 2, 14, 18, 13, 5, 10

Express the improper fraction as a mixed number.

13 $\frac{8}{3}$ = ☐ thirds

= ☐ thirds + ☐ thirds

= ☐ + ☐

= ☐ + ☐

= ☐ $\frac{☐}{☐}$

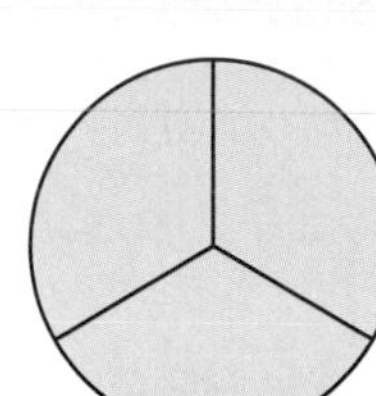

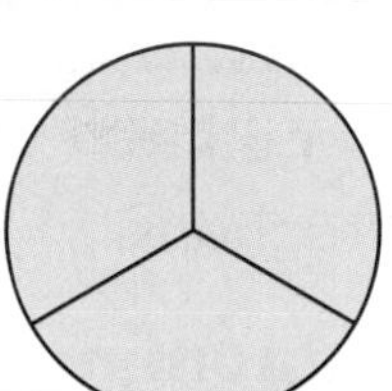

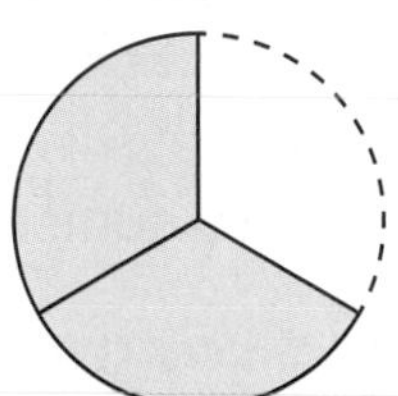

Express each improper fraction as a mixed number.
Use the division rule.

14 $\frac{13}{4}$ = ☐

15 $\frac{19}{5}$ = ☐

Add or subtract. Express the sum or difference in simplest form.

16 $\frac{5}{8} + \frac{1}{8} =$ ☐

17 $\frac{3}{10} - \frac{1}{10} =$ ☐

18 $\frac{1}{2} + \frac{3}{8} =$ ☐

19 $\frac{2}{3} + \frac{3}{4} + \frac{10}{12} =$ ☐

20 $\frac{4}{5} - \frac{3}{10} =$ ☐

21 $\frac{6}{7} - \frac{11}{14} =$ ☐

22 $1 - \frac{1}{6} - \frac{11}{18} =$ ☐

23 $3 - \frac{1}{3} - \frac{2}{9} =$ ☐

Express each fraction as a decimal.

24 $\frac{7}{10}$ ☐

25 $\frac{3}{100}$ ☐

26 $\frac{89}{100}$ ☐

Lesson

3.1 Adding Unlike Fractions

Lesson Objectives

- Add two unlike fractions where one denominator is not a multiple of the other.
- Estimate sums of fractions.

Vocabulary

multiple

least common multiple

least common denominator

equivalent fractions

benchmark

Learn Find common denominators to add unlike fractions.

A plank is painted $\frac{1}{2}$ red and $\frac{1}{3}$ green. The rest is painted yellow. What fraction of the plank is painted red and green?

$\frac{1}{2} + \frac{1}{3} = ?$

$\frac{1}{2}$ and $\frac{1}{3}$ are unlike fractions. To add, rewrite $\frac{1}{2}$ and $\frac{1}{3}$ as like fractions.

List the **multiples** of the denominators, 2 and 3.

Multiples of 2: 2, 4, 6, 8, ... Multiples of 3: 3, 6, 9, 12, ...

The **least common multiple** of 2 and 3 is 6.

So, 6 is the **least common denominator** of $\frac{1}{2}$ and $\frac{1}{3}$. Use it to rewrite $\frac{1}{2}$ and $\frac{1}{3}$ as like fractions.

$\frac{1 \times 3}{2 \times 3} = \frac{3}{6}$ $\frac{1 \times 2}{3 \times 2} = \frac{2}{6}$

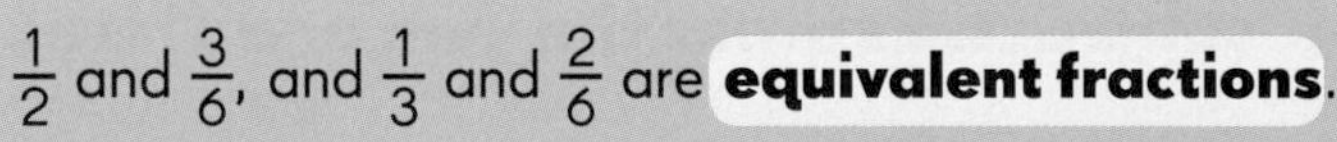

$\frac{1}{2}$ and $\frac{3}{6}$, and $\frac{1}{3}$ and $\frac{2}{6}$ are **equivalent fractions**.

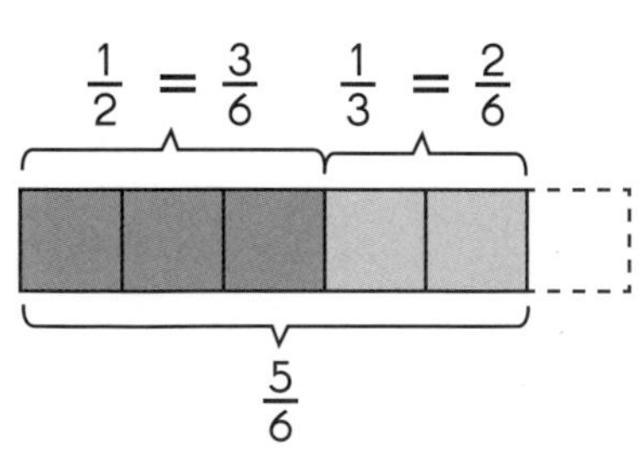

Since 6 is the least common multiple, I draw a model with 6 units.

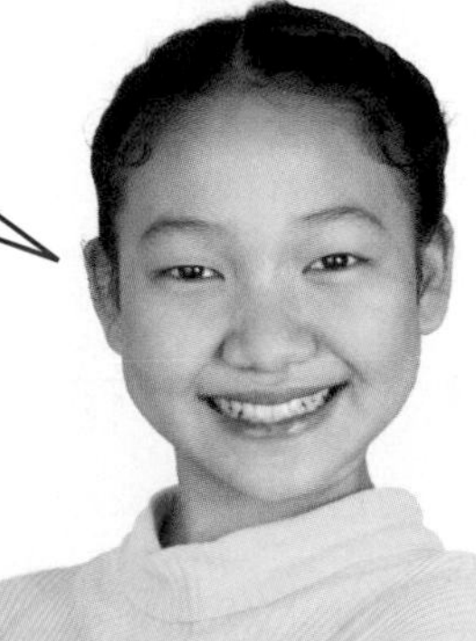

$$\frac{1}{2} + \frac{1}{3} = \frac{3}{6} + \frac{2}{6}$$
$$= \frac{5}{6}$$

$\frac{5}{6}$ of the plank is painted red and green.

Guided Learning

Add the fractions.

1 $\frac{1}{2} + \frac{2}{7}$

$\frac{1}{2} \xrightarrow{\times 7} \frac{7}{14}$ (numerator × 7, denominator × 7)

$\frac{2}{7} \xrightarrow{\times 2} \frac{4}{14}$ (numerator × 2, denominator × 2)

The least common multiple of 2 and 7 is 14.

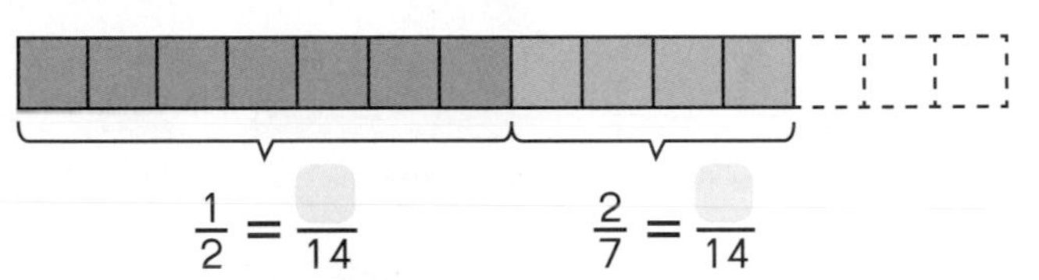

$\frac{1}{2} = \frac{\square}{14}$ $\frac{2}{7} = \frac{\square}{14}$

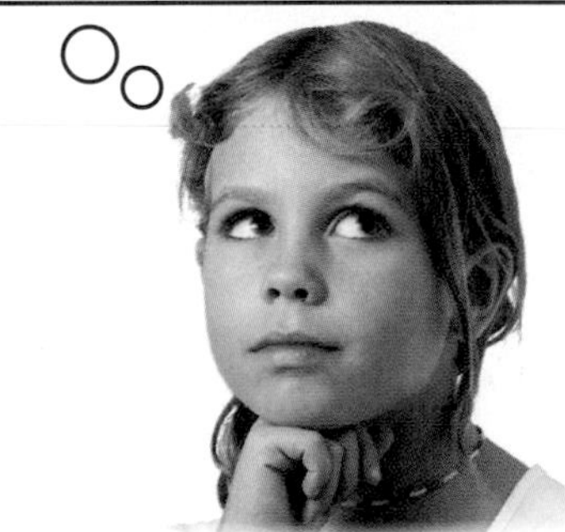

$\frac{1}{2} + \frac{2}{7} = \frac{\square}{14} + \frac{\square}{14}$

$= \frac{\square}{\square}$

2 $\frac{3}{4} + \frac{2}{3} = \frac{\square}{\square} + \frac{\square}{\square}$

$= \frac{\square}{\square}$

$= \frac{\square}{\square} + \frac{\square}{\square}$

$= \square\frac{\square}{\square}$

$\frac{3}{4} \xrightarrow{\times 3} \frac{\square}{\square}$ (numerator × 3, denominator × 3)

$\frac{2}{3} \xrightarrow{\times 4} \frac{\square}{\square}$ (numerator × 4, denominator × 4)

Hands-On Activity

Tech Connection

Use a computer drawing tool. Draw models that show the sum for each pair of fractions. Then find the sum.

1 $\frac{1}{2} + \frac{1}{4}$

2 $\frac{1}{5} + \frac{3}{4}$

3 $\frac{1}{4} + \frac{2}{3}$

Learn Use benchmarks to estimate sums of fractions.

Benchmarks are numbers that are easier to work with and to picture than others. They help compare numbers and estimate answers.

In estimating with fractions, you approximate each fraction to the closest benchmark. Common benchmarks for estimating with fractions are 0, $\frac{1}{2}$ and 1.

Estimate the sum of $\frac{11}{12}$, $\frac{2}{3}$ and $\frac{1}{6}$.

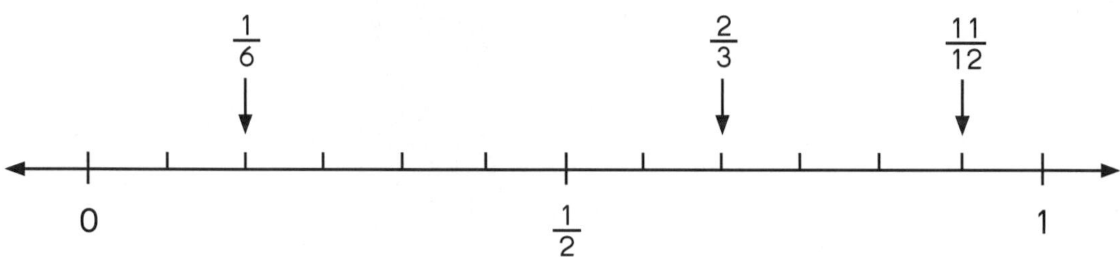

$\frac{11}{12}$ is about 1.

$\frac{2}{3}$ is about $\frac{1}{2}$.

$\frac{1}{6}$ is about 0.

$$\frac{11}{12} + \frac{2}{3} + \frac{1}{6}$$

$$\downarrow \quad \downarrow \quad \downarrow$$

$$1 + \frac{1}{2} + 0 = 1\frac{1}{2}$$

The sum of $\frac{11}{12}$, $\frac{2}{3}$ and $\frac{1}{6}$ is about $1\frac{1}{2}$.

Guided Learning

Use benchmarks to estimate each sum.

3 $\frac{1}{10} + \frac{2}{5}$ ______

4 $\frac{8}{9} + \frac{9}{10}$ ______

5 $\frac{1}{6} + \frac{7}{12} + \frac{5}{6}$ ______

Let's Explore!

1. Without solving, do you think the sum of $\frac{1}{3}$ and $\frac{3}{8}$ is less than 1? Explain your reasoning.
2. Do you think the sum of $\frac{5}{9}$ and $\frac{6}{11}$ is greater than 1? Why?
3. Can you tell if the sum of $\frac{5}{11}$ and $\frac{4}{7}$ is greater than or less than 1? Why or why not?

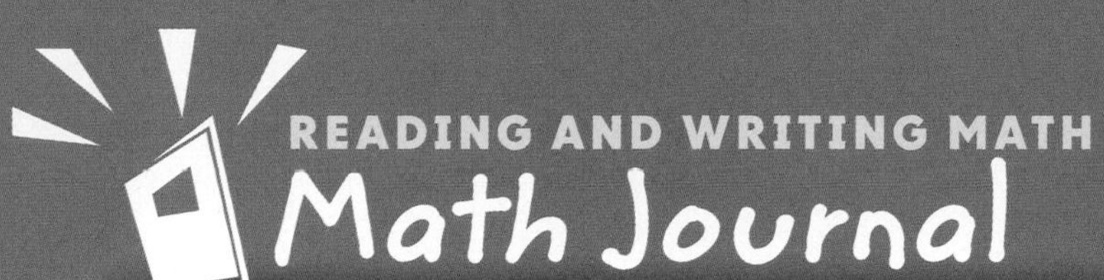

READING AND WRITING MATH

Math Journal

One of the three models shows the sum of $\frac{1}{2}$ and $\frac{1}{7}$. The other two models are incorrect.

Model 1: 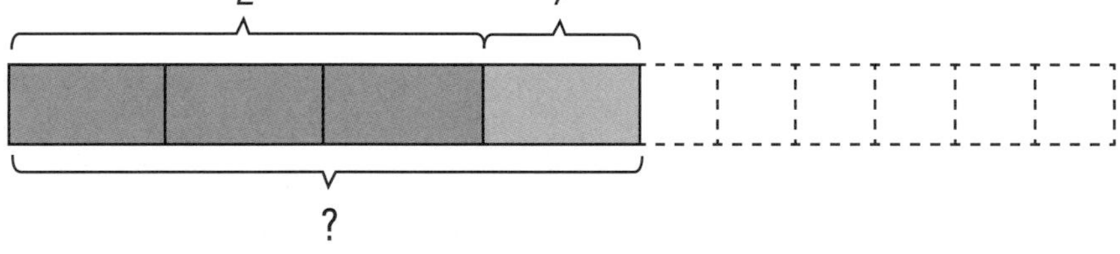

Model 2: 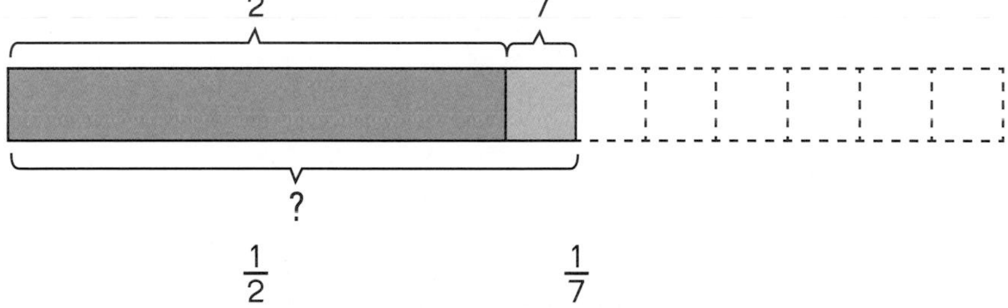

Model 3: 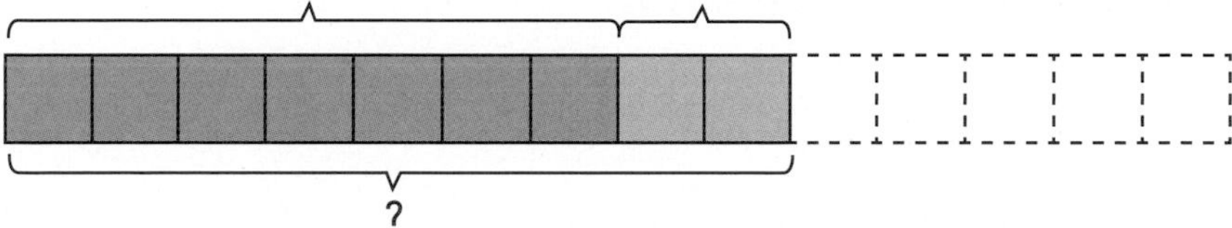

a. Identify the correct one of the three.

b. Explain why the other two are incorrect.

Let's Practice

Find the part of the model that shows the fractions $\frac{1}{2}$, $\frac{2}{5}$ and $\frac{9}{10}$. Then write two addition sentences using the fractions.

1

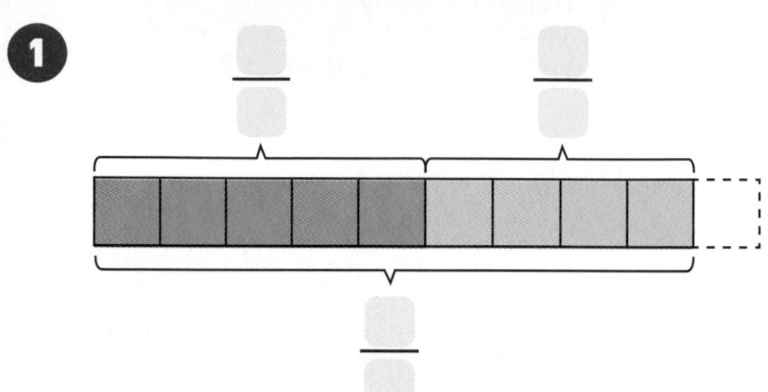

Draw a model to find each sum.

2 $\frac{1}{3}$ and $\frac{1}{4}$

3 $\frac{3}{5}$ and $\frac{1}{3}$

Add. Express each sum in simplest form.

4 $\frac{2}{3} + \frac{1}{8}$

5 $\frac{2}{3} + \frac{1}{12}$

6 $\frac{1}{5} + \frac{3}{10}$

7 $\frac{1}{4} + \frac{1}{6}$

8 $\frac{5}{9} + \frac{1}{2}$

9 $\frac{2}{5} + \frac{5}{6}$

10 $\frac{3}{4} + \frac{5}{12}$

11 $\frac{1}{6} + \frac{5}{8}$

Use benchmarks to estimate each sum.

12 $\frac{2}{5} + \frac{6}{7}$

13 $\frac{4}{9} + \frac{4}{10}$

14 $\frac{1}{8} + \frac{3}{5} + \frac{9}{10}$

ON YOUR OWN

Go to Workbook A:
Practice 1, pages 101–106

Lesson 3.2 Subtracting Unlike Fractions

Lesson Objectives

- Subtract two unlike fractions where one denominator is not a multiple of the other.
- Estimate differences between fractions.

Learn Find common denominators to subtract unlike fractions.

A carton contains $\frac{3}{4}$ quart of milk. Larry pours $\frac{1}{3}$ quart of the milk into a mug. How much milk is left in the carton?

$\frac{3}{4} - \frac{1}{3} = ?$

$\frac{1}{3}$ and $\frac{3}{4}$ are unlike fractions. To subtract, rewrite $\frac{1}{3}$ and $\frac{3}{4}$ as like fractions.

List the multiples of the denominators, 3 and 4.

Multiples of 3: 3, 6, 9, 12, ... Multiples of 4: 4, 8, 12, 16, ...

The least common multiple of 3 and 4 is 12.

So, 12 is the least common denominator of $\frac{1}{3}$ and $\frac{3}{4}$. Use it to rewrite $\frac{3}{4}$ and $\frac{1}{3}$ as like fractions.

$\frac{3}{4} = \frac{3 \times 3}{4 \times 3} = \frac{9}{12}$ $\frac{1}{3} = \frac{1 \times 4}{3 \times 4} = \frac{4}{12}$

$\frac{3}{4}$ and $\frac{9}{12}$, and $\frac{1}{3}$ and $\frac{4}{12}$ are equivalent fractions.

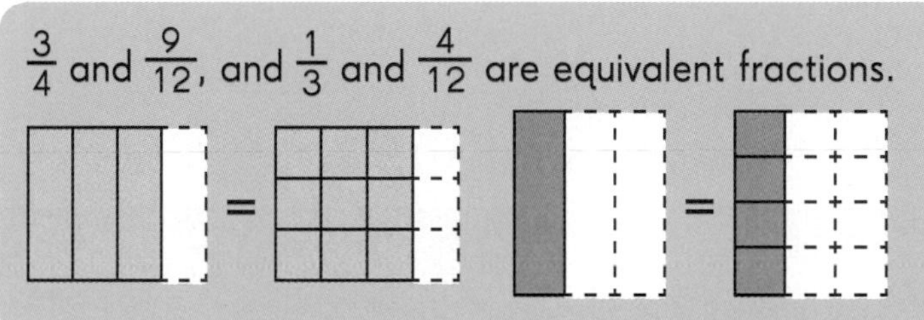

$\frac{3}{4} = \frac{9}{12}$

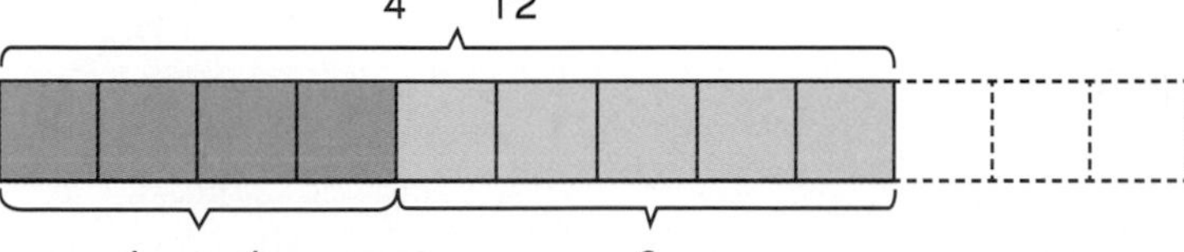

$\frac{1}{3} = \frac{4}{12}$?

$\frac{3}{4} - \frac{1}{3} = \frac{9}{12} - \frac{4}{12}$

$= \frac{5}{12}$

Since 12 is the least common multiple, I draw a model with 12 units.

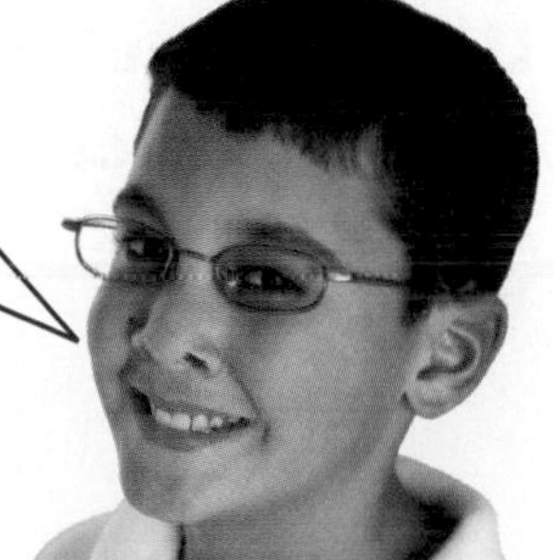

$\frac{5}{12}$ quart of milk is left in the carton.

Guided Learning

Subtract the fractions.

1 $\frac{2}{3} - \frac{1}{5}$

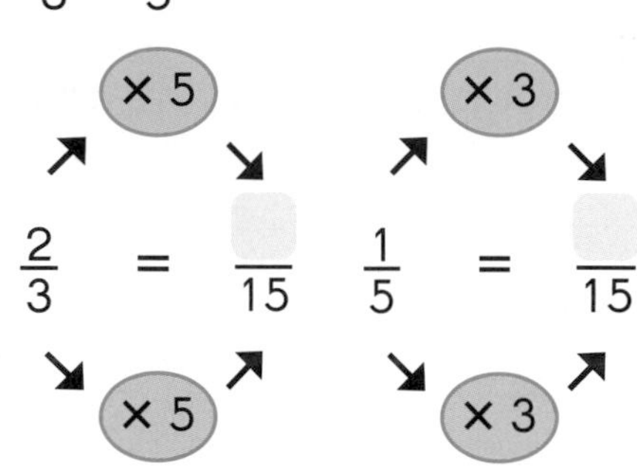

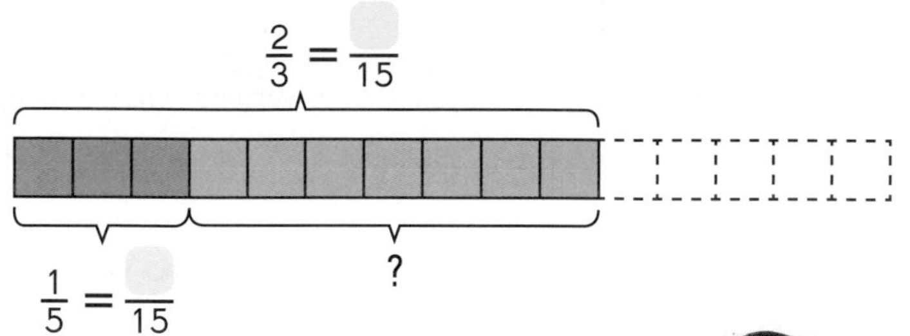

$\frac{2}{3} - \frac{1}{5} = \frac{?}{15} - \frac{?}{15}$

$= \frac{?}{15}$

2 $1 - \frac{1}{4} - \frac{1}{6} = 1 - \frac{?}{?} - \frac{?}{?}$

$= \frac{?}{?} - \frac{?}{?} - \frac{?}{?}$

$= \frac{?}{?}$

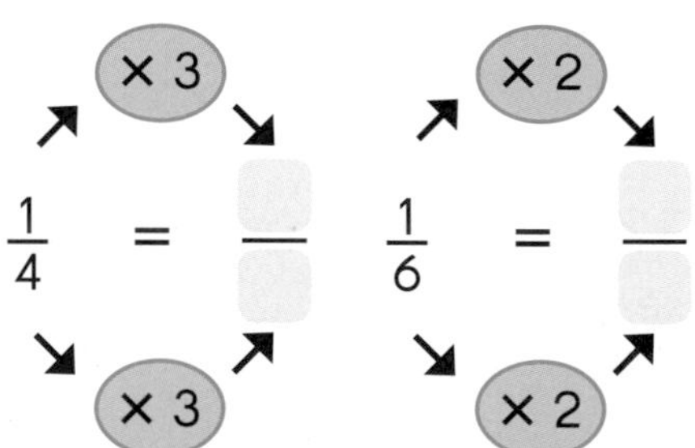

Hands-On Activity

Use a computer drawing tool. Draw models that show the difference for each pair of fractions. Then find the difference.

1 $\frac{1}{2} - \frac{2}{7}$ **2** $\frac{5}{6} - \frac{4}{9}$ **3** $\frac{3}{4} - \frac{3}{5}$

Learn: Use benchmarks to estimate differences between fractions.

Estimate the difference between $\frac{8}{9}$ and $\frac{4}{10}$.

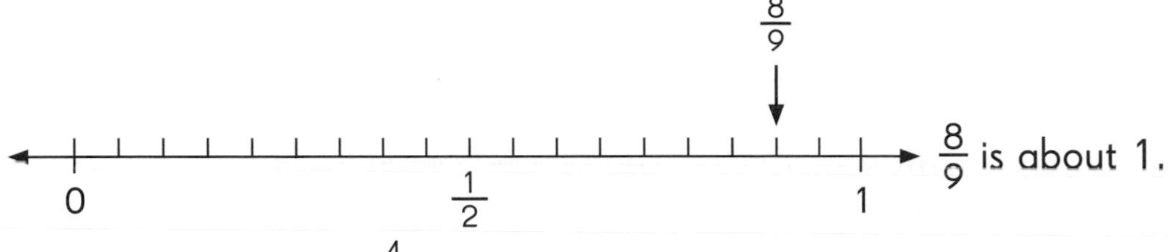

$\frac{8}{9}$ is about 1.

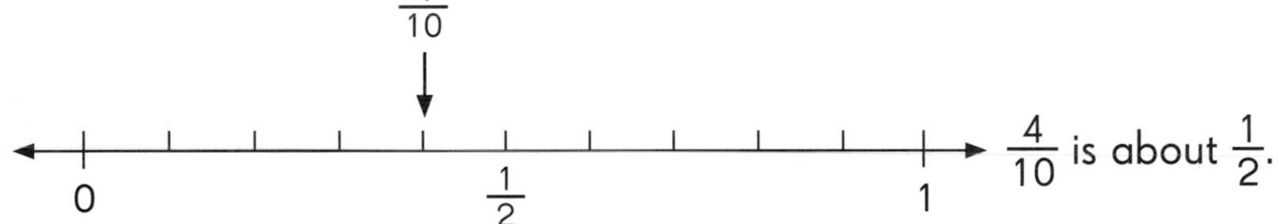

$\frac{4}{10}$ is about $\frac{1}{2}$.

$$\frac{8}{9} - \frac{4}{10}$$

$$1 - \frac{1}{2} = \frac{1}{2}$$

The difference between $\frac{8}{9}$ and $\frac{4}{10}$ is about $\frac{1}{2}$.

Guided Learning

Use benchmarks to estimate each difference.

3. $\frac{5}{6} - \frac{2}{5}$ ______

4. $\frac{9}{10} - \frac{1}{8}$ ______

5. $\frac{7}{12} - \frac{4}{9}$ ______

Let's Explore!

1. Without solving, do you think the difference between 1 and $\frac{3}{7}$ is greater than $\frac{1}{2}$? Explain your reasoning.
2. Do you think the difference between 1 and $\frac{7}{12}$ is less than $\frac{1}{2}$? Explain your reasoning.
3. Can you tell if the difference between $\frac{11}{12}$ and $\frac{1}{4}$ is greater than or less than $\frac{1}{2}$? Explain your reasoning.

Let's Practice

Find the part of the model that shows the fractions $\frac{1}{2}$, $\frac{3}{10}$ and $\frac{4}{5}$. Then write two subtraction sentences using the fractions.

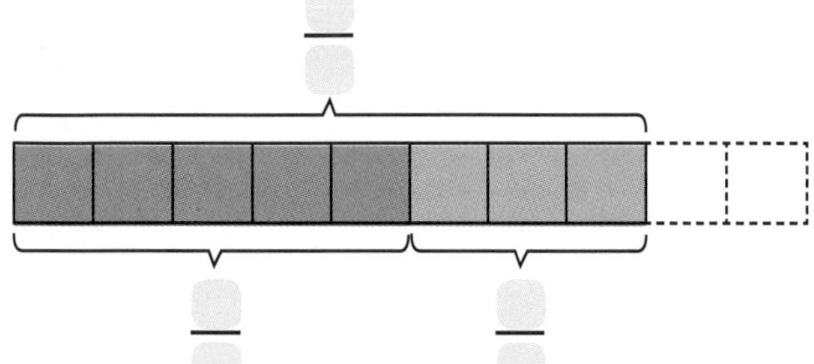

Draw a model to find each difference.

2. $\frac{5}{8} - \frac{1}{2}$

3. $\frac{4}{5} - \frac{1}{4}$

Subtract. Express each difference in simplest form.

4. $\frac{8}{9} - \frac{5}{6}$

5. $\frac{11}{12} - \frac{7}{8}$

6. $\frac{4}{5} - \frac{2}{7}$

7. $\frac{7}{9} - \frac{3}{4}$

8. $\frac{4}{7} - \frac{1}{6}$

9. $\frac{2}{3} - \frac{3}{8}$

10. $2 - \frac{1}{3} - \frac{9}{10}$

11. $4 - \frac{5}{6} - \frac{3}{8}$

Use benchmarks to estimate each difference.

12. $\frac{4}{5} - \frac{3}{7}$

13. $\frac{5}{8} - \frac{1}{9}$

14. $\frac{11}{12} - \frac{5}{6}$

ON YOUR OWN
Go to Workbook A:
Practice 2, pages 107–110

Lesson 3.3 Fractions, Mixed Numbers, and Division Expressions

Lesson Objective

- Understand and apply the relationships between fractions, mixed numbers, and division expressions.

Vocabulary
division expression
mixed number

Learn Rewrite division expressions as fractions.

Three friends share 2 pizzas equally.
What fraction of a pizza does each friend get?

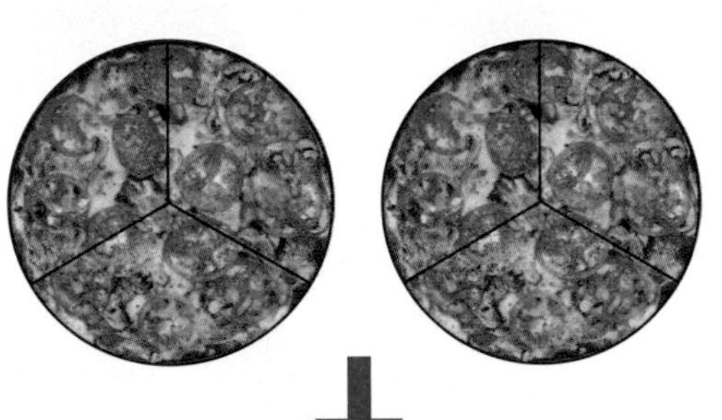

Each pizza is divided into 3 equal parts. Each part is $\frac{1}{3}$ of a pizza.

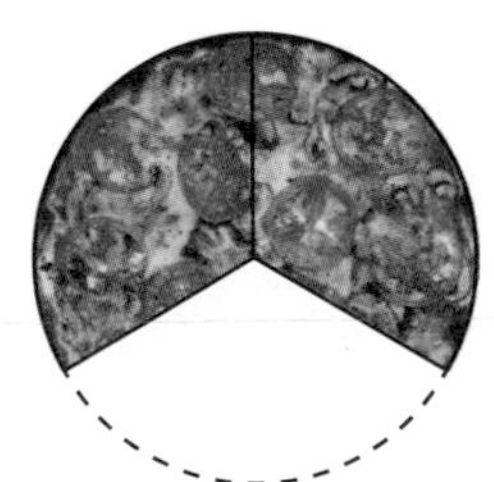

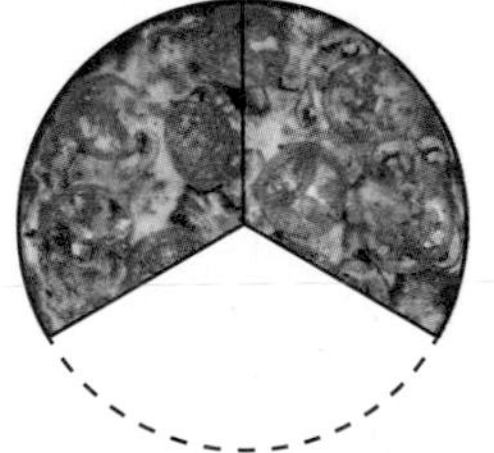

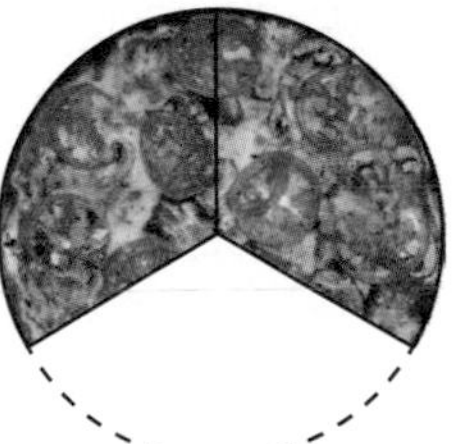

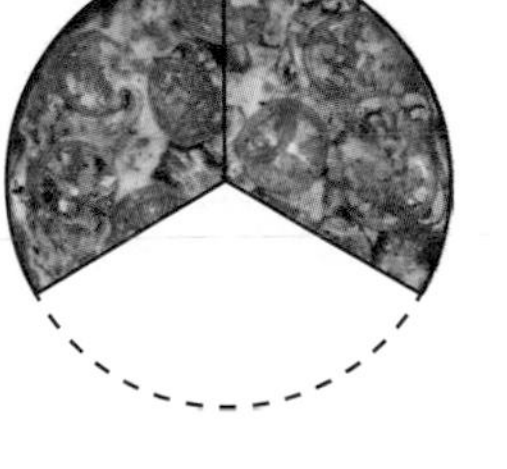

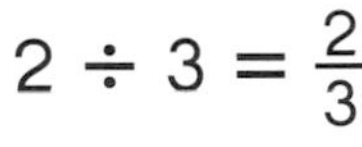

$2 \div 3 = \frac{2}{3}$

Each friend will get $\frac{2}{3}$ of a pizza.

2 divided by 3 is the same as $\frac{2}{3}$.

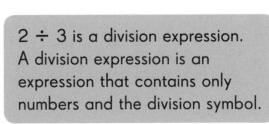

$2 \div 3$ is a division expression.
A division expression is an expression that contains only numbers and the division symbol.

Guided Learning

Solve.

1 Mr. Sheldon cuts 3 strawberry pies to share equally among 4 children. What fraction of a strawberry pie does each child get?

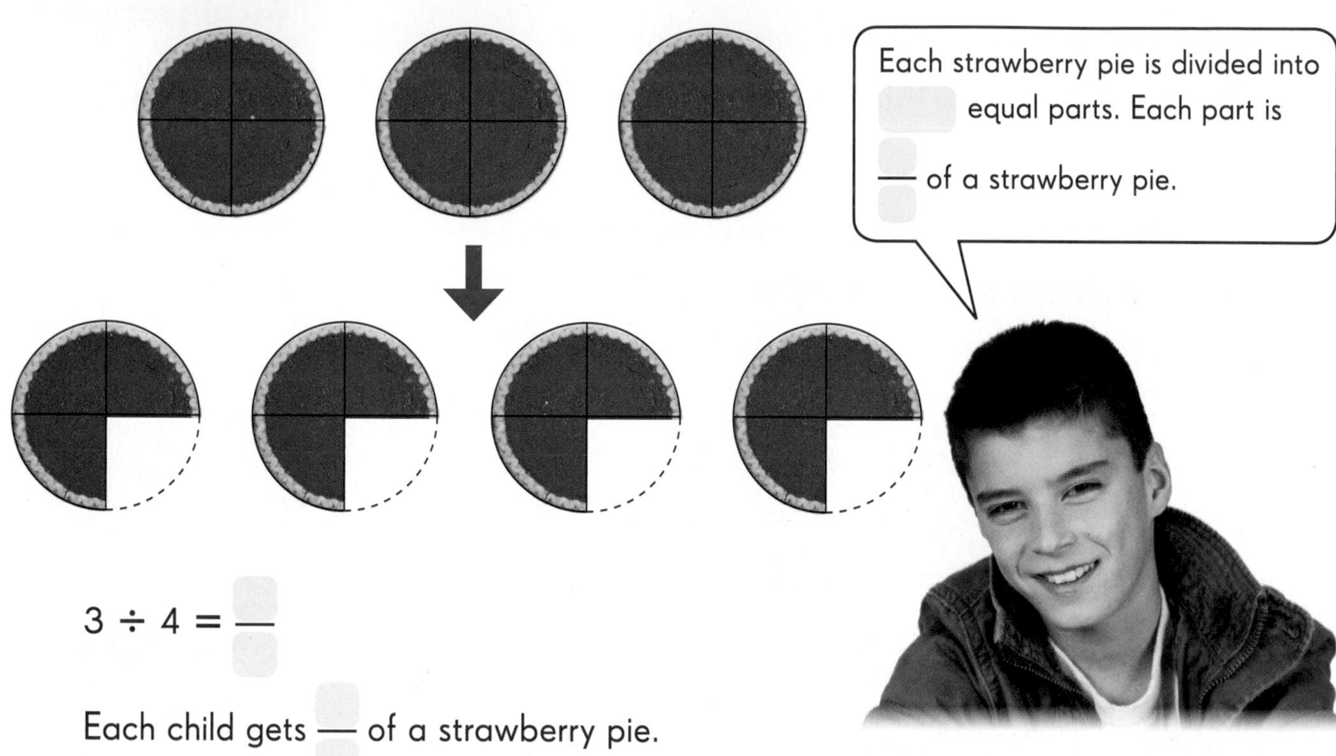

Each strawberry pie is divided into ___ equal parts. Each part is $\frac{\;}{\;}$ of a strawberry pie.

$3 \div 4 = \frac{\;}{\;}$

Each child gets $\frac{\;}{\;}$ of a strawberry pie.

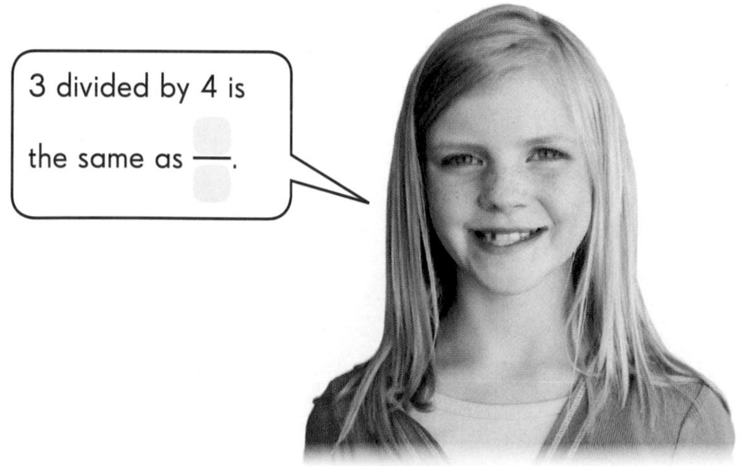

Hands-On Activity

Use paper strips of the same size and length. Use fewer paper strips than the number of students in your group.

STEP 1 Cut the strips into equal pieces so that each student gets the same number of pieces.

Example

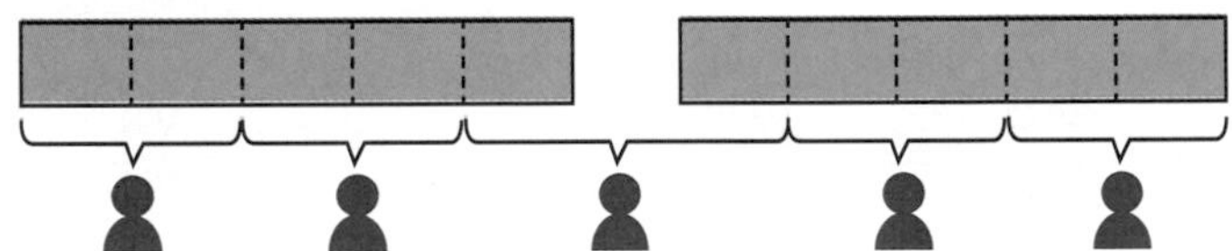

STEP 2 Write a division expression to show the fraction of a strip that each person gets. For example in STEP 1, write $2 \div 5 = \frac{2}{5}$.

Guided Learning

Rewrite each division expression as a fraction.

2. $4 \div 5 = \frac{\square}{\square}$

3. $7 \div 9 = \frac{\square}{\square}$

4. $5 \div 8 = \frac{\square}{\square}$

5. $7 \div 11 = \frac{\square}{\square}$

Rewrite each fraction as a division expression.

6. $\frac{3}{7} = \square \div \square$

7. $\frac{8}{12} = \square \div \square$

8. $\frac{3}{10} = \square \div \square$

9. $\frac{5}{6} = \square \div \square$

Learn Rewrite division expressions as mixed numbers.

Katie uses a mold to make 5 equal-sized pies. She then divides the 5 pies equally among 4 people. How many pies does each person get?

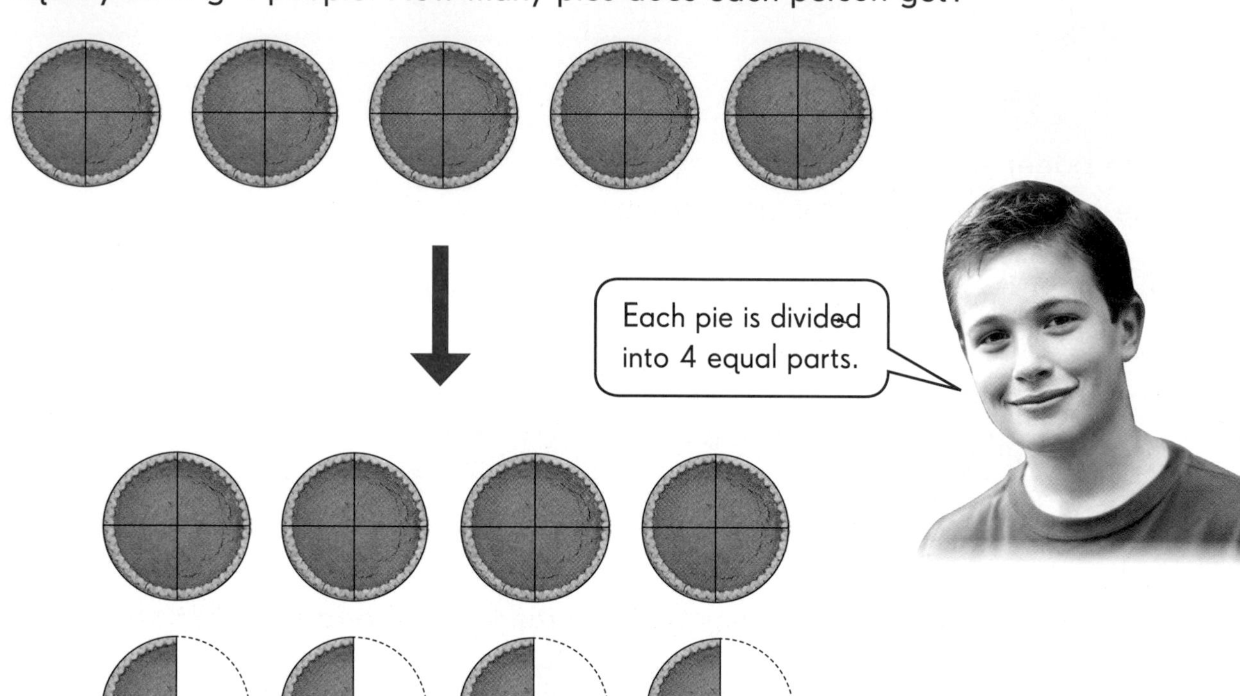
Each pie is divided into 4 equal parts.

Method 1

$$5 \div 4 = \frac{5}{4}$$
$$= \frac{4}{4} + \frac{1}{4}$$
$$= 1\frac{1}{4}$$

5 divided by 4 is the same as $\frac{5}{4}$ or $1\frac{1}{4}$.

Method 2

$$\begin{array}{r} 1 \\ 4\overline{)5} \\ \underline{4} \\ 1 \end{array}$$

1 ← number of wholes

1 ← number of fourths

$5 \div 4 = 1\frac{1}{4}$

Each person gets $1\frac{1}{4}$ pies.

Hands-On Activity

WORKING TOGETHER

Use paper strips of the same size and length. Use a greater number of paper strips than the number of students in your group.

STEP 1 Cut the strips into equal pieces so that each person gets the same number of pieces.

Example

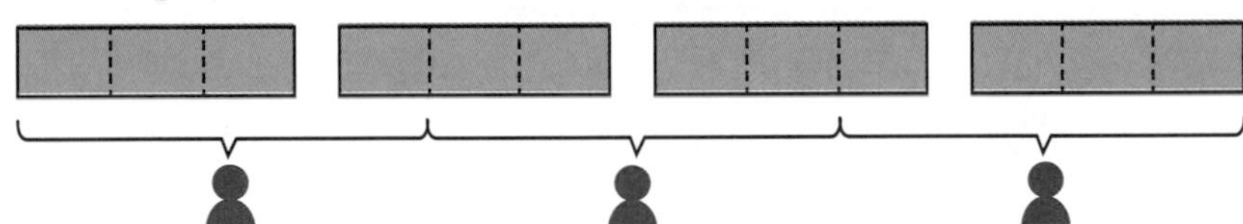

STEP 2 Write a division expression to show the number of strips each person gets. Then, express it as a fraction and a mixed number.

For example in STEP 1, write $4 \div 3 = \frac{4}{3} = 1\frac{1}{3}$.

Guided Learning

Express 14 ÷ 4 as a fraction in simplest form. Then rewrite the fraction as a mixed number.

10 $14 \div 4 = \frac{\square \div \square}{\square \div \square}$

$= \frac{\square}{\square}$

$= \square\frac{\square}{\square}$

Express each division expression as a fraction in simplest form. Then rewrite the fraction as a mixed number.

11. $19 \div 2$ ▢
12. $43 \div 4$ ▢
13. $49 \div 5$ ▢
14. $20 \div 8$ ▢

Let's Practice

Rewrite each fraction as a division expression.

1. $\frac{4}{7} = ▢ \div ▢$
2. $\frac{5}{11} = ▢ \div ▢$
3. $\frac{9}{13} = ▢ \div ▢$

Express each division expression as a fraction or mixed number in simplest form.

4. $10 \div 12 = \frac{▢}{▢}$
$= \frac{▢}{▢}$

5. $3 \div 2 = \frac{3}{2}$
$= \frac{▢}{▢} + \frac{▢}{▢}$
$= ▢\frac{▢}{▢}$

$2\overline{)3}$

6. $7 \div 3$ ▢
7. $11 \div 4$ ▢
8. $25 \div 7$ ▢

Express each division expression as a fraction in simplest form. Then rewrite the fraction as a mixed number.

9. $22 \div 4$ ▢
10. $32 \div 12$ ▢

ON YOUR OWN

Go to Workbook A: Practice 3, pages 111–114

Expressing Fractions, Division Expressions, and Mixed Numbers as Decimals

Lesson Objective

- Express fractions, division expressions, and mixed numbers as decimals.

Learn Express a fraction as a decimal by finding an equivalent fraction.

Express $\frac{2}{5}$ as a decimal.

Use a denominator of 10.

$$\frac{2}{5} = \frac{2 \times 2}{5 \times 2}$$
$$= \frac{4}{10}$$
$$= 0.4$$

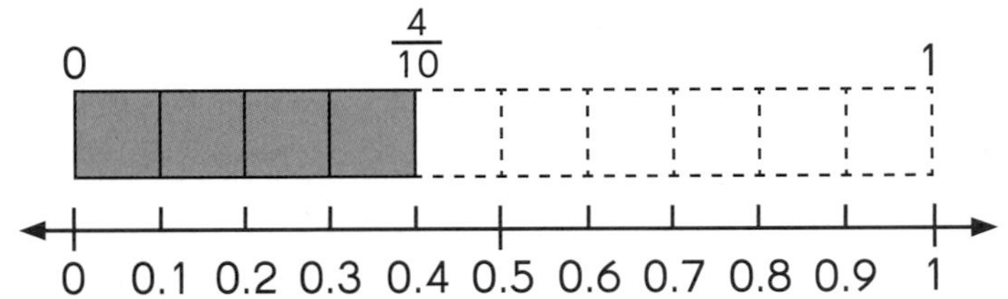

Read 0.4 as four tenths.

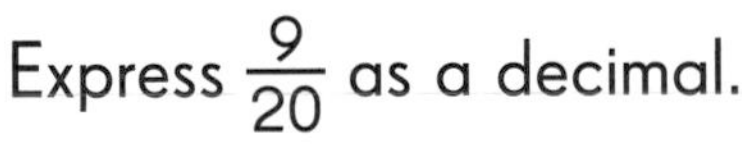

Express $\frac{9}{20}$ as a decimal.

Use a denominator of 100.

$$\frac{9}{20} = \frac{9 \times 5}{20 \times 5}$$
$$= \frac{45}{100}$$
$$= 0.45$$

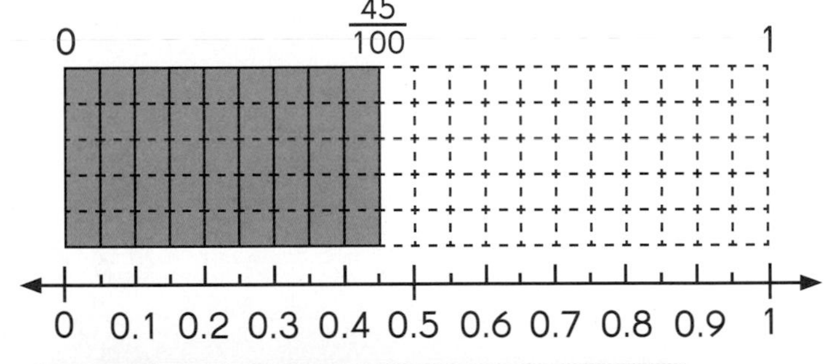

Read 0.45 as forty-five hundredths.

Guided Learning

Express each fraction as a decimal.

1 $\frac{4}{5} = \frac{\square}{10} = \square$

2 $\frac{7}{20} = \frac{\square}{100} = \square$

Learn Express division expressions as decimals.

Express $9 \div 6$ as a decimal.

$$9 \div 6 = \frac{9}{6} = 1 + \frac{3}{6} = 1 + \frac{1}{2} = 1 + 0.5 = 1.5$$

$$\frac{1}{2} = \frac{5}{10} = 0.5$$

(×5 numerator, ×5 denominator)

Learn Express mixed numbers as decimals.

Express $2\frac{1}{4}$ as a decimal.

$$2\frac{1}{4} = 2 + \frac{1}{4} = 2 + 0.25 = 2.25$$

$$\frac{1}{4} = \frac{25}{100} = 0.25$$

(×25 numerator, ×25 denominator)

Guided Learning

Express as a decimal.

3. $12 \div 5$ ___

4. $67 \div 25$ ___

5. $3\frac{3}{5}$ ___

6. $5\frac{7}{20}$ ___

Write a division expression for the problem. Then solve.

7. Mr. Jones has a bolt of cloth that is 6 yards long. He wants to divide it into 5 equal pieces. How long must each piece be?
Give your answer as

a. a mixed number, ___

b. a decimal. ___

Let's Practice

Express each fraction as a decimal.

1. $\frac{3}{5}$
2. $\frac{17}{20}$
3. $\frac{9}{25}$
4. $\frac{16}{25}$

Write a division expression for the problem. Then solve.

5. Jeff makes 16 quarts of lemonade. He then divides the lemonade equally among 5 jugs. How many quarts of lemonade are in each jug?

   Give your answer as

   a. a mixed number,
   b. a decimal.

6. The perimeter of a square court is 39 yards. What is the length of each of its sides?

   Give your answer as

   a. a mixed number,
   b. a decimal.

Express as a mixed number and as a decimal.

7. $7 \div 4$
8. $13 \div 10$
9. $36 \div 30$
10. $\frac{14}{5}$
11. $\frac{45}{20}$
12. $\frac{37}{25}$

ON YOUR OWN

Go to Workbook A:
Practice 4, pages 115–116

Lesson

3.5 Adding Mixed Numbers

Lesson Objectives

- Add mixed numbers with or without renaming.
- Estimate sums of mixed numbers.

Learn **Add mixed numbers without renaming.**

Maia bought $2\frac{1}{5}$ pounds of oranges. She also bought $1\frac{1}{2}$ pounds of grapes. What is the total weight of fruit that she bought?

$2\frac{1}{5} + 1\frac{1}{2} = ?$

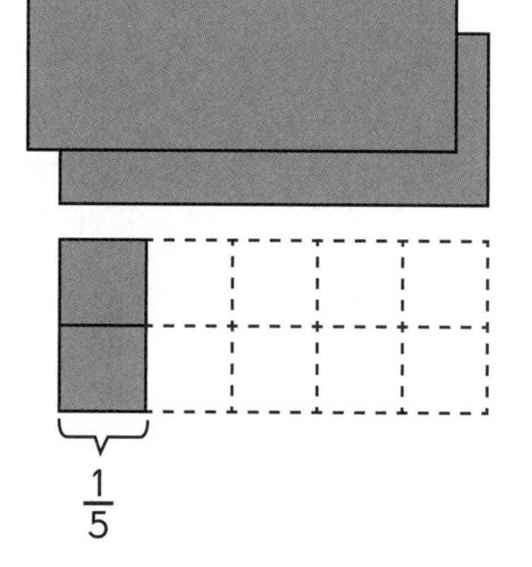

+

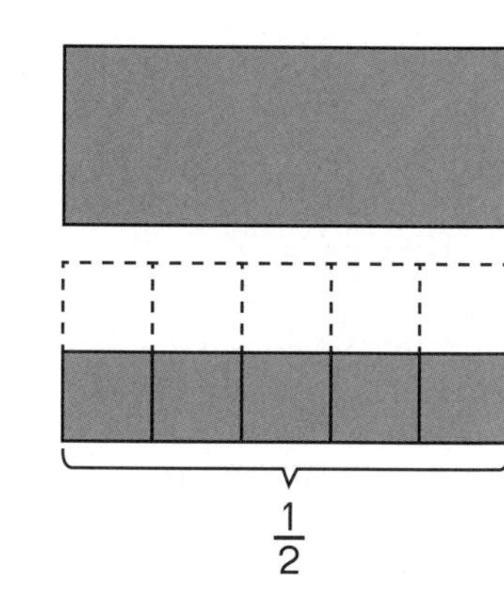

To add, rewrite the fractional parts as like fractions first. Then, add the fractional parts before adding the whole numbers.

$$2\frac{1}{5} + 1\frac{1}{2} = 2\frac{2}{10} + 1\frac{5}{10}$$
$$= 3\frac{7}{10}$$

Maia bought $3\frac{7}{10}$ pounds of fruit.

Guided Learning

Add.

1 $3\frac{1}{2} + 2\frac{4}{9}$

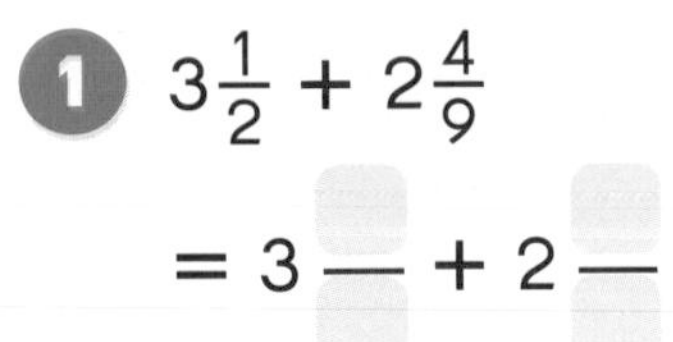

$= 3\frac{?}{} + 2\frac{?}{}$

$= ?\frac{?}{?}$

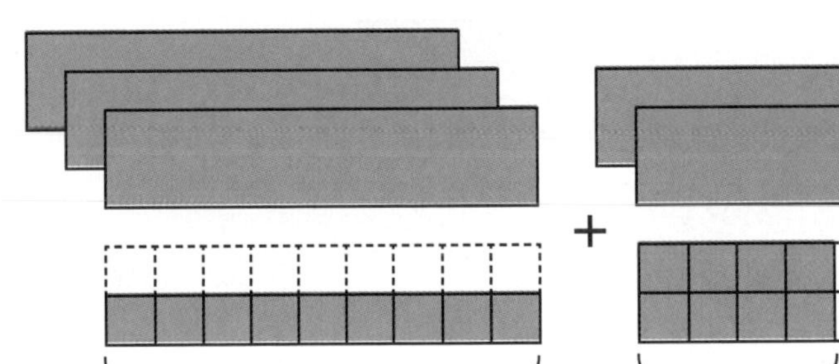

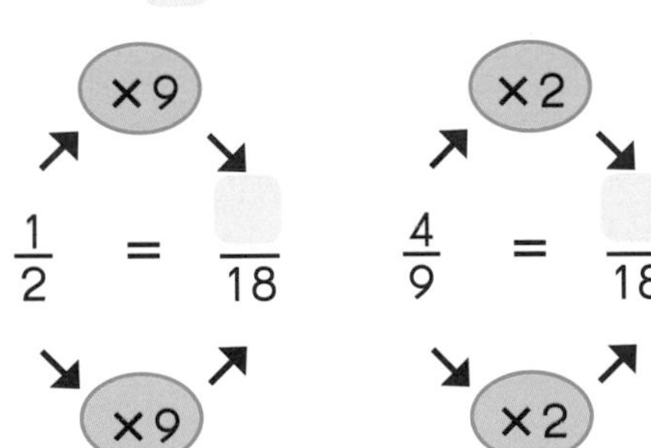

Learn: Add mixed numbers with renaming.

Serena jogged $2\frac{3}{4}$ miles and walked $1\frac{1}{2}$ miles. How many miles did she jog and walk altogether?

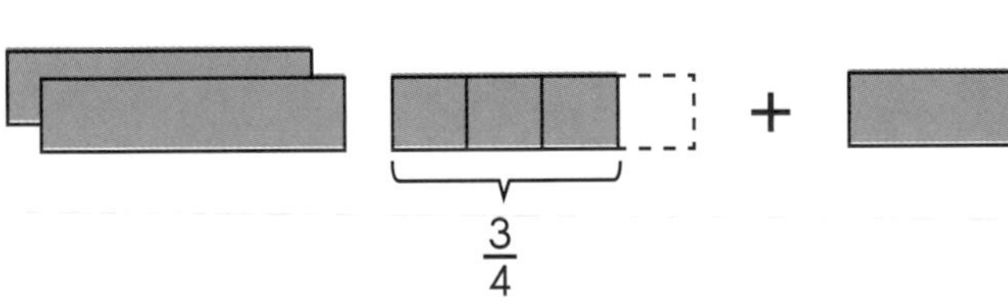

×2

$\frac{1}{2} = \frac{2}{4}$

×2

$$2\frac{3}{4} + 1\frac{1}{2} = 2\frac{3}{4} + 1\frac{2}{4}$$
$$= 3\frac{5}{4}$$
$$= 4\frac{1}{4}$$

$$3\frac{5}{4} = 3 + \frac{4}{4} + \frac{1}{4}$$
$$= 3 + 1 + \frac{1}{4}$$
$$= 4\frac{1}{4}$$

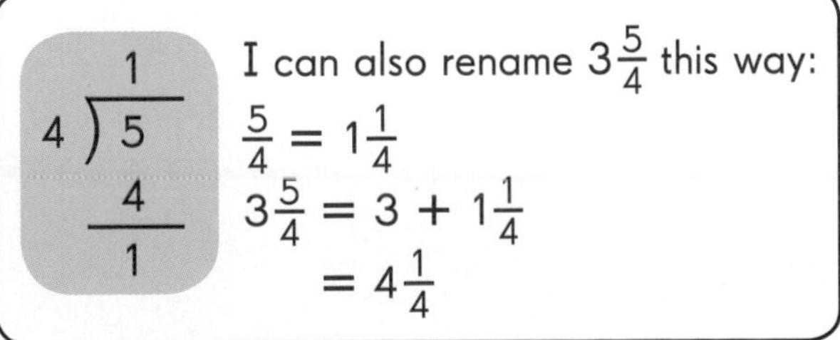

1
4) 5
4
1
I can also rename $3\frac{5}{4}$ this way:
$\frac{5}{4} = 1\frac{1}{4}$
$3\frac{5}{4} = 3 + 1\frac{1}{4}$
$= 4\frac{1}{4}$

Serena jogged and walked $4\frac{1}{4}$ miles altogether.

Guided Learning

Find the sum of the mixed numbers.

2 $2\frac{2}{3} + 3\frac{1}{2}$

$= 2\frac{\square}{\square} + 3\frac{\square}{\square}$

$= 5\frac{\square}{\square}$

$= \square\frac{\square}{\square}$

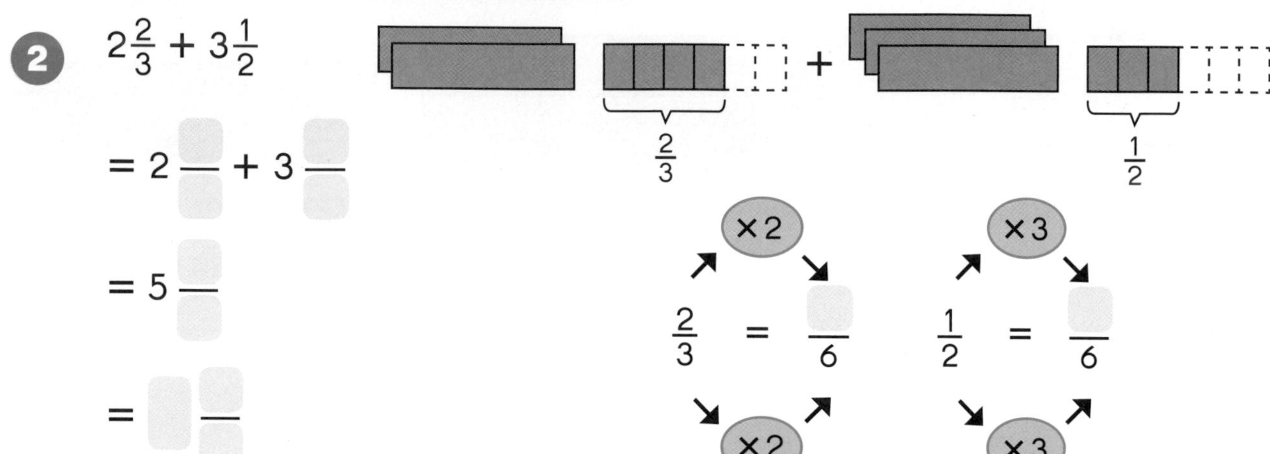

Learn: Use benchmarks to estimate sums of mixed numbers.

Estimate the sum of $2\frac{1}{3}$ and $3\frac{2}{5}$.

Compare the fractional part in each mixed number to the benchmarks,

0, $\frac{1}{2}$ and 1.

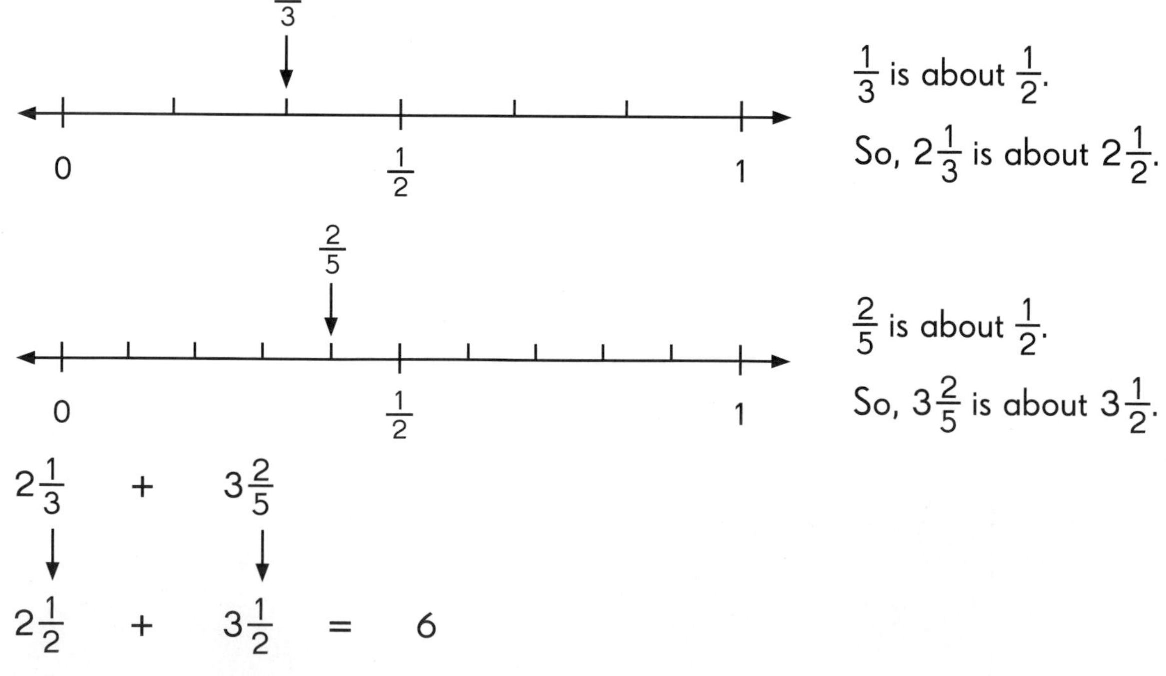

$\frac{1}{3}$ is about $\frac{1}{2}$.

So, $2\frac{1}{3}$ is about $2\frac{1}{2}$.

$\frac{2}{5}$ is about $\frac{1}{2}$.

So, $3\frac{2}{5}$ is about $3\frac{1}{2}$.

$2\frac{1}{3} + 3\frac{2}{5}$

$2\frac{1}{2} + 3\frac{1}{2} = 6$

The sum of $2\frac{1}{3}$ and $3\frac{2}{5}$ is about 6.

Guided Learning

Use benchmarks to estimate each sum.

3. $6\frac{7}{12} + 9\frac{3}{8}$

4. $11\frac{5}{6} + 5\frac{5}{9}$

5. $8\frac{3}{7} + 10\frac{1}{9}$

6. $32\frac{1}{5} + 14\frac{9}{10}$

7. $16\frac{9}{11} + 37\frac{2}{5}$

Let's Explore!

1. Without solving, do you think the sum of $1\frac{1}{4}$ and $3\frac{4}{9}$ is less than 5? Explain your reasoning.

2. Do you think the sum of $3\frac{5}{9}$ and $2\frac{7}{12}$ is greater than 6? Explain your reasoning.

3. Can you tell whether the sum of $3\frac{3}{8}$ and $5\frac{3}{5}$ is greater than or less than 9 by estimating? Explain your reasoning.

Let's Practice

Add. Express each sum in simplest form.

1. $1\frac{1}{4} + 2\frac{2}{5}$

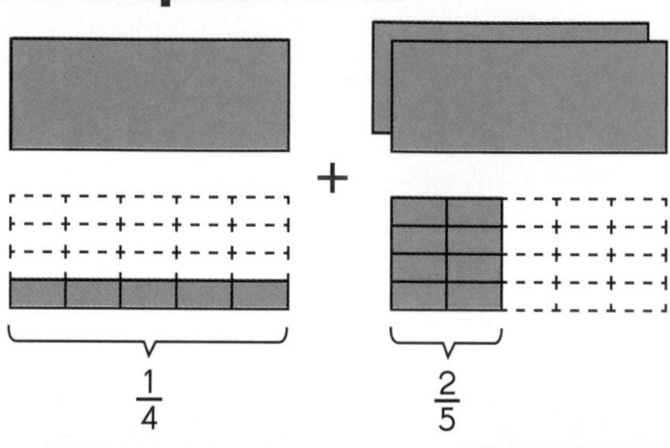

2. $3\frac{3}{8} + 4\frac{1}{3}$

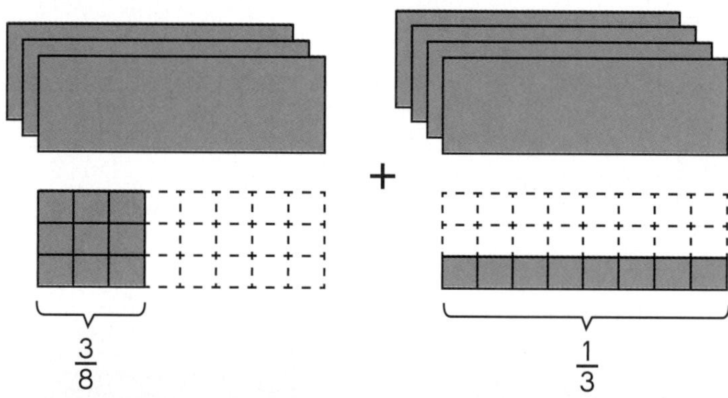

3. $5\frac{5}{6} + 3\frac{5}{12}$

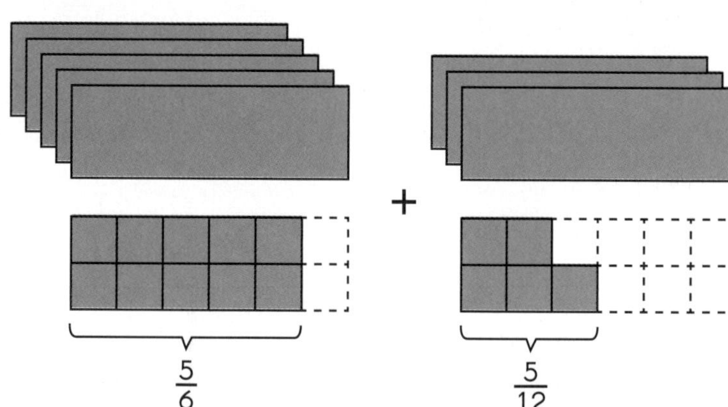

4. $1\frac{3}{5} + 2\frac{3}{8}$

5. $3\frac{3}{4} + 5\frac{2}{7}$

6. $5\frac{1}{6} + 2\frac{8}{9}$

Use benchmarks to estimate each sum.

7. $1\frac{3}{5} + 3\frac{4}{7}$

8. $5\frac{1}{8} + 7\frac{1}{12}$

9. $43\frac{5}{6} + 69\frac{5}{12}$

ON YOUR OWN

Go to Workbook A:
Practice 5, pages 117–120

Lesson 3.6 Subtracting Mixed Numbers

Lesson Objectives

- Subtract mixed numbers with or without renaming.
- Estimate differences between mixed numbers.

Learn Subtract mixed numbers without renaming.

Kim buys $2\frac{3}{4}$ yards of fabric. She cuts $1\frac{1}{8}$ yards to make a dress.
How much fabric does she have left?

$2\frac{3}{4} - 1\frac{1}{8} = ?$

To subtract, rewrite the fractional parts as like fractions first. Then subtract the fractional parts before subtracting the whole numbers.

$2\frac{3}{4} - 1\frac{1}{8} = 2\frac{6}{8} - 1\frac{1}{8}$

$= 1\frac{5}{8}$

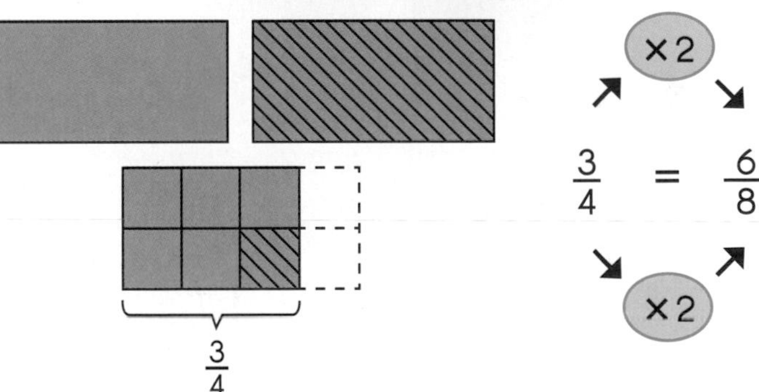

Kim has $1\frac{5}{8}$ yards of fabric left.

Guided Learning

Subtract.

1 $5\frac{5}{9} - 2\frac{1}{3} = 5\frac{?}{9} - 2\frac{?}{?}$

$= ?\frac{?}{?}$

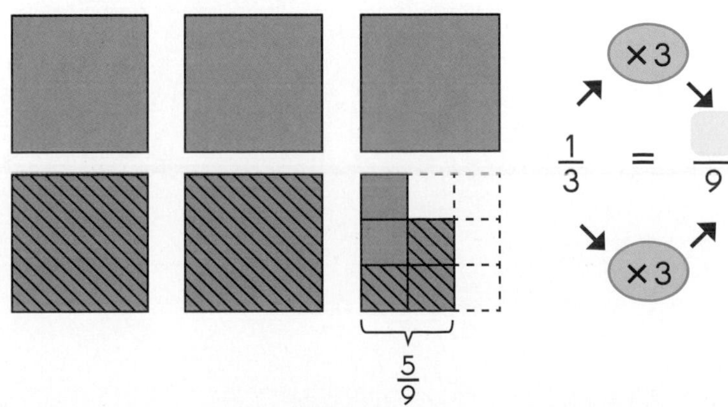

2 $3\frac{4}{5} - 2\frac{1}{2} = \square\frac{\square}{\square} - \square\frac{\square}{\square}$

$= \square\frac{\square}{\square}$

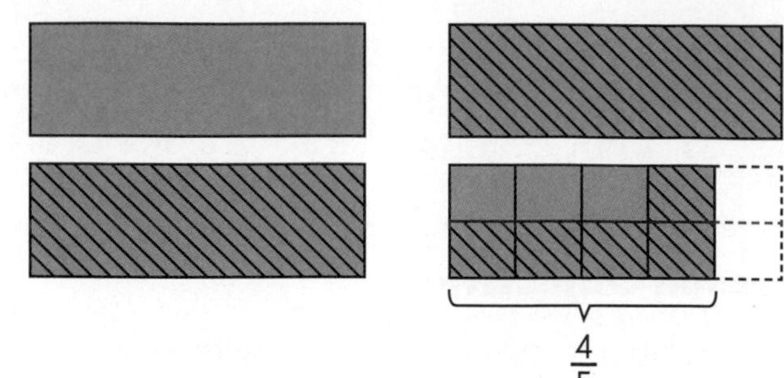

Learn Subtract mixed numbers with renaming.

A bottle contains $3\frac{1}{3}$ quarts of juice. Margaret uses $1\frac{3}{8}$ quarts of juice to make a fruit punch. How much juice is left in the bottle?

$3\frac{1}{3} - 1\frac{3}{8} = ?$

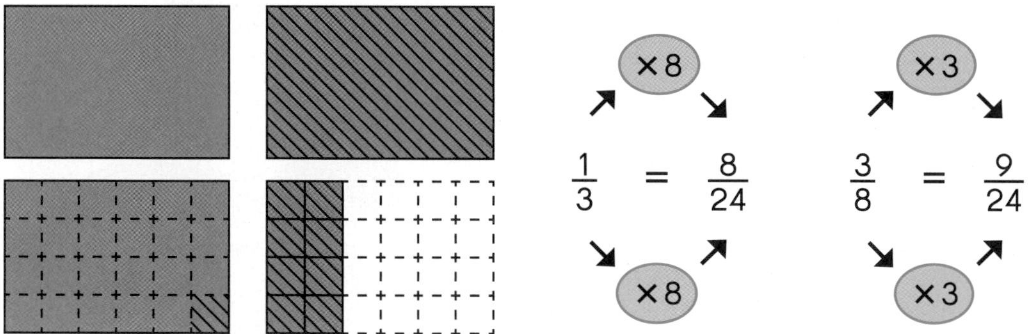

$3\frac{1}{3} - 1\frac{3}{8} = 3\frac{8}{24} - 1\frac{9}{24}$

$= 2\frac{32}{24} - 1\frac{9}{24}$

$= 1\frac{23}{24}$

$1\frac{23}{24}$ quarts of juice is left in the bottle.

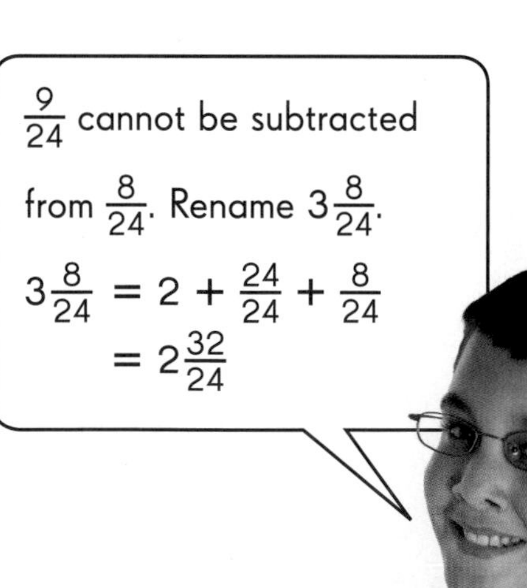

$\frac{9}{24}$ cannot be subtracted from $\frac{8}{24}$. Rename $3\frac{8}{24}$.
$3\frac{8}{24} = 2 + \frac{24}{24} + \frac{8}{24}$
$= 2\frac{32}{24}$

Guided Learning

Find the difference between the mixed numbers.

3 $4\frac{5}{9} - 3\frac{5}{6}$

$= 4\frac{\square}{\square} - 3\frac{\square}{\square}$

$= \square\frac{\square}{\square} - \square\frac{\square}{\square}$

$= \frac{\square}{\square}$

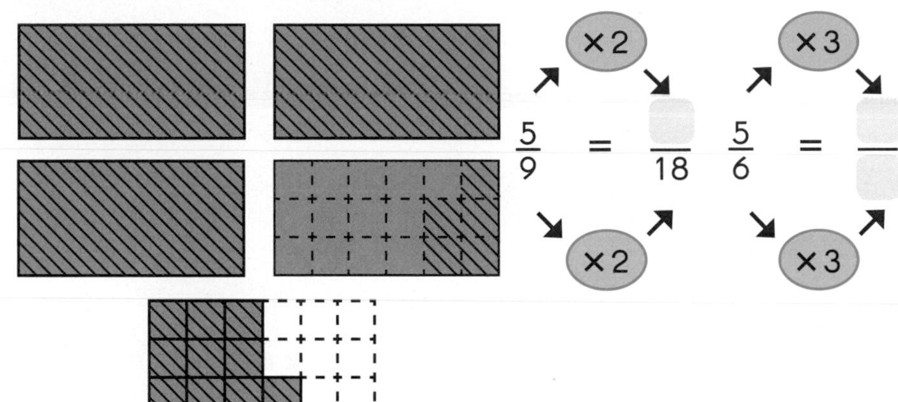

Learn: Use benchmarks to estimate differences between mixed numbers.

Estimate the difference between $4\frac{7}{8}$ and $3\frac{5}{12}$.

Compare the fractional part in each mixed number to the benchmarks,

0, $\frac{1}{2}$ and 1.

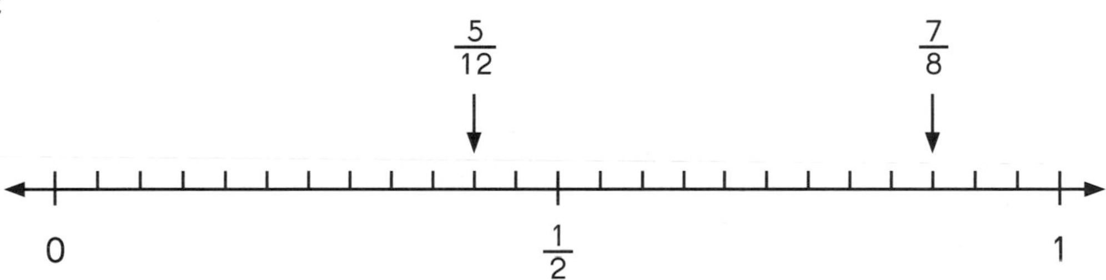

$\frac{7}{8}$ is about 1. So, $4\frac{7}{8}$ is about 5.

$\frac{5}{12}$ is about $\frac{1}{2}$. So, $3\frac{5}{12}$ is about $3\frac{1}{2}$.

$$4\frac{7}{8} \quad - \quad 3\frac{5}{12}$$
$$\downarrow \qquad\qquad \downarrow$$
$$5 \quad - \quad 3\frac{1}{2} \quad = \quad 1\frac{1}{2}$$

The difference between $4\frac{7}{8}$ and $3\frac{5}{12}$ is about $1\frac{1}{2}$.

Guided Learning

Use benchmarks to estimate each difference.

4. $7\frac{7}{9} - 3\frac{4}{7}$ ___

5. $23\frac{2}{5} - 17\frac{1}{6}$ ___

Let's Practice

Subtract. Express each difference in simplest form.

1. $3\frac{3}{4} - 1\frac{1}{2}$ ___

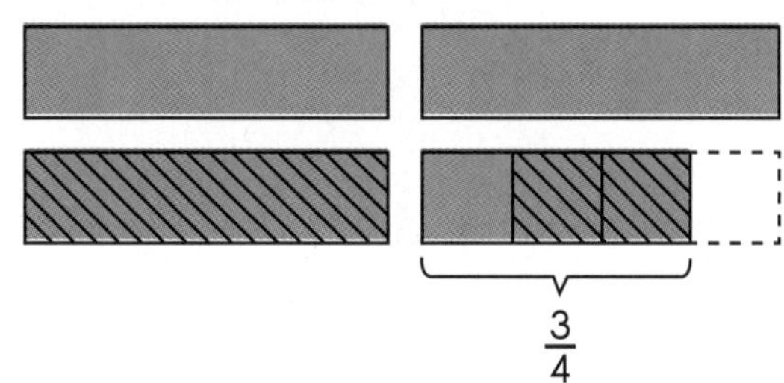

2. $5\frac{5}{6} - 2\frac{2}{3}$ ___

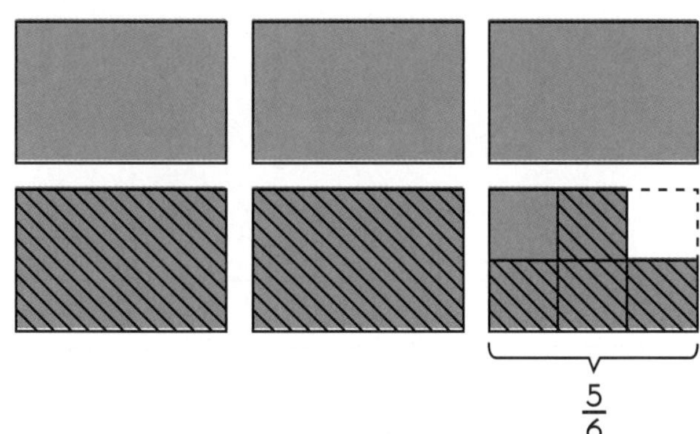

3. $4\frac{3}{8} - 1\frac{3}{4}$ ___

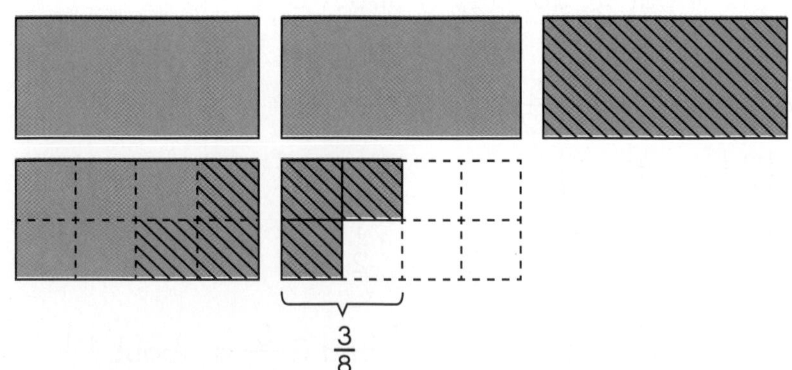

4 $3\frac{1}{4} - 1\frac{1}{3}$

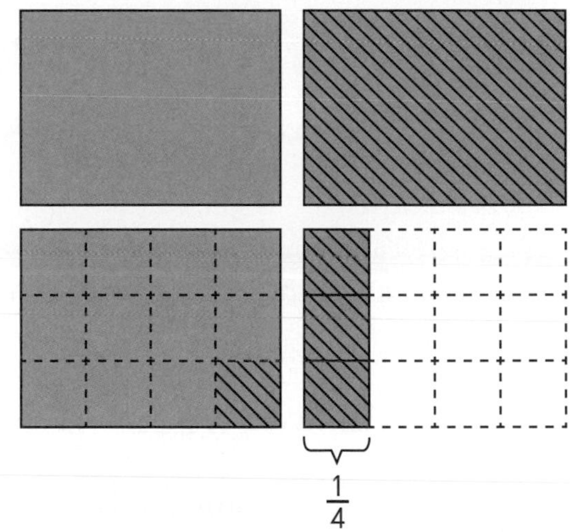

5 $4\frac{1}{6} - 3\frac{5}{8}$

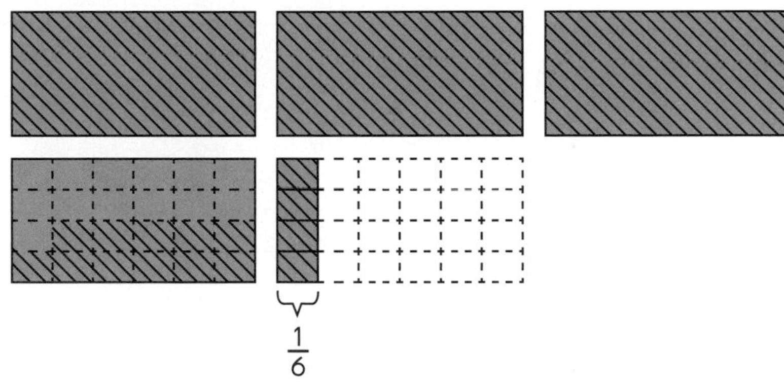

6 $7\frac{2}{3} - 4\frac{1}{2}$

7 $9\frac{4}{7} - 2\frac{1}{3}$

8 $6\frac{1}{10} - 3\frac{1}{5}$

9 $4\frac{1}{2} - 1\frac{7}{8}$

10 $5\frac{1}{4} - 2\frac{1}{3}$

11 $12\frac{7}{12} - 5\frac{8}{9}$

Use benchmarks to estimate each difference.

12 $6\frac{7}{10} - 4\frac{3}{5}$

13 $39\frac{4}{5} - 13\frac{5}{9}$

ON YOUR OWN

Go to Workbook A:
Practice 6, pages 121–124

Lesson 3.7 Real-World Problems: Fractions and Mixed Numbers

Lesson Objective

- Solve real-world problems involving fractions and mixed numbers.

Learn Write division expressions as fractions and mixed numbers.

Sheena bakes 5 pans of lasagna. She divides each of the 5 pans into 3 equal shares. How many pans are in each share?

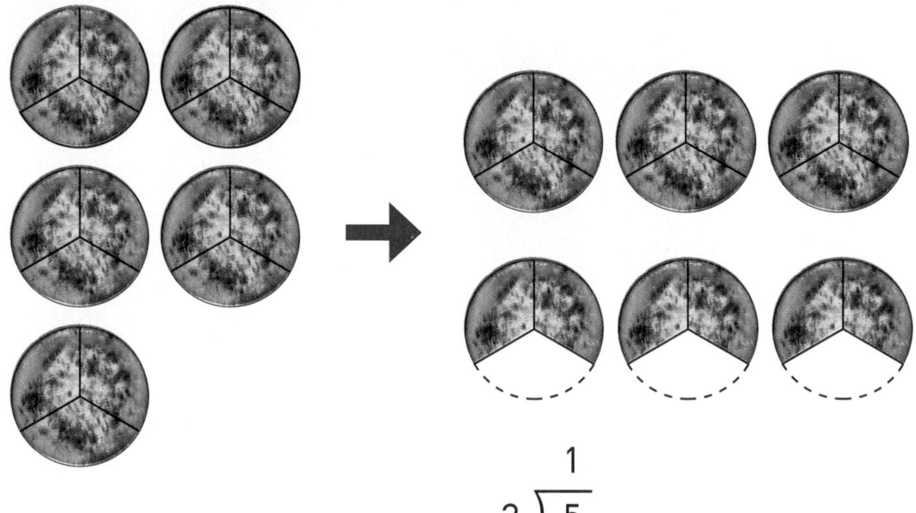

$$5 \div 3 = \frac{5}{3} = 1\frac{2}{3}$$

$$\begin{array}{r} 1 \\ 3\overline{)5} \\ \underline{3} \\ 2 \end{array}$$

There are $1\frac{2}{3}$ pans in each share.

Guided Learning

Solve.

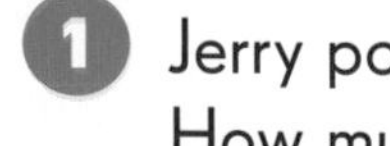

1. Jerry pours 12 quarts of spring water equally among 5 bottles. How much water is in each bottle?

$\square \div \square = \frac{\square}{\square} = \square\frac{\square}{\square}$

There are $\square\frac{\square}{\square}$ quarts of water in each bottle.

Learn Draw a model to solve a one-step problem.

Adam expected his homework to take $\frac{4}{5}$ hour. He completed it in $\frac{3}{4}$ hour. How much faster did Adam complete his homework than he expected?

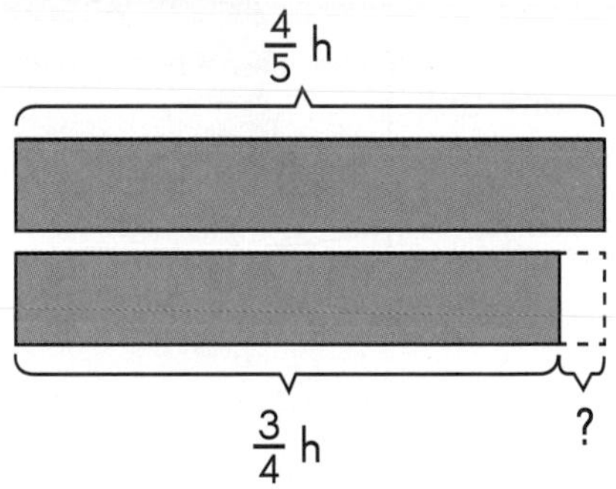

$$\frac{4}{5} - \frac{3}{4} = \frac{16}{20} - \frac{15}{20}$$
$$= \frac{1}{20}$$

Adam completed his homework $\frac{1}{20}$ hour faster.

Guided Learning

Solve.

2. Lisa has $1\frac{2}{9}$ pounds of peaches. She buys another $2\frac{1}{6}$ pounds of peaches. How many pounds of peaches does Lisa have now?

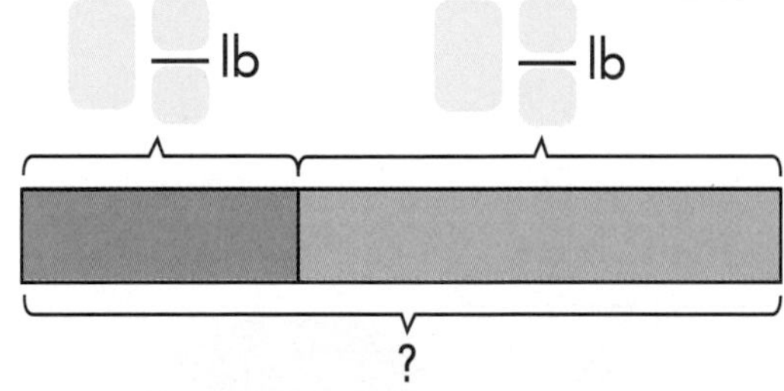

$\square\frac{\square}{\square} + \square\frac{\square}{\square} = \square\frac{\square}{\square} + \square\frac{\square}{\square}$

$= \square\frac{\square}{\square}$

Lisa has $\square\frac{\square}{\square}$ pounds of peaches now.

Learn Draw a model to solve a two-step problem.

Megan spent $\frac{1}{6}$ of her money on food and $\frac{5}{8}$ of her money on a new outfit. What fraction of Megan's money is left?

$\frac{1}{6} = \frac{4}{24}$ $\quad$ $\frac{5}{8} = \frac{15}{24}$

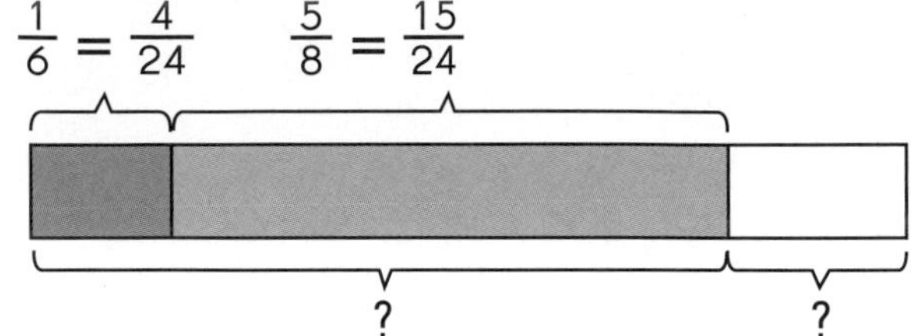

First, find the amount of money Megan spent on food and the new outfit.

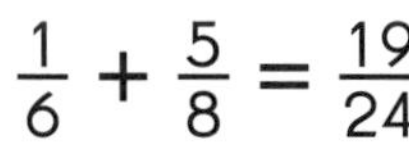

$\frac{1}{6} + \frac{5}{8} = \frac{19}{24}$

Megan spent $\frac{19}{24}$ of her money on food and the new outfit.

$1 - \frac{19}{24} = \frac{5}{24}$

$\frac{5}{24}$ of Megan's money is left.

Guided Learning

Solve.

3 Claire took $2\frac{3}{4}$ hours to read a book. Her brother, Dan, took $\frac{2}{3}$ hour less to read his book. How much time did they spend altogether reading their books?

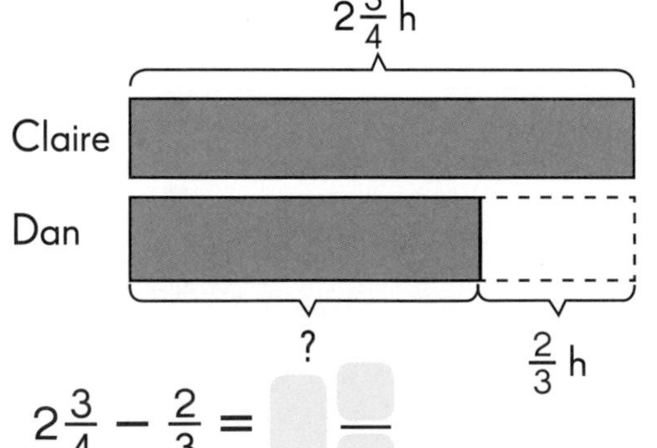

First, find the time Dan took to read the book.

$2\frac{3}{4} - \frac{2}{3} = \square\frac{\square}{\square}$

Dan read his book in $\square\frac{\square}{\square}$ hours.

$2\frac{3}{4} + \square\frac{\square}{\square} = \square\frac{\square}{\square}$

Claire and Dan spent $\square\frac{\square}{\square}$ hours altogether reading their books.

Let's Practice

Solve. Show your work.

1. The produce manager receives 5 containers of green beans, each weighing 7 pounds. She divides the total amount of green beans into 3 equal-weight portions. What is the weight of the beans in each portion?

2. Nisha spent $\frac{1}{4}$ of her money on Monday and $\frac{7}{10}$ of it on Tuesday. What fraction of her money did Nisha spend during the two days?

3. Lee drank $1\frac{2}{3}$ quarts of water today. He drank $\frac{2}{5}$ quart less water than Steve. How many quarts of water did Steve drink today?

4. Kathy uses $2\frac{5}{9}$ pounds of flour to make baked goods. She uses $\frac{5}{6}$ pounds more flour than Diana. How many pounds of flour does Diana use?

5. The Lido family has $2\frac{1}{2}$ pints of apple juice. They drink $\frac{7}{8}$ pint of the juice on Monday and $\frac{5}{12}$ pint on Tuesday. How many pints of apple juice are left?

6. A grocer sells $5\frac{2}{3}$ pounds of blueberries in the morning. In the afternoon, the grocer sells $\frac{11}{12}$ pound less blueberries. How many pounds of blueberries are sold in the morning and afternoon altogether?

ON YOUR OWN

Go to Workbook A:
Practice 7 and 8, pages 125–136

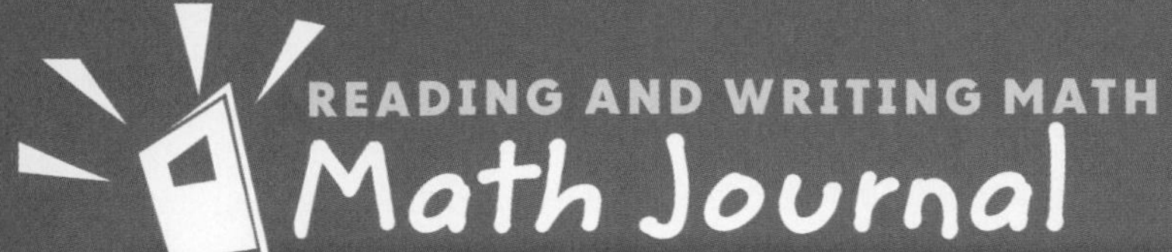

Leah, Marta and Noah each added these fractions.

$$\frac{5}{6} + \frac{7}{9} = ?$$

Leah's answer: $\frac{12}{15}$ Marta's answer: $2\frac{9}{18}$ Noah's answer: $1\frac{11}{18}$

Two of the three answers are incorrect.

a Whose answers are incorrect?

b Explain why.

> To add $\frac{5}{6}$ and $\frac{7}{9}$, I will have to rewrite them as like fractions.
>
> 6, 12, 18, 24, 30, ...
> 9, 18, 27, 36, 45, ...
>
> The least common multiple of 6 and 9 is $\square$.
>
> The least common denominator of $\frac{5}{6}$ and $\frac{7}{9}$ is $\square$.
>
> $\frac{5}{6} + \frac{7}{9} = \frac{\square}{\square} + \frac{\square}{\square}$
>
> $= \frac{\square}{\square}$
>
> $= \square\frac{\square}{\square}$
>
> The correct answer should be $\square\frac{\square}{\square}$.
>
> I can check Leah's, Marta's and Noah's answers against $\square\frac{\square}{\square}$ to spot the incorrect answers.

CRITICAL THINKING SKILLS

Put On Your Thinking Cap!

PROBLEM SOLVING

Jackie has two equal-sized bottles. The first bottle contains 1 quart of water. The second bottle has $\frac{5}{9}$ quart of water. What amount of water must Jackie pour from the first bottle into the second bottle so that both bottles contain the same amount of water? Express your answer as a fraction. Explain your answer using bar models.

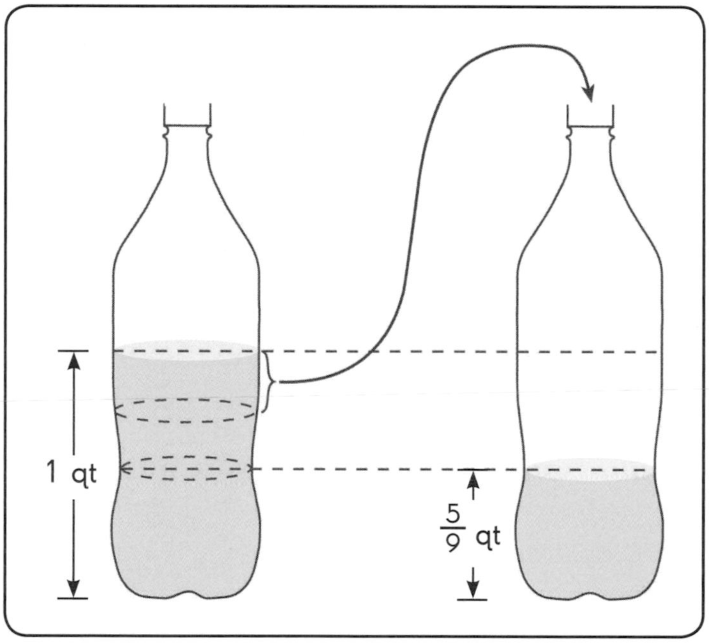

ON YOUR OWN

Go to Workbook A: Put on Your Thinking Cap! pages 137–138

Chapter Wrap Up

Study Guide

You have learned...

Fractions and Mixed Numbers

Adding and Subtracting Unlike Fractions

Find the least common multiple of their denominators. Use it to rewrite the fractions as like fractions. Then add or subtract.

$\frac{1}{4} + \frac{1}{6} = ?$

Multiples of 4: 4, 8, 12, ...
Multiples of 6: 6, 12, ...
12 is the least common multiple of 4 and 6.

$\frac{1}{4} + \frac{1}{6} = \frac{3}{12} + \frac{2}{12}$
$= \frac{5}{12}$

Adding and Subtracting Mixed Numbers

First rewrite the fractional parts as like fractions. Then add or subtract the fractional parts before adding or subtracting the whole numbers.

Without Renaming	With Renaming
$3\frac{1}{2} - 1\frac{1}{3}$	$3\frac{1}{2} - 1\frac{2}{3}$
$= 3\frac{3}{6} - 1\frac{2}{6}$	$= 3\frac{3}{6} - 1\frac{4}{6}$
$= 2\frac{1}{6}$	$= 2\frac{9}{6} - 1\frac{4}{6}$
	$= 1\frac{5}{6}$

Use Benchmarks to Estimate Sums and Differences

$\frac{4}{9} - \frac{7}{12}$	$2\frac{7}{8} + 2\frac{3}{5}$
↓ ↓	↓ ↓
$\frac{1}{2} - \frac{1}{2} = 0$	$3 + 2\frac{1}{2} = 5\frac{1}{2}$

▶ Add and subtract unlike fractions and mixed numbers by rewriting them with like denominators.

Fractions, Mixed Numbers and Division Expressions

Express division expressions as fractions or mixed numbers.

$$10 \div 6 = \frac{10 \div 2}{6 \div 2}$$
$$= \frac{5}{3}$$
$$= 1\frac{2}{3}$$

Express fractions as division expressions.

$$\frac{4}{5} = 4 \div 5$$

Expressing Fractions, Division Expressions and Mixed Numbers as Decimals

Express a fraction as a decimal by finding an equivalent fraction with a denominator of 10 or 100.

$$\frac{20}{25} = \frac{20 \times 4}{25 \times 4}$$
$$= \frac{80}{100}$$
$$= 0.8$$

Express division expressions and mixed numbers as decimals.

$$5 \div 4 = \frac{5}{4}$$
$$= 1 + \frac{1}{4}$$
$$= 1 + 0.25$$
$$= 1.25$$

Solve Real-World Problems

Chapter Review/Test

Vocabulary

Choose the correct word.

multiple
least common denominator
benchmark
mixed number
least common multiple
equivalent fractions
division expression

1. The first multiple that is the same for two numbers is called the ____.

2. $\frac{3}{4}$ and $\frac{6}{8}$ are ____. $2\frac{2}{3}$ is a ____.

3. In estimating with fractions, you approximate each fraction to the closest ____.

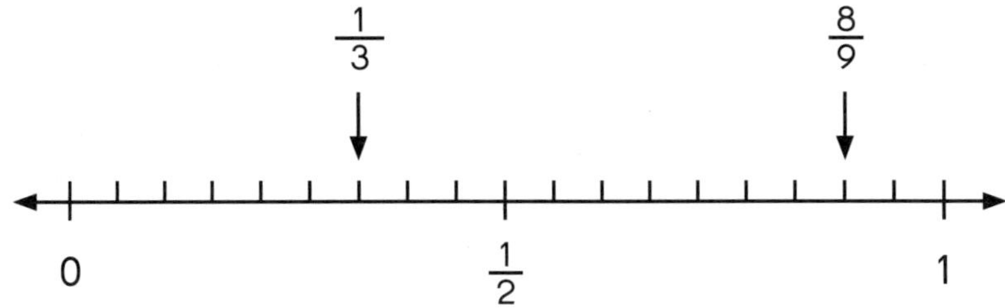

$\frac{1}{3}$ is about $\frac{1}{2}$. $\frac{8}{9}$ is about 1.

$\frac{1}{3} + \frac{8}{9} \longrightarrow \frac{1}{2} + 1$

$= 1\frac{1}{2}$

The sum of $\frac{1}{3}$ and $\frac{8}{9}$ is about $1\frac{1}{2}$.

4. $7 \div 6$ is a ____.

5. 14 is the ____ of $\frac{1}{7}$ and $\frac{1}{2}$.

6. 10 is a ____ of 2.

Concepts and Skills

Add or subtract. Express each sum or difference in simplest form.

7. $\frac{1}{2} + \frac{3}{7}$

8. $\frac{1}{6} + \frac{3}{10}$

9. $\frac{7}{8} - \frac{1}{2}$

10. $\frac{7}{9} - \frac{1}{4}$

Use benchmarks to estimate each sum or difference.

11. $\frac{4}{9} - \frac{3}{7}$

12. $\frac{7}{9} + \frac{4}{7} + \frac{1}{6}$

Express each division expression as a fraction or mixed number in simplest form.

13. $6 \div 8$

14. $10 \div 3$

Express each fraction as a decimal.

15. $\frac{1}{4}$

16. $\frac{18}{25}$

Express as a mixed number and as a decimal.

17. $21 \div 5$

18. $\frac{42}{8}$

Add or subtract. Express each sum or difference in simplest form.

19. $1\frac{2}{9} + 1\frac{1}{6}$

20. $3\frac{4}{5} + 2\frac{1}{2}$

21. $6\frac{3}{4} - 1\frac{1}{2}$

22. $5\frac{2}{9} - 3\frac{1}{3}$

Use benchmarks to estimate each sum or difference.

23. $4\frac{3}{5} + 2\frac{3}{8}$

24. $8\frac{11}{12} - 2\frac{11}{20}$

Problem Solving

Solve. Show your work.

25. Audrey bought 7 pounds of diced apples and shared them equally among 4 friends.

   a. How many pounds of apples did each person receive?

   b. Two of the friends put the portions they received together and then gave them to the food pantry. How many pounds of apples did they give to the food pantry?

   c. Audrey used $1\frac{2}{3}$ pounds of the apples the two friends gave to the food pantry to make apple sauce and the remaining to make apple pies. How many pounds of apples did Audrey use to make apple pies?

Multiplying and Dividing Fractions and Mixed Numbers

Lessons

4.1 Multiplying Proper Fractions

4.2 Real-World Problems: Multiplying with Proper Fractions

4.3 Multiplying Improper Fractions by Fractions

4.4 Multiplying Mixed Numbers and Whole Numbers

4.5 Real-World Problems: Multiplying with Mixed Numbers

4.6 Dividing Fractions and Whole Numbers

4.7 Real-World Problems: Multiplying and Dividing with Fractions

▶ Whole numbers, fractions, and mixed numbers can be multiplied or divided in any combination.

Recall Prior Knowledge

Finding equivalent fractions

$\frac{3}{4}$ is the same as $\frac{6}{8}$.

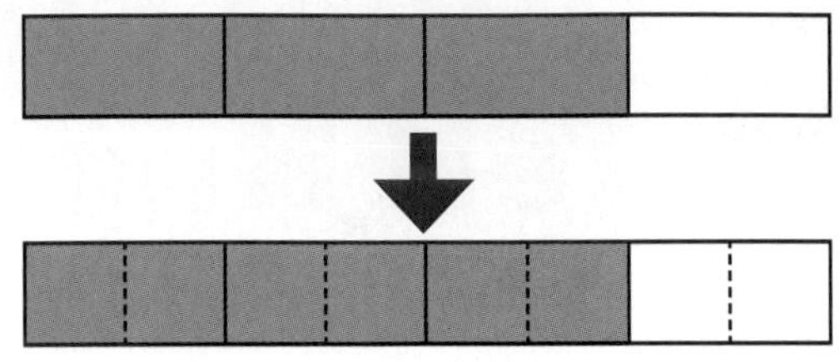

$$\frac{3}{4} = \frac{3 \times 2}{4 \times 2}$$
$$= \frac{6}{8}$$

Simplifying fractions

$$\frac{6}{8} = \frac{6 \div 2}{8 \div 2}$$ ← Divide the numerator and denominator by their greatest common factor.
$$= \frac{3}{4}$$

Adding and subtracting fractions

$$\frac{1}{4} + \frac{2}{4} = \frac{3}{4}$$

$$\frac{2}{5} + \frac{3}{10} = \frac{4}{10} + \frac{3}{10}$$
$$= \frac{7}{10}$$

$$\frac{4}{5} - \frac{3}{5} = \frac{1}{5}$$

$$\frac{7}{9} - \frac{2}{3} = \frac{7}{9} - \frac{6}{9}$$
$$= \frac{1}{9}$$

$$1 - \frac{3}{8} = \frac{8}{8} - \frac{3}{8}$$
$$= \frac{5}{8}$$

Expressing improper fractions as mixed numbers and mixed numbers as improper fractions

$$\frac{10}{3} = \frac{9}{3} + \frac{1}{3}$$
$$= 3 + \frac{1}{3}$$
$$= 3\frac{1}{3}$$

$$3\frac{1}{2} = 3 + \frac{1}{2}$$
$$= \frac{6}{2} + \frac{1}{2}$$
$$= \frac{7}{2}$$

Expressing fractions as decimals

$\frac{1}{4} = \frac{1 \times 25}{4 \times 25}$

$= \frac{25}{100}$

$= 0.25$

Multiplying fractions by whole numbers

$\frac{2}{5} \times 7 = \frac{2 \times 7}{5}$

$= \frac{14}{5}$

$= 2\frac{4}{5}$

Finding the number of units to solve a problem

7 tickets cost \$49. How much do 6 tickets cost?

7 units → \$49
1 unit → \$49 ÷ 7 = \$7
6 units → 6 × \$7 = \$42

6 tickets cost \$42.

Drawing a model to show what is stated

Three friends share a foot-long turkey sandwich. Jeff eats $\frac{1}{2}$ of the sandwich. Anne eats $\frac{1}{3}$ of the sandwich. Andy eats the rest.

Least common multiple: 2 × 3 = 6

$\frac{1}{2} = \frac{3}{6}$ $\frac{1}{3} = \frac{2}{6}$ $1 - \frac{3}{6} - \frac{2}{6} = \frac{1}{6}$

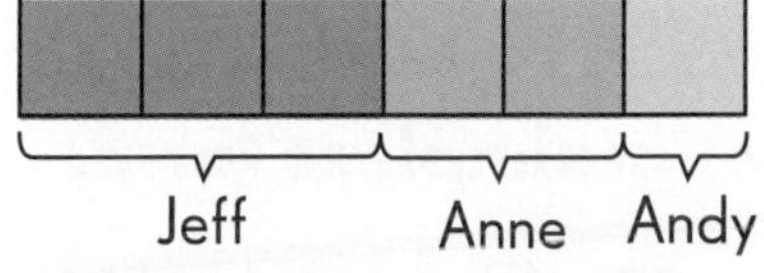

Using order of operations to simplify expressions

Simplify $(32 + 40) - 8 \times 6$.

First expression	$(32 + 40) - 8 \times 6$	Perform all operations in the parentheses first.
Second expression	$72 - 8 \times 6$	Then multiply.
Third expression	$72 - 48$	Finally subtract.
	24	

✔ Quick Check

Find an equivalent fraction.

1. $\frac{2}{3}$
2. $\frac{3}{4}$
3. $\frac{5}{6}$

Simplify.

4. $\frac{5}{10}$
5. $\frac{15}{25}$
6. $\frac{18}{32}$

Subtract.

7. $\frac{2}{3} - \frac{8}{15}$
8. $3 - \frac{5}{7}$
9. $4 - \frac{8}{11}$

Express each improper fraction as a mixed number in simplest form.

10. $\frac{17}{4}$
11. $\frac{22}{6}$
12. $\frac{40}{9}$

Express each mixed number as an improper fraction.

13 $3\frac{3}{7}$ ___ 14 $6\frac{5}{9}$ ___ 15 $8\frac{2}{5}$ ___

Express each fraction as a decimal.

16 $\frac{3}{4}$ ___ 17 $\frac{13}{20}$ ___ 18 $\frac{21}{25}$ ___

Find the product.

19 $\frac{1}{4} \times 12$ ___ 20 $\frac{3}{8} \times 10$ ___ 21 $\frac{5}{9} \times 24$ ___

Solve.

22 A store sells 5 DVDs for $15. How much do 3 DVDs cost?

5 DVDs ⟶ $15

1 DVD ⟶ $15 ÷ ___ = $___

3 DVDs ⟶ ___ × $___ = $___

3 DVDs cost $___.

Draw a model to show what is stated.

23 Miguel has some trading cards. $\frac{1}{2}$ of the cards are baseball cards, $\frac{2}{5}$ are soccer cards, and the rest are basketball cards. ___

Simplify.

24 (60 + 6 × 80) ÷ 20 ___

25 27 ÷ (1 + 2) × 5 − 9 ___

Lesson 4.1 Multiplying Proper Fractions

Lesson Objective

- Multiply proper fractions.

Vocabulary
product
common factor

Learn Use models to multiply fractions.

Find $\frac{1}{2} \times \frac{2}{3}$.

Margie drew a rectangle and colored $\frac{2}{3}$ of it blue.

She then drew stripes over $\frac{1}{2}$ of the blue parts.

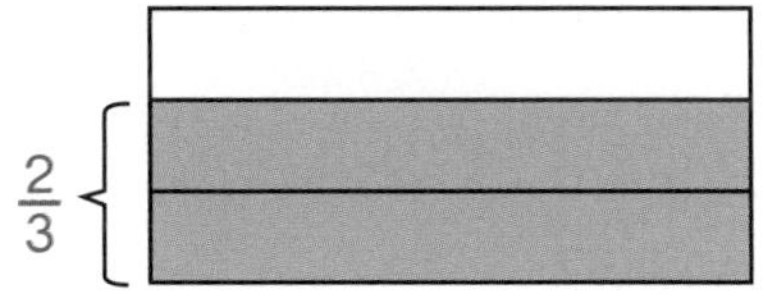

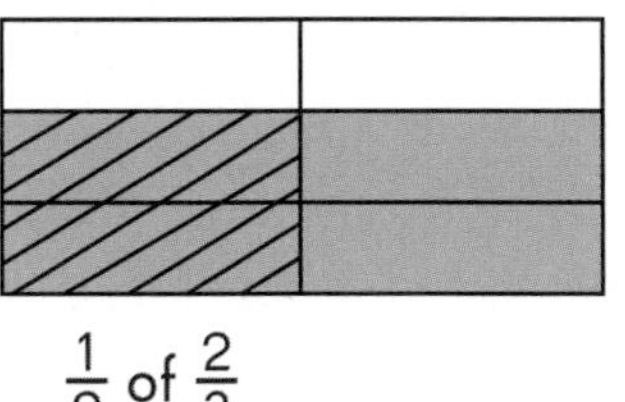

$$\frac{1}{2} \times \frac{2}{3} = \frac{1}{2} \text{ of } \frac{2}{3}$$

$= \frac{2}{6}$ ← Number of parts with stripes / Total number of parts

$= \frac{1}{3}$

Paul drew an identical rectangle and colored $\frac{1}{2}$ of it blue.

He then drew stripes over $\frac{2}{3}$ of the blue part.

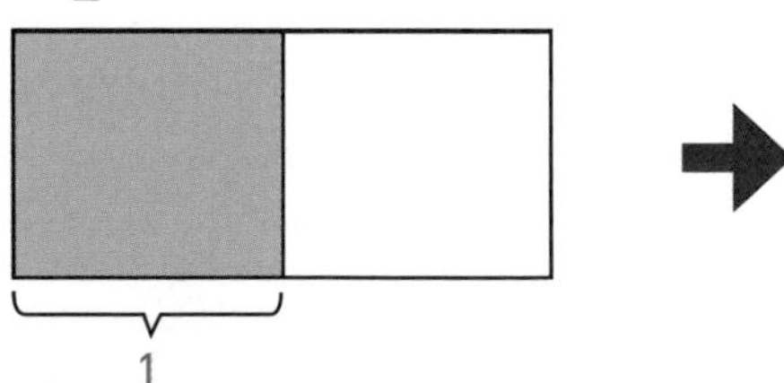

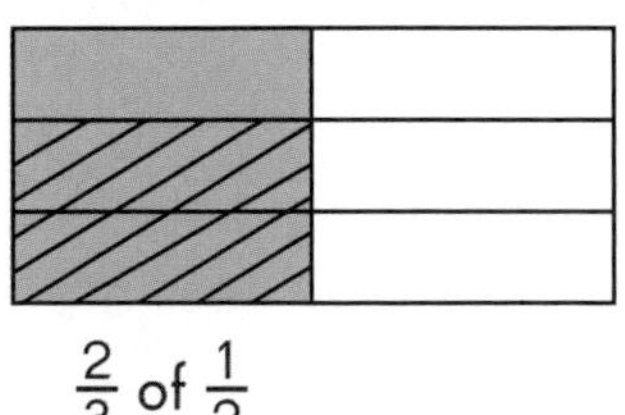

$$\frac{2}{3} \times \frac{1}{2} = \frac{2}{3} \text{ of } \frac{1}{2}$$

$= \frac{2}{6}$ ← Number of parts with stripes / Total number of parts

$= \frac{1}{3}$

Margie and Paul get the same **product**: $\frac{1}{3}$.

So, $\frac{1}{2} \times \frac{2}{3} = \frac{2}{3} \times \frac{1}{2}$.

Learn Multiply fractions without models.

Find $\frac{3}{4} \times \frac{8}{9}$.

Method 1

$\frac{3}{4} \times \frac{8}{9} = \frac{3 \times 8}{4 \times 9}$ ← Multiply the numerators. Multiply the denominators.

$= \frac{24}{36}$ ← Simplify the product.

$= \frac{2}{3}$

Method 2

$\frac{3}{4} \times \frac{8}{9} = \frac{3 \div 3}{4} \times \frac{8}{9 \div 3}$ ← Divide one numerator and one denominator by their **common factor**, 3.

$= \frac{1}{4 \div 4} \times \frac{8 \div 4}{3}$ ← Divide the other numerator and denominator by their common factor, 4.

$= \frac{1 \times 2}{1 \times 3}$ ← Multiply the numerators. Multiply the denominators.

$= \frac{2}{3}$

Division Rule
Other than zero, any number when divided by itself will give a quotient of 1.

So, $3 \div 3 = 1$

$4 \div 4 = 1$

Multiplication Property of 1
Any number multiplied by 1 will give a product that is equal to itself.

So, $1 \times 2 = 2$

$1 \times 3 = 3$

Guided Learning

Use models to find each product. Write each product in simplest form.

1. $\frac{1}{3} \times \frac{3}{4} = \frac{?}{?}$

2. $\frac{2}{5} \times \frac{5}{8} = \frac{?}{?}$

Find each product in simplest form.

3. $\frac{4}{10} \times \frac{5}{12} = \frac{?}{?}$

4. $\frac{3}{10} \times \frac{5}{9} = \frac{?}{?}$

Hands-On Activity

WORK IN PAIRS

Materials:
- grid paper
- 1 yellow crayon
- 1 blue crayon

Draw a 4×4 square on the grid paper.

Divide the square into four equal parts using horizontal lines. Color $\frac{3}{4}$ of it yellow.

Divide the square into four equal parts using vertical lines. Draw stripes on $\frac{1}{4}$ of the yellow parts with a blue crayon.

Refer to your model.

Complete: $\frac{1}{4} \times \frac{3}{4} = \frac{?}{?}$

Draw another 4×4 square.

Divide the square into four equal parts using horizontal lines. Color $\frac{1}{4}$ of it blue.

Divide the square into four equal parts using vertical lines. Draw stripes on $\frac{3}{4}$ of the blue parts with a yellow crayon.

Refer to your model.

Complete: $\frac{3}{4} \times \frac{1}{4} = \frac{?}{?}$

Do you get the same answer in both cases?

What can you say about $\frac{1}{4} \times \frac{3}{4}$ and $\frac{3}{4} \times \frac{1}{4}$?

Let's Explore!

1. Find the product of each pair of numbers.

$3 \times 4 = \square$ $5 \times 17 = \square$

$9 \times 8 = \square$ $12 \times 7 = \square$

Notice that each product is greater than each of its factors. Explain why.

2. Find the product of each pair of fractions.

$\frac{1}{2} \times \frac{3}{4} = \frac{\square}{\square}$ $\frac{3}{4} \times \frac{4}{5} = \frac{\square}{\square}$

$\frac{2}{7} \times \frac{3}{4} = \frac{\square}{\square}$ $\frac{1}{6} \times \frac{5}{9} = \frac{\square}{\square}$

Notice that each product is less than each of its factors. Explain why.

Let's Practice

Find each product in simplest form.

1. $\frac{1}{3} \times \frac{6}{7}$ $\square$
2. $\frac{6}{8} \times \frac{4}{9}$ $\square$
3. $\frac{10}{15} \times \frac{3}{4}$ $\square$
4. $\frac{7}{10}$ of $\frac{5}{10}$ $\square$
5. $\frac{3}{8}$ of $\frac{4}{6}$ $\square$
6. $\frac{7}{12}$ of $\frac{9}{14}$ $\square$

ON YOUR OWN

Go to Workbook A: Practice 1, pages 139–140

Lesson 4.2 Real-World Problems: Multiplying with Proper Fractions

Lesson Objective

- Solve real-world problems involving multiplication of proper fractions.

Learn Multiply fractions to solve real-world problems.

Maurice has $\frac{3}{4}$ quart of chicken stock. He uses $\frac{2}{3}$ of it to make some soup.

a How much chicken stock does he use to make the soup?

b How much chicken stock does he have left?

Method 1

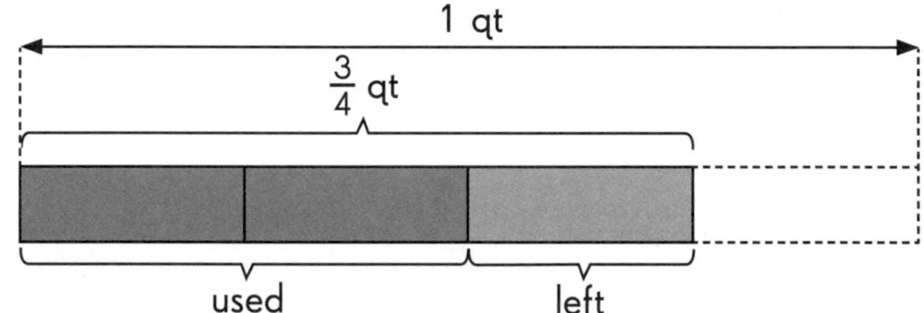

The model shows that:

4 units → 1 qt

1 unit → $\frac{1}{4}$ qt

2 units → $\frac{1}{2}$ qt

a Maurice uses $\frac{1}{2}$ quart of chicken stock to make the soup.

b He has $\frac{1}{4}$ quart of chicken stock left.

Method 2

a $\frac{2}{3} \times \frac{3}{4} = \frac{6}{12} = \frac{1}{2}$

Maurice uses $\frac{1}{2}$ quart of chicken stock to make the soup.

b $\frac{3}{4} - \frac{1}{2} = \frac{3}{4} - \frac{2}{4}$

$= \frac{1}{4}$

He has $\frac{1}{4}$ quart of chicken stock left.

Guided Learning

Solve.

1 Michelle has $\frac{4}{5}$ gallon of paint. She uses $\frac{3}{4}$ of it to paint a door.

a How much paint does she use?

b How much paint is left?

Method 1

? gal

? gal

The model shows that:

? units → ? gal

? unit → $\frac{?}{?}$ gal

? units → $\frac{?}{?}$ gal

a Michelle uses $\frac{?}{?}$ gallon of paint.

b There is $\frac{?}{?}$ gallon of paint left.

Method 2

a $\frac{3}{4} \times \frac{?}{?} = \frac{12}{20}$

$= \frac{?}{?}$

Michelle uses $\frac{?}{?}$ gallon of paint.

b $\frac{4}{5} - \frac{?}{?} = \frac{?}{?}$

There is $\frac{?}{?}$ gallon of paint left.

Learn: Give the answer as a fractional remainder.

Len received some money for a vacation job. He saved $\frac{1}{4}$ of the money, spent $\frac{4}{9}$ of the remainder on a DVD, and spent the rest on a T-shirt.

a What fraction of his money was spent on the DVD?

b What fraction of his money was spent on the T-shirt?

Method 1

$1 - \frac{1}{4} = \frac{3}{4}$

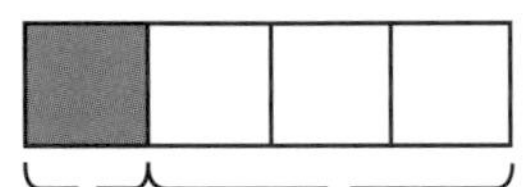

saved remainder

Remainder ⟶ 3 parts

To show $\frac{4}{9}$ of the remainder is spent on the DVD, I have to further divide the remainder into 9 parts.

Least common multiple of 3 and 9 = 9

By equivalent fractions:

$\frac{3}{4} = \frac{9}{12}$ (× 3, × 3)

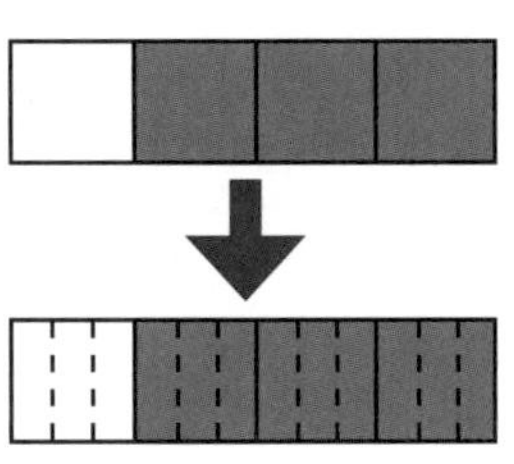

I need to draw a model with 12 equal units to show the problem.

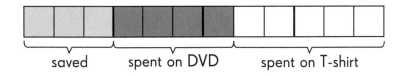

saved spent on DVD spent on T-shirt

$\frac{1}{4}$ of 12 units = 3 units

$\frac{4}{9}$ of 9 units = 4 units

The model shows that:

Number of units spent on DVD = 4

Number of units spent on T-shirt = 5

Total number of units in 1 whole = 12

a $\frac{4}{12} = \frac{1}{3}$

Len spent $\frac{1}{3}$ of his money on the DVD.

b Len spent $\frac{5}{12}$ of his money on the T-shirt.

Method 2

a $1 - \frac{1}{4} = \frac{3}{4}$

$\frac{3}{4}$ of Len's money is left after he saves $\frac{1}{4}$ of it.

$\frac{4}{9} \times \frac{3}{4} = \frac{12}{36} = \frac{1}{3}$

Len spent $\frac{1}{3}$ of his money on the DVD.

b $\frac{3}{4} - \frac{1}{3} = \frac{9}{12} - \frac{4}{12}$

$= \frac{5}{12}$

Len spent $\frac{5}{12}$ of his money on the T-shirt.

Guided Learning

Solve.

2 Janice picks some strawberries. She uses $\frac{3}{5}$ of the strawberries to make jam. She gives $\frac{3}{4}$ of the remainder to her neighbor.

a What fraction of the strawberries does she give to her neighbor?

b What fraction of the strawberries does she have left?

Method 1

$1 - \frac{3}{5} = \frac{2}{5}$

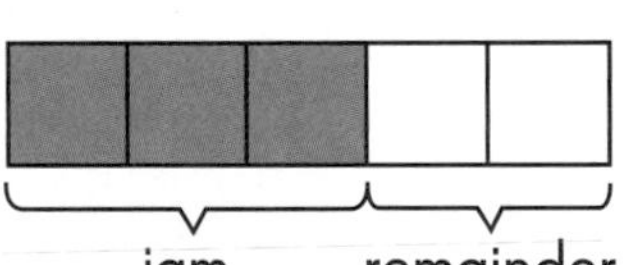

Remainder ⟶ 2 parts

To show $\frac{3}{4}$ of the remainder is given to Janice's neighbor, I have to further divide the remainder into 4 parts.

Least common multiple of 2 and 4 = 4

By equivalent fractions:

$\frac{2}{5} \xrightarrow{\times 2} = \frac{4}{10}$ (numerator × 2, denominator × 2)

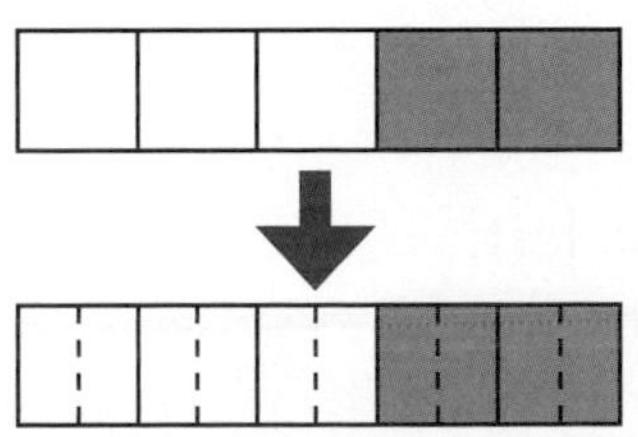

I need to draw a model with 10 equal units to show the problem.

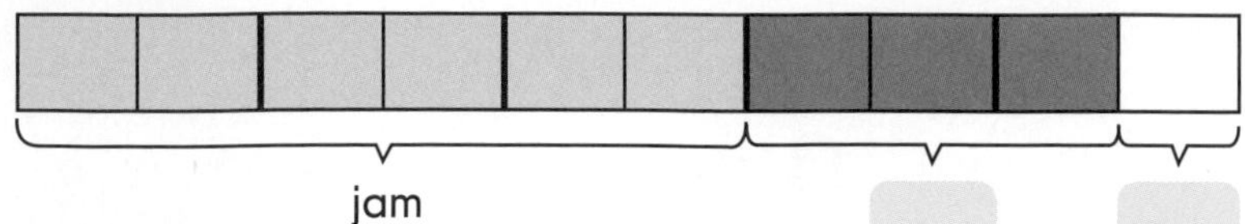

$\frac{3}{5}$ of 10 units = 6 units

$\frac{3}{4}$ of 4 units = 3 units

The model shows that:
Number of units given to the neighbor = ___
Total number of units in 1 whole = ___

(a) She gives $\frac{\square}{\square}$ of the strawberries to her neighbor.

(b) She has $\frac{\square}{\square}$ of the strawberries left.

Method 2

(a) $1 - \frac{\square}{\square} = \frac{\square}{\square}$

$\frac{\square}{\square}$ of Janice's strawberries is left after she makes jam with $\frac{3}{5}$ of them.

$\frac{3}{4} \times \frac{\square}{\square} = \frac{6}{20}$

$= \frac{\square}{\square}$

She gives $\frac{\square}{\square}$ of the strawberries to her neighbor.

(b) $\frac{\square}{\square} - \frac{\square}{\square} = \frac{\square}{\square} - \frac{\square}{\square}$

$= \frac{\square}{\square}$

She has $\frac{\square}{\square}$ of the strawberries left.

Let's Practice

Solve. Show your work.

1. Mrs. Smith has a plot of land. She plants flowers on $\frac{3}{4}$ of the land. $\frac{2}{3}$ of the flowers are sunflowers. What fraction of the land is planted with sunflowers? ______

2. Justin spends $\frac{7}{9}$ of his homework time on math and social studies. He spends $\frac{4}{7}$ of this time on math. What fraction of the total time does he spend on social studies? ______

3. Priya has a piece of string $\frac{5}{6}$ yard long. She cuts $\frac{3}{5}$ of the piece of string for a craft. What is the length of the string left? ______

4. Jeff spends $\frac{1}{2}$ of his paycheck. He then gives $\frac{1}{3}$ of the remainder to charity and puts the rest in the bank. What fraction of his paycheck does he put in the bank? ______

5. Mrs. Kong uses $\frac{1}{3}$ of a stick of butter in a sauce. She then uses $\frac{5}{8}$ of the remaining butter to make garlic bread. What fraction of the stick of butter is left? ______

6. Gia spends $\frac{2}{5}$ of her money on a shirt. She then spends $\frac{4}{9}$ of her remaining money on a pair of shoes. What fraction of her money is left? ______

7. Ben sells $\frac{7}{12}$ of the pottery he made. Of the remaining pottery, $\frac{3}{5}$ are vases and the rest are bowls. What fraction of all the pottery is the unsold bowls? ______

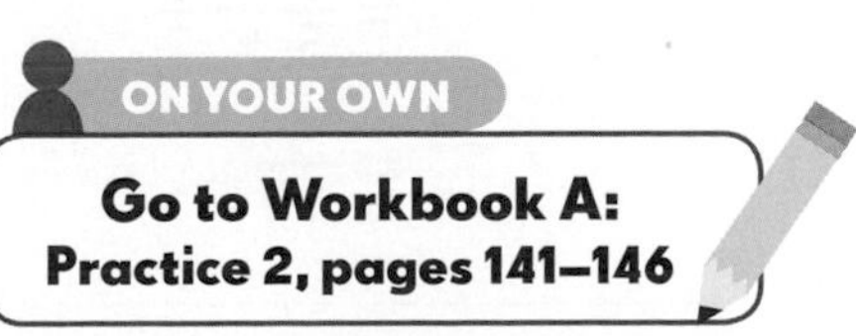

ON YOUR OWN
Go to Workbook A:
Practice 2, pages 141–146

Lesson 4.3

Multiplying Improper Fractions by Fractions

Lesson Objective

- Multiply improper fractions by proper fractions.

Vocabulary
proper fraction
improper fraction

Learn Multiply improper fractions by proper fractions.

Find the product of $\frac{6}{5}$ and $\frac{3}{4}$.

Method 1

$\frac{6}{5} \times \frac{3}{4}$

$= \frac{3}{4} \times \frac{6}{5}$

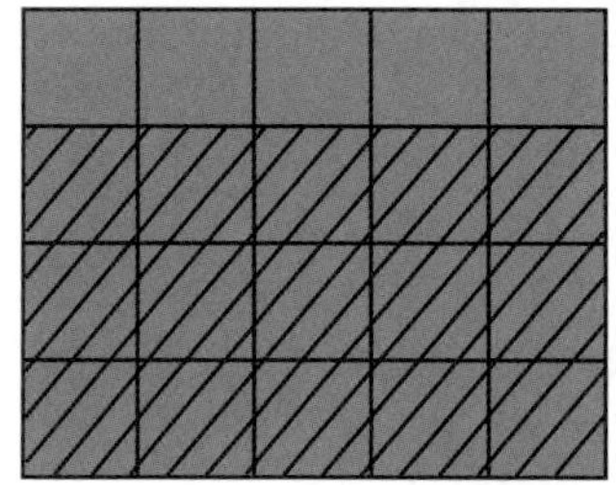

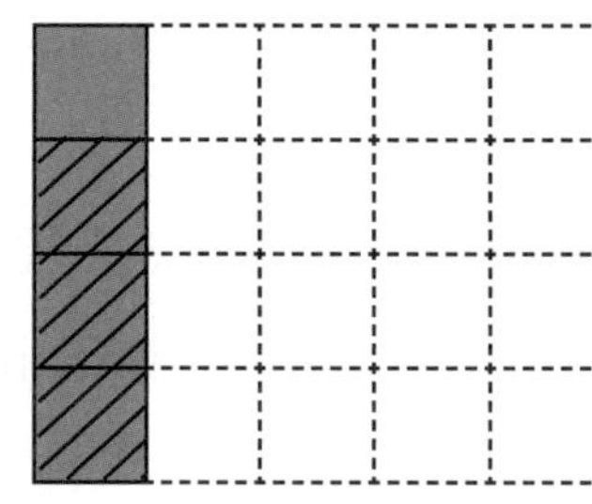

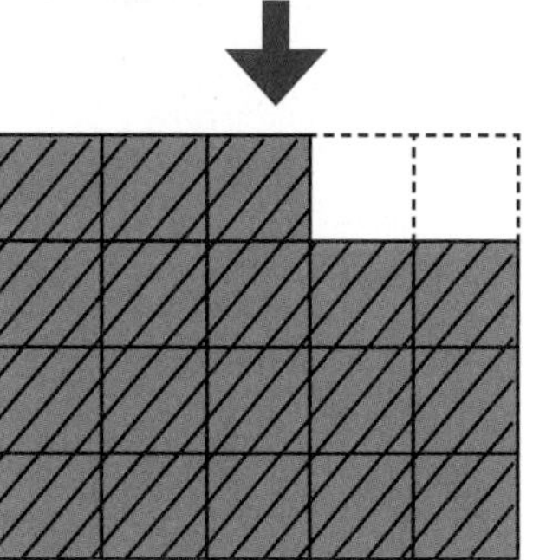

$\frac{18}{20} = \frac{9}{10}$

In $\frac{3}{4}$, the numerator is less than the denominator. $\frac{3}{4}$ is a **proper fraction**.

In $\frac{6}{5}$, the numerator is greater than the denominator. $\frac{6}{5}$ is an **improper fraction**.

Method 2

$\frac{6}{5} \times \frac{3}{4} = \frac{6 \div 2}{5} \times \frac{3}{4 \div 2}$

$= \frac{3 \times 3}{5 \times 2}$

$= \frac{9}{10}$

Divide both the numerator and denominator by their common factor, 2.

Guided Learning

Multiply. Express the product in simplest form.

1. $\frac{1}{3} \times \frac{7}{5}$

2. $\frac{2}{7} \times \frac{21}{12}$

Multiply. Express the product as a whole number or a mixed number in simplest form.

3. $\frac{3}{7} \times \frac{14}{5}$

4. $\frac{5}{9} \times \frac{24}{7}$

5. $\frac{9}{4} \times \frac{10}{3}$

6. $\frac{7}{5} \times \frac{9}{2}$

7. $\frac{27}{6} \times \frac{15}{8}$

8. $\frac{16}{3} \times \frac{9}{4}$

Let's Practice

Multiply. Express the product as a whole number or a mixed number in simplest form.

1. $\frac{22}{6} \times \frac{3}{11}$

2. $\frac{15}{6} \times \frac{4}{5}$

3. $\frac{21}{8} \times \frac{10}{7}$

4. $\frac{32}{12} \times \frac{15}{4}$

5. $\frac{17}{3} \times \frac{21}{5}$

6. $\frac{15}{9} \times \frac{11}{3}$

7. $\frac{28}{11} \times \frac{44}{12}$

8. $\frac{23}{10} \times \frac{11}{3}$

ON YOUR OWN

Go to Workbook A: Practice 3, pages 147–150

Lesson

4.4 Multiplying Mixed Numbers and Whole Numbers

Lesson Objectives

- Multiply a mixed number by a whole number.
- Compare the size of a product to the size of its factors.

Vocabulary
mixed number

Learn

Multiply mixed numbers by whole numbers.

There are 6 students in a group. Each student works $1\frac{1}{2}$ hours on a group project. What is the total amount of time they spend working on the project?

Method 1

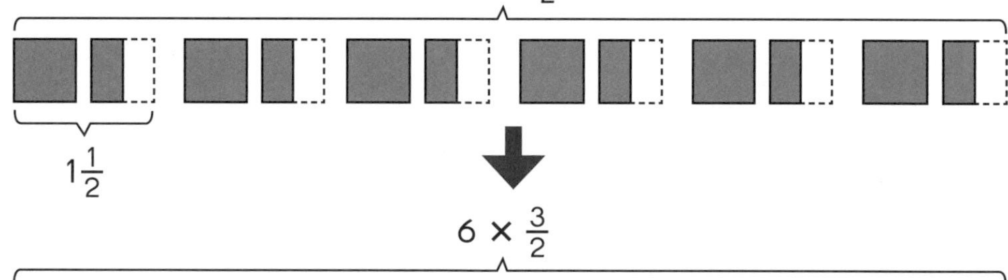

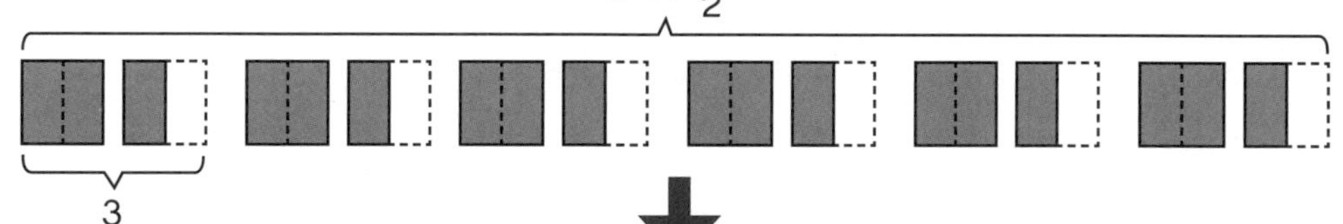

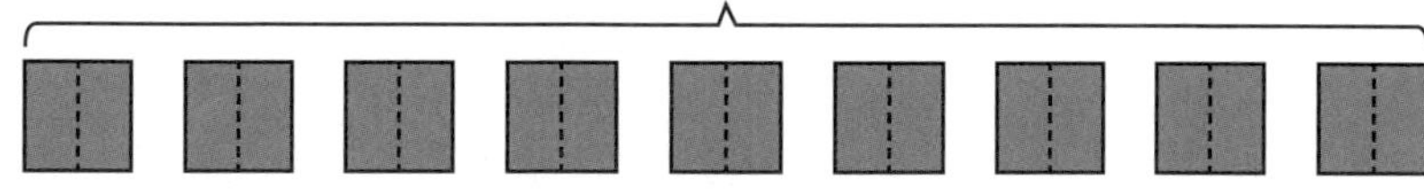

The group works on the project for a total of 9 hours.

Method 2

$$1\frac{1}{2} \times 6 = \frac{3}{2} \times 6$$
$$= \frac{18}{2}$$
$$= 9$$

$1\frac{1}{2} = \frac{3}{2}$
So, $1\frac{1}{2} \times 6$ is the same as 6 groups of $\frac{3}{2}$.

The group works on the project for a total of 9 hours.

Guided Learning

Find the product of $2\frac{1}{3}$ and 5.

1 ***Method 1***

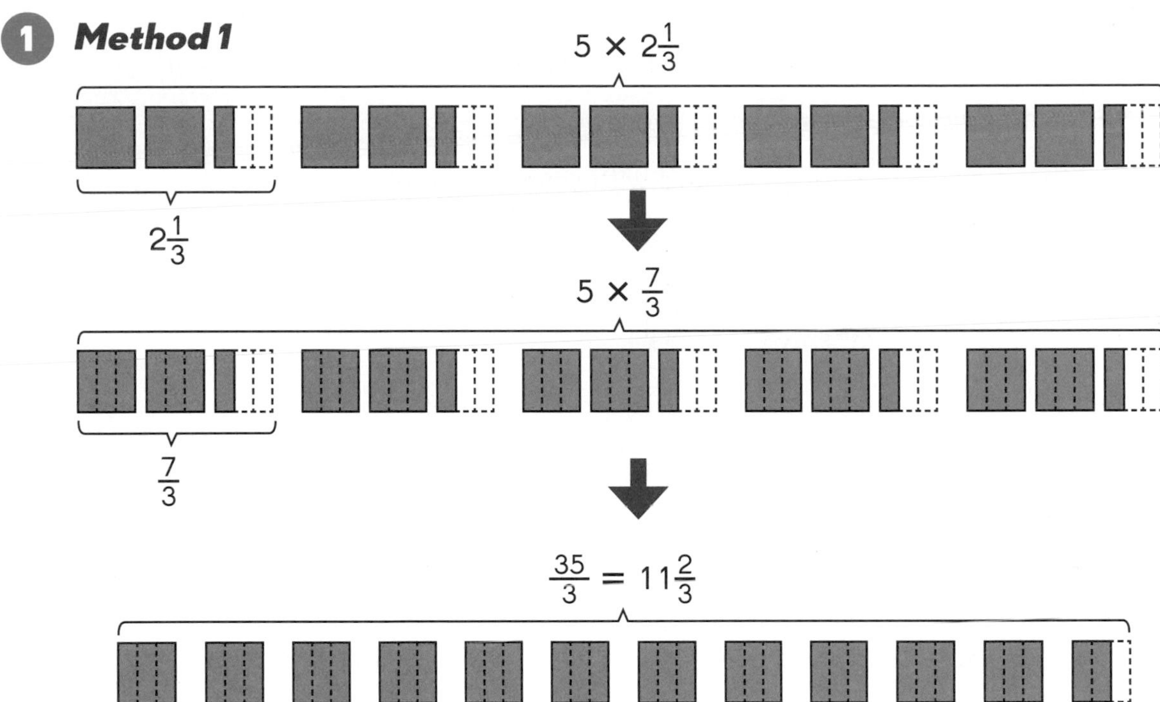

Method 2

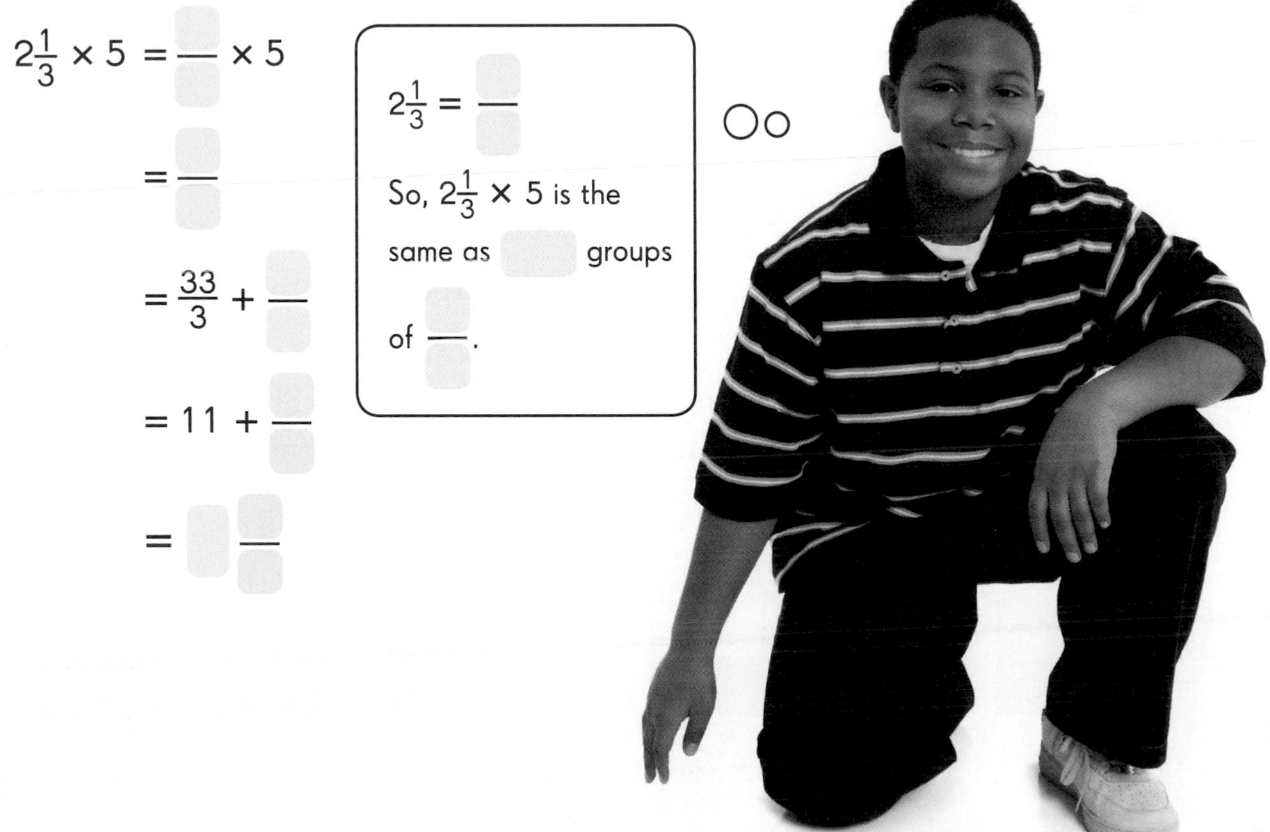

$2\frac{1}{3} \times 5 = \frac{\square}{\square} \times 5$
$= \frac{\square}{\square}$
$= \frac{33}{3} + \frac{\square}{\square}$
$= 11 + \frac{\square}{\square}$
$= \square\frac{\square}{\square}$
$2\frac{1}{3} = \frac{\square}{\square}$
So, $2\frac{1}{3} \times 5$ is the same as ___ groups of $\frac{\square}{\square}$.

Hands-On Activity

STEP 1 Use a sheet of paper to represent 1 whole. Next, fold another sheet of paper into half and cut it into two equal pieces. Use one of these pieces to represent $\frac{1}{2}$. Do this with several pieces.

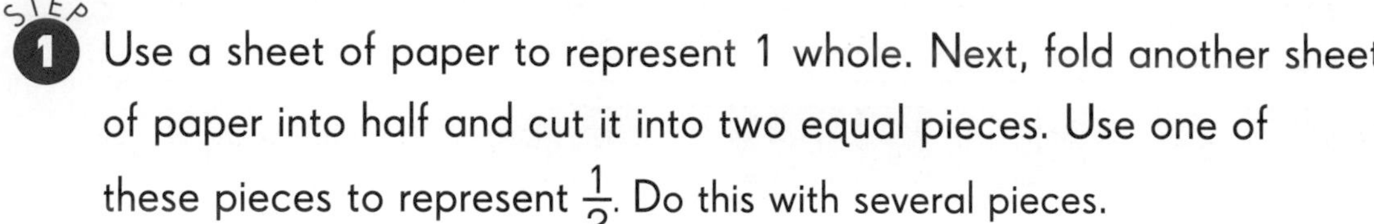

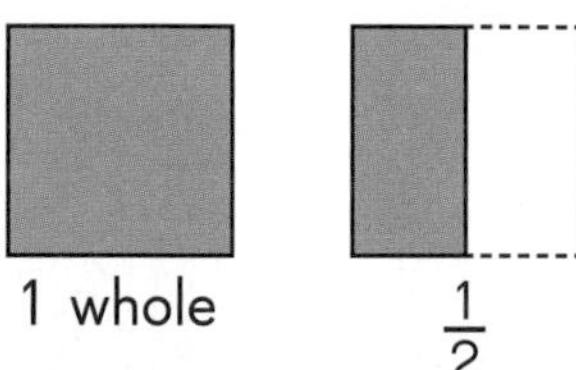

1 whole $\quad \frac{1}{2}$

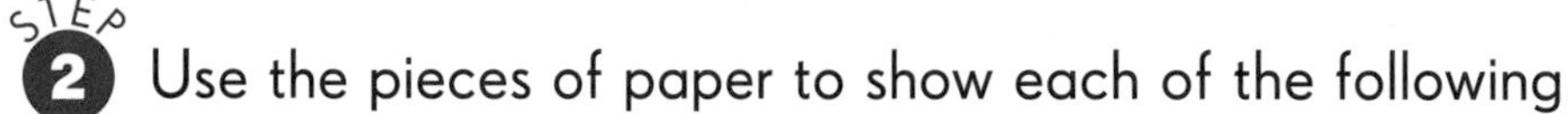

STEP 2 Use the pieces of paper to show each of the following.

a $3\frac{1}{2}$ **b** $4 \times 3\frac{1}{2}$ **c** $3\frac{1}{2} \times 5$

d Rearrange the pieces of paper representing $4 \times 3\frac{1}{2}$. How many wholes are in $4 \times 3\frac{1}{2}$?

STEP 3 Consider $3\frac{1}{2} \times 4\frac{1}{2}$. Use the results of **STEP 2** to predict, without multiplying, whether the product is greater than or less than $3\frac{1}{2}$. Explain your reasoning.

STEP 4 Suppose you multiply $3\frac{1}{2}$ by any number greater than 1. Will the product be greater than or less than $3\frac{1}{2}$? Explain your reasoning.

STEP 5 Draw horizontal lines on some of the pieces as shown. Shade an amount equal to the product.

a $2\frac{1}{2} \times \frac{1}{2}$

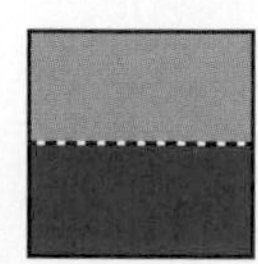

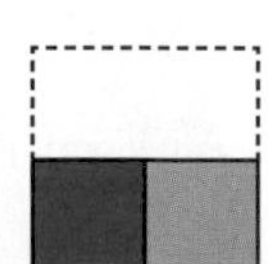

b $\frac{1}{4} \times 2\frac{1}{2}$

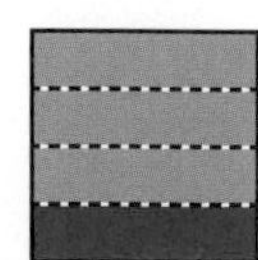

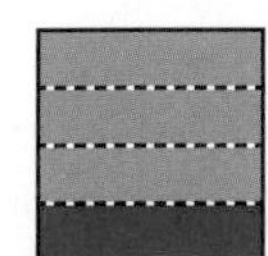

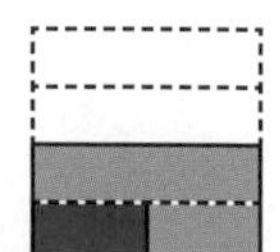

STEP 6 Consider the product of $2\frac{1}{2} \times \frac{3}{4}$. Use the results of **STEP 5** to predict, without multiplying, whether the product is greater than or less than $2\frac{1}{2}$.

STEP 7 Suppose you multiply $2\frac{1}{2}$ by any number less than 1. Will the product be greater than or less than $2\frac{1}{2}$? Explain your reasoning.

Let's Explore!

The model shows $4\frac{1}{2}$.

    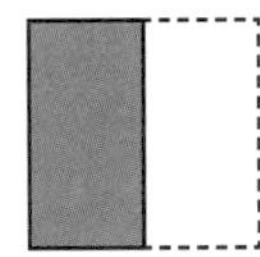

1 Express this product as a product of another mixed number and a whole number.

$4\frac{1}{2} = \square\frac{\square}{\square} \times 2$

$2 \times \square = 4$

$2 \times \frac{\square}{\square} = \frac{1}{2}$

2 Use the same method to find the missing number below.

a $8\frac{1}{4} = \square\frac{\square}{\square} \times 2$

b $9\frac{1}{2} = \square\frac{\square}{\square} \times 3$

Let's Practice

Complete. Express each product as a mixed number. Use the model to help you.

1. $1\frac{1}{2} \times 3 = \square\frac{\square}{\square}$

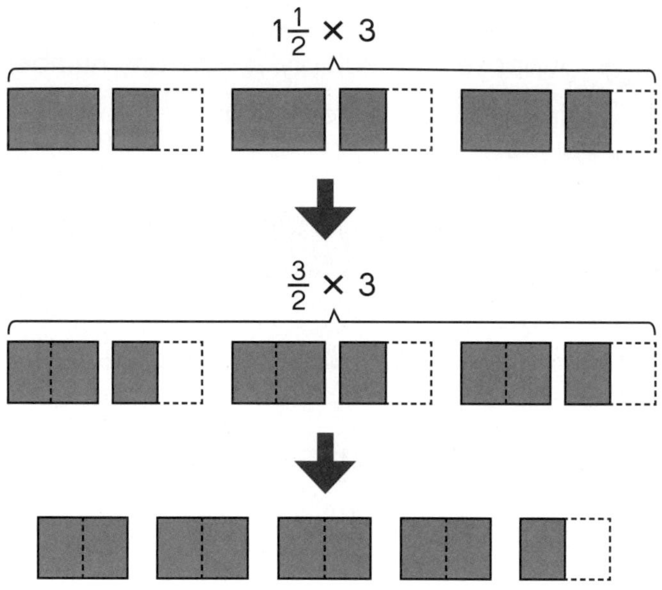

2. $2\frac{1}{3} \times 2 = \square\frac{\square}{\square}$

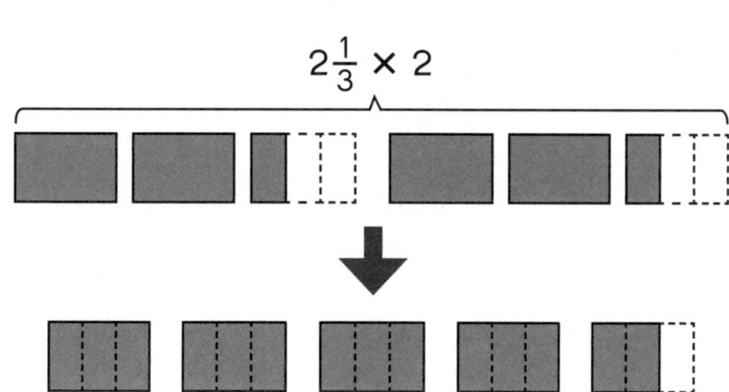

Multiply. Express each product as a whole number or a mixed number in simplest form.

3. $3\frac{9}{11} \times 33$ $\square$

4. $14 \times 2\frac{3}{5}$ $\square$

5. $38 \times 5\frac{2}{7}$ $\square$

6. Name a whole number that you can multiply $4\frac{3}{4}$ by to get a product greater than $4\frac{3}{4}$. Name a mixed number that would give a similar result. $\square$

7. Name a number you can mutiply $3\frac{5}{6}$ by to get a product less than $3\frac{5}{6}$. $\square$

ON YOUR OWN

Go to Workbook A: Practice 4, pages 151–154

Lesson 4.5

Real-World Problems: Multiplying with Mixed Numbers

Lesson Objective

- Solve real-world problems involving multiplication of whole numbers and mixed numbers.

Learn **Multiply mixed numbers by whole numbers to solve real-world problems.**

There are 40 guests at a party. Each guest eats $2\frac{3}{4}$ mini pizzas. How many mini pizzas do the guests eat altogether?

1 guest → $2\frac{3}{4}$ mini pizzas

40 guests → $40 \times 2\frac{3}{4}$ mini pizzas

$= 40 \times \frac{11}{4}$

$= \frac{440}{4}$

$= 110$

The guests eat 110 mini pizzas.

Guided Learning

Solve.

1. Ken uses $2\frac{1}{4}$ feet of tape to wrap a package. How many feet of tape does he use to wrap 20 of these packages?

1 package → $2\frac{1}{4}$ ft

20 packages → ___ $\times 2\frac{1}{4}$

$=$ ___ $\times \frac{\_\_\_}{\_\_\_}$

$= \frac{\_\_\_}{\_\_\_}$

$=$ ___ ft

He uses ___ feet of tape.

Learn Express the product of a mixed number and a whole number as a decimal.

Justina has 5 ribbons, each $2\frac{1}{4}$ feet long. What is the total length of the ribbons? Express your answer as a decimal.

$$2\frac{1}{4} \times 5 = \frac{9}{4} \times 5$$
$$= \frac{45}{4}$$
$$= 11\frac{1}{4}$$
$$= 11\frac{25}{100}$$
$$= 11.25$$

The total length of the ribbons is 11.25 feet.

Guided Learning

Solve.

2 Andrew's rectangular garden has a length of $12\frac{3}{4}$ yards and a width of 7 yards. Find the area of Andrew's garden. Express your answer as a decimal.

Area of Andrew's rectangular garden = length × width

$$= \square\frac{\square}{\square} \times \square$$
$$= \frac{\square}{\square} \times \square$$
$$= \frac{\square}{\square}$$
$$= \square\frac{\square}{\square}$$
$$= \square\frac{\square}{100}$$
$$= \square \text{ yd}^2$$

The area of Andrew's garden is ☐ square yards.

Learn Solve two-step problems involving multiplication with mixed numbers.

Ms. Gupta buys 4 packages of chicken. Each package weighs $2\frac{3}{5}$ pounds. The price of the chicken is $2 per pound. How much does Ms. Gupta pay for the 4 packages of chicken?

1 package of chicken → $2\frac{3}{5}$ lb

4 packages of chicken → $4 \times 2\frac{3}{5}$

$= 10\frac{2}{5}$ lb

$$4 \times 2\frac{3}{5} = 4 \times \frac{13}{5} = \frac{52}{5} = 10\frac{2}{5}$$

The weight of the 4 packages of chicken is $10\frac{2}{5}$ pounds.

1 pound of chicken → $2

$10\frac{2}{5}$ pounds of chicken → $10\frac{2}{5} \times \$2$

$= \$20\frac{4}{5}$

$= \$20\frac{8}{10}$

$= \$20.80$

$$10\frac{2}{5} \times 2 = \frac{52}{5} \times 2 = \frac{104}{5} = 20\frac{4}{5}$$

Ms. Gupta pays $20.80 for the 4 packages of chicken.

Guided Learning

Solve.

3. A chef uses 3 bottles of olive oil to make salad dressing. Each bottle contains $1\frac{1}{2}$ quarts of oil. The cost of 1 quart of olive oil is $5. Find the total cost of the oil she uses.

1 bottle → $\square\frac{\square}{\square}$ qt

3 bottles → $3 \times \square\frac{\square}{\square}$

$= \square\frac{\square}{\square}$ qt

3 bottles contain $\square\frac{\square}{\square}$ quarts of olive oil.

1 qt of olive oil → $5

$\square\frac{\square}{\square}$ qt of olive oil → $\square\frac{\square}{\square} \times \$5$

$= \frac{\square}{\square} \times \$5$

$= \$\square$

The total cost of the olive oil is $ ___.

Let's Practice

Solve.

1. There are 6 children at a birthday party. Each child gets $2\frac{1}{3}$ cups of fruit punch. How many cups of fruit punch are needed for all 6 children?

2. Amin cuts a ball of string into 14 equal pieces. The length of each piece of string is $2\frac{1}{4}$ yards. What is the original length of the ball of string?

3. Regan uses $4\frac{1}{8}$ ounces of paint to paint a chair. How many ounces of paint will he need to paint 9 such chairs?

4. At a zoo, each adult elephant gets $70\frac{1}{4}$ pounds of bananas every day. The zoo keeps 5 adult elephants. How many pounds of bananas will the zoo need for all 5 adult elephants in a day?

5. Mr. Richards bought 3 packages of meat for a neighborhood barbecue. Each package weighs $7\frac{1}{2}$ pounds. The price of the meat is $3 per pound. How much did he pay for all the meat he bought?

6. Ms. Scutter is tiling a bathroom with a length of 9 feet and a width of $8\frac{1}{2}$ feet. The tile that she chose sells at $4 per square foot. How much will Ms. Scutter need to pay for the tiles she needs?

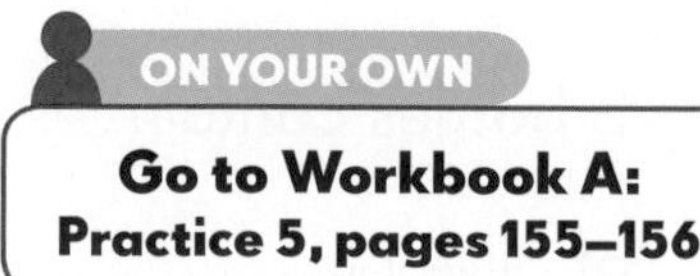
ON YOUR OWN
Go to Workbook A:
Practice 5, pages 155–156

Lesson 4.6 Dividing Fractions and Whole Numbers

Lesson Objectives
- Divide a fraction by a whole number.
- Divide a whole number by a unit fraction.

Vocabulary
reciprocal

Learn Divide a fraction by a whole number.

Maura cuts a rectangular piece of clay in half. She then divides one half into 3 equal parts. What fraction of the whole piece of clay is each of the 3 parts?

Method 1

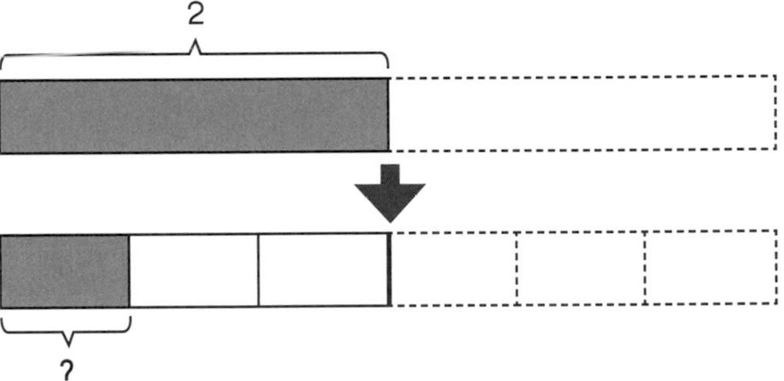

$\frac{1}{2} \div 3 = \frac{1}{6}$

The model shows that each part is $\frac{1}{6}$ of the whole piece of clay.

Method 2

$$\begin{aligned}\frac{1}{2} \div 3 &= \frac{1}{3} \text{ of } \frac{1}{2} \\ &= \frac{1}{3} \times \frac{1}{2} \\ &= \frac{1}{6}\end{aligned}$$

Each part is $\frac{1}{3}$ of $\frac{1}{2}$ the piece of clay.

Each part is $\frac{1}{6}$ of the whole piece of clay.

Method 3

$$\begin{aligned}\frac{1}{2} \div 3 &= \frac{1}{2} \div \frac{3}{1} \\ &= \frac{1}{2} \times \frac{1}{3} \\ &= \frac{1}{6}\end{aligned}$$

$\frac{1}{3}$ is the **reciprocal** of $\frac{3}{1}$ or 3. Dividing by a number is the same as multiplying by the reciprocal of the number.

Each part is $\frac{1}{6}$ of the whole piece of clay.

Guided Learning

Solve.

1 A roll of wire, $\frac{3}{5}$ feet long, is cut into 6 equal pieces. How long is each piece?

Method 1

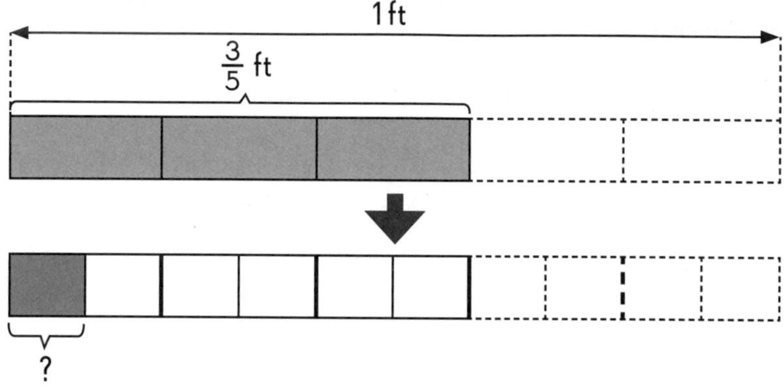

$\frac{3}{5} \div 6 = \frac{\square}{\square}$

The model shows that each piece is $\frac{\square}{\square}$ feet long.

Method 2

$\frac{3}{5} \div 6 = \frac{1}{6}$ of $\frac{3}{5}$

$= \frac{\square}{\square} \times \frac{\square}{\square}$

$= \frac{\square}{\square}$

$= \frac{\square}{\square}$

Each piece is $\frac{\square}{\square}$ feet long.

Method 3

$\frac{3}{5} \div 6 = \frac{3}{5} \div \frac{6}{1}$

$= \frac{3}{5} \times \frac{\square}{\square}$

$= \frac{\square}{\square}$

$= \frac{\square}{\square}$

Each piece is $\frac{\square}{\square}$ feet long.

Learn Divide a fraction by a whole number.

A $\frac{4}{5}$-pound cantaloupe is cut into 2 equal pieces. What is the weight of each piece of cantaloupe?

Method 1

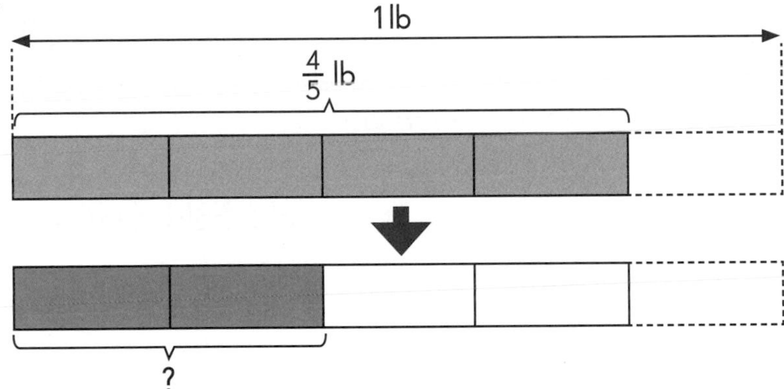

The model shows that the weight of each piece of cantaloupe is $\frac{2}{5}$ pound.

Method 2

$$\frac{4}{5} \div 2 = \frac{4}{5} \times \frac{1}{2}$$
$$= \frac{2}{5}$$

The weight of each piece of cantaloupe is $\frac{2}{5}$ pound.

Guided Learning

Solve.

2 Find $\frac{9}{11} \div 3$.

Method 1

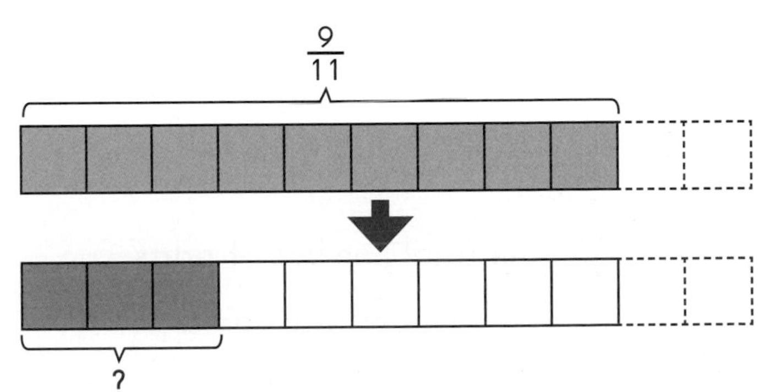

The model shows that

$\frac{9}{11} \div 3 = \frac{\square}{\square}$.

Method 2

$$\frac{9}{11} \div 3 = \frac{9}{11} \times \frac{\square}{\square}$$
$$= \frac{\square}{\square}$$

Hands-On Activity

WORK IN PAIRS

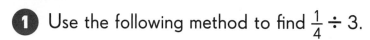

Materials:
- paper
- colored pencil

1 Use the following method to find $\frac{1}{4} \div 3$.

STEP 1 Use a piece of paper to represent 1 whole. Fold it into fourths. (Do not unfold the piece of paper just yet.)

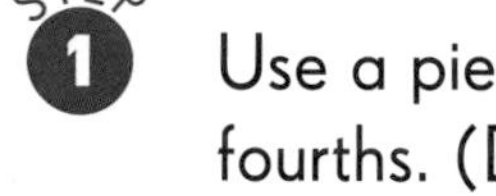

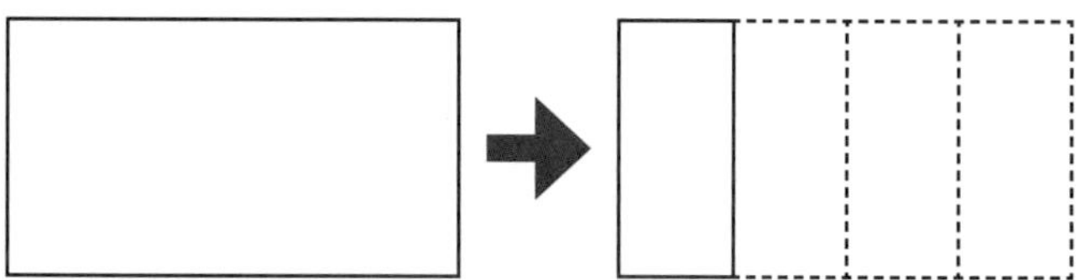

STEP 2 Continue to fold the paper further into thirds. Color any one side.

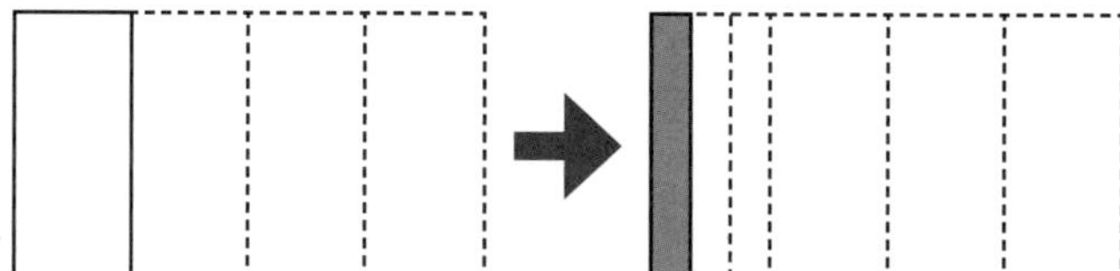

STEP 3 Unfold the paper to reveal the total number of parts.

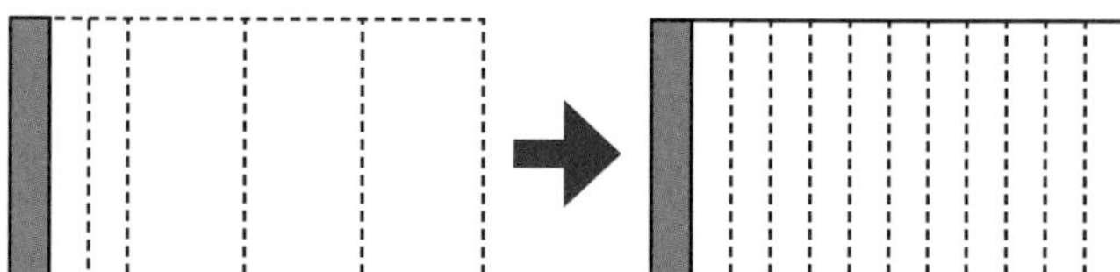

Count:

a. the total number of parts,

b. the number of colored parts.

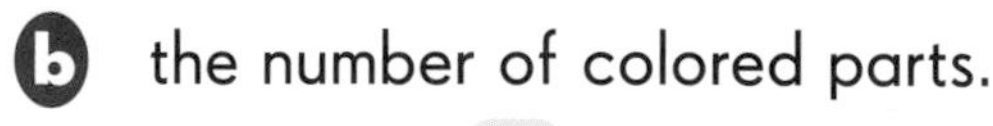

$\frac{1}{4} \div 3 = \frac{\square}{\square}$

Check!

$\frac{\square}{\square} \times 3 = \frac{\square}{\square}$

$= \frac{\square}{\square}$

2 Use a similar method to divide $\frac{1}{4}$ by 4.

Learn Divide a whole number by a unit fraction.

Laura uses $\frac{1}{3}$ yard of ribbon to decorate a greeting card. How many similar greeting cards can she decorate with 4 yards of ribbon?

Number of greeting cards $= 4 \div \frac{1}{3}$

  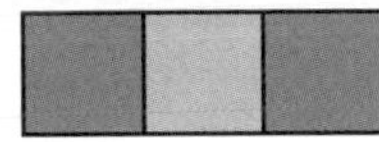 

The model shows that:

Number of $\frac{1}{3}$ yard pieces in 1 yard $= 3$

Number of $\frac{1}{3}$ yard pieces in 3 yards $= 4 \times 3$

So, $4 \div \frac{1}{3} = 4 \times 3$ ← Rewrite as a multiplication expression using the reciprocal of the divisor.

$= 12$ ← Then multiply.

Laura can decorate 12 similar greeting cards with 4 yards of ribbon.

Check!

$12 \times \frac{1}{3} = \frac{12 \times 1}{3}$

$= \frac{12}{3}$

$= 4$

In general, dividing by a number is the same as multiplying by the reciprocal of the number.

$4 \div \mathbf{\frac{1}{3}} = 4 \times \mathbf{3}$

$\frac{1}{3}$ and 3 are reciprocals.

Guided Learning

Divide. You may draw models to help you.

3 $3 \div \frac{1}{5}$ ☐

4 $7 \div \frac{1}{4}$ ☐

Let's Practice

Divide. Express the quotient in simplest form. You may draw models to help you.

1. $\frac{2}{3} \div 8 = \frac{\square}{\square}$
2. $\frac{3}{4} \div 12 = \frac{\square}{\square}$
3. $\frac{6}{7} \div 9 = \frac{\square}{\square}$
4. $\frac{5}{8} \div 10 = \frac{\square}{\square}$

Divide. Express the quotient in simplest form.

5. $\frac{6}{11} \div 3 = \frac{\square}{\square}$
6. $\frac{8}{9} \div 4 = \frac{\square}{\square}$
7. $\frac{3}{7} \div 2 = \frac{\square}{\square}$
8. $\frac{3}{5} \div 7 = \frac{\square}{\square}$

Divide. You may draw models to help you.

9. $5 \div \frac{1}{7}$ $\square$
10. $9 \div \frac{1}{6}$ $\square$
11. $3 \div \frac{1}{8}$ $\square$
12. $6 \div \frac{1}{10}$ $\square$
13. $8 \div \frac{1}{12}$ $\square$
14. $10 \div \frac{1}{9}$ $\square$

Solve. Show your work.

15. The area of a rectangular piece of fabric is $\frac{4}{9}$ square yards. Julie cuts the fabric into 3 smaller pieces of the same size. What is the area of each smaller piece of fabric? $\square$

16 Mel made a quesadilla. He cut $\frac{1}{10}$ of the quesadilla to save for later. Mel then shared the remaining portion of the quesadilla among himself and 2 friends. What fraction of the whole quesadilla did each person get?

17 A water cooler holds 10 gallons of water. How many pint-sized water bottles can be filled from the cooler?

18 Mrs. Pena spent $\frac{1}{3}$ of her paycheck on groceries and household goods and paid bills with $\frac{5}{12}$ of the paycheck. She then deposited the rest of the money equally in 3 accounts. What fraction of her paycheck did she deposit in each account?

19 Christine bought $\frac{5}{9}$ pound of granola. She repacked it equally in 20 bags to use as party favors.

a Find the weight of 1 bag of granola in pounds.

b After the party, 7 bags were left over. How many pounds of granola were left over?

20 Sandra uses $\frac{1}{9}$ of a bottle of honey to make 1 pitcher of lemonade. How many pitchers of lemonade can she make with 3 bottles of honey?

21 Lewis needs $\frac{1}{8}$ quart of paint to cover 10 square yards. How many square yards can he paint with 4 quarts of paint?

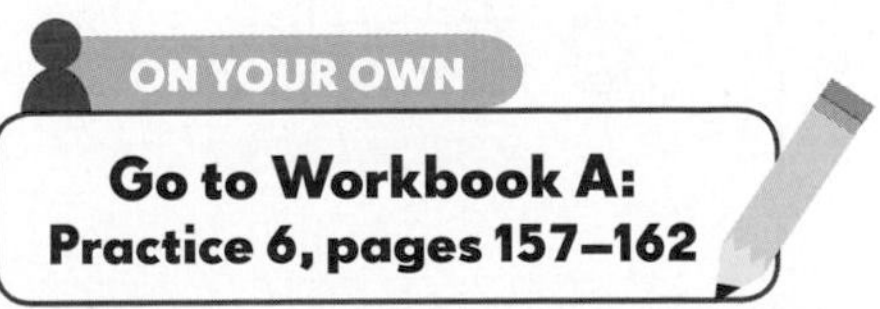

ON YOUR OWN
Go to Workbook A:
Practice 6, pages 157–162

Real-World Problems: Multiplying and Dividing with Fractions

Lesson Objective

- Solve real-world problems involving multiplication and division of fractions and whole numbers.

Learn Find parts of a whole to solve real-world problems.

A vendor at the farmers' market has 240 pieces of fruit. She sells $\frac{1}{2}$ of it to one customer and $\frac{1}{3}$ of it to another customer.

ⓐ How many pieces of fruit does the vendor sell?

ⓑ How many pieces of fruit does she have left?

Method 1

The least common multiple of 2 and 3 is 6. Draw a model with 6 equal units.

$\frac{1}{2}$ of 6 units $= \frac{1}{2} \times 6$
$= 3$ units

$\frac{1}{3}$ of 6 units $= \frac{1}{3} \times 6$
$= 2$ units

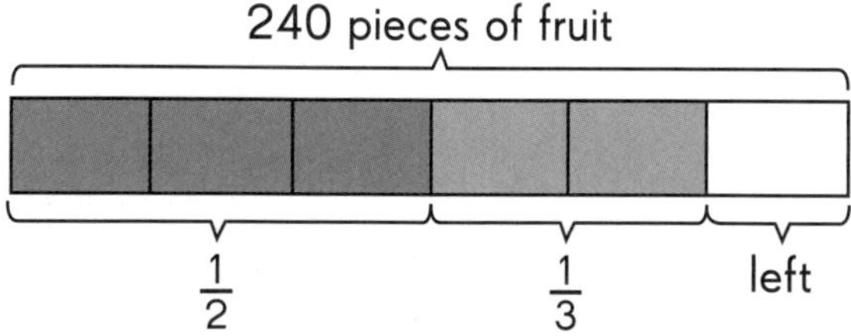

The model shows that:

6 units ⟶ 240 pieces of fruit

1 unit ⟶ $240 \div 6 = 40$ pieces of fruit

5 units ⟶ $5 \times 40 = 200$ pieces of fruit

ⓐ The vendor sells 200 pieces of fruit.

ⓑ She has 40 pieces of fruit left.

Method 2

$\frac{1}{2} = \frac{3}{6}$ $\frac{1}{3} = \frac{2}{6}$

Fraction of fruit sold:

$\frac{3}{6} + \frac{2}{6} = \frac{5}{6}$

$\frac{5}{6}$ of $240 = \frac{5}{6} \times 240 = 200$

a The vendor sells 200 pieces of fruit.

b She has $240 - 200 = 40$ pieces of fruit left.

Method 3

$\frac{1}{2} \times 240 = 120$

$\frac{1}{3} \times 240 = 80$

a The vendor sells $120 + 80 = 200$ pieces of fruit.

b She has $240 - 200 = 40$ pieces of fruit left.

Guided Learning

Solve.

1 Kim has 48 plants in her garden. Of the 48 plants, $\frac{2}{3}$ are carrots and $\frac{1}{4}$ are tomatoes. The rest of the plants are pumpkins. How many pumpkin plants are in the garden?

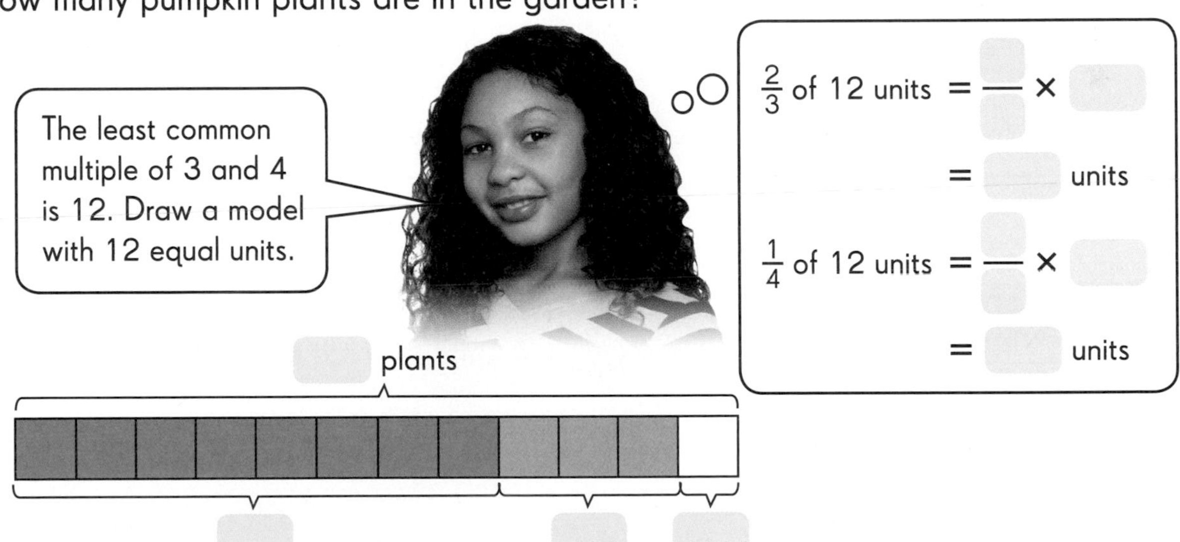
The least common multiple of 3 and 4 is 12. Draw a model with 12 equal units.
$\frac{2}{3}$ of 12 units = — ×
= units
$\frac{1}{4}$ of 12 units = — ×
= units
plants

The model shows that:

units → plants

1 unit → ÷ = plants

Kim has pumpkin plants.

Learn Find fractional parts of a whole and the remainder.

Sofia has \$480. She uses $\frac{1}{3}$ of the money to buy a winter coat. She then spends $\frac{1}{4}$ of the remainder on a pair of winter boots. How much money does she have left?

Method 1

$1 - \frac{1}{3} = \frac{2}{3}$

Remainder ⟶ 2 parts

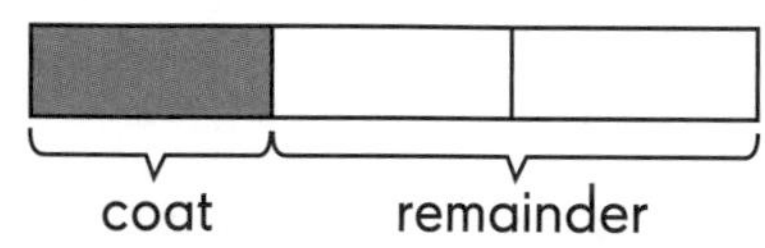

To show $\frac{1}{4}$ of the remainder is spent on the boots, I have to further divide the remainder into 4 parts.

Least common multiple of 2 and 4 = 4

By equivalent fractions:

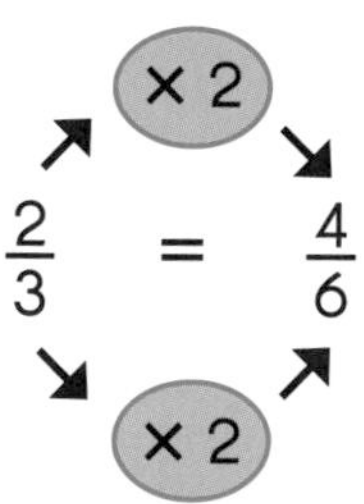

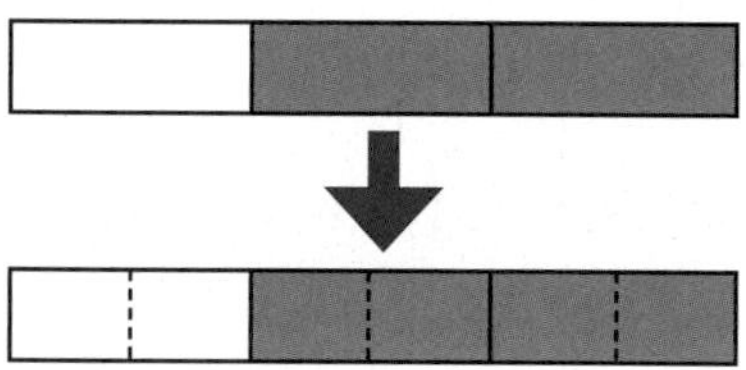

I need to draw a model with 6 equal units to show the problem.

\$480

coat | boots | left

$\frac{1}{3}$ of 6 units = 2 units

$\frac{1}{4}$ of 4 units = 1 unit

The model shows that:

6 units ⟶ \$480

1 unit ⟶ \$480 ÷ 6 = \$80

3 units ⟶ 3 × \$80

= \$240

She has \$240 left.

Method 2

$\frac{1}{3}$ of 480 $= \frac{1}{3} \times 480$
$= 160$

Sofia spends \$160 on the coat.

$480 - 160 = 320$

After buying the coat, she has \$320 left.

$1 - \frac{1}{4} = \frac{3}{4}$

$\frac{3}{4}$ of 320 $= \frac{3}{4} \times 320$
$= 240$

She has \$240 left.

Learn Find fractional parts and wholes given one fractional part.

Ben took a test with three sections, A, B, and C. Ben spent $\frac{1}{5}$ of his time on Section A and $\frac{1}{3}$ of the remaining time on Section B. He spent 48 minutes on Section C. How much time did Ben take to complete the whole test?

Method 1

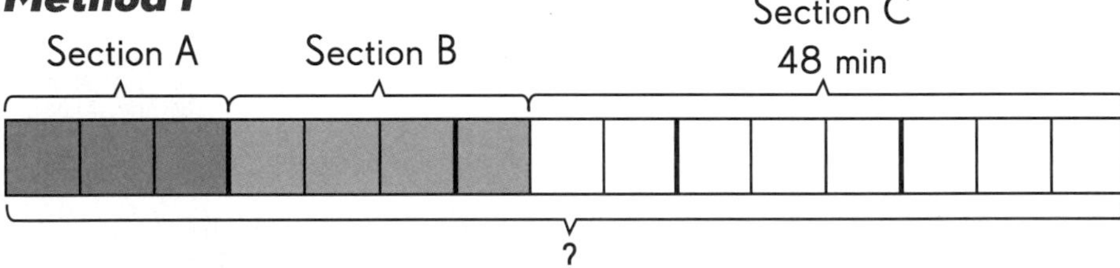

The model shows that:

8 units ⟶ 48 min
1 unit ⟶ 6 min
15 units ⟶ 90 min

Ben took 90 minutes to complete the test.

Method 2

Fraction of the total time Ben spent on Section B

$= \frac{1}{3} \times \frac{4}{5} = \frac{4}{15}$

Fraction of the total time he spent on Sections A and B

$= \frac{1}{5} + \frac{4}{15} = \frac{3}{15} + \frac{4}{15}$
$= \frac{7}{15}$

Fraction of the total time he spent on Section C

$= 1 - \frac{7}{15} = \frac{8}{15}$

$\frac{8}{15}$ ⟶ 48 min

$\frac{1}{15}$ ⟶ 6 min

$\frac{15}{15}$ ⟶ 90 min

Ben took 90 minutes to complete the test.

Guided Learning

Solve.

2 Jermaine prepares a mixture of apple, carrot, and strawberry juices. Of the total amount, $\frac{1}{3}$ of the mixture is apple juice. $\frac{2}{5}$ of the remainder is strawberry juice. Jermaine uses 315 milliliters of strawberry juice in the mixture. How many milliliters of the mixture are carrot juice?

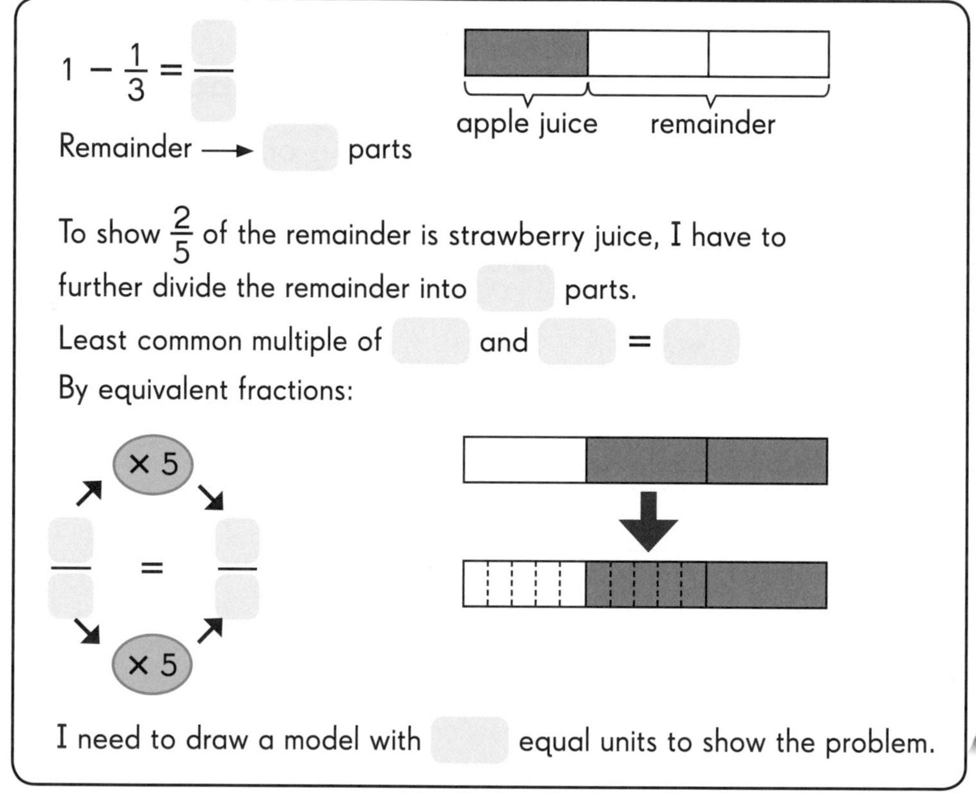

$1 - \frac{1}{3} = \frac{\square}{\square}$
Remainder → ___ parts
apple juice
remainder
To show $\frac{2}{5}$ of the remainder is strawberry juice, I have to further divide the remainder into ___ parts.
Least common multiple of ___ and ___ = ___
By equivalent fractions:
× 5
=
× 5
I need to draw a model with ___ equal units to show the problem.

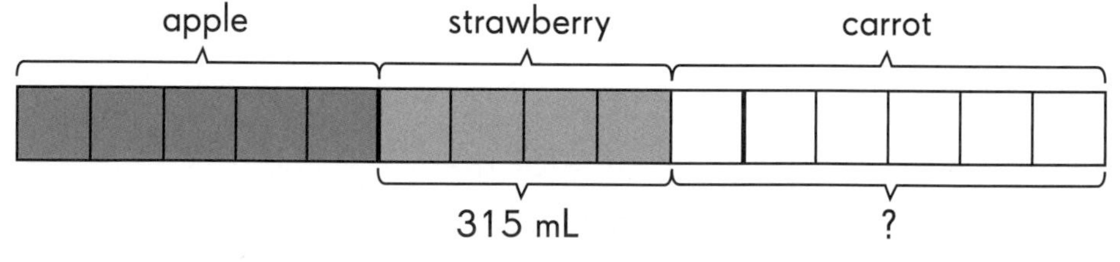

$\frac{1}{3}$ of ___ units
$= \frac{1}{3} \times$ ___ units
$=$ ___ units

$\frac{2}{5}$ of ___ units
$= \frac{2}{5} \times$ ___ units
$=$ ___ units

The model shows that:

4 units → 315 mL

1 unit → 315 ÷ 4 = ___ mL

6 units → 6 × ___ = ___ mL

___ milliliters of the mixture are carrot juice.

3 Gomez collects stamps as a hobby. He gives his cousin $\frac{1}{3}$ of his stamp collection. He then gives his sister $\frac{5}{6}$ of the remainder and has 80 stamps left. How many stamps did he have at first?

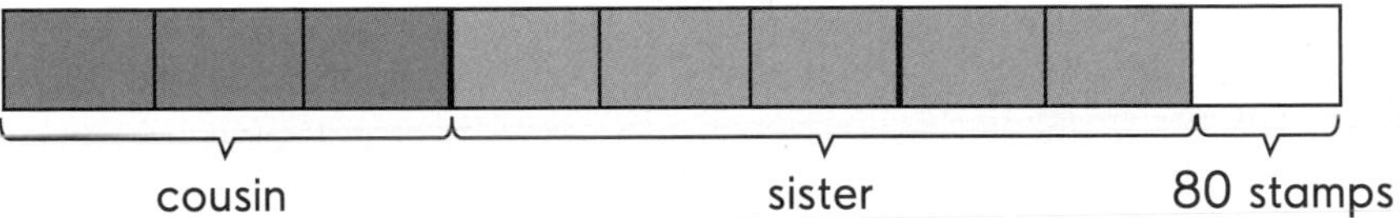

The model shows that:

1 unit → ___ stamps

___ units → 9 × ___ = ___ stamps

Gomez had ___ stamps at first.

Learn Find fractional parts of a remainder when given wholes.

Alana makes $\frac{4}{5}$ gallon of lemonade. She pours $\frac{1}{4}$ of the lemonade into a pitcher and the remaining lemonade equally among 6 glasses. How much lemonade is in each glass?

Method 1

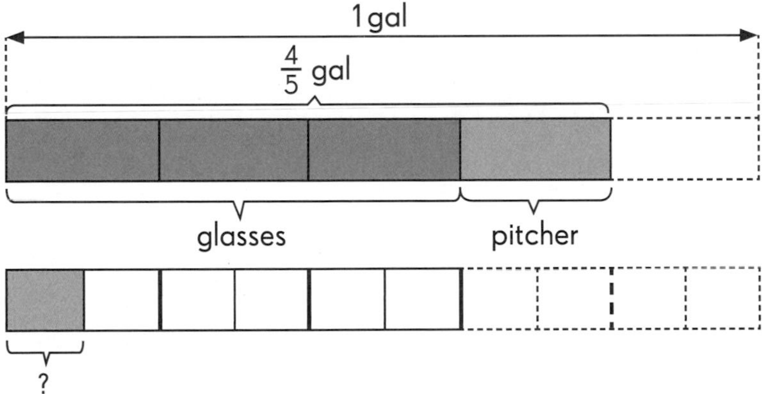

The model shows that:

10 units → 1 gal

1 unit → $\frac{1}{10}$ gal

There is $\frac{1}{10}$ gallon of lemonade in each glass.

Continued on next page

Method 2

Fraction of lemonade remaining $= 1 - \frac{1}{4} = \frac{3}{4}$

Amount of lemonade in 6 glasses $= \frac{3}{4} \times \frac{4}{5} = \frac{3}{5}$ gal

Amount of lemonade in 1 glass $= \frac{3}{5} \div 6$

$= \frac{3}{5} \times \frac{1}{6}$

$= \frac{1}{10}$ gal

There is $\frac{1}{10}$ gallon of lemonade in each glass.

Guided Learning

Solve.

4 Jeff buys $\frac{3}{4}$ pound of beads. $\frac{1}{6}$ of the beads are pink and the rest are green. Jeff packs the green beads equally into 10 jars. What is the weight of beads in each jar?

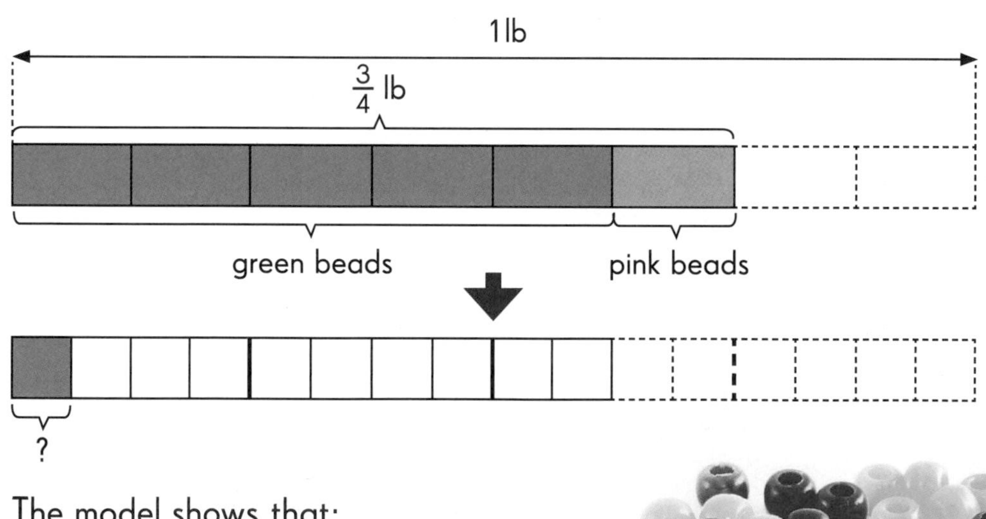

The model shows that:

16 units → ▢ lb

1 unit → $\frac{▢}{▢}$ lb

There is $\frac{▢}{▢}$ pound of beads in each jar.

Learn

Divide a whole number by a unit fraction to solve real-world problems.

Philip buys 5 square yards of wrapping paper for a large gift box and some small gift boxes. He uses 2 square yards of the paper to wrap the large box, and uses the rest to wrap the small boxes. He uses $\frac{1}{2}$ square yard of paper for each small box. How many small boxes does Philip wrap?

Method 1

Wrapping paper used for the small gift boxes
$= 5 - 2$
$= 3$ square yards

Number of small gift boxes = number of $\frac{1}{2}$ square yards in 3 square yards

2 yd^2 of wrapping paper for the large gift box

3 yd^2 of wrapping paper for the small gift boxes

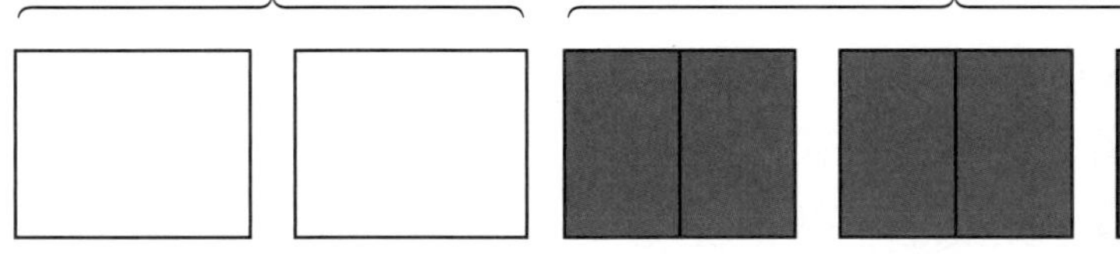

The model shows that:
Number of $\frac{1}{2}$ square yards in 3 square yards = 6

Philip wraps 6 small gift boxes.

Method 2

Wrapping paper used for the small gift boxes
$= 5 - 2$
$= 3$ square yards

$$\text{Number of small gift boxes} = 3 \div \frac{1}{2}$$
$$= 3 \times 2$$
$$= 6$$

Philip wraps 6 small gift boxes.

Guided Learning

Solve.

5. Mason is watering some plants. He has 7 gallons of water. He uses 2 gallons of water for a plot of land and uses the rest to water some potted plants. If he uses $\frac{1}{6}$ gallon of water for each potted plant, how many potted plants can he water?

Let's Practice

Solve. Show your work.

1. Jan has 288 tickets to sell for charity. She sells $\frac{2}{9}$ of the tickets to her family and $\frac{1}{3}$ of them to her friends.
   a. How many tickets are sold to both her family and friends?
   b. How many tickets are not sold?

2. Maggie has $960. She spends $\frac{1}{4}$ of it on a mountain bike and $\frac{1}{6}$ of the remainder on bicycle clothing and accessories. She keeps the rest of the money. How much money does she keep?

3. Jeb took 1 hour 40 minutes to complete a road race that was three laps around a section of the city. He took $\frac{1}{4}$ of the total time to run the first lap and $\frac{1}{3}$ of the remaining time to run the second lap. The rest of the time was used to run the third lap.
   a. How many minutes did it take Jeb to complete the race?
   b. How many minutes did he take to run the third lap of the race?

4 In a middle school glee club, $\frac{2}{5}$ of the singers are sopranos, $\frac{1}{3}$ are altos, and the rest are tenors. If there are 90 students in the glee club, how many of them are tenors?

5 Mr. Young has a piece of rope. He uses $\frac{1}{4}$ of it to tie some boxes together. He then uses $\frac{5}{9}$ of the remainder to make a jumprope for his daughter. After this, 120 centimeters are left. What is the length of rope Mr. Young used to tie the boxes together?

6 Sean has a piece of string $\frac{7}{8}$ meter long. He uses $\frac{1}{5}$ of the piece of string to tie a package and cuts the rest into 5 equal pieces. What is the length of each piece?

7 Callie bought a bag of dried fruit: cherries, pears, and apples. In the bag, $\frac{1}{4}$ of the dried fruit is cherries and $\frac{2}{3}$ of the remainder is pears. There are 48 pear pieces. How many pieces of fruit are apples?

8 Vanessa has 3 bottles of ceramic glaze for her art project. She buys 5 more bottles of ceramic glaze. If she uses $\frac{1}{4}$ of a bottle of ceramic glaze to coat a piece of sculpture, how many similar pieces of sculpture can she coat with all the ceramic glaze?

ON YOUR OWN
Go to Workbook A:
Practice 7, pages 163–170

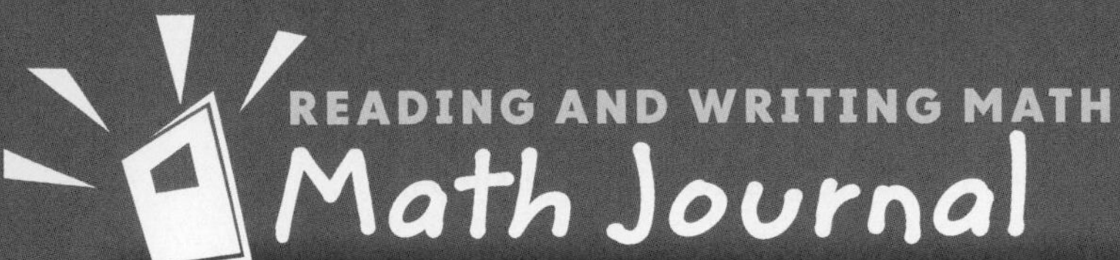

Amelia and Bart were each given a problem to solve.

1. Amelia: $\frac{2}{9} \div 3$
2. Bart: $\frac{2}{9} \times \frac{4}{11}$

They obtained answers to the problems as follows:

1. Amelia: $\frac{2}{9} \div 3 = \frac{2}{3}$
2. Bart: $\frac{2}{9} \times \frac{4}{11} = \frac{6}{20}$

Their answers however are incorrect. Give explanations as to how they could have possibly arrived at these incorrect answers. Write the correct way to solve each problem.

$\frac{2}{9} \div 3 = \frac{2}{3}$

$9 \; ? \; 3 = 3$

Amelia got the answer $\frac{2}{3}$ by ?.

The correct way to solve the problem should have been:

$\frac{2}{9} \div 3 = \frac{2}{9} \; ? \; \frac{1}{?}$

$= \frac{?}{?}$

$\frac{2}{9} \times \frac{4}{11} = \frac{6}{20}$

$2 \; ? \; 4 = 6$

$9 \; ? \; 11 = 20$

Bart got the answer $\frac{6}{20}$ by ?.

The correct way to solve the problem should have been:

$\frac{2}{9} \times \frac{4}{11} = \frac{? \times ?}{? \times ?}$

$= \frac{?}{?}$

CRITICAL THINKING SKILLS

Put On Your Thinking Cap!

PROBLEM SOLVING

1. Find the missing mass in each pattern.

   a. 2,000 g $\quad \frac{1}{3}$ of 18 kg $\quad$ 18,000 g $\quad$ ___ kg $\quad \frac{1}{3}$ of 486 kg

   b. 7,000 g $\quad$ ___ kg $\quad \frac{1}{2}$ of 38 kg $\quad$ 31 kg $\quad 1\frac{1}{4}$ of 37,600 g

2. Danny was the 31st person in line at the cafeteria. His position in line was just behind $\frac{5}{9}$ of the total number of students in line. How many students were in line?

3. Keith bought 10 similar model cars. Brad bought $1\frac{1}{2}$ times as many of the same model cars as Keith. All cars were of the same price. The total cost of the model cars the two boys bought was $75. What was the cost of each model car?

ON YOUR OWN

Go to Workbook A: Put on Your Thinking Cap! pages 171–172

Chapter Wrap Up

Study Guide

You have learned...

▶ Whole numbers, fractions, and mixed numbers can be multiplied or divided in any combination

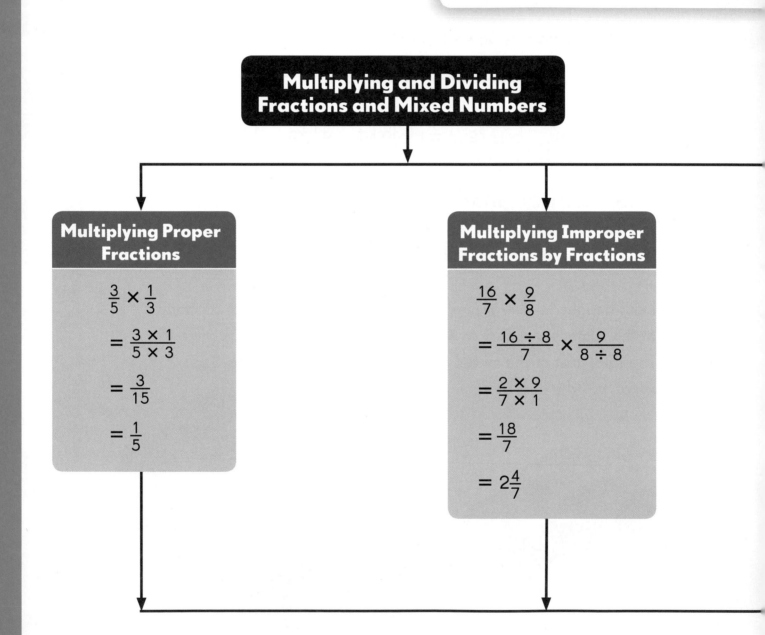

Multiplying and Dividing Fractions and Mixed Numbers

Multiplying Proper Fractions

$$\frac{3}{5} \times \frac{1}{3}$$
$$= \frac{3 \times 1}{5 \times 3}$$
$$= \frac{3}{15}$$
$$= \frac{1}{5}$$

Multiplying Improper Fractions by Fractions

$$\frac{16}{7} \times \frac{9}{8}$$
$$= \frac{16 \div 8}{7} \times \frac{9}{8 \div 8}$$
$$= \frac{2 \times 9}{7 \times 1}$$
$$= \frac{18}{7}$$
$$= 2\frac{4}{7}$$

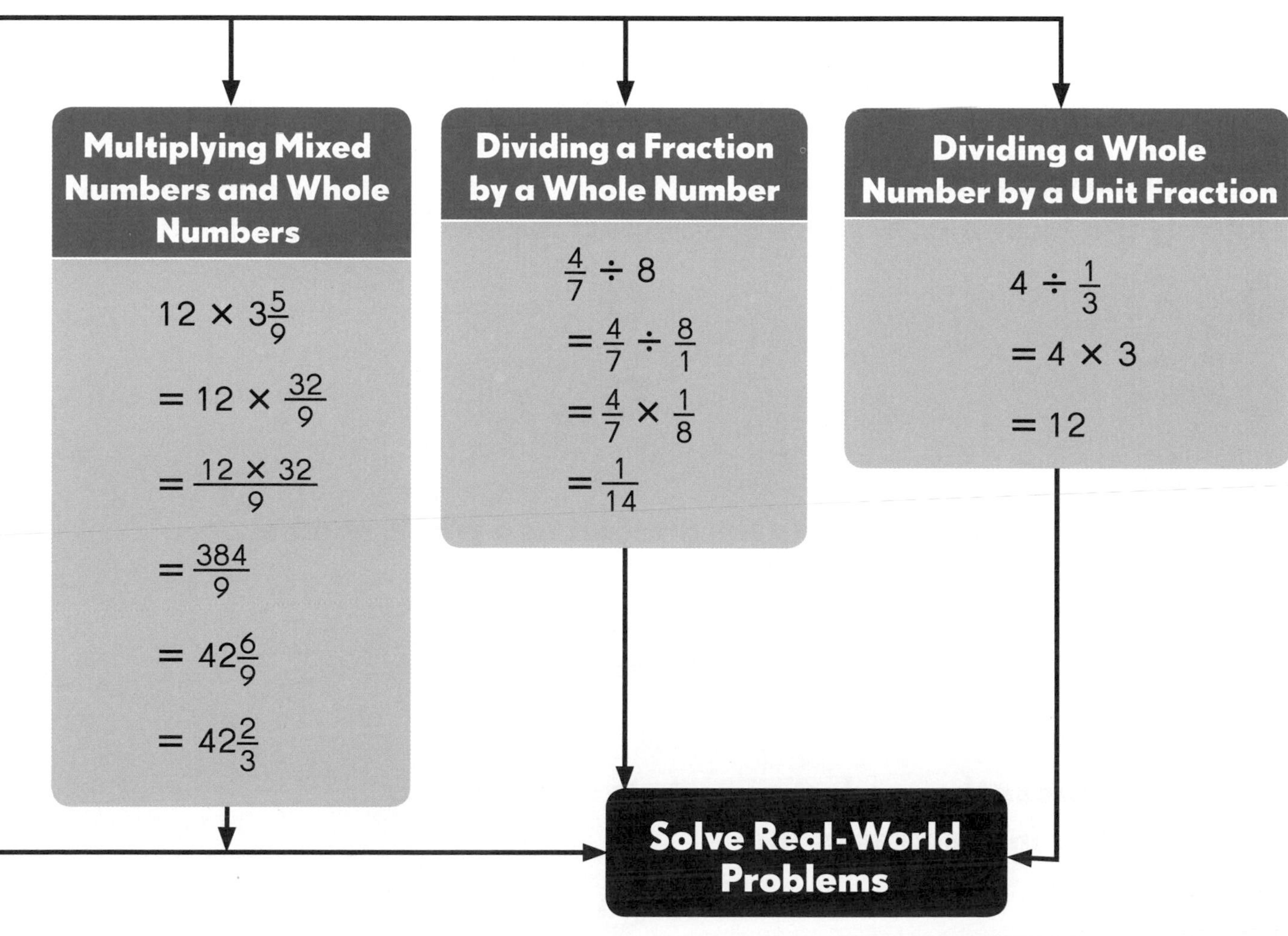
Multiplying Mixed Numbers and Whole Numbers
$12 \times 3\frac{5}{9}$
$= 12 \times \frac{32}{9}$
$= \frac{12 \times 32}{9}$
$= \frac{384}{9}$
$= 42\frac{6}{9}$
$= 42\frac{2}{3}$
Dividing a Fraction by a Whole Number
$\frac{4}{7} \div 8$
$= \frac{4}{7} \div \frac{8}{1}$
$= \frac{4}{7} \times \frac{1}{8}$
$= \frac{1}{14}$
Dividing a Whole Number by a Unit Fraction
$4 \div \frac{1}{3}$
$= 4 \times 3$
$= 12$
Solve Real-World Problems

Chapter Review/Test

Vocabulary

Choose the correct word.

product
common factor
proper fraction
improper fraction
mixed number
reciprocal

1. A fraction whose numerator is greater than the denominator is called an ____.

2. A number that has a whole number part and a fractional part is called a ____.

3. When the same number is a factor of two numbers, it is called a ____.

4. The ____ of $\frac{9}{1}$ or 9 is $\frac{1}{9}$.

Concepts and Skills

Multiply the fractions. Express the product in simplest form.

5. $\frac{1}{2} \times \frac{4}{7}$ ____

6. $\frac{2}{3} \times \frac{9}{10}$ ____

7. $\frac{3}{8} \times \frac{2}{5}$ ____

8. $\frac{11}{3} \times \frac{1}{4}$ ____

Multiply the fractions. Express the product as a whole number or a mixed number in simplest form.

9. $\frac{20}{6} \times \frac{12}{5}$ ____

10. $\frac{16}{9} \times \frac{12}{8}$ ____

Multiply. Express the product as a whole number or a mixed number in simplest form.

11. $5\frac{1}{4} \times 8$ ____

12. $14 \times 3\frac{5}{6}$ ____

13. $17 \times 2\frac{5}{8}$ ____

Divide. Express the quotient in simplest form.

14. $\frac{2}{9} \div 4$

15. $\frac{7}{12} \div 2$

16. $\frac{3}{10} \div 9$

17. $\frac{15}{19} \div 5$

18. $6 \div \frac{1}{4}$

19. $5 \div \frac{1}{5}$

20. $10 \div \frac{1}{2}$

21. $6 \div \frac{1}{8}$

Problem Solving

Solve. Show your work.

22. Pat has some T-shirts. $\frac{1}{4}$ of the T-shirts are pink, $\frac{1}{2}$ of the remainder are white, and the rest are purple.
What fraction of the T-shirts are purple?

23. Donald works $1\frac{3}{4}$ hours a day at a book store. If he is paid $9 an hour, how much money does he earn in 5 days?

24. Jody has a rectangular piece of fabric $\frac{7}{8}$ yard long and $\frac{4}{5}$ yard wide.
    a. What is the area of the piece of fabric?
    b. Jody decides to share the piece of fabric equally with her friend. What is the area of the piece of fabric each person gets?

25. Of the total number of spectators at a circus show, $\frac{1}{4}$ are men. $\frac{2}{5}$ of the remaining spectators are women. There are 132 women at the circus show. How many children are at the circus show?

Algebra

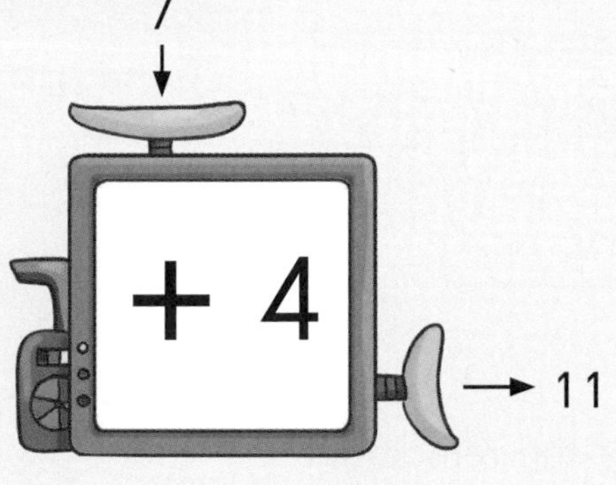

This machine adds 4 to the number put in.

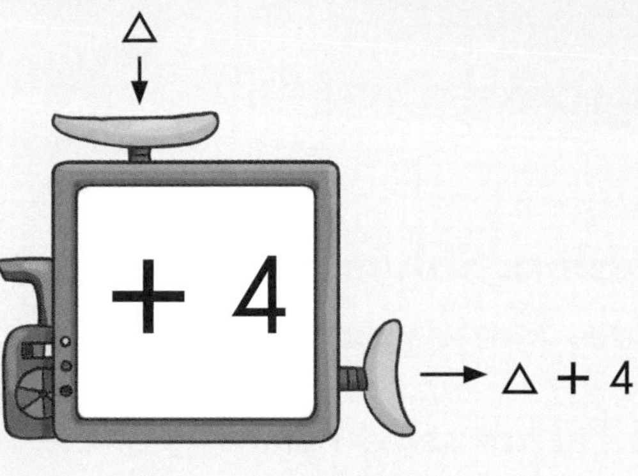

This machine multiplies the number put in by 3.

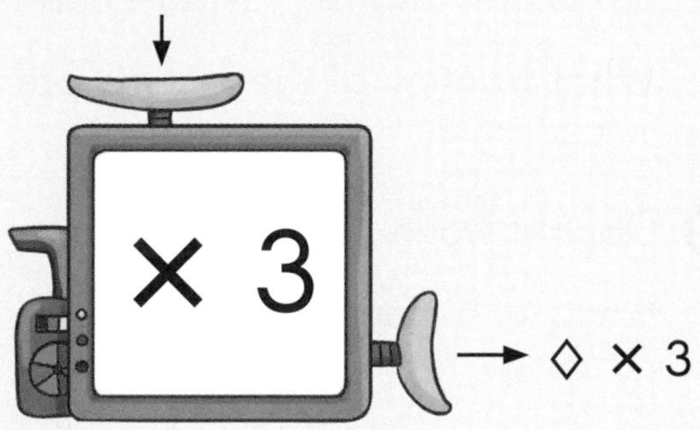

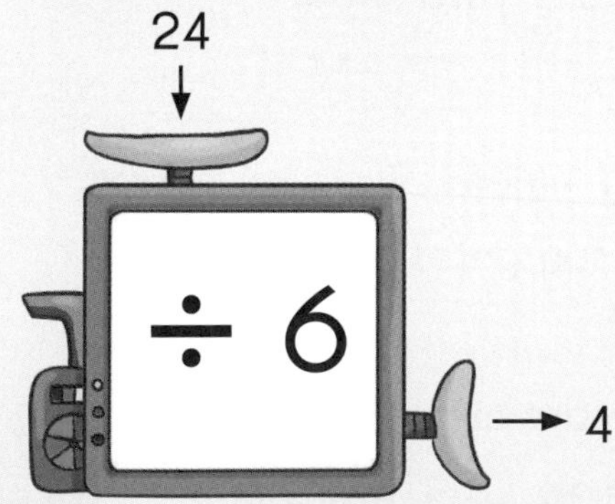

What does this machine do?

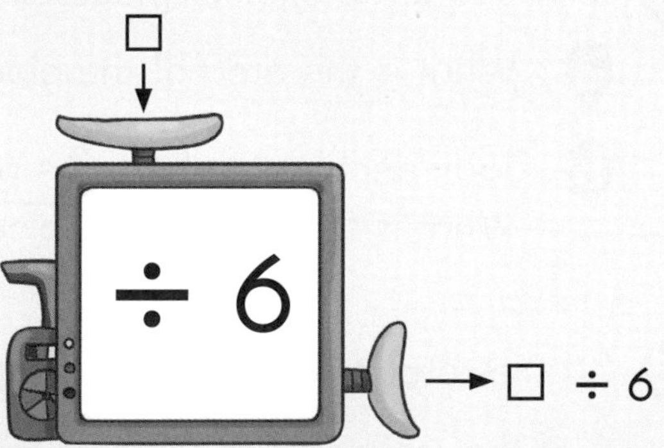

Lessons

5.1 Number Patterns and Relationships
5.2 Using Letters as Numbers
5.3 Simplifying Algebraic Expressions
5.4 Inequalities and Equations
5.5 Real-World Problems: Algebra

BIG IDEA

- Algebraic expressions can be used to describe situations and solve real-world problems.

Recall Prior Knowledge

Comparing numbers with symbols

Symbol	Meaning	Example
$=$	is equal to	$4 + 6 = 10 \rightarrow 4 + 6$ is equal to 10.
$>$	is greater than	$15 > 6 \rightarrow 15$ is greater than 6.
$<$	is less than	$4 < 10 \rightarrow 4$ is less than 10.

Multiplication is the same as repeated addition.

8	8	8	8

$8 + 8 + 8 + 8 = 4 \times 8$

Number properties

1. Commutative properties
   $2 + 3 = 3 + 2$
   $4 \times 5 = 5 \times 4$

2. Associative properties
   $(6 + 7) + 8 = 6 + (7 + 8)$
   $(9 \times 10) \times 11 = 9 \times (10 \times 11)$

3. Identity properties
   $13 + 0 = 13$
   $14 \times 1 = 14$

4. Distributive properties
   $12 \times 2 = (10 \times 2) + (2 \times 2)$
   $9 \times 4 = (10 \times 4) - (1 \times 4)$

5. Zero property of multiplication
   $16 \times 0 = 0$

Inverse operations

Inverse operations are operations that have opposite effects.

Addition and subtraction are one pair of inverse operations.

Multiplication and division are another pair of inverse operations.

You can use inverse operations to find missing numbers.

In $\square + 7 = 15$,

$\square = 15 - 7$

$= 8$

In $\square \times 4 = 24$,

$\square = 24 \div 4$

$= 6$

Order of operations

Work inside the parentheses, then brackets, and then braces.

Multiply and divide from left to right.

Add and subtract from left to right.

First expression: **(30 + 42)** − 3 × 8 ← Perform all operations in the parentheses first.

Second expression: **72 − 3 × 8** ← Then multiply.

Third expression: 72 − **24** ← Finally, subtract.

48

Complete with =, >, or <.

1. 101 ◯ 99
2. 49 ◯ 51
3. 8 + 5 ◯ 4 + 9

Complete.

4. 7 + 7 = ____ × 7
5. 5 + 5 + 5 = ____ × 5
6. 23 + 23 = 2 ◯ 23
7. 16 + 16 + 16 + 16 = 4 ◯ 16

Write True or False.

8. 25 + 39 gives the same sum as 39 + 25. ____
9. (3 × 4) × 9 gives a different product from 3 × (4 × 9). ____
10. The sum of any number and 0 is the same number. ____
11. 64 × 9 is the same as (60 × 9) − (4 × 9). ____
12. The product of any number and 0 is 0. ____

Find the missing number.

13. 7 + ____ = 11
14. ____ − 3 = 18
15. 6 × ____ = 54
16. ____ ÷ 6 = 10

Simplify each expression.

17. 2 + (8 − 3) × 4 ____
18. (12 − 8) ÷ 4 + 5 ____

Lesson 5.1 Number Patterns and Relationships

Lesson Objectives

- Identify and extend number patterns.
- Identify the relationship between two sets of numbers.

Vocabulary
number pattern
term

Learn Identify and extend a number pattern.

Look at this number pattern.

a 1, 3, 9, 27, ...

The first **term** is 1.
The second term is $3 = 1 \times 3$.
The third term is $9 = 3 \times 3$.
The fourth term is $27 = 9 \times 3$.
The fifth term will be $27 \times 3 = 81$.
The sixth term will be $81 \times 3 = 243$.

Multiply each term by 3 to get the next term.

Here is another number pattern.

b 1, 3, 6, 10, 15, ...

The first term is 1.
The second term is $3 = 1 + 2$.
The third term is $6 = (1 + 2) + 3$.
The fourth term is $10 = (1 + 2 + 3) + 4$.
The fifth term is $15 = (1 + 2 + 3 + 4) + 5$.
The sixth term will be $21 = (1 + 2 + 3 + 4 + 5) + 6$.
The seventh term will be $28 = (1 + 2 + 3 + 4 + 5 + 6) + 7$.

To get the eighth term, add 8 to the seventh term.

To get the twelfth term, add 12 to the eleventh term.

Guided Learning

1. Find the next three terms in number pattern (a).

2. Find the next four terms in number pattern (b).

Learn: Identify the relationship between two sets of numbers.

(a) Look at this table.

Rico's Age (yr)	11	12	13	14	15
His Sister's Age (yr)	8	9	10	11	12

To get his sister's age, subtract 3 from Rico's age.

The table shows that Rico's sister is 3 years younger than him.

(b) Here is another table.

Length of Side of Square (cm)	1	2	3	4	5
Perimeter of Square (cm)	4	8	12	16	20

To get the perimeter, multiply the length by 4.

This table shows that the perimeter of a square is 4 times the length of its side.

Guided Learning

Use Table (a) to answer these questions.

3. How old will his sister be when Rico is 23 years old?

4. How old will Rico be when his sister is 27 years old?

Use Table (b) to answer these questions.

5. What is the perimeter of a square with a side 17 centimeters long?

6. What is the length of each side of a square with a perimeter of 52 centimeters?

Hands-On Activity

WORK IN PAIRS

STEP 1 Draw the next three rectangular arrays of circles. In each array, the number of circles on the longer side is one more than the number of circles on the shorter side.

○○ ○○○
   ○○○

What are the first 5 terms in this number pattern?

STEP 2 A car is traveling at constant speed. You and your partner should each choose a different speed for the car. Then copy and complete the table below.

Time (h)	1	2	3	4	5
Distance Traveled (km)					

Based on your table, ask two questions for your partner to answer.

Let's Practice

Find the next three terms of each number pattern.

1. 2, 8, 32, 128, ...

2. 64, 32, 16, 8, ...

3. 1, 4, 9, 16, ...

4. $\frac{1}{2}, \frac{1}{4}, \frac{1}{6}, \frac{1}{8}, \frac{1}{10}, \ldots$

5. Complete the table and answer the questions that follow.

Number of Pens	1	2	3	4	5
Cost of Each ($)	1.50				

6. What is the cost of
   a. 8 pens?
   b. 14 pens?

7. How many pens cost
   a. $16.50?
   b. $33?

8. The width of a rectangle is 6 centimeters. Complete the table and answer the questions that follow.

Length of Rectangle (cm)	7	8	9	10	11
Area of Rectangle (sq cm)	42				

9. What is the area of a rectangle when its length is
   a. 15 centimeters?
   b. 12.5 centimeters?

10. What is the length of a rectangle when its area is
    a. 108 square centimeters?
    b. 69 square centimeters?

11. Write the first five terms of the number pattern that is all the multiples of 7. To get the sixth term, do you add or multiply the fifth term by 7? Explain your reasoning.

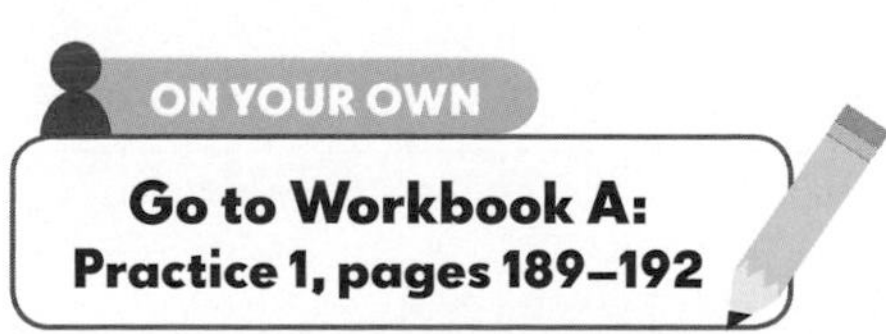
ON YOUR OWN
Go to Workbook A:
Practice 1, pages 189–192

Lesson

5.2 Using Letters as Numbers

Lesson Objective

- Recognize, write, and evaluate simple algebraic expressions in one variable.

Vocabulary

variable	numerical expression
evaluate	algebraic expression

Learn

Write a numerical expression to show how numbers in a situation are related.

Randy is now 12 years old.

a Write an expression to show Randy's age one year from now.

	Randy's age (in years)
Now	12
1 year from now	12 + 1 = 13

An expression is a number or group of numbers with operation symbols.

Randy's age one year from now is (12 + 1) or 13 years.

b Write an expression to show Randy's age two years ago.

	Randy's age (in years)
Now	12
1 year ago	12 − 1
2 years ago	12 − 2 = 10

Randy's age two years ago was (12 − 2) or 10 years.

Learn Use variables to represent unknown numbers and form expressions involving addition and subtraction.

Mr. Haskin is a fifth-grade teacher. His students do not know his age.

a Write an expression to show Mr. Haskin's age one year from now.

I do not know Mr. Haskin's age. How can I write an expression to show his age one year from now?
You can use a letter, called a variable, to represent the unknown number. You can then write an expression for Mr. Haskin's age in the same way as if you know it.

Let x stand for Mr. Haskin's age now (in years).

	Mr. Haskin's age (in years)
Now	x
1 year from now	$x + 1$

Mr. Haskin's age one year from now is $(x + 1)$ years.

A variable can take on different values. x is a variable, so it can take on different values. If Mr. Haskin is 47 years old, then x is 47. If Mr. Haskin is 38 years old, then x is 38.

b Write an expression to show Mr. Haskin's age two years ago. Use the same variable, x.

	Mr. Haskin's age (in years)
Now	x
1 year ago	$x - 1$
2 years ago	$x - 2$

Mr. Haskin's age two years ago was $(x - 2)$ years.

$x + 1$, $x - 1$ and $x - 2$ are examples of **algebraic expressions** in terms of x.

An algebraic expression is an expression that contains at least one variable.

Guided Learning

Complete.

1. What is Mr. Haskin's age in terms of x?

	Mr. Haskin's Age (in Years)
Now	x
4 years from now	
10 years from now	
5 years ago	
8 years ago	

Learn A variable can be used in place of a number in an algebraic expression.

a. Add 2 to 6.
$6 + 2$

b. Add x to 6.
$6 + x$

c. Subtract 3 from 4.
$4 - 3$

d. Subtract 3 from y.
$y - 3$

e. Find 4 more than 8.
$8 + 4$

f. Find x more than 8.
$8 + x$

g. Find 5 less than 9.
$9 - 5$

h. Find 5 less than y.
$y - 5$

Guided Learning

Write the algebraic expression for each of the following.

2. Add 5 to z.
3. Add z to 8.
4. Subtract 7 from z.
5. Subtract z from 10.
6. Find 9 more than z.
7. Find z more than 9.
8. Find 11 less than z.
9. Find z less than 11.

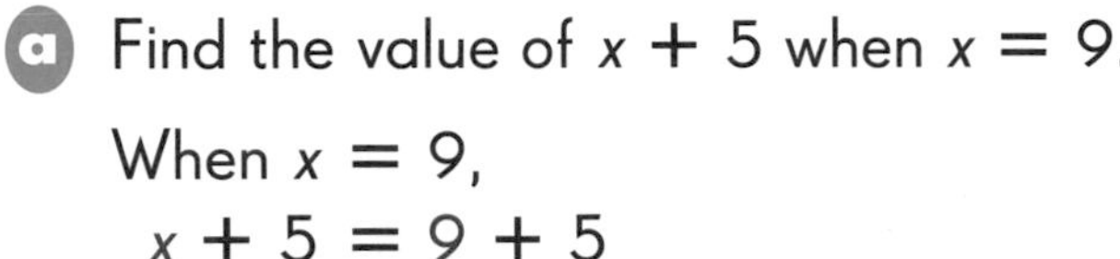

Algebraic expressions can be evaluated for given values of the variable.

a Find the value of $x + 5$ when $x = 9$.

When $x = 9$,
$$x + 5 = 9 + 5$$
$$= 14$$

b Find the value of $5 + x$ when $x = 23$.

When $x = 23$,
$$5 + x = 5 + 23$$
$$= 28$$

c Find the value of $y - 7$ when $y = 15$.

When $y = 15$,
$$y - 7 = 15 - 7$$
$$= 8$$

d Find the value of $30 - y$ when $y = 7$.

When $y = 7$,
$$30 - y = 30 - 7$$
$$= 23$$

To evaluate an expression for a given value of the variable, substitute the given value for the variable and then find the value of the expression.

Guided Learning

Complete. Evaluate each algebraic expression for the given values of *x*.

10

Expression	Value of Expression When	
	$x = 8$	$x = 30$
$x + 4$	$8 + 4 = 12$	$30 + 4 = 34$
$12 + x$		
$x - 6$		
$40 - x$		

Learn Use variables to form expressions involving multiplication.

A box has 12 plums. How many plums are in 2 such boxes?

$2 \times 12 = 24$

2 — Number of boxes
12 — Number of plums in each box

There are (2×12) or 24 plums in 2 such boxes.

A box has n plums.

a How many plums are in 2 such boxes?

$2 \times n = 2 \times n$

2 — Number of boxes
n — Number of plums in each box

There are $(2 \times n)$ plums in 2 such boxes.

b How many plums are in 3 such boxes?

$3 \times n = 3 \times n$

3 — Number of boxes
n — Number of plums in each box

There are $(3 \times n)$ plums in 3 such boxes.

Write $2 \times n$ as $2n$ and $3 \times n$ as $3n$.

The expressions $2n$ and $3n$ are examples of algebraic expressions involving multiplication in terms of n.

> $2n$ and $3n$ are how $2 \times n$ and $3 \times n$ are written in algebra.

$3n$ is $3 \times n$ or 3 groups of n or $n \times 3$ or n groups of 3.

$1 \times n = n \times 1$
$= 1n$
$= n$

$12p$ is $12 \times p$ or 12 groups of p or $p \times 12$ or p groups of 12.

Guided Learning

Write each of the following in at least three other ways.

11 $4k$

12 $7 \times j$

13 5 groups of p

14 q groups of 8

Complete.

15 There are n stickers in 1 package. Find the number of stickers in terms of n. Then, find the number of stickers for the given values of n.

Number of Packages	Number of Stickers	Number of Stickers When	
		$n = 15$	$n = 20$
1	n	15	20
4			
7			
10			
15			

To find the number of stickers for any value of n, substitute the value of n into the expression for the number of stickers. Then, find the value of the expression.

Learn Use variables to form expressions involving division.

A carton has 6 juice boxes. The boxes are put into 2 equal groups. How many boxes are in each group?

$$6 \div 2 = 3$$

6 ↑ Number of juice boxes

2 ↑ Number of groups

There are $(6 \div 2)$ or 3 juice boxes in each group.

A carton has m juice boxes.

a If the juice boxes are put into 2 equal groups, how many boxes are in each group?

$$m \div 2$$

m ↑ Number of juice boxes

2 ↑ Number of groups

There are $(m \div 2)$ juice boxes in each group.

b If the juice boxes are put into 3 equal groups, how many boxes are in each group?

$$m \div 3$$

m ↑ Number of juice boxes

3 ↑ Number of groups

There are $(m \div 3)$ juice boxes in each group.

Write $m \div 2$ as $\frac{m}{2}$ and $m \div 3$ as $\frac{m}{3}$.

The expressions $\frac{m}{2}$ and $\frac{m}{3}$ are examples of algebraic expressions involving division in terms of m.

$\frac{m}{2}$ and $\frac{m}{3}$ are how $m \div 2$ and $m \div 3$ are written in algebra.

$\frac{m}{1}$ is equal to m.

$\frac{s}{6}$ means $s \div 6$.

Guided Learning

Complete.

16 A package of m pretzel sticks is to be shared equally among some children. Find the number of pretzel sticks each child gets in terms of m. Then, find the number of pretzel sticks for the given values of m.

Number of Children	Number of Pretzel Sticks Each Child Gets	Number of Pretzel Sticks Each Child Gets When	
		$m = 24$	$m = 48$
1	m	24	48
3	$\frac{m}{3}$	$\frac{24}{3} = 8$	
6	$\frac{\square}{\square}$		
8	$\frac{\square}{\square}$		
12	$\frac{\square}{\square}$		

17 Find the expression that belongs to each box in terms of p. For each circle on the right, find the value of the expression in the box next to it when $p = 6$.

$p \xrightarrow{\times 1} p \xrightarrow{+7} p + 7 \xrightarrow{\text{when } p = 6}$ ○

$3 \xrightarrow{\times p} \square \xrightarrow{-8} \square \xrightarrow{\text{when } p = 6}$ ○

$p \xrightarrow{+4} \square \xrightarrow{\div 2} \square \xrightarrow{\text{when } p = 6}$ ○

$p \xrightarrow{\div 2} \square \xrightarrow{+2} \square \xrightarrow{\text{when } p = 6}$ ○

$11 \xrightarrow{-p} \square \xrightarrow{\div 5} \square \xrightarrow{\text{when } p = 6}$ ○

Find the value of each expression when $r = 1{,}728$.

18 $23r - 89$

19 $\frac{11{,}640 - r}{28}$

20 $\frac{11r}{24} + 2{,}399$

21 $\frac{14r + 7{,}392}{32}$

Hands-On Activity

WORK IN PAIRS

Materials:
- 5 letter cards
- 5 number cards

STEP 1 Choose one letter card and one number card.

STEP 2 Write as many algebraic expressions as you can with the two cards. For example, if you draw the cards x and 8, you can write: '$x + 8$', '$8 + x$', '$x - 8$', '$8 - x$', '$8x$', '$\frac{x}{8}$' and '$\frac{8}{x}$'.

STEP 3 Repeat STEP 1 and STEP 2 until all the cards have been chosen.

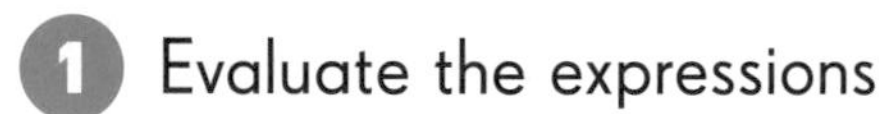

Let's Explore!

1. Evaluate the expressions:

   a. $\frac{y}{2}$ b. $\frac{1}{2} \times y$

   for $y = 6$ and $y = 14$.

   Choose any other three values for y and use your calculator to evaluate the expressions. What can you conclude about the expressions?

2. Evaluate the expressions:

   a. $\frac{y - 2}{3}$ b. $(y - 2) \div 3$ c. $\frac{1}{3} \times (y - 2)$

   for $y = 8$ and $y = 17$.

   Choose any other three values for y and use your calculator to evaluate the expressions. What can you conclude about the expressions?

3. Write the expression $(x + 4) \div 6$ in two other ways.

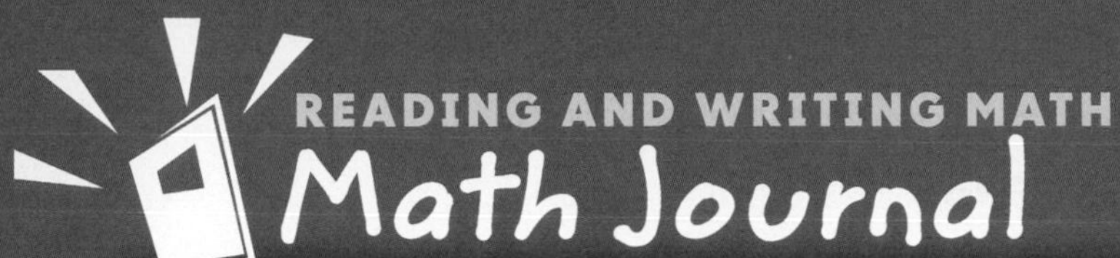

Write two real-world problems that can be described by these expressions.

1. $m - 20$
2. $5m$

Let's Practice

Write each expression in one or two other ways.

1. $5 \times w$
2. $v \times 15$
3. $x \div 3$
4. $\frac{1}{4} \times y$
5. $\frac{z + 4}{5}$
6. $\frac{1}{2} \times (a - 7)$

Write an expression for each of the following.

7. Add *b* to 9.
8. Subtract 4 from *b*.
9. Subtract *b* from 10.
10. Multiply *b* by 3.
11. Multiply 7 by *b*.
12. Divide *b* by 5.
13. Half of *b*.
14. Add 10 to *b*, then divide by 7.
15. Multiply *b* by 6, then subtract 11.
16. Divide *b* by 3, then add 8.

Write an expression in terms of x for each of the following. Then evaluate the expression when $x = 18$.

John is now x years old.

17. The age of his brother, who is 5 years older.
18. The age of his sister, who is 3 years younger.
19. The age of his aunt, who is twice as old as him.
20. The age of his cousin, who is half his age.

Write an expression in terms of n for each of the following. Then evaluate the expression when $n = 24$.

There are n strawberries in a carton.

21. The number of strawberries left after 6 pieces have been eaten.
22. The number of strawberries each child gets when the carton of strawberries is shared equally among 4 children.
23. The total number of strawberries in 10 similar cartons.
24. The number of strawberries each child gets when one carton and 11 strawberries are shared equally among 5 children.

Evaluate each expression when $y = 18{,}324$.

25. $y + 967$
26. $y - 1{,}259$
27. $25{,}283 - y$
28. $5y$
29. $y \div 4$

ON YOUR OWN

Go to Workbook A: Practice 2, pages 193–200

Lesson

5.3 Simplifying Algebraic Expressions

Lesson Objective

- Simplify algebraic expressions in one variable.

Vocabulary
simplify   like terms

Learn Algebraic expressions can be simplified.

A rod of length a centimeters is joined to another rod of the same length. What is the total length of the 2 rods?

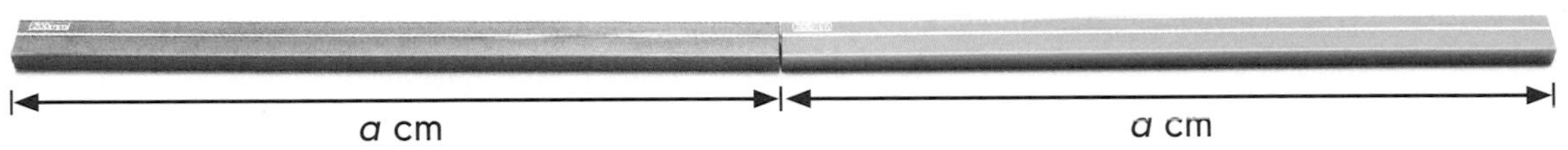

a cm a cm

$a + a = 2 \times a$

Simplify $(a + a)$ by writing:

$a + a = 2a$

The total length of the 2 rods is $2a$ centimeters.

3	3

$3 + 3 = 2 \times 3$

4	4

$4 + 4 = 2 \times 4$

a	a

$a + a = 2 \times a$

$2 \times a$ is the same as $2a$.

The picture shows 3 rods, each b centimeters long. What is the total length of the 3 rods?

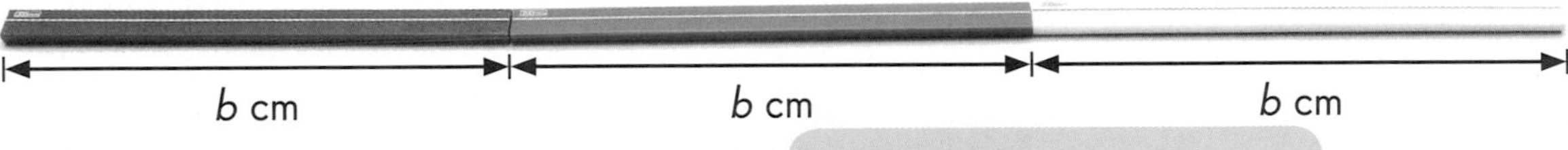

b cm b cm b cm

$b + b + b = 3 \times b$

Simplify $(b + b + b)$ by writing:

$b + b + b = 3b$

5	5	5

$5 + 5 + 5 = 3 \times 5$

b	b	b

$b + b + b = 3 \times b$

$3 \times b$ is the same as $3b$.

The total length of the 3 rods is $3b$ centimeters.

Continued on next page

The figure shows 5 sticks, each r centimeters long.
What is the total length of the 5 sticks?

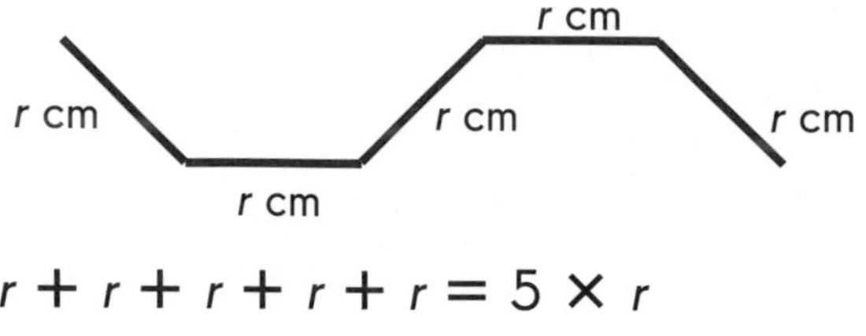

$r + r + r + r + r = 5 \times r$
$= 5r$

r	r	r	r	r

$r + r + r + r + r = 5 \times r$

$5 \times r$ is the same as $5r$.

The total length of the 5 sticks is $5r$ centimeters.

Guided Learning

Simplify each expression.

1. $x + x$
2. $y + y + y$
3. $a + a + a + a + a$
4. $b + b + b + b + b + b$
5. $c + c + c + c + c + c + c$

Learn **Like terms can be added.**

Simplify $a + 2a$.

$a + 2a = a + a + a$
$= 3a$

a	a	a

(a | $2a$)

a and $2a$ are the terms of the expression, $a + 2a$. You call a and $2a$ like terms.

Guided Learning

Complete.

6. Simplify $2a + 3a$.

$2a + 3a =$

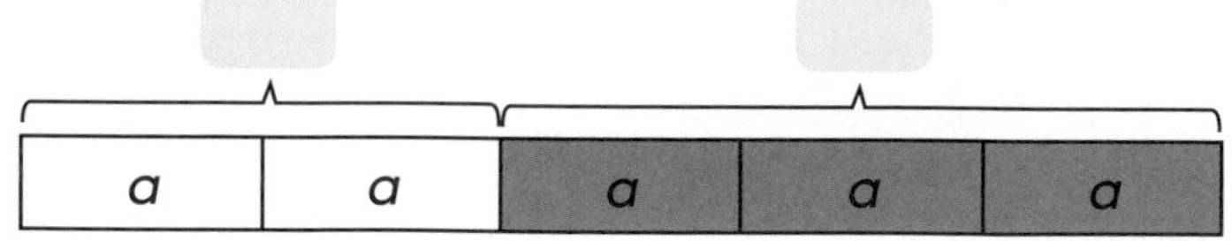

Simplify each expression.

7. $a + 3a$
8. $4x + x$
9. $2z + 5z$
10. $3y + 6y$
11. $b + 2b + 3b$
12. $4c + 2c + 10c$

Learn A variable subtracted from itself results in zero.

A ribbon is a centimeters long. Jenny uses the whole ribbon to decorate a present.
How much ribbon is left?

$a - a = 0$

There are 0 centimeters of ribbon left.

Compare this with:
$2 - 2 = 0$
$7 - 7 = 0$
$14 - 14 = 0$

Guided Learning

Simplify each expression.

13 $x - x$ ____

14 $2y - 2y$ ____

15 $10z - 10z$ ____

Learn Like terms can be subtracted.

Simplify $3a - a$.

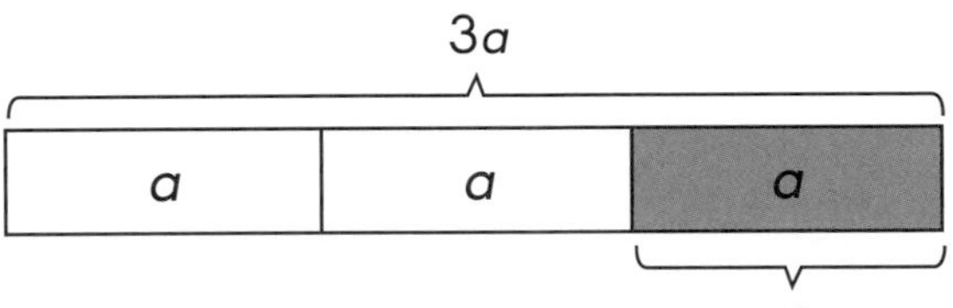

$3a - a = 2a$

From the model,
$3a - a = a + a$
$a + a = 2 \times a = 2a$
So, $3a - a = 2a$

Simplify $4a - 2a$.

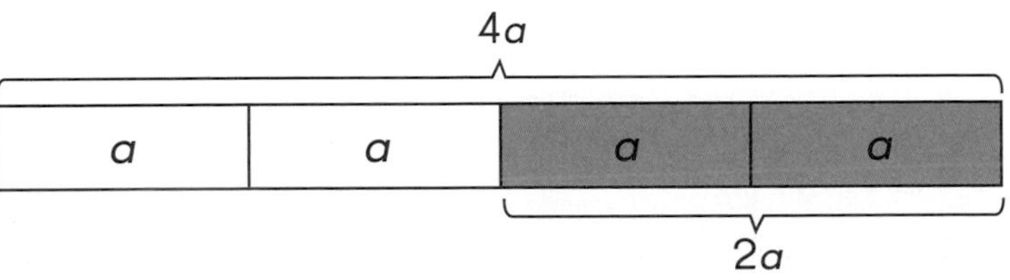

$4a - 2a = 2a$

From the model,
$4a - 2a = a + a$
$a + a = 2 \times a = 2a$
So, $4a - 2a = 2a$

Guided Learning

Complete.

16 Simplify $5a - 2a$.

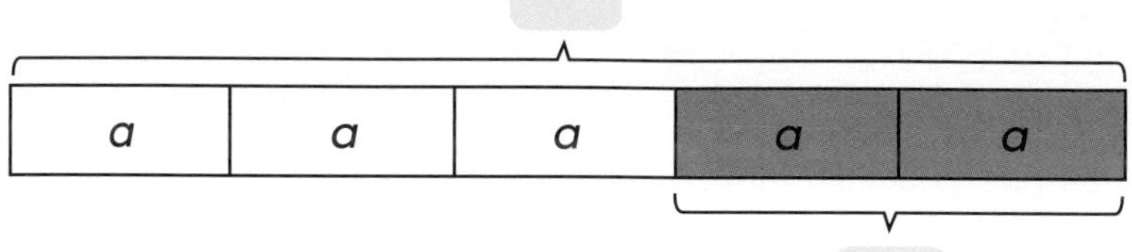

$5a - 2a =$ ___

Simplify each expression.

17 $4a - a$ ___

18 $7a - 3a$ ___

19 $5x - 4x$ ___

20 $10x - 6x$ ___

21 $8y - 3y - 5y$ ___

22 $12y - 7y - y$ ___

Learn Use the order of operations to simplify algebraic expressions.

a Simplify $6a + 3a - 2a$.

Working from left to right,

$$6a + 3a - 2a = 9a - 2a$$
$$= 7a$$

b Simplify $6a - 2a + 3a$.

Working from left to right,

$$6a - 2a + 3a = 4a + 3a$$
$$= 7a$$

Guided Learning

Simplify each expression.

23 $2x + 3x - 4x$ ___

24 $x + 5x - 6x$ ___

25 $9a - 3a + 4a$ ___

26 $12a - 7a + 2a$ ___

Learn: Collect like terms to simplify algebraic expressions.

Find the distance between point A and point B.

$a + 4 + a + 2$ ← Identify like terms.

$= a + a + 4 + 2$ ← Change the order of terms to collect like terms. Then simplify.

$= 2a + 6$

The distance between point A and point B is $(2a + 6)$ kilometers.

Commutative Property of Addition:

Two numbers can be added in any order.

So, $4 + a = a + 4$.

Simplify $4x + 6 - 2x$.

$4x + 6 - 2x$ ← Identify like terms.

$= 6 + 4x - 2x$ ← Change the order of terms to collect like terms. Then simplify.

$= 6 + 2x$

$4x + 6 = 6 + 4x$

Guided Learning

Simplify each expression.

27. $b + 5 + b + 5$ ☐

28. $3b + 4b + 2 + 6$ ☐

29. $5s + 9 - 3s$ ☐

30. $8s + 6 - 2s - 1$ ☐

Hands-On Activity

Materials:

- 20 craft sticks

Let the length of each craft stick equal p units.

STEP 1 Form a closed figure using 3 or more craft sticks.

Example

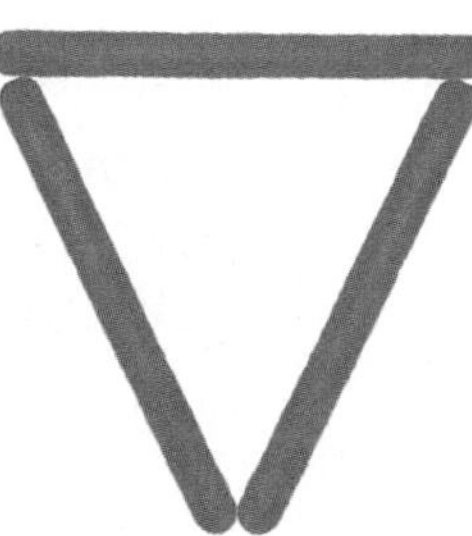

STEP 2 Write the total length of the craft sticks used.

Example

Total length of craft sticks $= p + p + p$

$= 3p$ units

STEP 3 Remove, then add craft sticks to form another figure.

Example

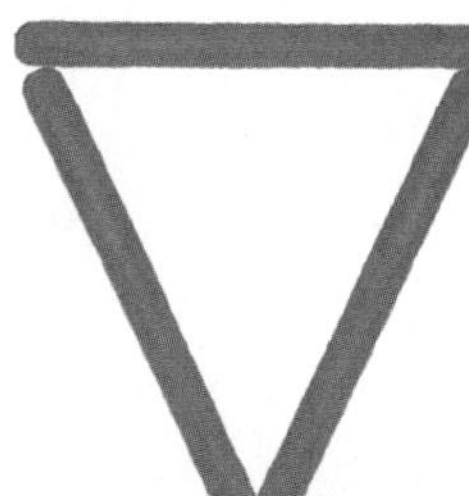

remove 1 craft stick,
add 3 craft sticks

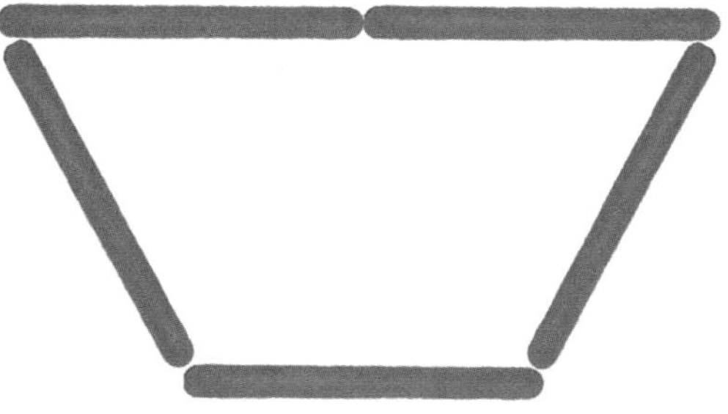

STEP 4 Write the total length of the craft sticks used in the new figure. Subtract the total length of the craft sticks removed and add the total length of the craft sticks added.

Example

To form a second figure, 1 craft stick was removed and 3 craft sticks were added.

Total length of craft sticks $= 3p - p + 3p$

$= 5p$ units

STEP 5 Check your answer in STEP 4 by counting the number of craft sticks used in the new figure to find the total length.

Example

Total number of craft sticks used = 5

Total length of craft sticks = $5 \times p$

$= 5p$ units

STEP 6 Repeat the activity with other figures.

Let's Practice

Simplify each expression.

1. $2a + 5a$
2. $a + 7a$
3. $3a + 3a + 6a$
4. $4x - 2x$
5. $6x - 5x$
6. $10x - 2x - 8x$
7. $7y - 5y + 4y$
8. $9y + 3y - 5y$
9. $a + a + 5$
10. $b + 4 + 4 + b$
11. $2s + 7 - 6 + s$
12. $9r + 10 + 2 - 3r$

ON YOUR OWN

Go to Workbook A:
Practice 3, pages 201–204

Lesson

5.4 Inequalities and Equations

Lesson Objectives

- Write and evaluate inequalities.
- Solve simple equations.

Vocabulary

inequality	equation
solve	true
equality properties	

Learn

Algebraic expressions can be used in inequalities and equations.

Serena buys 2 bags of apples and 1 bag of 8 oranges. Each bag has the same number of apples. Are there more oranges or apples?

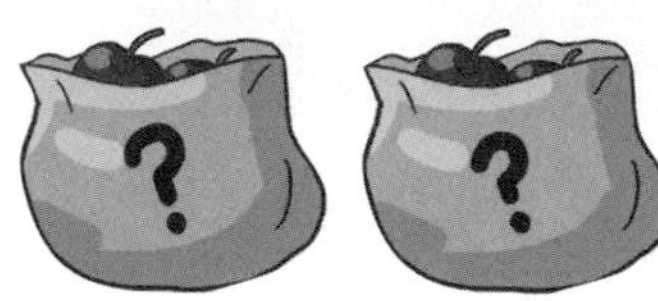

Let each bag of apples contain x apples.

$x + x = 2x$

There are $2x$ apples.

To compare $2x$ and 8, you need to know the value of x.

When $x = 3$, $2x = 2 \times 3 = 6$

$6 < 8$, so $2x < 8$.

When $x = 3$, there are more oranges than apples.

When $x = 4$, $2x = 2 \times 4 = 8$

$8 = 8$, so $2x = 8$.

When $x = 4$, there is the same number of oranges and apples.

When $x = 5$, $2x = 2 \times 5 = 10$

$10 > 8$, so $2x > 8$.

When $x = 5$, there are more apples than oranges.

The statement $2x = 8$ is an equation.
The statements $2x < 8$ and $2x > 8$ are inequalities.

Guided Learning

Complete with >, <, or =.

1. When $y = 6$, $3y$ ◯ 18.
2. When $y = 10$, $3y$ ◯ 18.
3. When $y = 5$, $3y$ ◯ 18.
4. When $y = 9$, $3y$ ◯ 18.

Learn

Algebraic expressions can be compared by evaluating them for a given value of the variable.

When $b = 8$, is $4b - 6$ greater than, less than, or equal to 26?

Evaluate the expression to compare:

When $b = 8$,

$$\begin{aligned} 4b - 6 &= (4 \times 8) - 6 \\ &= 32 - 6 \\ &= 26 \end{aligned}$$

$26 = 26$

So, when $b = 8$, $4b - 6 = 26$.

Two expressions that have the same value are said to be equal.
When two equal expressions are related by an '=' sign, they form an equation.

When $c = 15$, is $3c \div 5$ greater than, less than, or equal to $c - 8$?

Evaluate both expressions to compare:

When $c = 15$,

$$\begin{aligned} 3c \div 5 &= (3 \times 15) \div 5 \\ &= 45 \div 5 \\ &= 9 \end{aligned}$$

$$\begin{aligned} c - 8 &= 15 - 8 \\ &= 7 \end{aligned}$$

$9 > 7$

So, when $c = 15$, $3c \div 5 > c - 8$.

When two expressions with different values are related by an '>' or '<' sign, they form an inequality.

Guided Learning

Complete.

5 When $d = 6$, is $2d + 10$ greater than, less than, or equal to $4d$?

When $d = 6$, $2d + 10 = (2 \times \underline{\quad}) + 10$ $\qquad$ $4d = 4 \times \underline{\quad}$

$= \underline{\quad} + 10$ $\qquad$ $= \underline{\quad}$

$= \underline{\quad}$

So, $2d + 10$ is ___ $4d$, when $d = 6$.

Complete with >, <, or =.

6 When $e = 4$, $3e \div 6$ ___ $e - 2$.

7 When $f = 9$, $8f - 4$ ___ $6f + 10$.

Learn

Equality properties

You can add the same number to or subtract the same number from both sides of an equation. The new equation will still be **true** for the same value of variable.

Look at the balance.

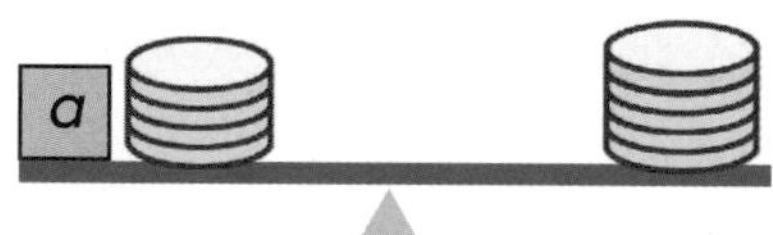

(counter) represents 1.

a represents a counters.

a counters together with 4 counters on the left side balance 5 counters on the right side.

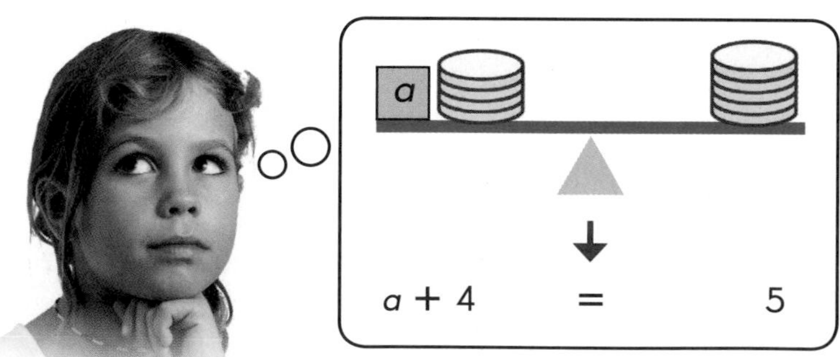

You have the equation $a + 4 = 5$.
Compare $a + 4 = 5$ with $1 + 4 = 5$. You can see that $a = 1$.
This equation is true for $a = 1$.

a Add 2 counters to both sides of the equation.
The two sides still balance.

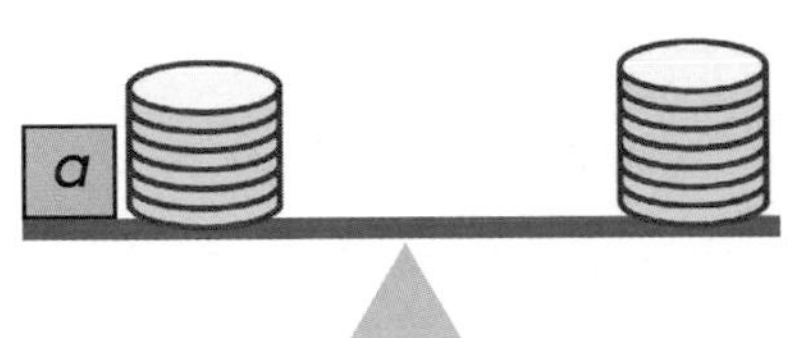

You have a new equation:
$a + 4 + 2 = 5 + 2$, that is, $a + 6 = 7$.

Substitute 1 for a:
$a + 6 = 1 + 6 = 7$

The new equation $a + 6 = 7$ is still true for $a = 1$.

b Take away 2 counters from both sides of the equation.
The two sides still balance.

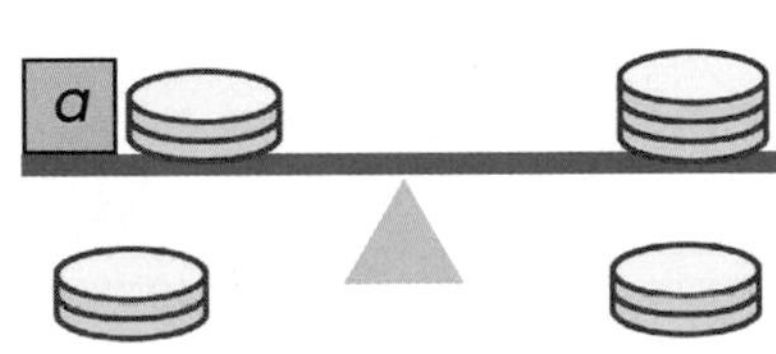

You have a new equation:
$a + 4 - 2 = 5 - 2$, that is, $a + 2 = 3$.

Substitute 1 for a:
$a + 2 = 1 + 2 = 3$

The new equation $a + 2 = 3$ is still true for $a = 1$.

You can multiply or divide both sides of an equation by the same nonzero number. The new equation will still be true for the same value of the variable.

Look at the balance.

$4a$ counters on the left side balance 8 counters on the right side.

You have the equation, $4a = 8$. Compare $4a = 8$ with $4 \times 2 = 8$.
You can see that $a = 2$. This equation is true for $a = 2$.

a Multiply the number of counters on both sides by 2.
The two sides still balance.

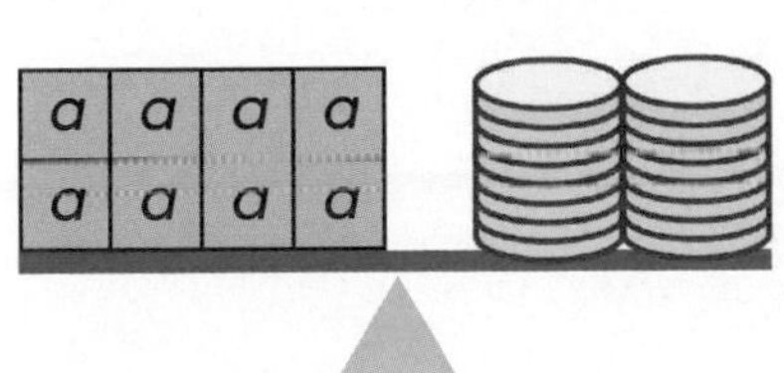

You have a new equation:
$4a \times 2 = 8 \times 2$, that is, $8a = 16$.

Substitute 2 for a:
$8a = 8 \times 2 = 16$

The new equation $8a = 16$ is still true for $a = 2$.

b Divide the number of counters on both sides by 2.
The two sides still balance.

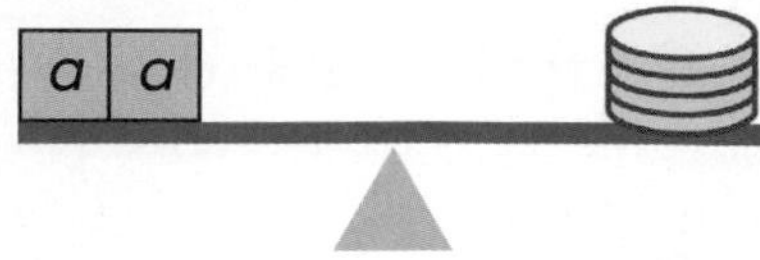

a a

You have a new equation:
$4a \div 2 = 8 \div 2$, that is, $2a = 4$.

Substitute 2 for a:
$2a = 2 \times 2 = 4$

The new equation $2a = 4$ is still true for $a = 2$.

Learn Solve equations with variables on one side of the equal sign.

For what value of y will $5y - 2 = 13$ be true?

To find the value of y that makes $5y - 2 = 13$ true, you simply need to find the value of y that makes $5y - 2$ equal to 13.

In finding the value of y that makes $5y - 2 = 13$ true, you are also said to be solving $5y - 2 = 13$.

Method 1

If $y = 2$,

$$\begin{aligned} 5y - 2 &= (5 \times 2) - 2 \\ &= 10 - 2 \\ &= 8 \\ &\neq 13 \end{aligned}$$

'$\neq$' means 'is not equal to'.

The value of $5y - 2$ is too small when $y = 2$.

Try $y = 3$.

If $y = 3$,

$$\begin{aligned} 5y - 2 &= (5 \times 3) - 2 \\ &= 15 - 2 \\ &= 13 \end{aligned}$$

$5y - 2 = 13$ is true when $y = 3$.

Method 2

'Building up': $y \xrightarrow{\times 5} 5y \xrightarrow{-2} 5y - 2$

'Breaking down': $y \xleftarrow{\div 5} 5y \xleftarrow{+2} 5y - 2$

$$5y - 2 = 13$$

$$5y - 2 + 2 = 13 + 2$$ ← Add 2 to both sides of the equation.

$$5y = 15$$

$$5y \div 5 = 15 \div 5$$ ← Divide both sides of the equation by 5.

$$y = 3$$

$5y - 2 = 13$ is true when $y = 3$.

Check!

Evaluate the expression $5y - 2$ for the value of y you have found.

$5y - 2 = (5 \times 3) - 2$
$= 15 - 2$
$= 13$

The answer is correct.

Guided Learning

Fill in ◯ with +, −, ×, or ÷ and ▭ with the correct number.

8 For what value of p will $6p + 7 = 37$ be true?

$$6p + 7 = 37$$

$$6p + 7 \bigcirc \square = 37 \bigcirc \square$$

$$6p = \square$$

$$6p \bigcirc \square = \square \bigcirc \square$$

$$p = \square$$

$6p + 7 = 37$ is true when $p = \square$.

Solve each equation.

9 $5r + 5 = 60$ ▭

10 $3q - 12 = 15$ ▭

Learn Solve equations with variables on both sides of the equal sign.

For what value of y will $6y - 7 = 2y + 9$ be true?

Guess and check.

Method 1

y	$6y - 7$	$2y + 9$	Both sides equal?
2	$6 \times 2 - 7 = 12 - 7$ $= 5$	$2 \times 2 + 9 = 4 + 9$ $= 13$	No
3	$6 \times 3 - 7 = 18 - 7$ $= 11$	$2 \times 3 + 9 = 6 + 9$ $= 15$	No
4	$6 \times 4 - 7 = 24 - 7$ $= 17$	$2 \times 4 + 9 = 8 + 9$ $= 17$	Yes

$6y - 7 = 2y + 9$ is true when $y = 4$.

Method 2

$$6y - 7 = 2y + 9$$

$$6y - 7 + 7 = 2y + 9 + 7$$ ← Add 7 to both sides of the equation.

$$6y = 2y + 16$$

$$6y - 2y = 2y - 2y + 16$$ ← Subtract $2y$ from both sides of the equation.

$$4y = 16$$

$$4y \div 4 = 16 \div 4$$ ← Divide both sides of the equation by 4.

$$y = 4$$

$6y - 7 = 2y + 9$ is true when $y = 4$.

Check!

Substitute the value of y into both sides of the equation.

Left side:

$$\begin{aligned} 6y - 7 &= 6 \times 4 - 7 \\ &= 24 - 7 \\ &= 17 \end{aligned}$$

Right side:

$$\begin{aligned} 2y + 9 &= 2 \times 4 + 9 \\ &= 8 + 9 \\ &= 17 \end{aligned}$$

$y = 4$ is the correct answer.

Solve $3p + 4 = 5p - 6$.

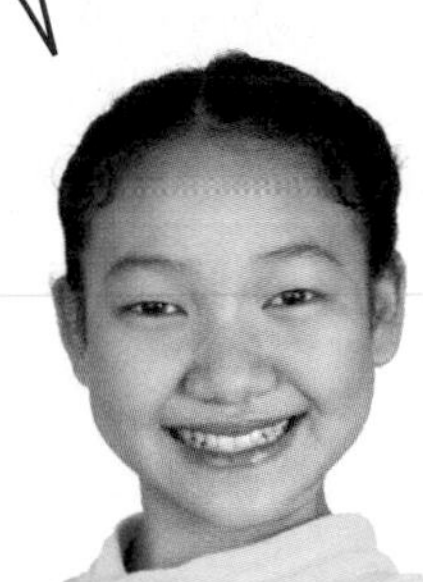

Method 1

y	$3p + 4$	$5p - 6$	Both sides equal?
2	$3 \times 2 + 4 = 6 + 4$ $= 10$	$5 \times 2 - 6 = 10 - 6$ $= 4$	No
4	$3 \times 4 + 4 = 12 + 4$ $= 16$	$5 \times 4 - 6 = 20 - 6$ $= 14$	No
5	$3 \times 5 + 4 = 15 + 4$ $= 19$	$5 \times 5 - 6 = 25 - 6$ $= 19$	Yes

$p = 5$

Method 2

$$3p + 4 = 5p - 6$$

$$3p + 4 + 6 = 5p - 6 + 6$$ ← Add 6 to both sides of the equation.

$$3p + 10 = 5p$$

$$3p - 3p + 10 = 5p - 3p$$ ← Subtract $3p$ from both sides of the equation.

$$10 = 2p$$

$$2p = 10$$

$$2p \div 2 = 10 \div 2$$ ← Divide both sides of the equation by 2.

$$p = 5$$

I can either subtract 4 from both sides of the equation or add 6 to both sides. Which do I know how to do?

Subtract 4:
$3p + 4 - 4 = 5p \underbrace{- 6 - 4}_{?}$

Add 6:
$3p + 4 + 6 = 5p - 6 + 6$

I do not know how to simplify '$- 6 - 4$'. I will add 6 to both sides instead.

Check!

Substitute the value of p into both sides of the equation.

Left side:
$3p + 4 = 3 \times 5 + 4$
$= 15 + 4$
$= 19$

Right side:
$5p - 6 = 5 \times 5 - 6$
$= 25 - 6$
$= 19$

$p = 5$ is the correct answer.

Guided Learning

Fill in $\bigcirc$ with +, −, ×, or ÷ and $\square$ with the correct number.

11 For what value of q will $8q - 7 = 5q + 11$ be true?

$$8q - 7 = 5q + 11$$
$$8q - 7 \bigcirc \square = 5q + 11 \bigcirc \square$$
$$8q = 5q \bigcirc \square$$
$$8q \bigcirc 5q = 5q \bigcirc 5q \bigcirc \square$$
$$3q = \square$$
$$3q \bigcirc \square = \square \bigcirc \square$$
$$q = \square$$

$8q - 7 = 5q + 11$ is true when $q = \square$.

12 For what value of m will $3m + 9 = 5m - 11$ be true?

$$3m + 9 = 5m - 11$$
$$3m + 9 \bigcirc \square = 5m - 11 \bigcirc \square$$
$$3m \bigcirc \square = 5m$$
$$3m \bigcirc 3m + \square = 5m \bigcirc 3m$$
$$\square = 2m$$
$$2m = \square$$
$$2m \bigcirc \square = \square \bigcirc \square$$
$$m = \square$$

$3m + 9 = 5m - 11$ is true when $m = \square$.

I can either subtract $\square$ from both sides of the equation or add $\square$ to both sides. Which do I know how to do?

Subtract $\square$:

$3m + 9 - \square = 5m - 11 - \square$

?

Add $\square$:

$3m + 9 + \square = 5m - 11 + \square$

I do not know how to simplify '$- \square \bigcirc \square$'. I will add $\square$ to both sides instead.

Let's Practice

Complete with >, <, or =.

1. When $z = 5$, $4z$ ◯ 24.
2. When $z = 8$, $4z$ ◯ 24.
3. When $z = 6$, $4z$ ◯ 24.
4. When $z = 2$, $4z$ ◯ 24.

Complete with =, >, or < for $a = 9$.

5. $a + 7$ ◯ 16
6. $2a - 5$ ◯ 11
7. $(12 + a) - 21$ ◯ 1
8. $15 - a$ ◯ $a - 2$
9. $4a \div 6$ ◯ $17 - a$
10. $13 + (72 \div a)$ ◯ $2a + 2$

Solve each equation.

11. $6j - 24 = 12$
12. $8k + 19 = 35$
13. $5m - 9 = 3m + 7$
14. $10n + 6 = 15n - 9$

Check your solution by substituting it for the variable in the given equation.

ON YOUR OWN

Go to Workbook A: Practice 4, pages 205–206

Lesson 5.5

Real-World Problems: Algebra

Lesson Objective

- Solve real-world problems involving algebraic expressions.

Learn Write an addition or subtraction expression for a real-world problem and evaluate it.

Tyrone has y compact discs (CDs). John has 3 times as many CDs as Tyrone. John buys another 7 CDs.

a) How many more CDs does John have than Tyrone?

John has $(3y + 7)$ CDs.

$$3y + 7 - y = 7 + 3y - y$$
$$= 7 + 2y$$

John has $(7 + 2y)$ more CDs than Tyrone.

b) If Tyrone has 25 CDs, how many more CDs does John have than Tyrone?

$$7 + 2y = 7 + 2 \times 25$$
$$= 7 + 50$$
$$= 57$$

John has 57 more CDs than Tyrone.

Guided Learning

Complete.

1. Ray has m dollars. Ben has \$15 more than Ray.

a) Find the amount of money they have altogether in terms of m.

Ben has ___ dollars.

They have ___ dollars altogether.

b) If Ray has \$75, how much money do they have altogether?

If $m = 75$, they have \$___ altogether.

Learn Write a multiplication or division expression for a real-world problem and evaluate it.

Salma has x dollars in her wallet. She buys a shirt for \$15 and spends the rest of her money on 3 movie tickets.

a Find the price of 1 movie ticket in terms of x.

Price of 3 movie tickets = $\$(x - 15)$

$(x - 15) \div 3 = \frac{x - 15}{3}$

The price of 1 movie ticket is $\frac{x - 15}{3}$ dollars.

b If Salma has \$39, what is the price of 1 movie ticket?

$$\begin{aligned}\frac{x - 15}{3} &= \frac{39 - 15}{3} \\ &= \frac{24}{3} \\ &= 8\end{aligned}$$

The price of 1 movie ticket is \$8.

Guided Learning

Complete.

2 A man has y dollars in his wallet. He withdraws \$200 from an ATM and spends half the total amount on groceries.

a Find the amount of money he has left in terms of y.

Total amount the man had upon withdrawing \$200 from the ATM = \$(▢)

▢ $\div 2 = \frac{▢}{▢}$

He has $\frac{▢}{▢}$ dollars left.

b If $y = 80$, how much money does he have left?

If $y = 80$, he has \$ ▢ left.

Learn Use algebraic expressions to compare quantities and solve equations.

Andy and Cathy each have some pencils. Andy has his pencils in 4 boxes. 3 of the boxes have an equal number of pencils. There are p pencils in each of the 3 boxes. The remaining box has 3 pencils fewer. Cathy has 2 boxes of pencils each with p pencils and 13 extra pencils.

a Write the number of pencils Andy and Cathy each have, in terms of p.

Andy has $3p + (p - 3)$ pencils. So, Andy has $(4p - 3)$ pencils.
Cathy has $(2p + 13)$ pencils.

b Write an inequality to show who has more pencils if $p = 9$.

If $p = 9$,

$$\begin{aligned} 4p - 3 &= (4 \times 9) - 3 \\ &= 36 - 3 \\ &= 33 \end{aligned} \qquad \begin{aligned} 2p + 13 &= (2 \times 9) + 13 \\ &= 18 + 13 \\ &= 31 \end{aligned}$$

$4p - 3 > 2p + 13$.

Andy has more pencils if $p = 9$.

c For what value of p will Andy and Cathy have the same number of pencils?

$$\begin{aligned} 4p - 3 &= 2p + 13 \\ 4p - 3 + 3 &= 2p + 13 + 3 \\ 4p &= 2p + 16 \\ 4p - 2p &= 2p + 16 - 2p \\ 2p &= 16 \\ 2p \div 2 &= 16 \div 2 \\ p &= 8 \end{aligned}$$

Andy and Cathy will have the same number of pencils, if $p = 8$.

Guided Learning

Fill in ◯ with +, −, ×, or ÷ and ▭ with the correct number.

3. Lenny has $2y - 7$ marbles. Max has $y + 9$ marbles.

   a. Write an inequality to show who has more marbles if $y = 18$.

   If $y = 18$,

   $2y - 7 = (2 \times \square) - 7$
   $= \square - 7$
   $= \square$

   $y + 9 = \square + 9$
   $= \square$

   $2y - 7 \bigcirc y + 9$

   ▭ has more marbles if $y = 18$.

   b. For what value of y will Lenny and Max have the same number of marbles?

   $2y - 7 = y + 9$
   $2y - 7 + \square = y + 9 + \square$
   $2y = y + \square$
   $2y \bigcirc \square = y + \square \bigcirc \square$
   $y = \square$

   They will have the same number of marbles if $y = \square$.

Let's Practice

Solve. Show your work.

1. José is r years old. Keith is 3 times as old as he is. Lara is 4 years younger than Keith.

   a. Find Keith's age in terms of r. ▭
   b. Find Lara's age in terms of r. ▭
   c. If $r = 5$, how old is Lara? ▭

2. Aida bought a belt for x dollars and a handbag that cost twice as much as the belt. She gave the cashier \$100.

   a. Find the amount that Aida spent in terms of x.
   b. Find the amount of change Aida received in terms of x.
   c. If $x = 15$, how much change did Aida receive?

3. Paul scored z points playing a math game. Meghan scored 4 times as many points as Paul. Kieran scored 5 more points than Meghan.

   a. Find the number of points Meghan scored in terms of z.
   b. Find the number of points Kieran scored in terms of z.
   c. Find the total number of points the three players scored in terms of z.

4. A plumber has a copper pipe and a steel pipe. The copper pipe is $(3p + 2)$ feet long and the steel pipe is $(4p - 3)$ feet long.

   a. If $p = 8$, which pipe is longer?
   b. For what value of p will the two pipes be of the same length?

5. A group of 3 friends made m bracelets. They sold the bracelets for \$14 each and shared the money equally.

   a. How much did each person get? Give your answer in terms of m.
   b. If there were 18 bracelets, how much did each person get?

6. A pail and a pitcher contain q quarts of water altogether. The pail contains 9 times as much water as the pitcher.

   a. Find the amount of water in the pitcher in terms of q.
   b. If the pail and the pitcher contain 25 quarts of water altogether, find the amount of water in the pail in quarts. Express your answer as a decimal.

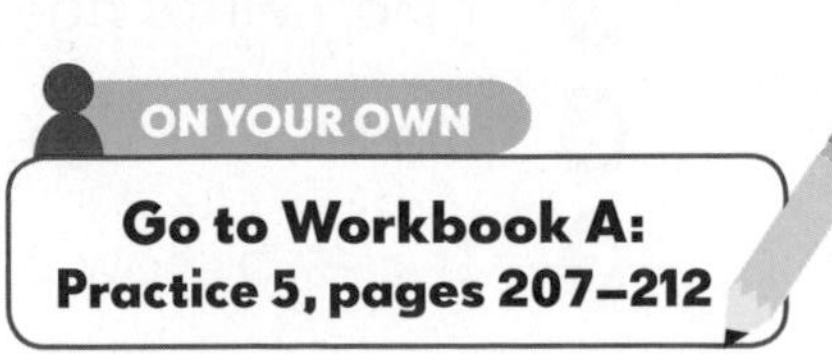
ON YOUR OWN
Go to Workbook A:
Practice 5, pages 207–212

1. Explain in words what the expression $3x$ means.

2. Rita says that $a + a = 2a$ can be thought of as:
   1 apple + 1 apple = 2 apples.
   Is her thinking correct? If not, what is the correct way to think of $a + a = 2a$?

CRITICAL THINKING SKILLS
Put On Your Thinking Cap!

PROBLEM SOLVING

Grace thinks of a number. First, she multiplies it by 2. Then, she adds 12. Finally, she subtracts twice the number that she originally thought of. What is the answer that she will get?

ON YOUR OWN

Go to Workbook A: Put on Your Thinking Cap! pages 213–214

Chapter Wrap Up

Study Guide

You have learned...

Algebraic Expressions

Number Patterns and Relationships

- Identify and extend number patterns.

  1, 6, 11, 16, ...
- Identify number relationships between two sets of numbers.

Counting numbers	1	2	3	4	5
Even numbers	2	4	6	8	10

Using Letters as Numbers

- Letters in algebra, called variables, stand for numbers.
- $x + 4$, $2y - 5$, $4z$ and $\frac{b}{3}$ are examples of algebraic expressions.
- Operations can be performed on variables.
- Algebraic expressions can be evaluated for given values of the variable.

  For $x = 4$,

  $$\begin{aligned} 2x + 3 &= (2 \times 4) + 3 \\ &= 8 + 3 \\ &= 11 \end{aligned}$$

Solve Real-World Problems

▶ Algebraic expressions can be used to describe a situation and solve real-world problems.

Simplifying Algebraic Expressions

Algebraic expressions can be simplified by adding or subtracting like terms.

$y + y + y = 3y$

$3y + 2y = 5y$

$8y + 10 - 4y - 5 = 4y + 5$

Inequalities and Equations

- Algebraic expressions can be compared by evaluating them for a given value of the variable.

  When $a = 3$, $4a + 2 > 2a + 4$
- Two equal expressions related by an '$=$' sign, form an equation.
- Two expressions related by an "$>$" or "$<$" sign, they form an inequality.
- Equations can be solved.

$$\begin{aligned} 6a - 5 &= 4a + 3 \\ 6a &= 4a + 8 \\ 2a &= 8 \\ a &= 4 \end{aligned}$$

Chapter Review/Test

Vocabulary

Choose the correct word.

numerical expression
number pattern
term
variable
algebraic expression
evaluate
simplify
like terms
inequality
equation
true
equality properties
solve

1. A letter used to represent a number is called a ___.
2. An expression which contains variables is called an ___.
3. To find the value of an expression for a given value of the variable is to ___ the expression.
4. When two expressions are compared using '$>$' or '$<$', the whole statement is an ___. If the two expressions have the same value, the statement is an ___.
5. To find the value of the variable that will make an equation true is to ___ the equation.

Concepts and Skills

Write the next three terms of each number pattern.

6. 3, 5, 7, 9, ... ___
7. 1, 10, 100, 1,000, ... ___
8. 4, 5, 7, 10, ... ___
9. 92, 87, 82, 77, ... ___

Write an expression for each of the following.

10. Add 4 to x. ___
11. Subtract x from 8. ___
12. Multiply x by 7. ___
13. Divide x by 2. $\frac{\square}{\square}$

Evaluate each expression for $y = 9$.

14. $y + 2$ ___
15. $y - 5$ ___
16. $9y$ ___
17. $\frac{y}{9}$ ___

Simplify each expression.

18 $2a + a$

19 $3a - 2a$

20 $5a - 2a + a$

21 $a + 6 + a - 2$

Complete with =, >, or < for $b = 9$.

22 $b + 2$ ◯ 15

23 $2b + 8$ ◯ $3b - 4$

24 $(b \div 3) \times 6$ ◯ $2b$

25 $5b \div 5$ ◯ $b \div 3$

Solve each equation.

26 $5p = 25$

27 $3p - 4 = 8$

28 $2p + 6 = 4p - 10$

29 $10p - 4 = 8p + 16$

Problem Solving

Solve. Show your work.

30 A florist buys 12 dozen carnations. What are some ways in which the florist could make bouquets of the same size using all 144 flowers?

Number of Flowers in Bouquet	2	3	4	6	8	9	12	16	18
Number of Bouquets	72	48	36	24	18				

a Copy and complete the table.

b What are three more sizes of bouquets that the florist could make?

c Why can't the florist make bouquets with 10 flowers?

31 At a parade, there are m women and 3 times as many men as women. There are 6,352 fewer children than men.

a Find the number of men and the number of children respectively in terms of m.

b If $m = 7{,}145$, how many people are at the parade?

32 Andy has $3r - 3$ baseball cards. Micah has $2r + 5$ baseball cards.

a If $r = 14$, who has more cards?

b For what value of r will the two boys have the same number of cards?

Chapter

6 Area

Lessons

- **6.1** Finding the Area of a Rectangle with Fractional Side Lengths
- **6.2** Base and Height of a Triangle
- **6.3** Finding the Area of a Triangle

BIG IDEA

▶ Base and height are measurements that are used to find the area of a triangle.

Recall Prior Knowledge

Forming angles

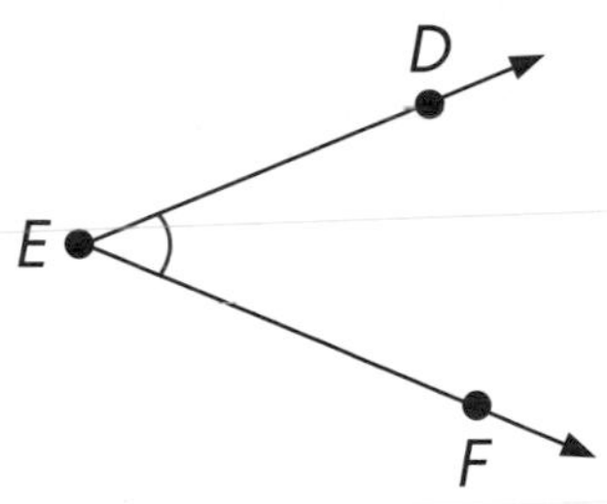

An angle is formed by two rays with the same endpoint.

Rays *ED* and *EF* form $\angle DEF$.

Classifying angles

Acute Angle	Right Angle	Obtuse Angle
$< 90^\circ$	90°	$> 90^\circ$

Identifying perpendicular line segments

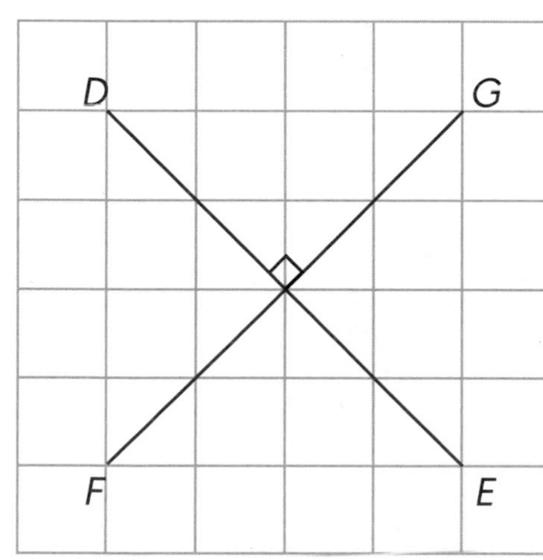

$\overline{DE}$ and $\overline{FG}$ intersect at right angles.

$\overline{DE}$ is perpendicular to $\overline{FG}$.

Area is the amount of surface covered.

The measures of the shaded parts are the areas of the figures.

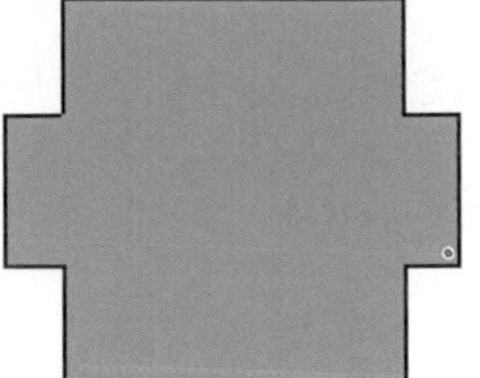

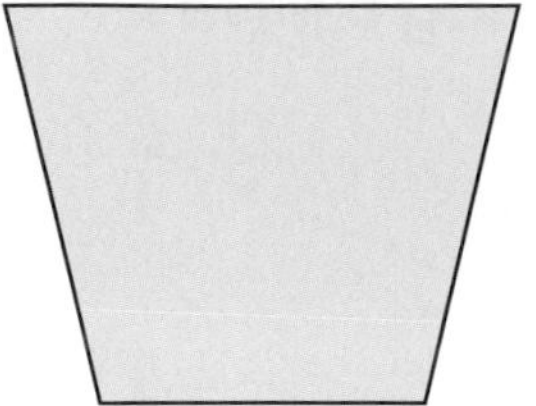

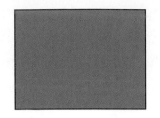

Finding area by counting square units

A square that is one unit long and one unit wide has an area of one square unit. Area is measured in square units, such as square centimeters (cm^2), or square inches ($in.^2$).

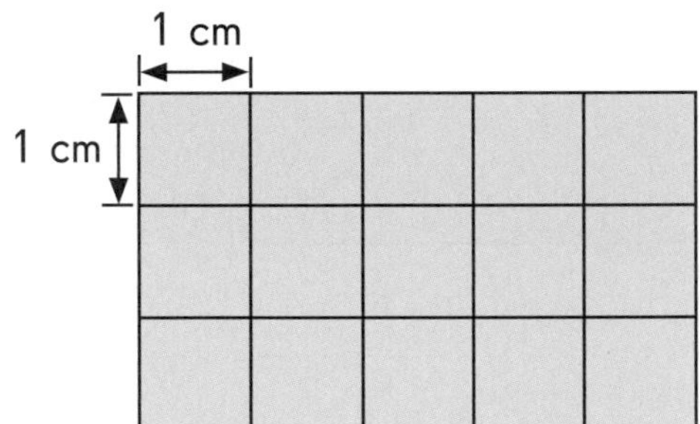

There are 15 square units.

Area of the rectangle = 15 cm^2

Finding area by using formulas

A = side × side
= 4 × 4
= 16 cm^2

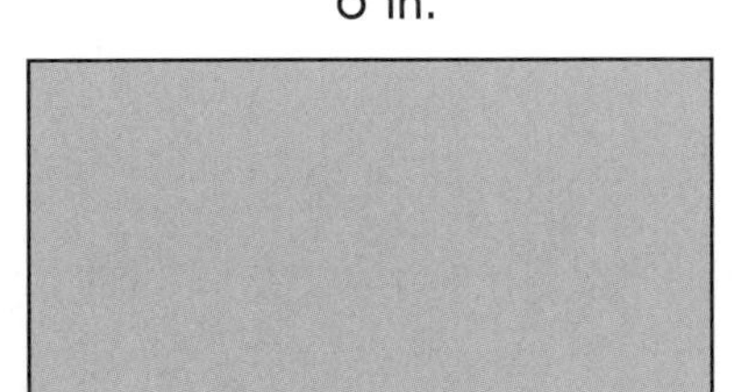

A = length × width
= 6 × 3
= 18 $in.^2$

Classify the angles as acute angles, right angles, and obtuse angles. Use a piece of paper that is folded in fourths to help you.

1

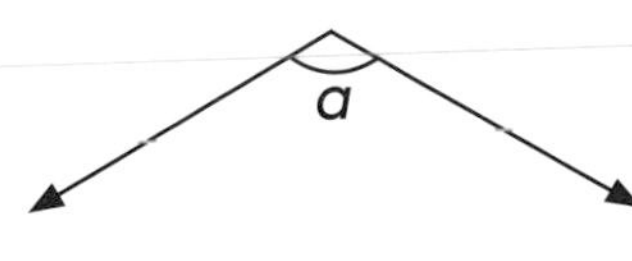

b

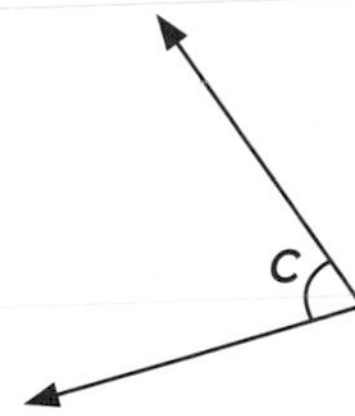

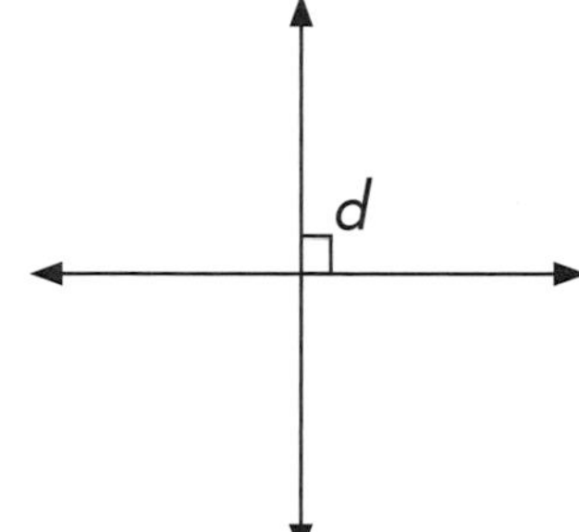

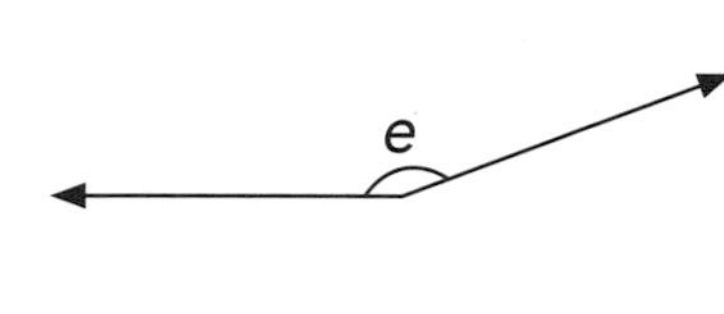

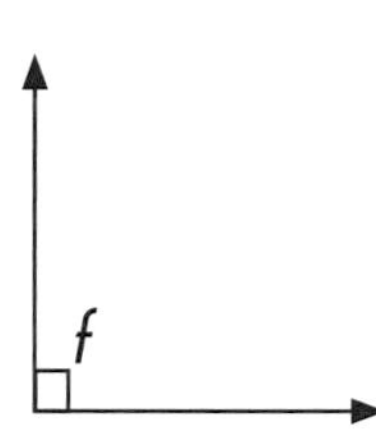

Acute angles: ______

Right angles: ______

Obtuse angles: ______

State whether the line segments are perpendicular. Use a piece of paper that is folded in fourths to help you.

2

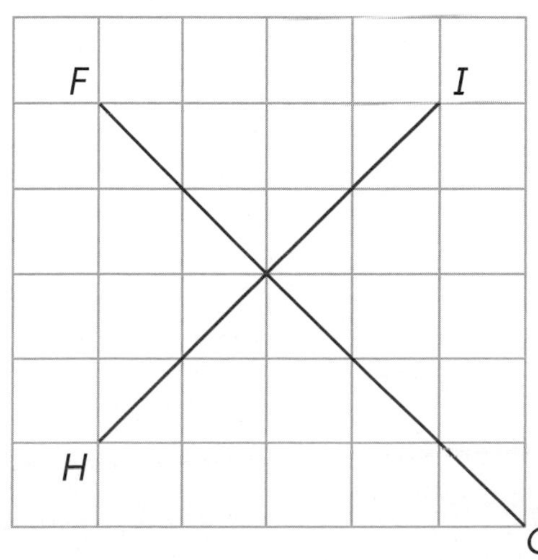

______

3

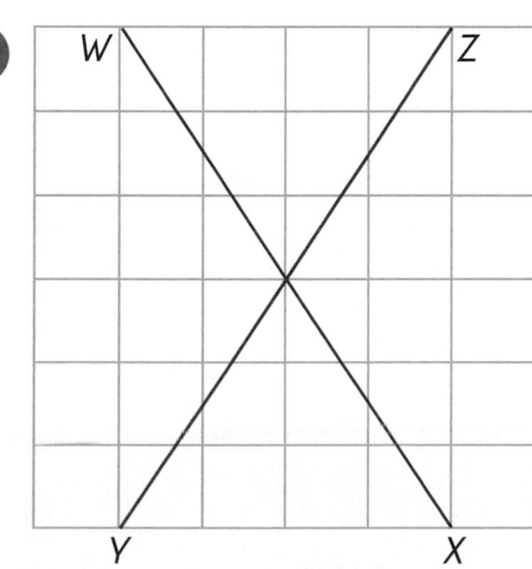

______

Find the area of each figure.

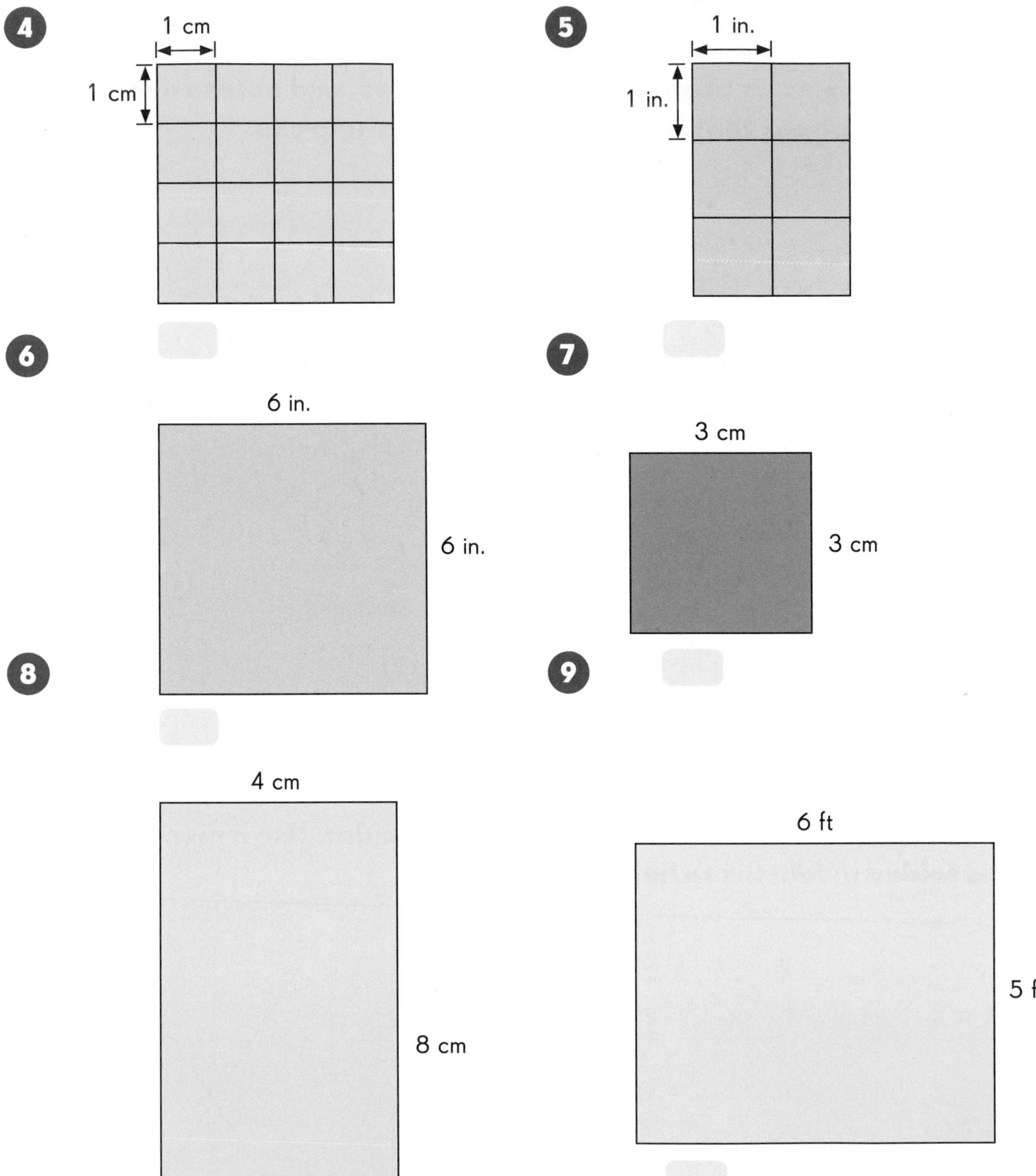

Finding the Area of a Rectangle with Fractional Side Lengths

Lesson Objective

- Find the area of a rectangle with fractional side lengths by counting square units, and by using a formula.

Learn Find the area of a rectangle with fractional side lengths.

Find the area of a rectangle that is $\frac{3}{5}$ foot by $\frac{4}{5}$ foot.

Method 1

Use a model. Draw a square and divide it into fractional units.

$\frac{3}{5}$ ft (across the first three columns); $\frac{4}{5}$ ft (down the first four rows)

	$\frac{1}{5}$	$\frac{1}{5}$	$\frac{1}{5}$	$\frac{1}{5}$	$\frac{1}{5}$
$\frac{1}{5}$	$\frac{1}{25}$	$\frac{1}{25}$	$\frac{1}{25}$	$\frac{1}{25}$	$\frac{1}{25}$
$\frac{1}{5}$	$\frac{1}{25}$	$\frac{1}{25}$	$\frac{1}{25}$	$\frac{1}{25}$	$\frac{1}{25}$
$\frac{1}{5}$	$\frac{1}{25}$	$\frac{1}{25}$	$\frac{1}{25}$	$\frac{1}{25}$	$\frac{1}{25}$
$\frac{1}{5}$	$\frac{1}{25}$	$\frac{1}{25}$	$\frac{1}{25}$	$\frac{1}{25}$	$\frac{1}{25}$
$\frac{1}{5}$	$\frac{1}{25}$	$\frac{1}{25}$	$\frac{1}{25}$	$\frac{1}{25}$	$\frac{1}{25}$

Each small square has an area of $\frac{1}{25}$ square foot.

There are 12 squares in the shaded rectangle.

So, the area of the rectangle with sides of $\frac{3}{5}$ foot and $\frac{4}{5}$ foot is $\frac{12}{25}$ square foot.

Method 2

Use the formula A = length × width.

$\frac{3}{5}$ ft

$\frac{4}{5}$ ft

$$\begin{aligned} A &= \text{length} \times \text{width} \\ &= \frac{4}{5} \times \frac{3}{5} \\ &= \frac{12}{25}\ \text{ft}^2 \end{aligned}$$

The area of the rectangle is $\frac{12}{25}$ square foot.

Guided Learning

1 Find the area of a rectangle that is $\frac{3}{4}$ foot by $\frac{2}{3}$ foot in two ways.

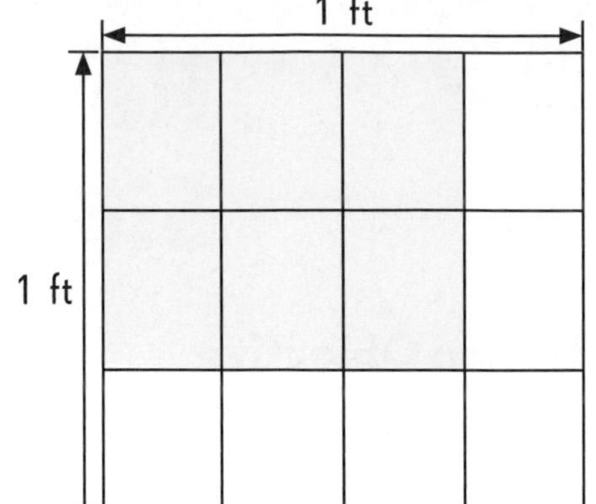

a Counting equal parts

The square foot is divided into ___ equal parts.

___ parts are shaded.

$\frac{?}{?}$ of the square foot is shaded.

The area of a rectangle $\frac{2}{3}$ foot by $\frac{3}{4}$ foot is $\frac{?}{?}$ square foot.

b Using the formula A = length × width

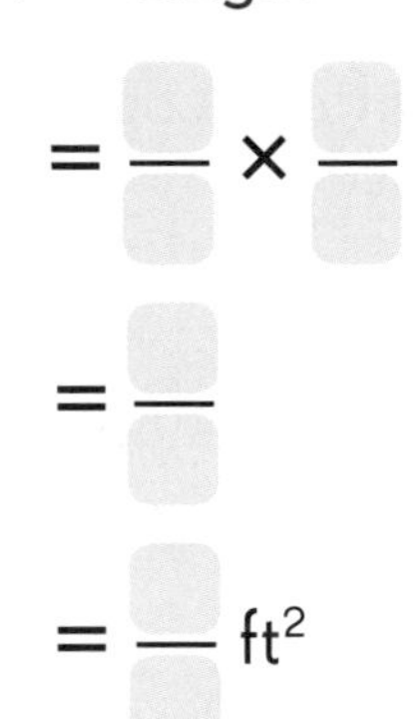

$= \frac{?}{?} \times \frac{?}{?}$

$= \frac{?}{?}$

$= \frac{?}{?}$ ft^2

Learn

Find the area of a rectangle whose side lengths are mixed numbers.

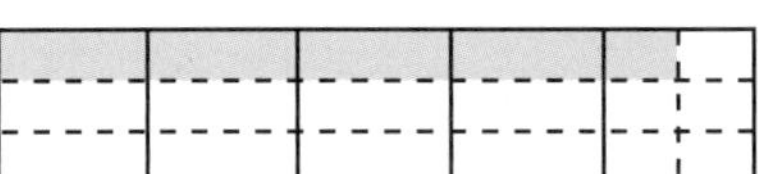

To find the area of the shaded rectangle, count the number of parts of each size. There are:

4 squares that are $\frac{1}{3}$ shaded, and

1 part that is $\frac{1}{3}$ of $\frac{1}{2} = \frac{1}{6}$ of a square

Total shaded squares: $\frac{4}{3} + \frac{1}{6} = \frac{8}{6} + \frac{1}{6}$

$= \frac{9}{6}$

$= 1\frac{1}{2}$

The total area of the rectangle is $1\frac{1}{2}$ square units.

You can also find the area by using the formula for the area of a rectangle.

$$A = \text{length} \times \text{width}$$
$$= 4\frac{1}{2} \times \frac{1}{3}$$
$$= \frac{9}{2} \times \frac{1}{3}$$
$$= \frac{9}{6}$$
$$= 1\frac{1}{2} \text{ square units}$$

You can simplify $\frac{9}{2} \times \frac{1}{3}$ by dividing out the common factor 3, either before you multiply or after.

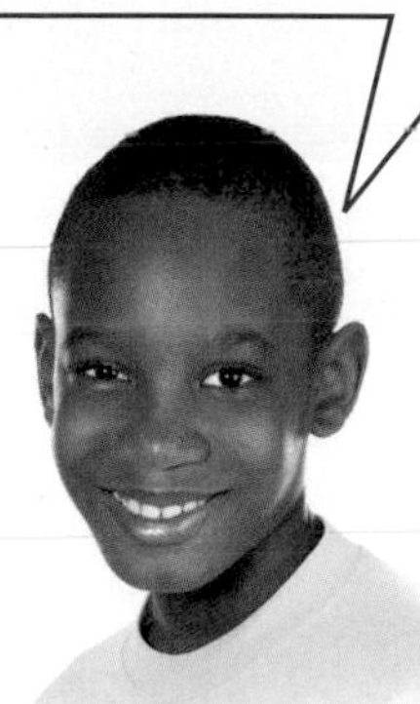

Guided Learning

2 Find the area of the shaded rectangle.

$A = \text{length} \times \text{width}$

$= \square\frac{\square}{\square} \times \frac{\square}{\square}$

$= \frac{\square}{\square}$ square units

Let's Practice

Find the area of the rectangle.

1

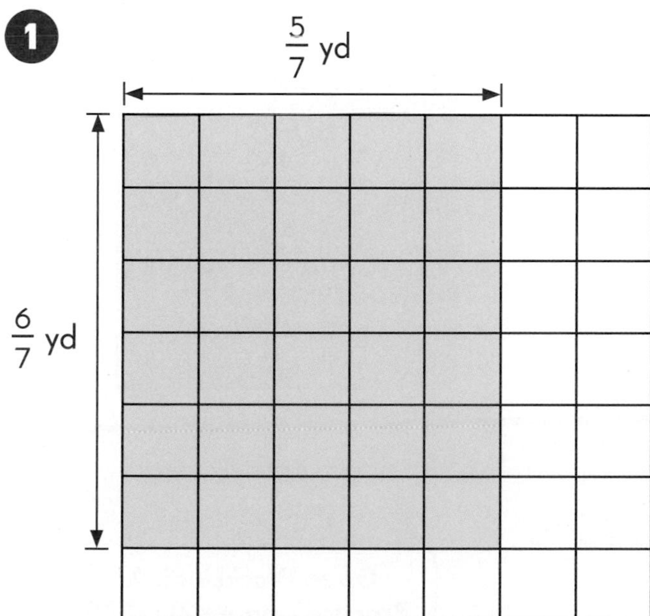

Find the area of each figure.

2

$\frac{3}{4}$ ft

$\frac{2}{7}$ ft

3

$\frac{5}{8}$ in.

$\frac{3}{8}$ in.

4

$3\frac{3}{10}$ cm

5 cm

5

$\frac{4}{9}$ yd

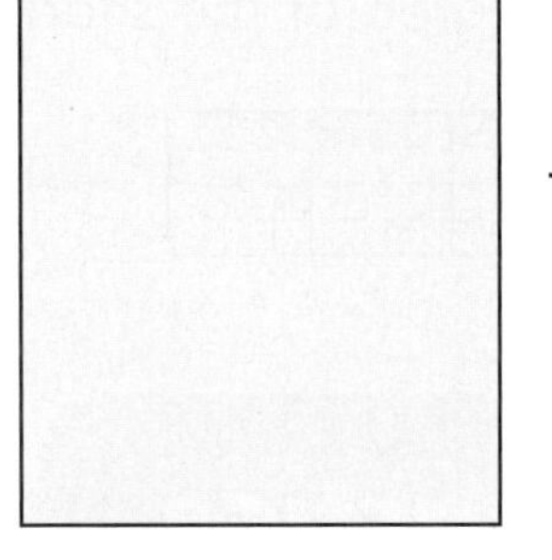

$\frac{2}{3}$ yd

6

$2\frac{5}{6}$ in.

$1\frac{3}{7}$ in.

7

$4\frac{1}{2}$ ft

$4\frac{1}{2}$ ft

ON YOUR OWN

Go to Workbook A: Practice 1, pages 215–220

Lesson 6.2 Base and Height of a Triangle

Lesson Objectives

- Identify the base given the height of a triangle.
- Identify the height given the base of a triangle.

Vocabulary

vertex	side	angle
base	height	perpendicular

Learn A triangle has three vertices, three sides and three angles.

ABC is a triangle.

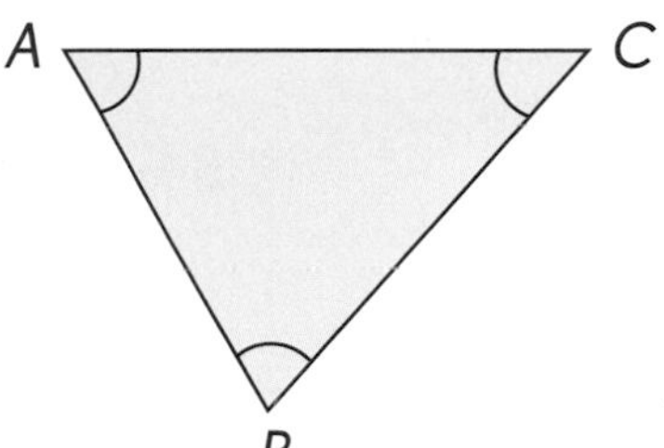

It has:

three vertices — points *A*, *B* and *C*

three sides — $\overline{AB}$, $\overline{BC}$, and $\overline{CA}$

three angles — $\angle ABC$, $\angle ACB$ and $\angle BAC$

Learn Any one side of a triangle can be its base.

The base of an object is the face or side on which it lies.

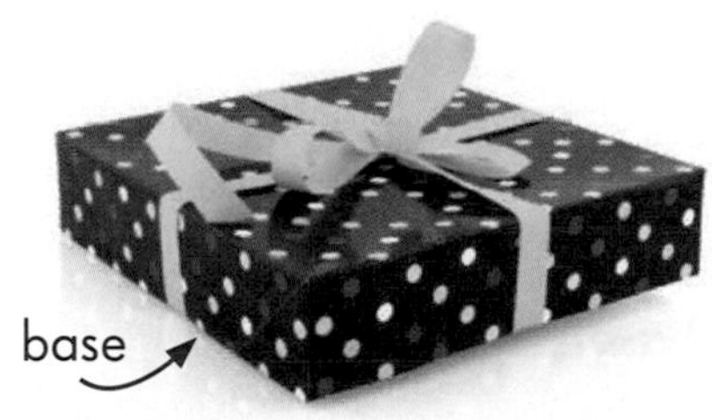

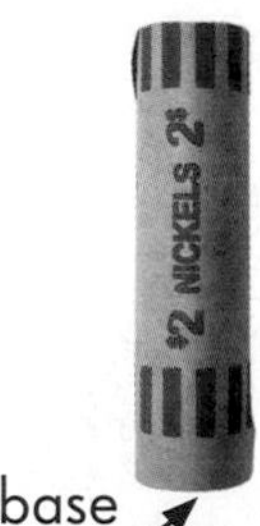

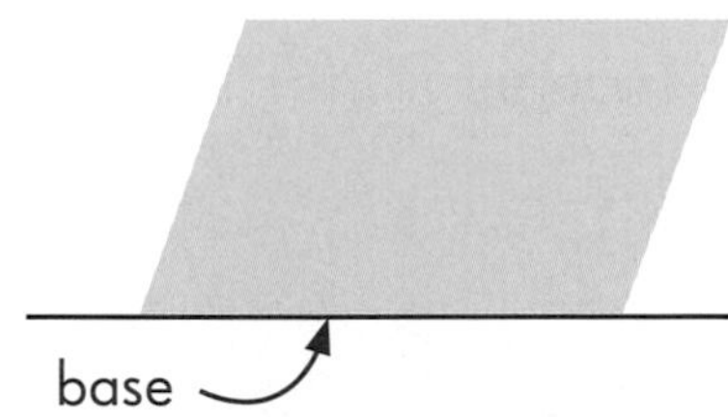

A triangle can be pictured to be lying on any one side. So, in a triangle, any one side can be its base.

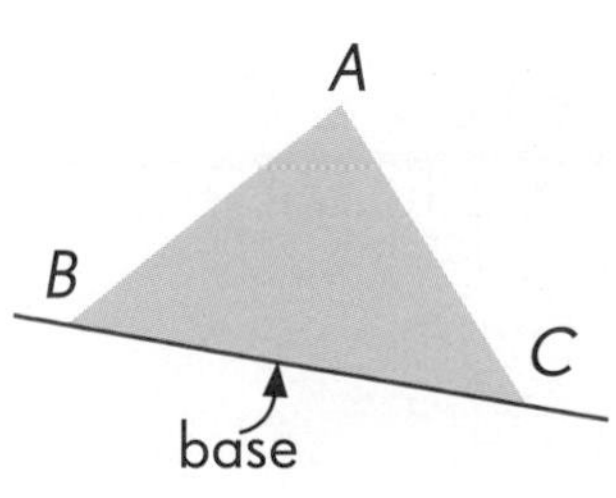

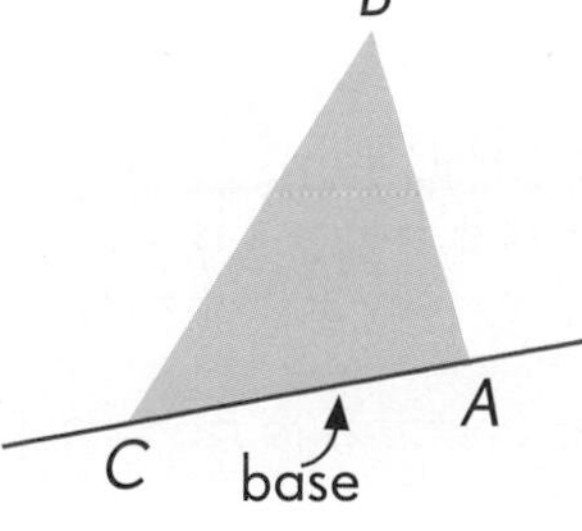

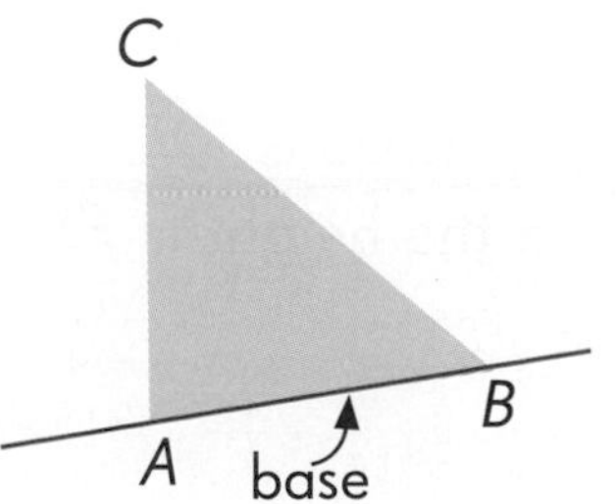

Learn A triangle is measured by its base and its height.

You measure a triangle by its base and its height:
— the base being the side chosen as such;
— the height being the **perpendicular** distance from the base to the opposite vertex.

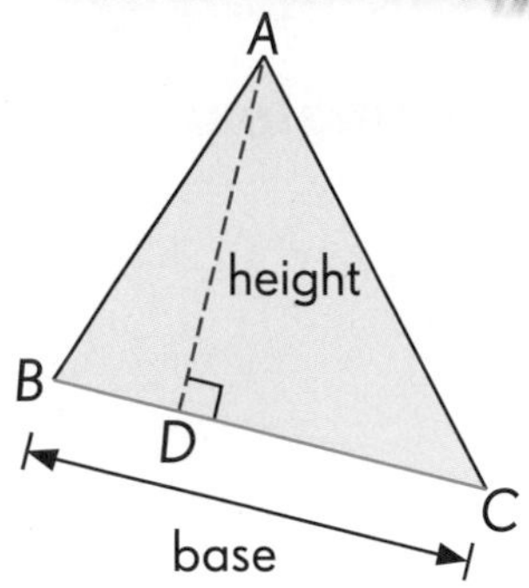

You can take the length of $\overline{BC}$ and the height AD to be the measurements of triangle ABC.

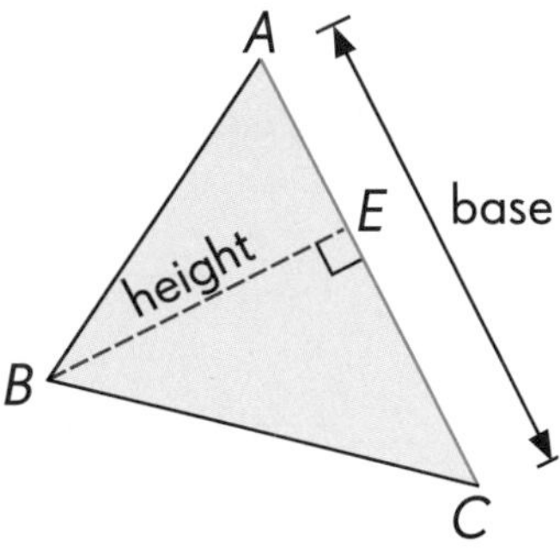

You can take the length of $\overline{AC}$ and the height BE to be the measurements of triangle ABC.

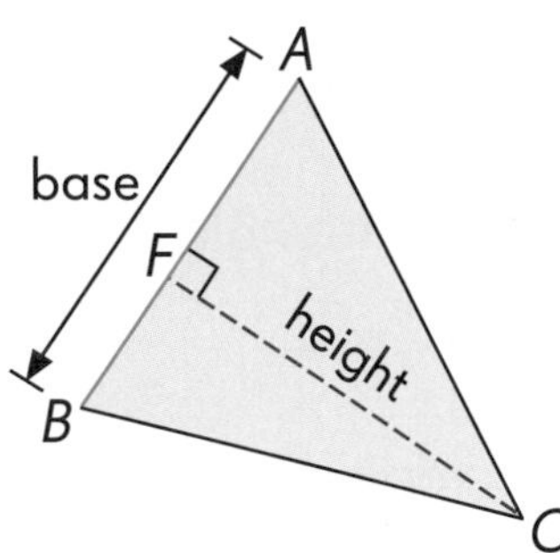

You can take the length of $\overline{AB}$ and the height CF to be the measurements of triangle ABC.

Learn Sometimes the height is not part of the triangle.

In triangle PQR:

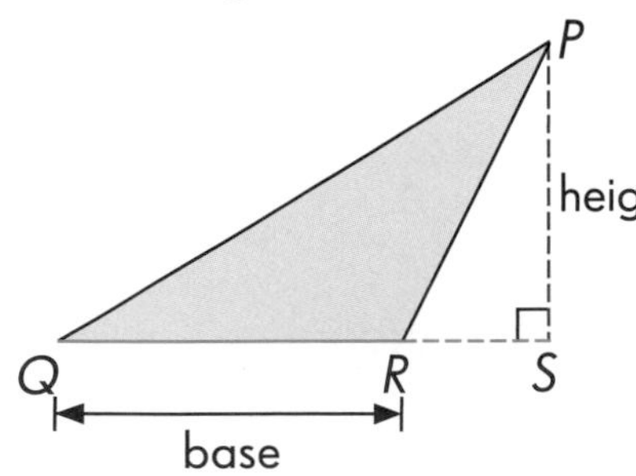

If the base is $\overline{QR}$, then the height is PS.

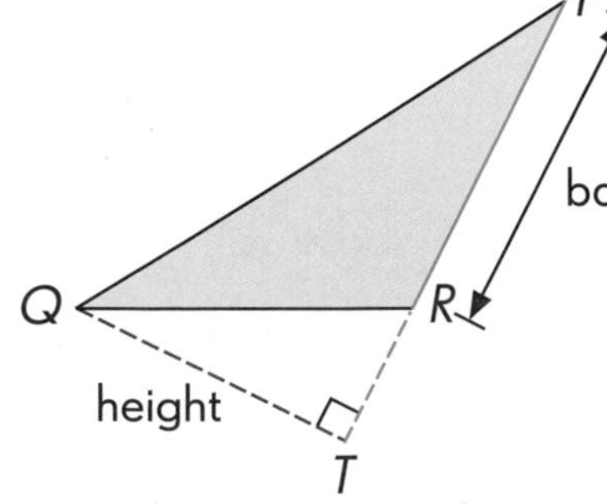

If the base is $\overline{PR}$, then the height is QT.

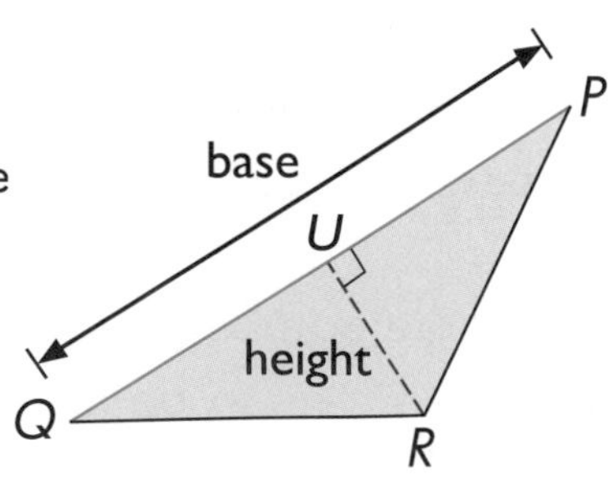

If the base is $\overline{QP}$, then the height is RU.

The height of a triangle is always perpendicular to its base.

Guided Learning

Complete. Identify both the base and the height in each triangle.

1. 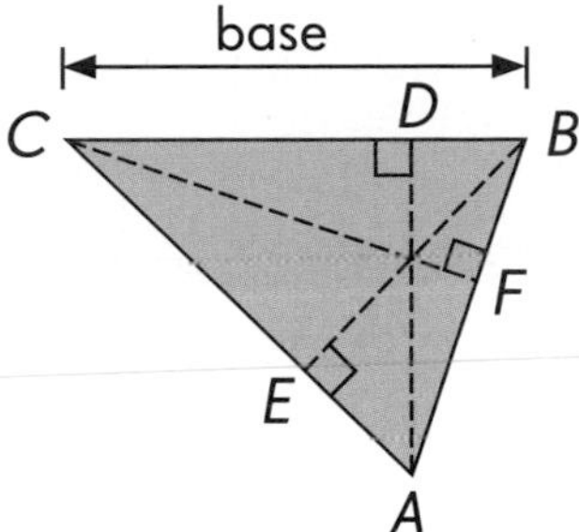

Base:

Height:

2. 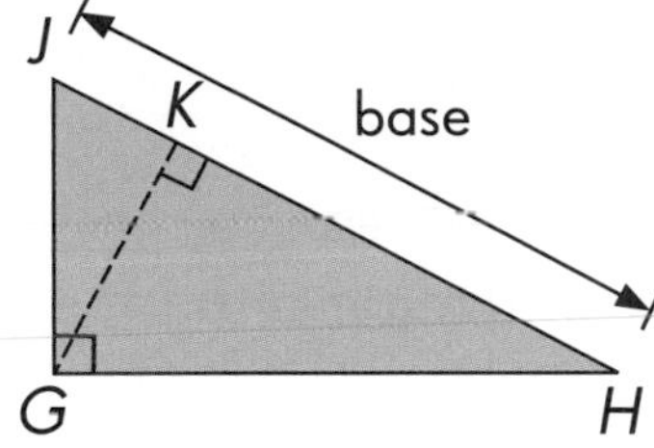

Base:

Height:

3. 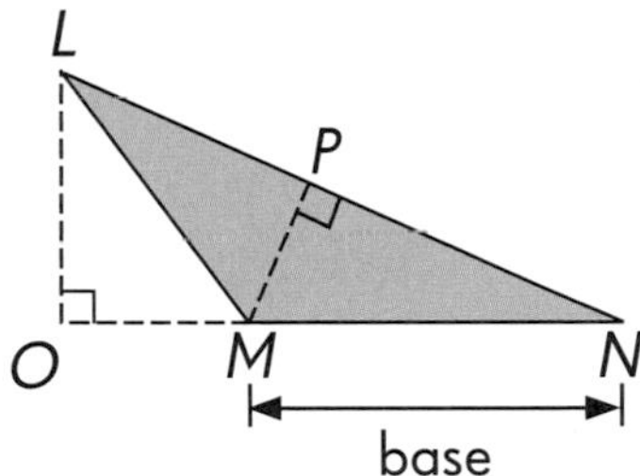

Base:

Height:

4. 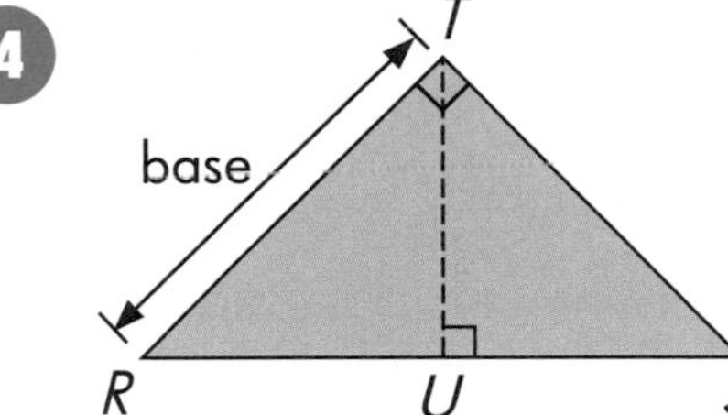

Base:

Height:

5. 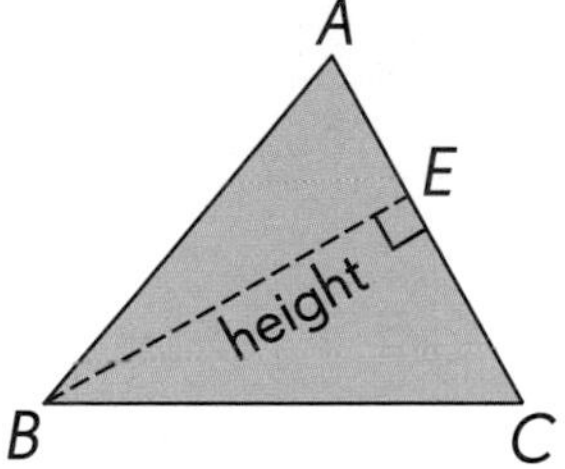

Height:

Base:

6. 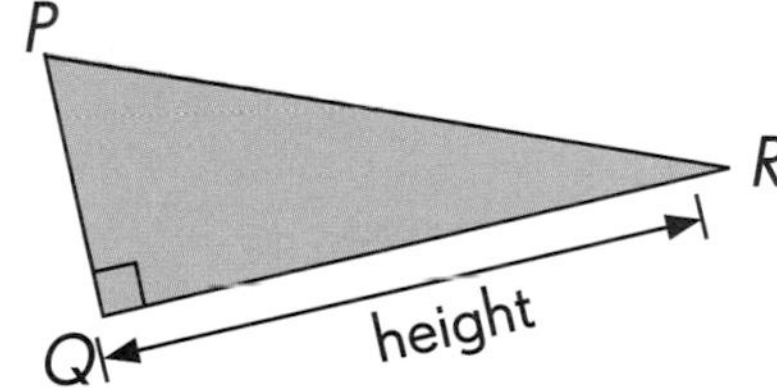

Height:

Base:

7. 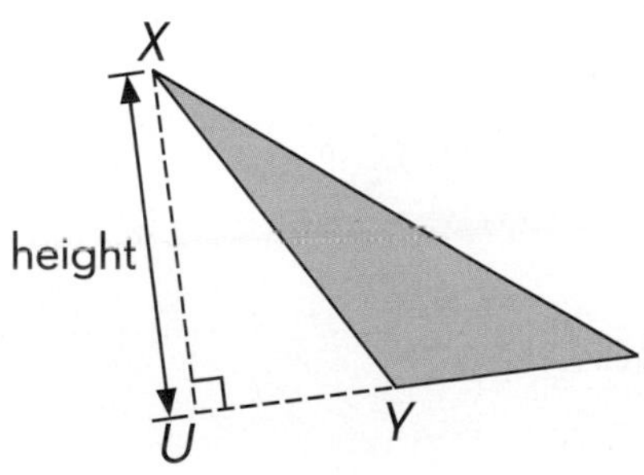

Height:

Base:

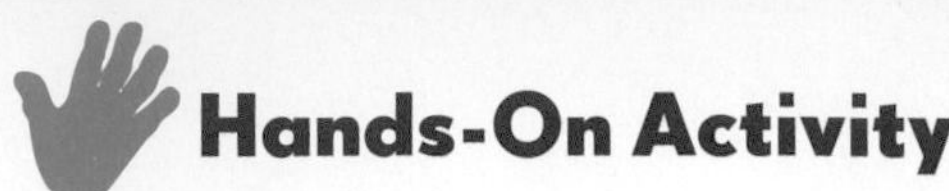

Hands-On Activity

WORKING TOGETHER

STEP 1 Draw a triangle and label it *ABC*.

Examples

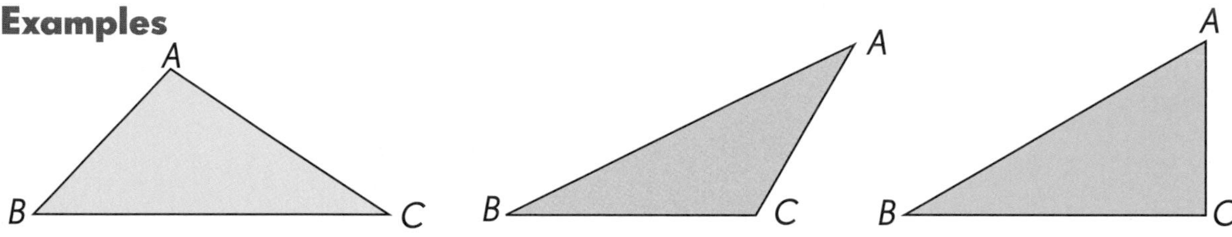

STEP 2 For each base, $\overline{AB}$, $\overline{BC}$, and $\overline{CA}$, identify the height.

STEP 3 Using a drawing triangle, draw the three heights of your triangle. Label them *AD*, *BE*, and *CF*.

STEP 4 Look at all the triangles drawn. What do you notice about the heights *AD*, *BE*, and *CF*?

Let's Practice

Complete. Identify both the base and the height in each triangle.

1. 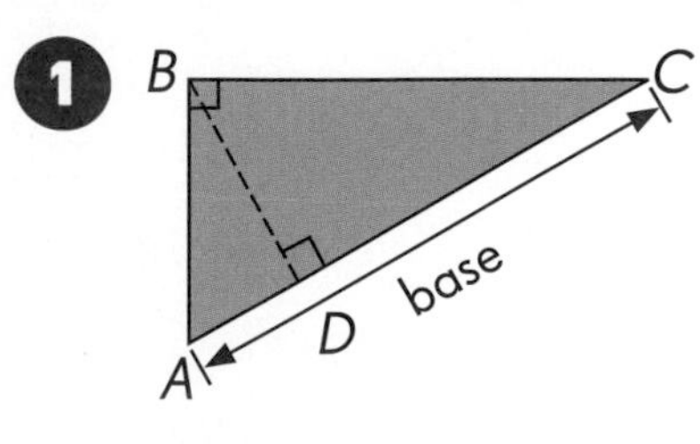

Base: ___

Height: ___

2. 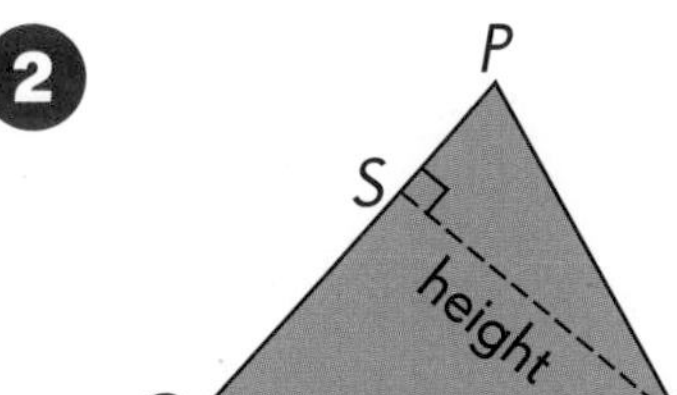

Height: ___

Base: ___

The height of triangle *ABC* is as given. Name its base.

3 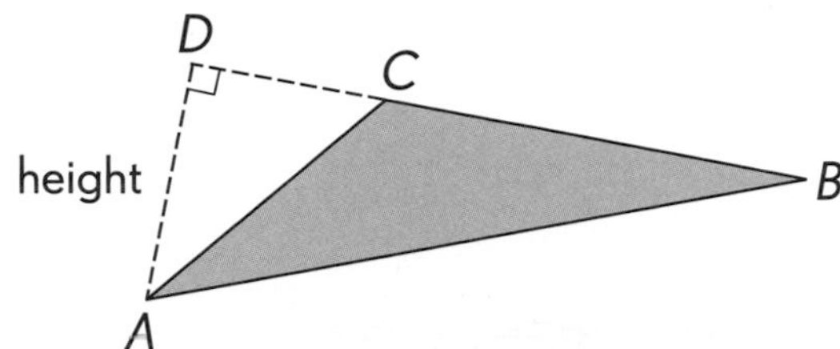

Height: *AD*

Base: ______

The base of triangle *DEF* is as labeled. Make a copy of triangle *DEF* and mark its height on the copy.

4 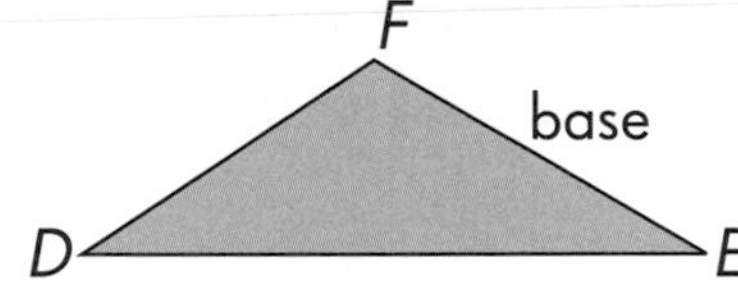

List all the possible pairs of bases and heights for triangle *ABC*.

5 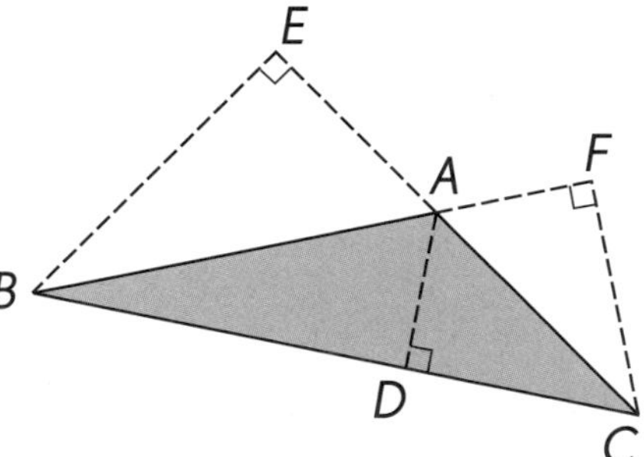

Base: ______; Height: ______

Base: ______; Height: ______

Base: ______; Height: ______

Complete.

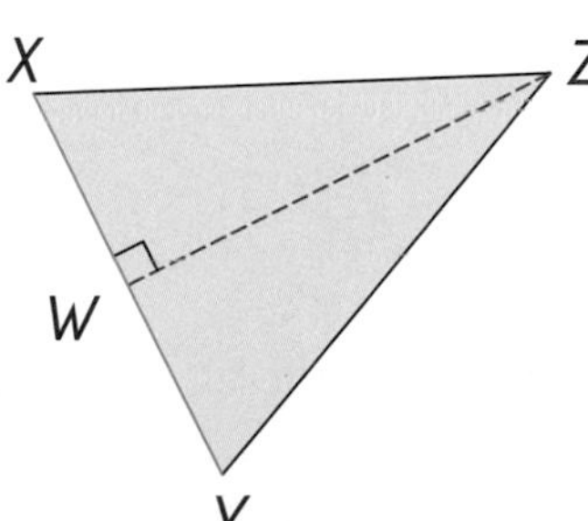

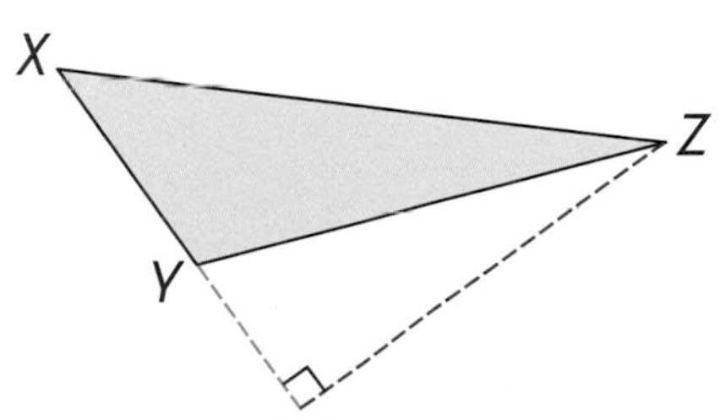

6 In both triangles, ______ is perpendicular to $\overline{XY}$.

7 In both triangles, ______ is the height and ______ is the base.

ON YOUR OWN

Go to Workbook A: Practice 2, pages 221–222

Finding the Area of a Triangle

Lesson Objective

- Find the area of a triangle given its base and its height.

Vocabulary
area
right triangle

Learn **The area of a triangle is half the area of a rectangle with the same 'base' and 'height' or half its base times height.**

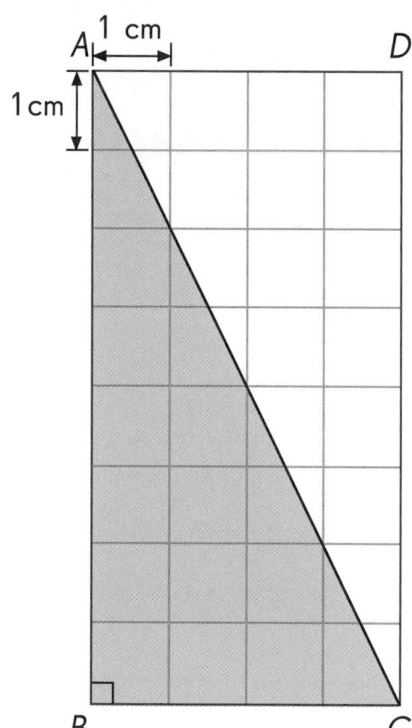

The area of triangle ABC is half the area of rectangle $ABCD$.

$ABCD$ is a rectangle.

In triangle ABC, $\overline{AB}$ is perpendicular to $\overline{BC}$.

$\overline{BC}$ is the base and AB is the height.

The length of the base $\overline{BC}$ = 4 cm and the height AB = 8 cm.

$$\begin{aligned}\text{Area of triangle } ABC &= \tfrac{1}{2} \times \text{area of rectangle } ABCD \\ &= \tfrac{1}{2} \times 4 \times 8 \\ &= \tfrac{1}{2} \times BC \times AB \\ &= \tfrac{1}{2} \times \text{base} \times \text{height}\end{aligned}$$

The length 4 cm and the width 8 cm of rectangle $ABCD$ are exactly the base and the height of **right triangle** ABC.

So, $\frac{1}{2} \times 4 \times 8 = \frac{1}{2} \times BC \times AB$

$= \frac{1}{2} \times \text{base} \times \text{height}$

A right triangle is a triangle with exactly one right angle.

Hands-On Activity

WORKING TOGETHER

On page 276, you saw that a right triangle *ABC* has an area that is half the area of the corresponding rectangle or $\frac{1}{2}$ × base × height. You now need to check if the same is true for other triangles.

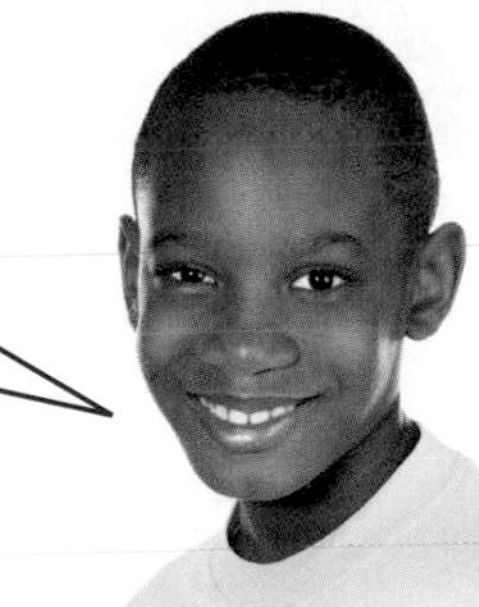

1 In triangle *DEF*, all the angles have measures less than 90°. $\overline{EF}$ is the base and *DG* is the height.

STEP **1** Use a copy of Figure 1. Cut out triangles *DLM* and *DMN*. Rearrange the two triangles as shown in Figure 2.

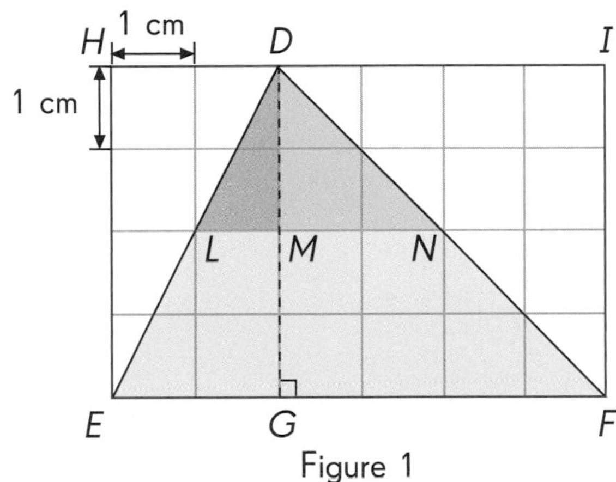

Figure 1

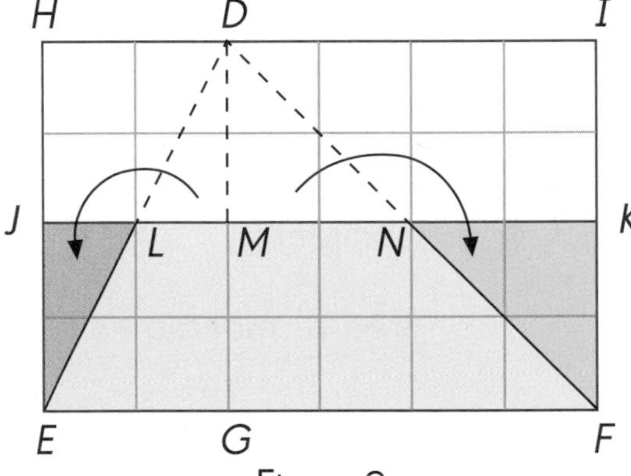

Figure 2

STEP **2** Complete.

Area of triangle *DEF* = area of rectangle ______

$= \frac{1}{2} \times$ area of rectangle ______

$= \frac{1}{2} \times EF \times IF$

$= \frac{1}{2} \times EF \times$ ______

$= \frac{1}{2} \times \text{base} \times$ ______

2 In triangle PQR, one angle has a measure greater than 90°. $\overline{QR}$ is the base and PS is the height.

STEP 1 Use a copy of Figure 3. Cut out triangles PVX and VRX. Then rearrange the two triangles as shown in Figure 4.

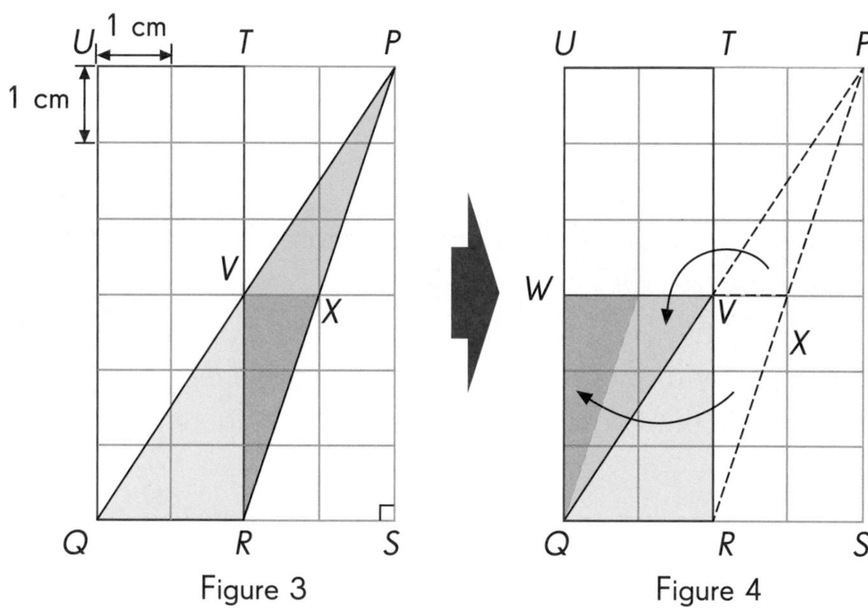

Figure 3 Figure 4

STEP 2 Complete.

Area of triangle PQR = area of rectangle ____

$= \frac{1}{2} \times$ area of rectangle ____

$= \frac{1}{2} \times QR \times TR$

$= \frac{1}{2} \times QR \times$ ____

$= \frac{1}{2} \times \text{base} \times$ ____

What can you say about the area of triangle DEF in Step 1? How about triangle PQR above?

Learn Find the area of a triangle using the 'area of a triangle' formula.

Find the area of triangle PQR.

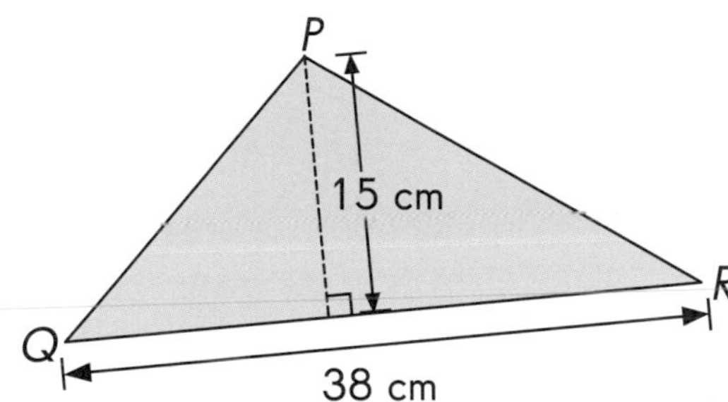

$$\begin{aligned} A &= \frac{1}{2} \times \text{base} \times \text{height} \\ &= \frac{1}{2} \times 38 \times 15 \\ &= 285 \text{ cm}^2 \end{aligned}$$

Hands-On Activity

In triangle *ABC*, ∠BAC is a right angle and *AD* is perpendicular to *BC*.

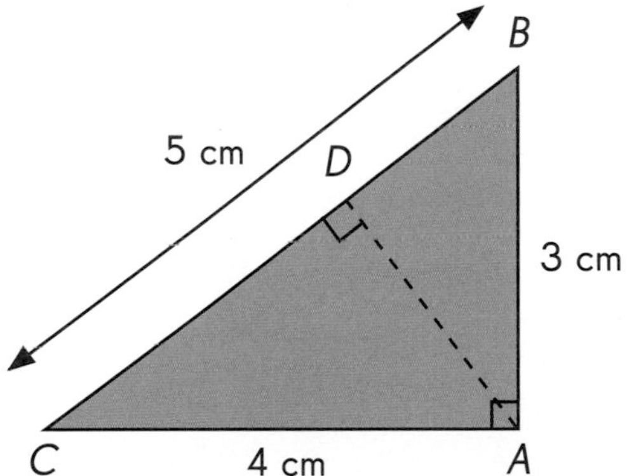

Measure the height *AD* in centimeters to the nearest tenth.

Using each side $\overline{AB}$, $\overline{AC}$, and $\overline{BC}$ as the base, find the area of the triangle. Are all three answers the same?

Guided Learning

Find the area of each shaded triangle.

1

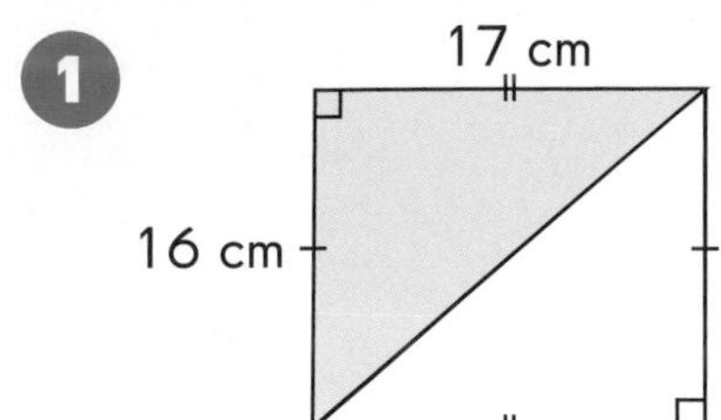

2

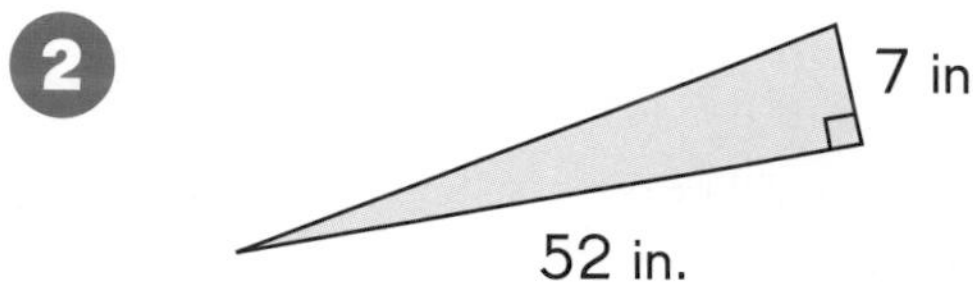

3

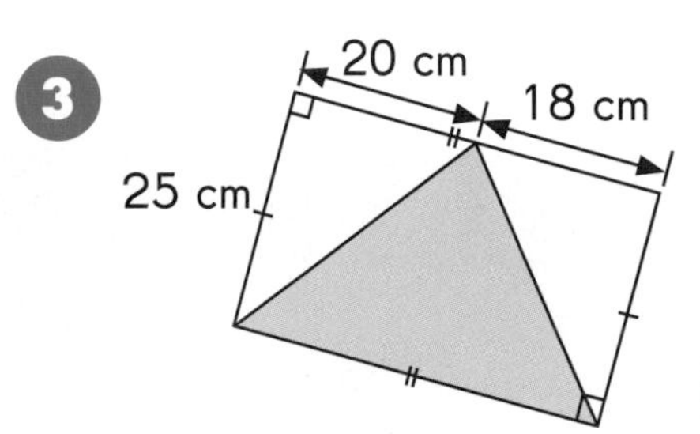

4

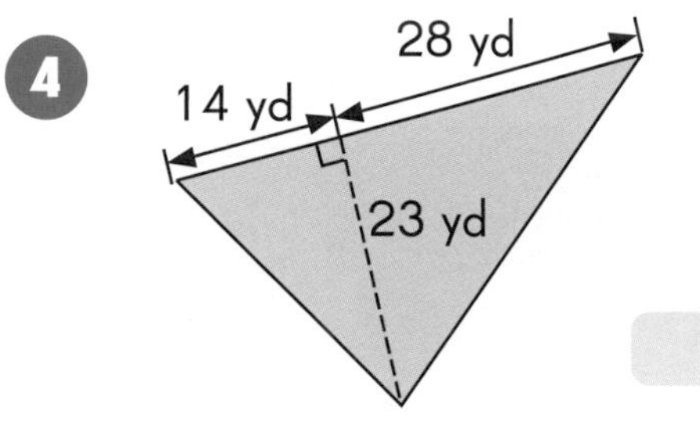

5

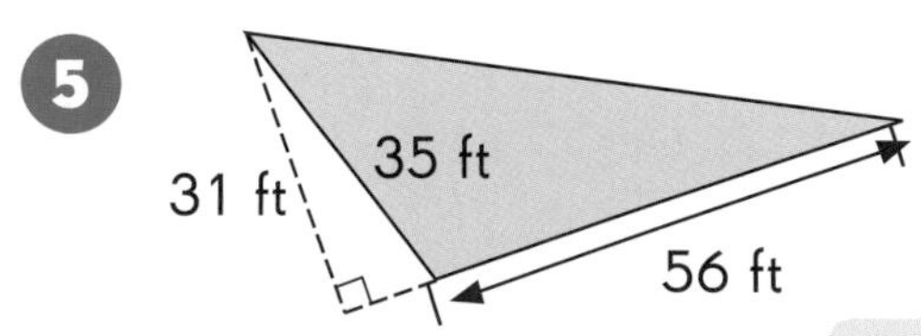

6

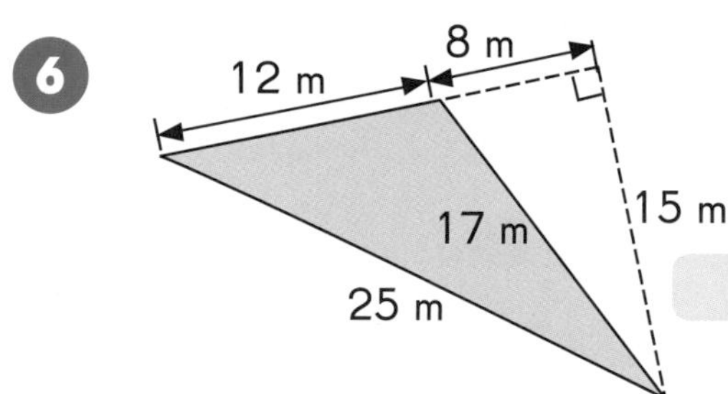

Let's Practice

Find the area of each shaded triangle.

1

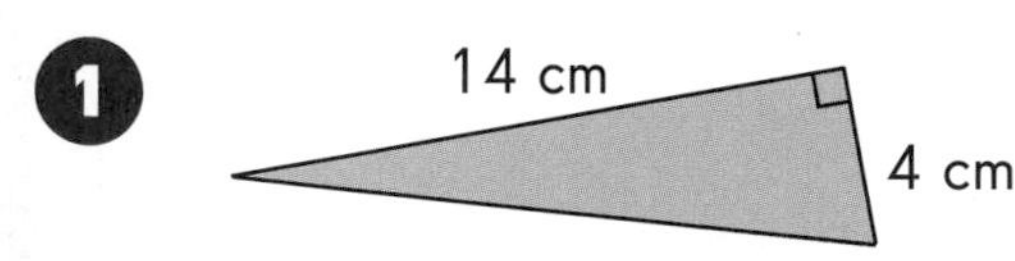

2

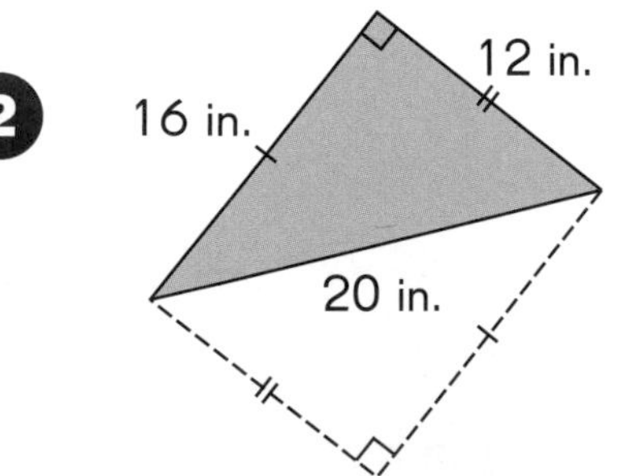

3

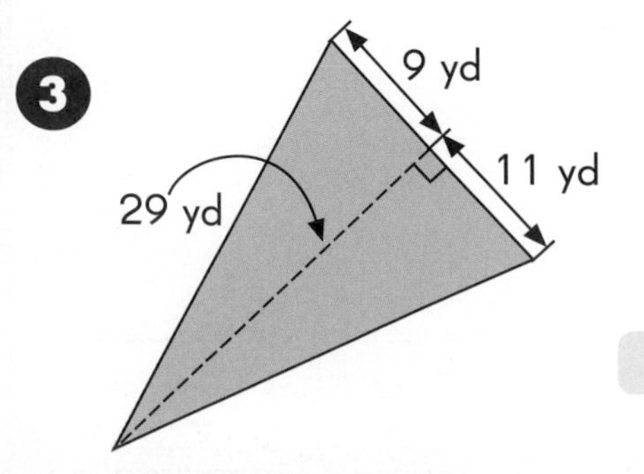

4

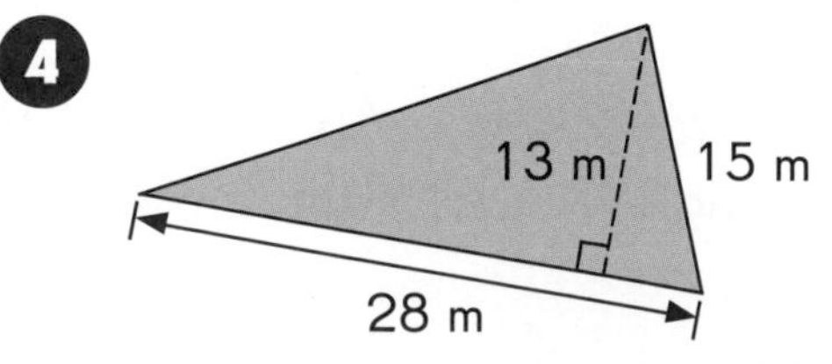

5 In triangle ABC, $BC = 44$ cm and $AD = 27$ cm. Find the area of triangle ABC.

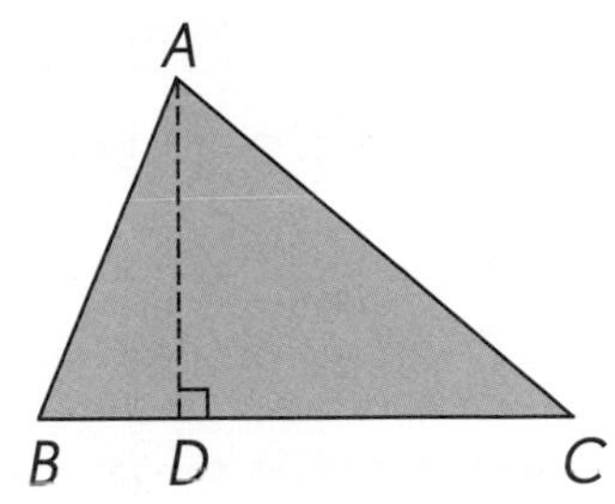

6 In the figure, $QR = 26$ in., $QS = 20$ in. and $PS = 26$ in. Find the area of triangle PQR.

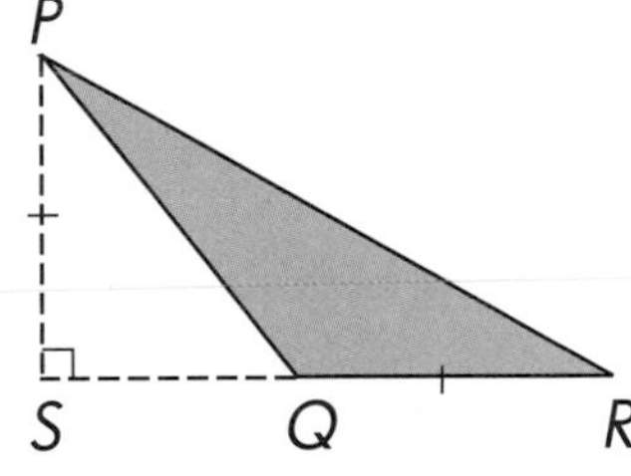

7 In the figure, $LM = 18$ ft, $KM = 16$ ft and $KN = 14$ ft. Find the area of triangle KLM.

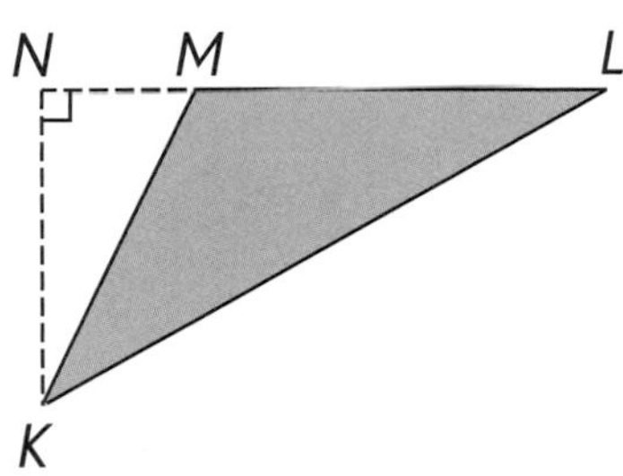

8 Triangle STU represents a triangular table top. It is given that $SU = 32$ in. and $UT = 25$ in. Find the area of the triangular table top.

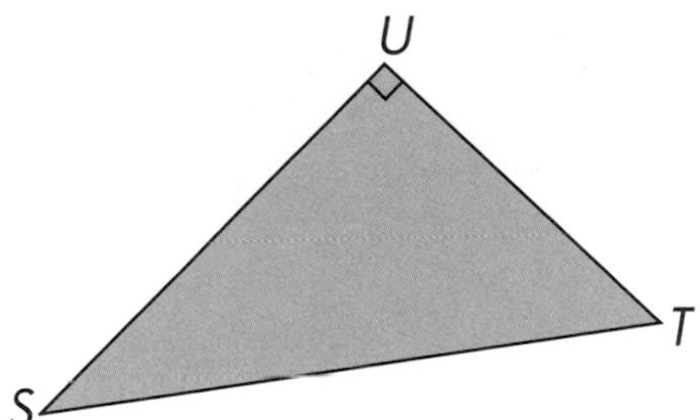

9 In the figure, triangle PQR represents a plot of land. $PQ = 10$ yd, $RS = 21$ yd and $PQ = QS$. Find the area of the land.

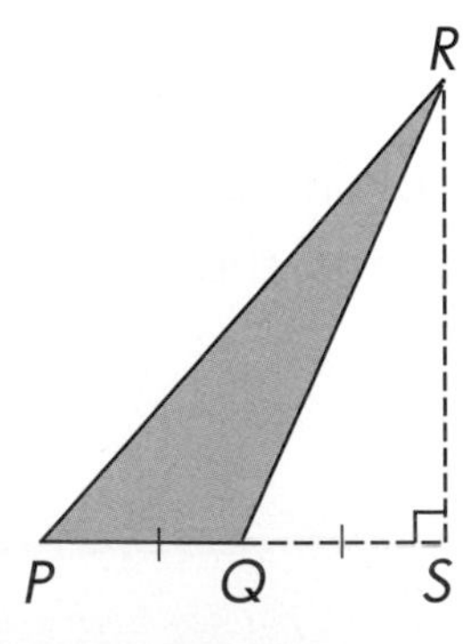

ON YOUR OWN

Go to Workbook A: Practice 3, pages 223–226

Let's Explore!

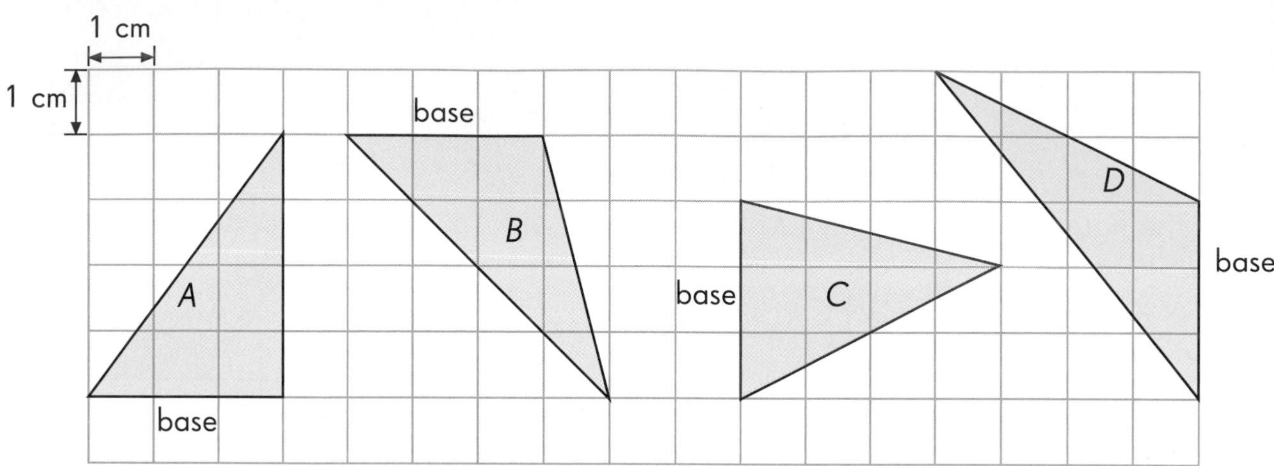

For each triangle, find the height. Then find its area.
What can you say about the bases and heights of these triangles?

Different triangles with equal bases and equal ______ have the same ______.

CRITICAL THINKING SKILLS

Put On Your Thinking Cap!

PROBLEM SOLVING

ABCD is a rectangle. *BE* = *ED*.
Explain how you can find the area of the shaded triangle *ABE*.

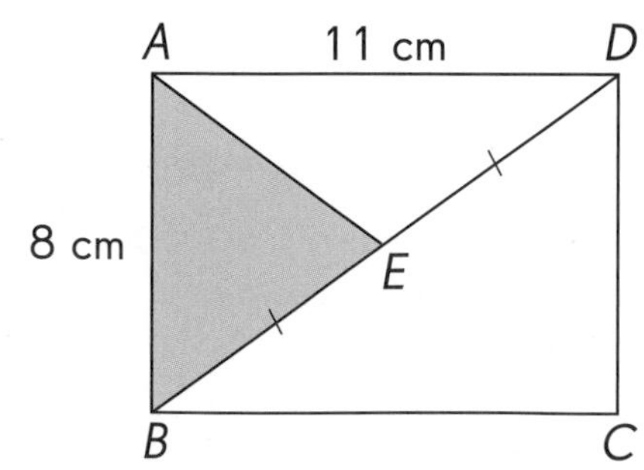

ON YOUR OWN

Go to Workbook A: Put on Your Thinking Cap! pages 227–232

Chapter Wrap Up

▶ Base and height are measurements that are used to find the area of a triangle.

Study Guide

You have learned...

Area

Base and Height of a Triangle

- You measure a triangle by its base and its height:
  - the base can be any side;
  - the height is the perpendicular distance from the base to the opposite vertex.

Example

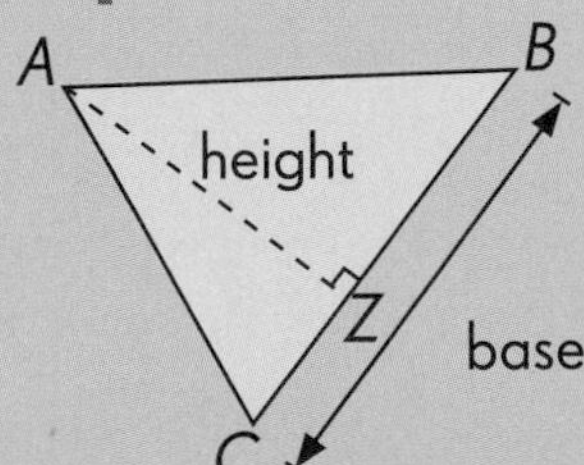

- You can take the length of $\overline{BC}$ and the height, AZ to be the measurements of triangle ABC.

Area of a Triangle

- The area of a triangle is half the area of a rectangle with the same 'base' and 'height' or $\frac{1}{2} \times$ base $\times$ height.

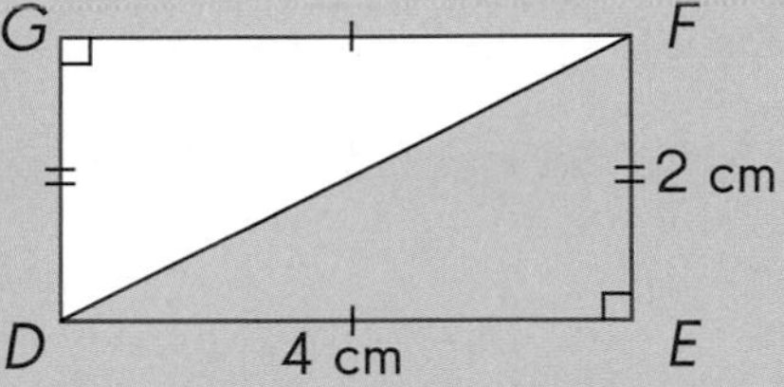

Area of triangle DEF

$= \frac{1}{2} \times \text{base} \times \text{height}$

$= \frac{1}{2} \times DE \times EF$

$= \frac{1}{2} \times 4 \times 2$

$= 4 \text{ cm}^2$

Area of a Rectangle with Fractional Side Lengths

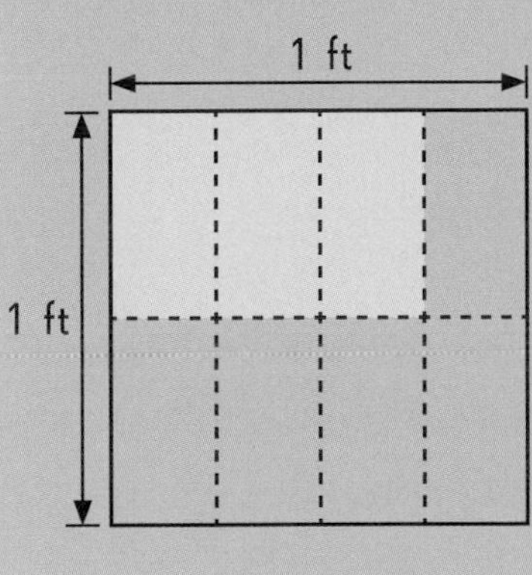

- The area of a rectangle with fractional side lengths can be found by:
  - counting fractions of a whole square unit;

    $A = \frac{1}{8} + \frac{1}{8} + \frac{1}{8}$
  - using the area formula.

    $A = \text{length} \times \text{width}$

    $= \frac{3}{4} \times \frac{1}{2}$

    $= \frac{3}{8}$

Chapter Review/Test

Vocabulary

Fill in the blanks.

vertex
side
angle
base
height
perpendicular
area
right triangle

1. Two lines that intersect at a right angle are said to be ______ to each other.
2. Any side of a triangle can be the ______ and the line segment that is perpendicular to that side is the ______.
3. The amount of surface covered by a triangle is its ______.
4. A triangle with one 90° angle is a ______.

Concepts and Skills

Complete to give both the base and the height in each triangle.

5.

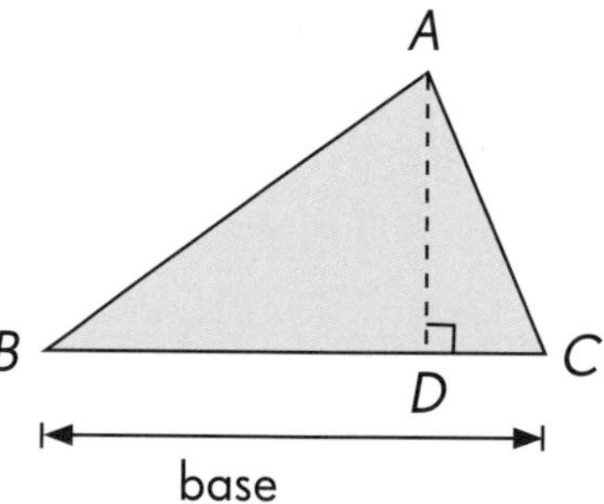

Base: ______

Height: ______

6.

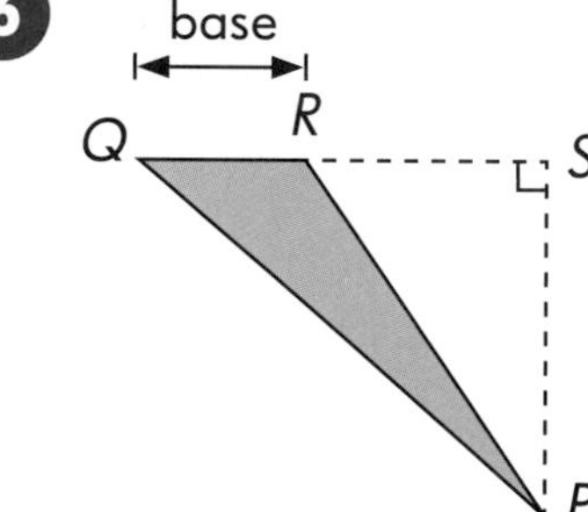

Base: ______

Height: ______

7.

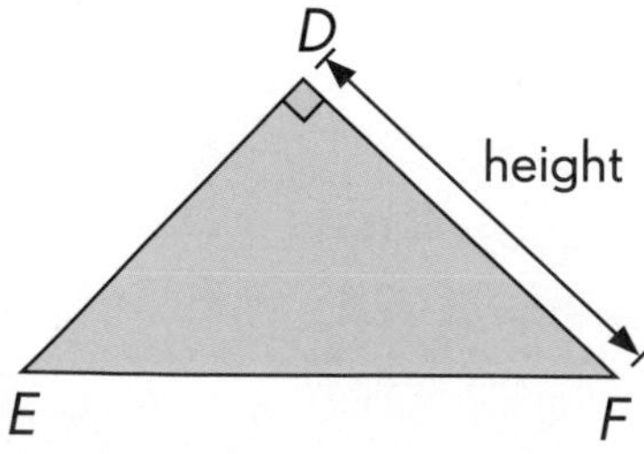

Height: ______

Base: ______

8.

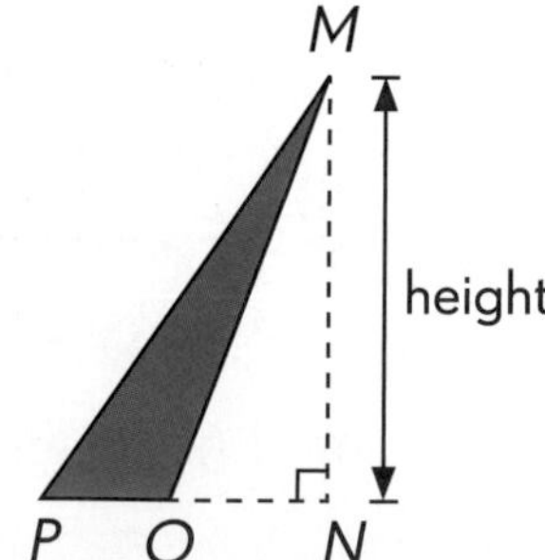

Height: ______

Base: ______

Find the area of each figure.

9

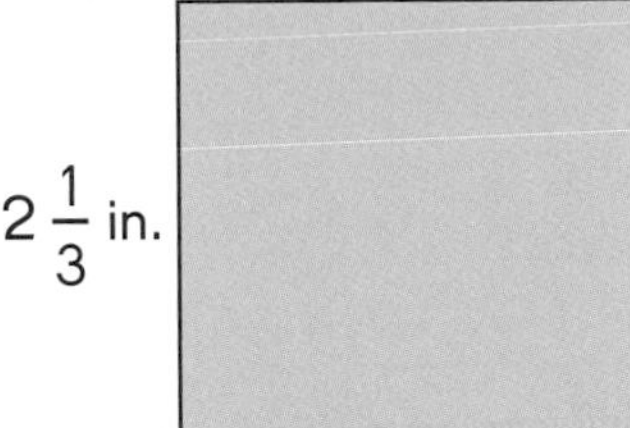

10

11

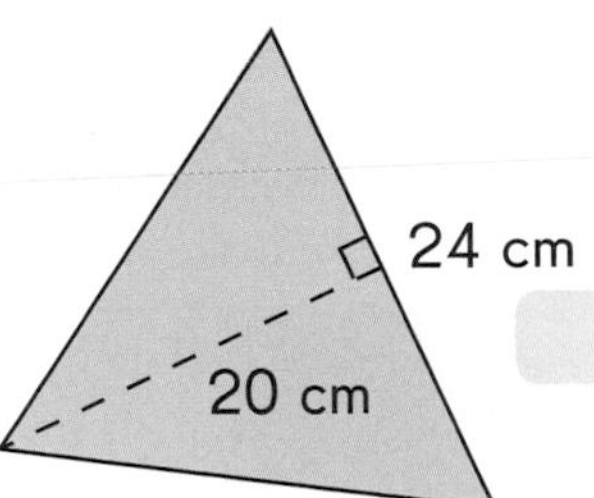

12

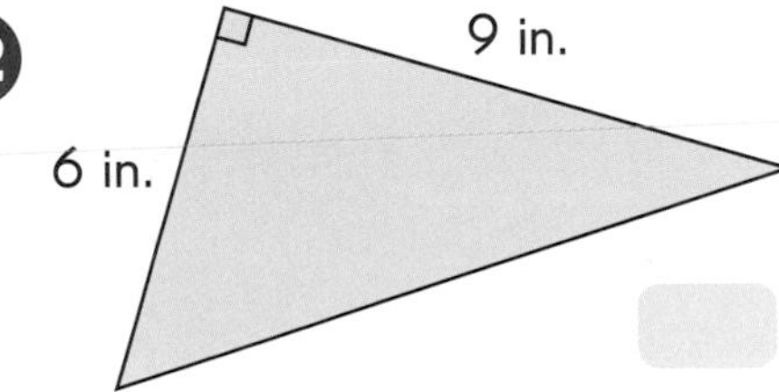

13

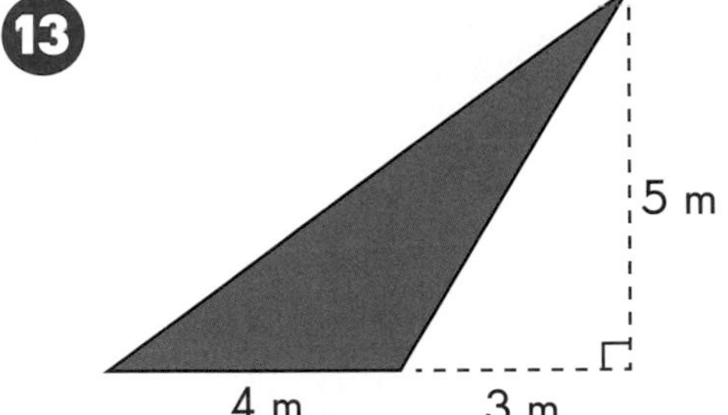

14

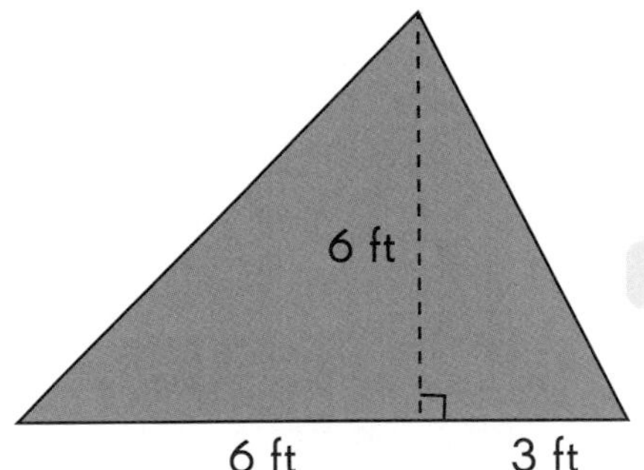

Problem Solving

Use the figure to answer Exercises 15 to 17.

ABCD is a rectangle of perimeter 48 cm. *AB* = 6 cm and *CD* = *DE*.

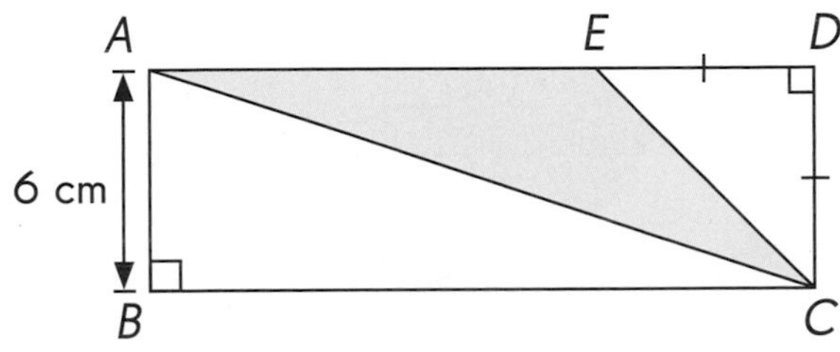

15 Find the length of rectangle *ABCD*.

16 Find the area of triangle *ACD*.

17 Find the area of the shaded triangle *ACE*.

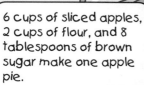

Chapter 7

Ratio

Lessons

- **7.1** Finding Ratio
- **7.2** Equivalent Ratios
- **7.3** Real-World Problems: Ratios
- **7.4** Ratios in Fraction Form
- **7.5** Comparing Three Quantities
- **7.6** Real-World Problems: More Ratios

BIG IDEA

▶ Two numbers can be compared by subtraction. Two or more numbers or quantities can also be compared by division and the comparison expressed as a ratio.

Recall Prior Knowledge

Comparing numbers using subtraction

$15 - 9 = 6$

6 is 9 less than 15.

15 is 9 more than 6.

Understanding fractions

A fraction is part of a whole.

The numerator represents the number of parts and the denominator represents the whole.

$\frac{3}{5}$ is 3 out of 5 parts.

Writing fractions in simplest form

Write $\frac{16}{28}$ in simplest form.

Factors of 16:

$16 = (1) \times 16$
$= (2) \times 8$
$= (4) \times 4$

Factors of 28:

$28 = (1) \times 28$
$= (2) \times 14$
$= (4) \times 7$

Common factors of 16 and 28 are 1, 2, and 4.

Greatest common factor (G.C.F.) of 16 and 28 is 4.

$\frac{16 \div 4}{28 \div 4}$ ← Divide both numerator and denominator by the G.C.F., 4

$= \frac{4}{7}$

Using models to solve problems

Find the value of each set using the model.

a 4 units

b 1 unit

c 3 units

d 7 units

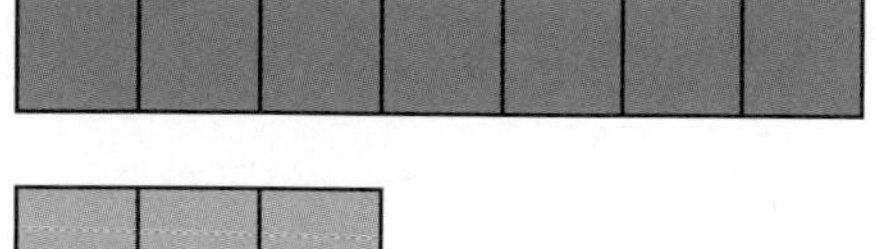

From the model,

a 4 units → 24

b 1 unit → 6

c 3 units → 18

d 7 units → 42

✔ Quick Check

Complete using the number bond on the right.

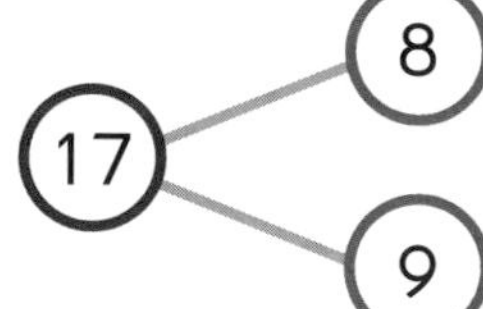

1 ___ is 9 less than 17.

2 17 is 8 more than ___.

State how many parts of the whole are represented by each fraction.

3 $\frac{1}{3}$ ___

4 $\frac{4}{8}$ ___

Write each fraction in simplest form.

5 $\frac{15}{20}$ ___

6 $\frac{4}{24}$ ___

Find the value of each set using the model.

7 7 units ___

8 1 unit ___

9 2 units ___

10 9 units ___

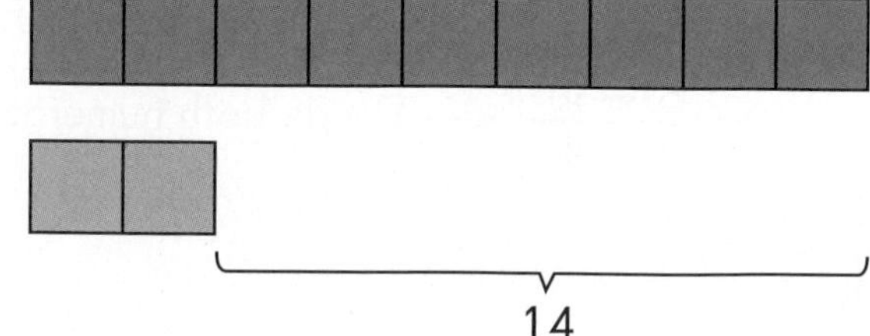

Lesson 7.1 Finding Ratio

Lesson Objective

- Read and write ratios.

Vocabulary
ratio term

Learn Use a ratio to compare two numbers or quantities by division.

You can compare two quantities or numbers by division.
To compare two quantities or numbers by division, you write them as a ratio.

There are 2 bran muffins and 1 blueberry muffin. You can compare the number of one type of muffin to the number of the other by division.

a To compare the number of bran muffins to the number of blueberry muffins, you write them as a ratio as shown.

1st		2nd		1st term		2nd term
Number of bran muffins	to	**Number of blueberry muffins**	→	**2**	:	**1**

Say: The ratio of the number of bran muffins to the number of blueberry muffins is '2 to 1'.

The two quantities you are comparing form the **terms** of the ratio.

The first term of the ratio is the first quantity in the comparison. The second term of the ratio is the second quantity.

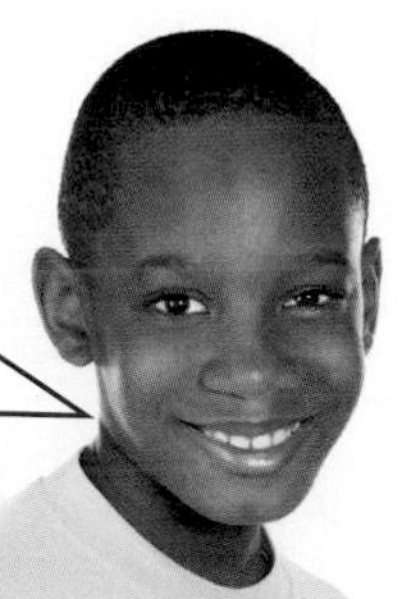
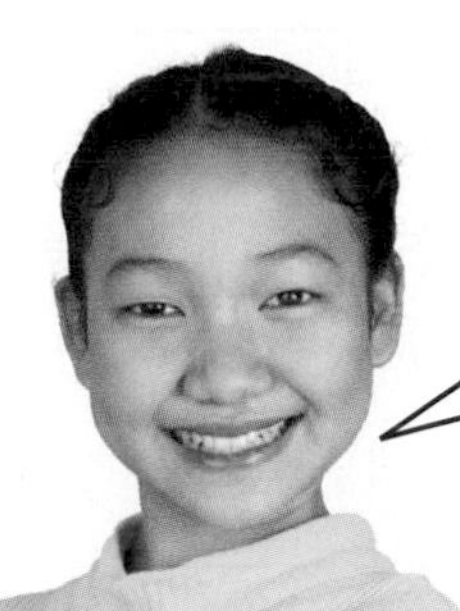

The ratio '2 : 1' tells us that 'there are 2 bran muffins to 1 blueberry muffin' or 'there is 1 blueberry muffin to 2 bran muffins'.

Continued on next page

b To compare the number of blueberry muffins to the number of bran muffins, you write them as a ratio as shown.

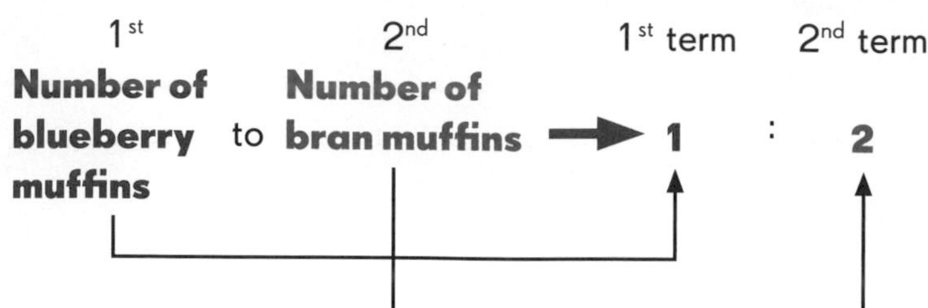
1st
2nd
1st term
2nd term
Number of blueberry muffins
to
Number of bran muffins
1 : 2

Say: The ratio of the number of blueberry muffins to the number of bran muffins is '1 to 2'.

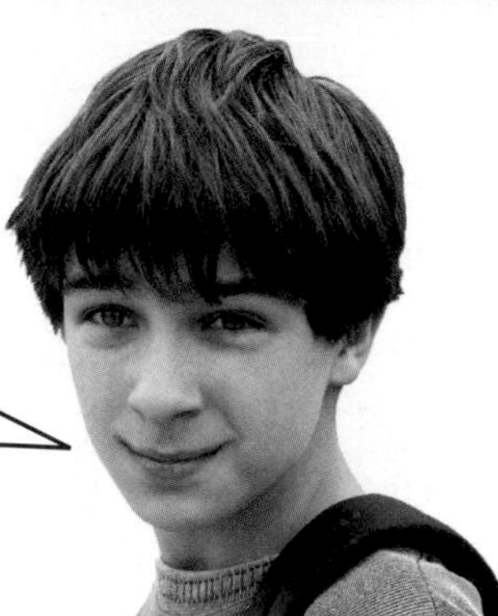

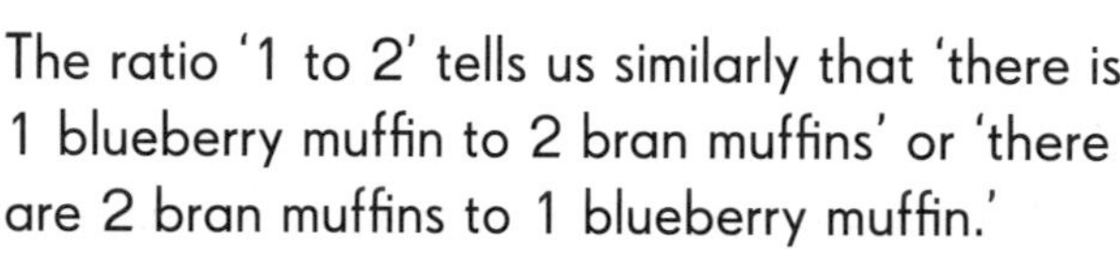
The ratio '1 to 2' tells us similarly that 'there is 1 blueberry muffin to 2 bran muffins' or 'there are 2 bran muffins to 1 blueberry muffin.'

Guided Learning

Complete.

1. The ratio of the number of blue pennants to the number of yellow pennants is ___ : ___.

2. The ratio of the number of yellow pennants to the number of blue pennants is ___ : ___.

The ratio ___ : ___ tells us that 'there are ___ blue pennants to ___ yellow pennants' or 'there are ___ yellow pennants to ___ blue pennants'.

The ratio ___ : ___ tells us that 'there are ___ yellow pennants to ___ blue pennants' or 'there are ___ blue pennants to ___ yellow pennants'.

Learn A ratio may not give the actual quantities compared.

The manager of a sporting goods store set up bins of baseballs and lacrosse balls for a sale. There are 2 bins of lacrosse balls and 3 bins of baseballs. Each bin has an equal number of balls.

2 bins to 3 bins is 2 : 3.

You know that there is an equal number of balls in each bin. The ratio does not tell you the actual number of balls.

The ratio of the number of lacrosse balls to the number of baseballs is 2 : 3.

The ratio of the number of baseballs to the number of lacrosse balls is 3 : 2.

1 unit

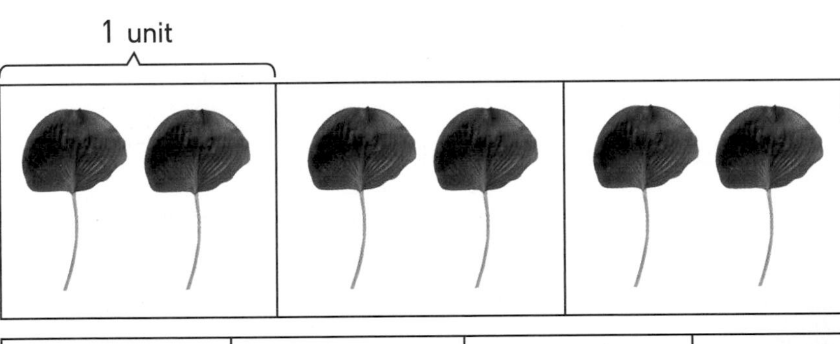

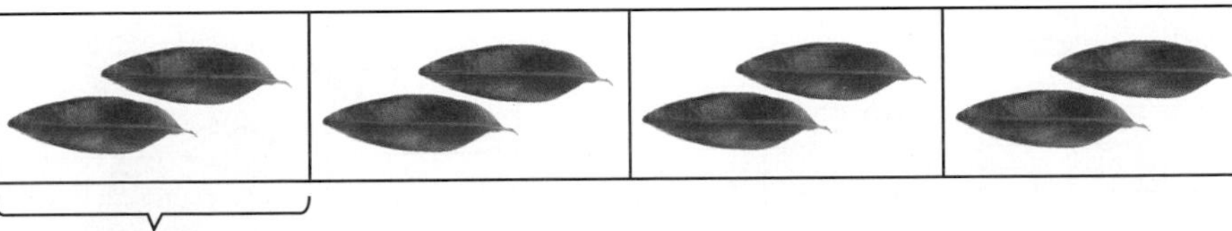

1 unit

1 unit = 2 leaves
So, a ratio need not give the actual quantities compared.

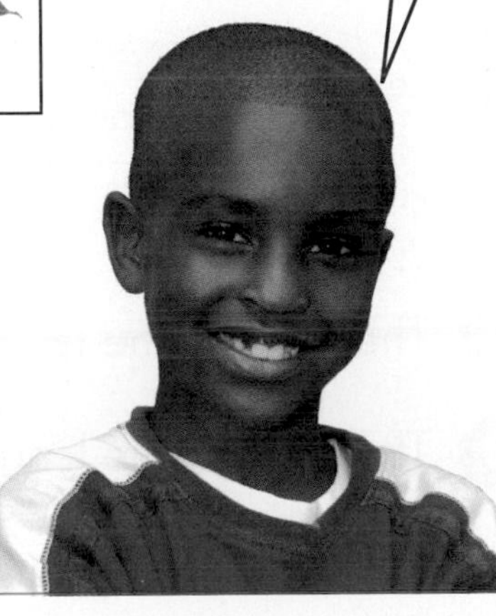

The ratio of the number of fan-shaped leaves to the number of lance-shaped leaves is 3 : 4.

The ratio of the number of lance-shaped leaves to the number of fan-shaped leaves is 4 : 3.

Guided Learning

Complete.

3. The ratio of the number of grape juice boxes to the number of apple juice boxes is ___ : ___.

4. The ratio of the number of apple juice boxes to the number of grape juice boxes is ___ : ___.

Ronald bought 2 pounds of pears and 5 pounds of oranges.

To compare as a ratio, the items must be in the same unit. The ratio however has no units.

5. The ratio of the weight of the pears to the weight of the oranges is ___ : ___.

6. The ratio of the weight of the oranges to the weight of the pears is ___ : ___.

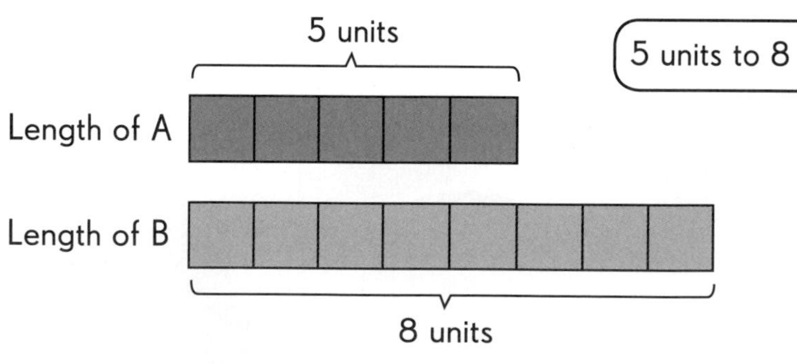

5 units to 8 units

7. The ratio of the length of A to the length of B is ___ : ___.

8. The ratio of the length of B to the length of A is ___ : ___.

Learn Use a part-whole model to show a ratio.

Jim cuts a piece of wood, 24 centimeters long, into two pieces. The shorter piece is 7 centimeters long. Find the ratio of the length of the shorter piece to the length of the longer piece.

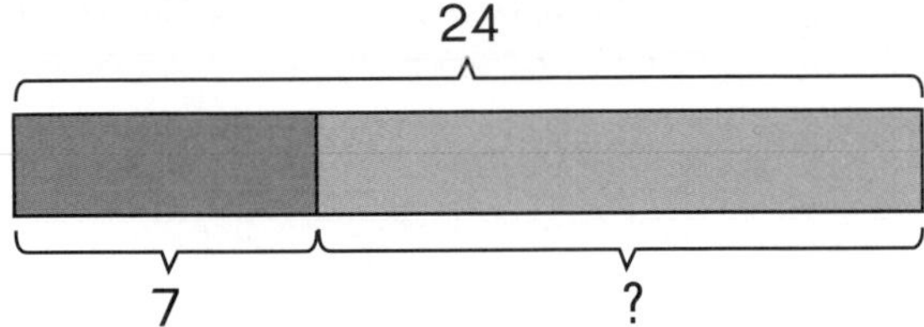

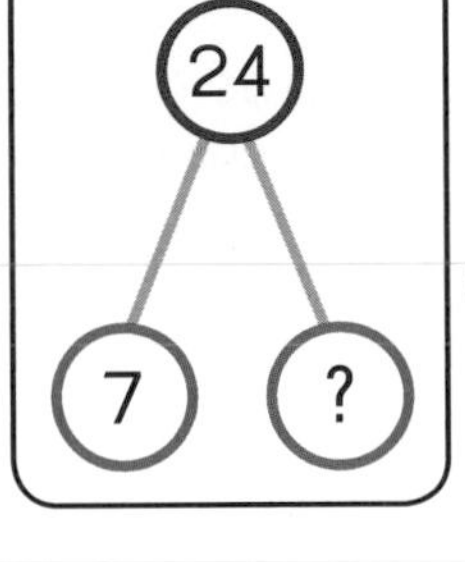

The length of the shorter piece of wood is 7 centimeters.

$24 - 7 = 17$

The length of the longer piece of wood is 17 centimeters.

The ratio of the length of the shorter piece to the length of the longer piece is 7 : 17.

Guided Learning

Solve.

9 Mr. Larson had 15 pounds of green beans to sell at his vegetable stand. He sold 7 pounds of green beans. Find the ratio of the weight of beans sold to the weight of beans left.

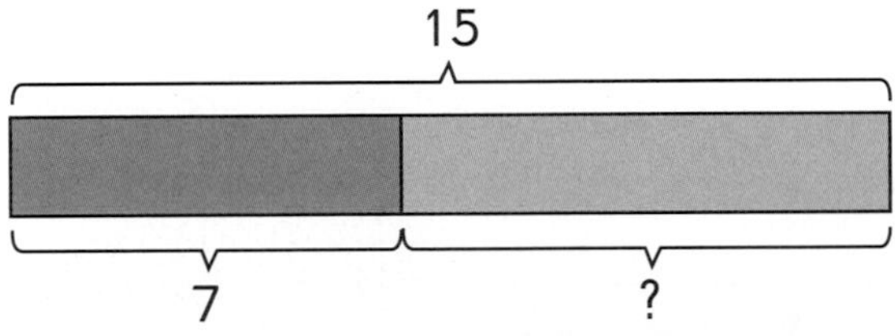

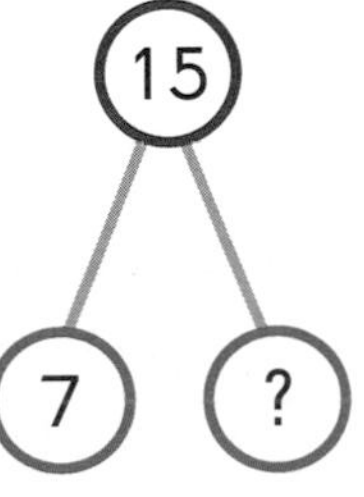

The weight of beans sold is 7 pounds.

____ − 7 = ____

The weight of beans left is ____ pounds.

The ratio of the weight of beans sold to the weight of beans left is ____ : ____.

Let's Practice

Complete.

1 The table shows the masses of shellfish sold at a seafood market one afternoon.

Shellfish	Mussels	Shrimp	Crabs	Lobsters	Scallops
Mass	2 kg	5 kg	3 kg	11 kg	8 kg

Copy and complete the table. Then, write six more ratios from the data.

Example

	Ratio
Mass of mussels to mass of shrimp	2 : 5
Mass of lobsters to mass of scallops	___ : ___
⋮	⋮
Mass of crabs to mass of shellfish in total	___ : ___

Draw a model to show each ratio.

Example

A : B = 2 : 5

A ▭▭

B ▭▭▭▭▭

2 A : B = 4 : 9

3 A : B = 11 : 7

Write two ratios to compare Set A and Set B.

4

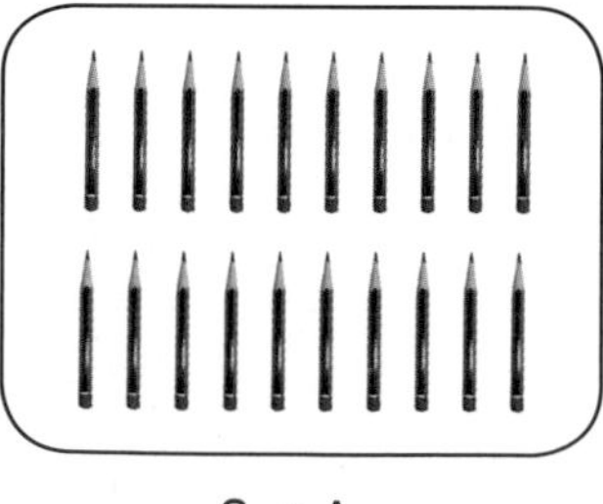

Set A

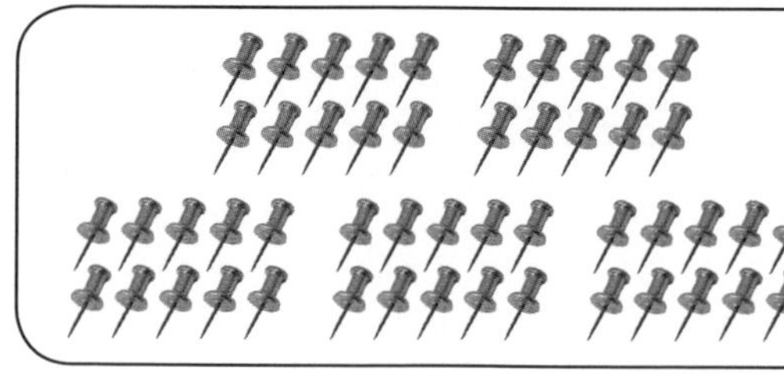

Set B

___ : ___ and ___ : ___

Write two ratios to compare the sets of leaves and flowers.

5 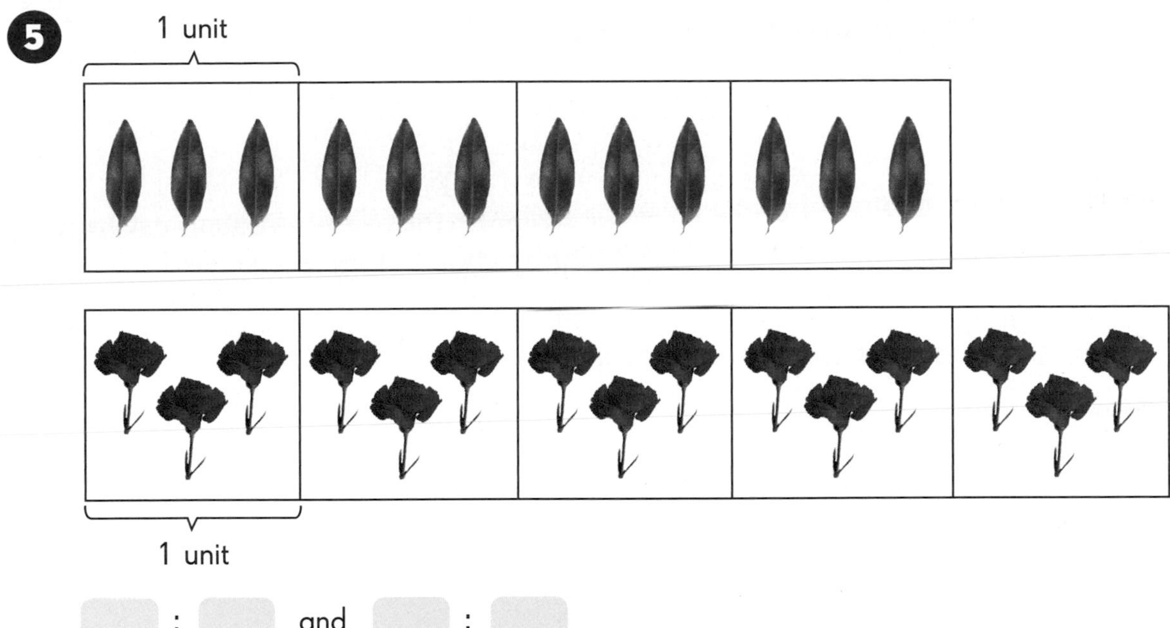

___ : ___ and ___ : ___

Solve.

6 A large checkered tablecloth is 5 feet wide and 7 feet long. Find the ratio of the length of the tablecloth to its width. ___

7 James has $88. He gives $35 to charity A and the rest to charity B. Find the ratio of the amount of money he gives to charity A to the amount of money he gives to charity B. ___

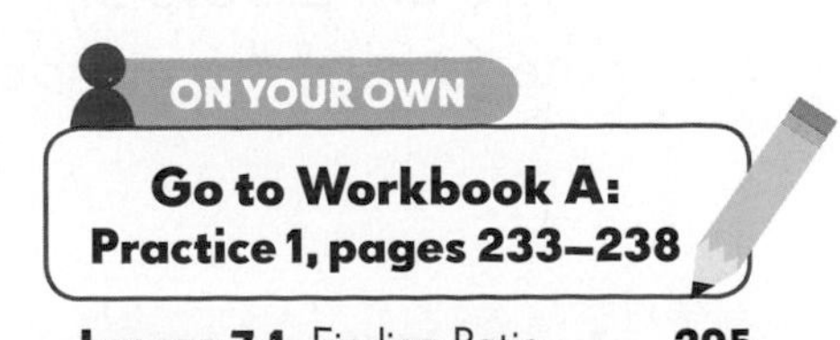

ON YOUR OWN
Go to Workbook A:
Practice 1, pages 233–238

Lesson

7.2 Equivalent Ratios

Lesson Objective

- Find equivalent ratios.

Vocabulary
equivalent ratios
simplest form
greatest common factor

Learn

Equivalent ratios show the same comparisons of numbers or quantities.

Jack has 4 red apples and 8 green apples. The ratio of the number of red apples to the number of green apples is 4 : 8.

Jack puts 2 apples of the same color on each tray.

2 trays of red apples

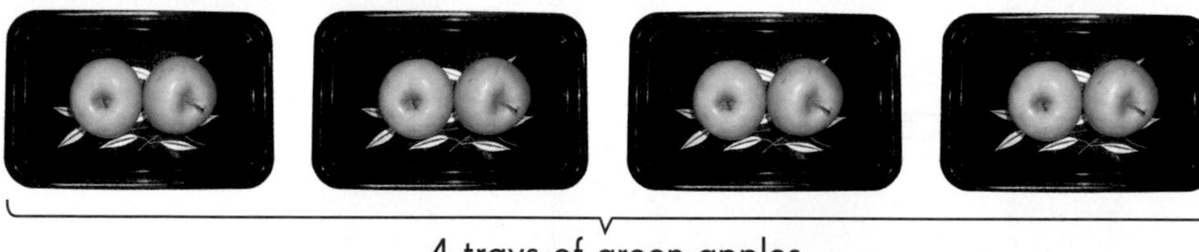

4 trays of green apples

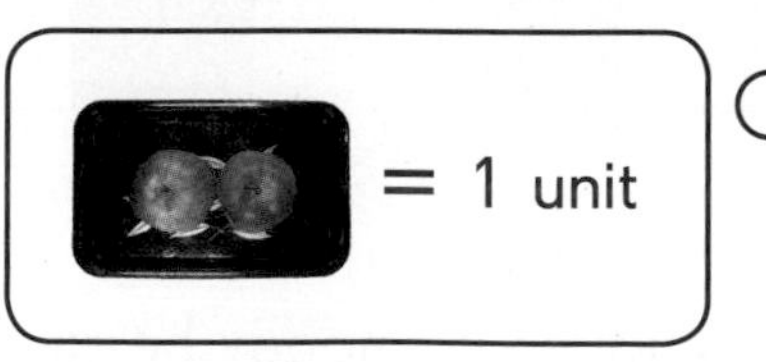

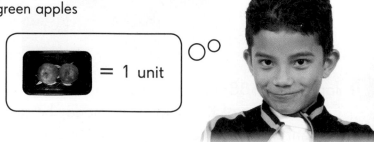

= 1 unit

There are 2 trays of red apples and 4 trays of green apples.
The ratio of the number of red apples to the number of green apples is 2 : 4.

Next, he puts 4 apples of the same color on each tray.

1 tray of red apples

2 trays of green apples

There is 1 tray of red apples and 2 trays of green apples.
The ratio of the number of red apples to the number of green apples is 1 : 2.

All three ratios 4 : 8, 2 : 4, and 1 : 2 compare the same numbers of red apples and green apples.
These ratios are equivalent ratios.

4 : 8 = 2 : 4 = 1 : 2
The ratio in **simplest form** is 1 : 2.

The ratio that shows the actual numbers of red apples and green apples is 4 : 8.

Guided Learning

Complete.

1. 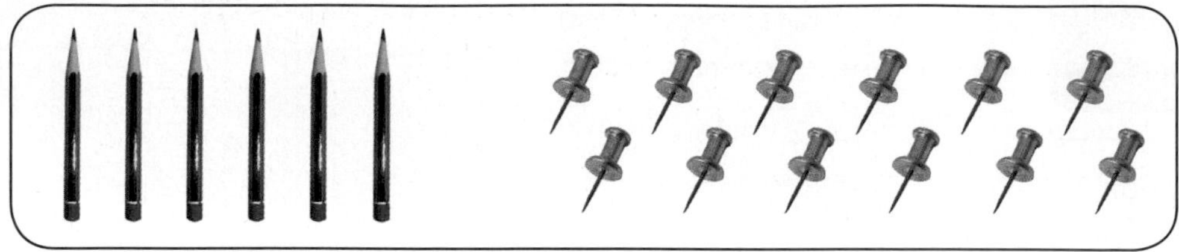

The ratio of the number of pencils to the number of push pins is ___ : ___.

2. 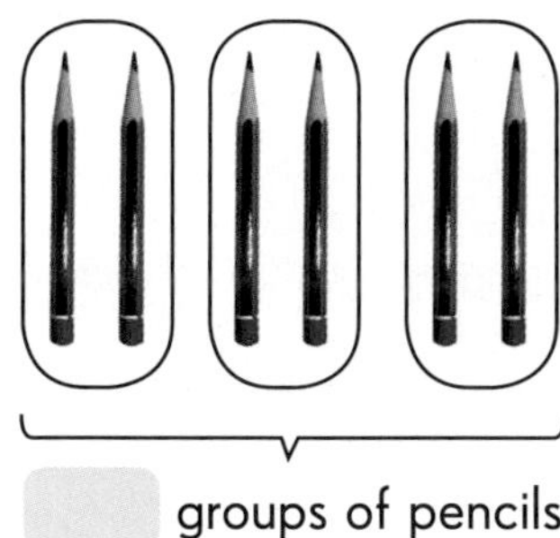 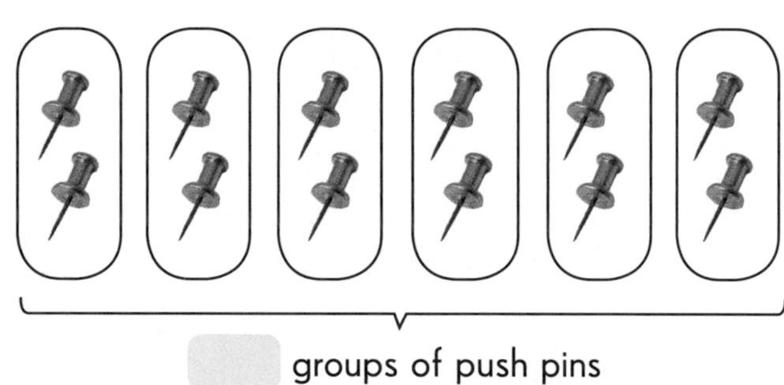

___ groups of pencils ___ groups of push pins

The ratio of the number of pencils to the number of push pins is ___ : ___.

3. 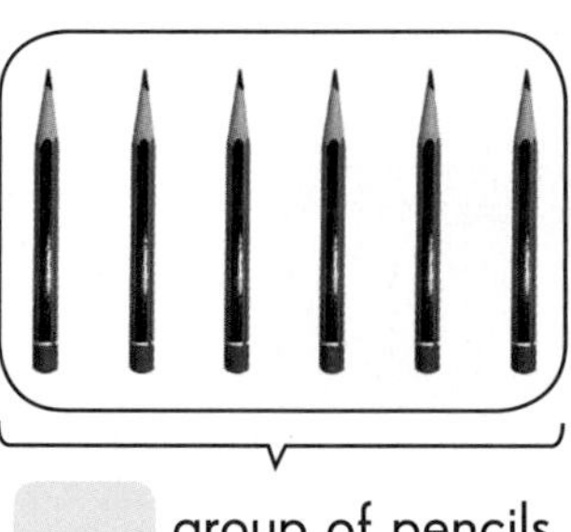 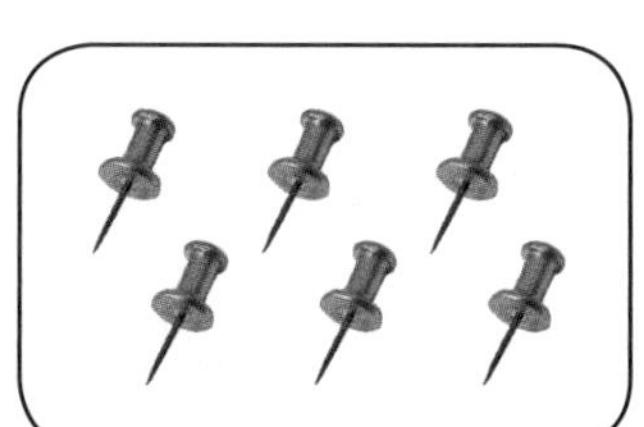 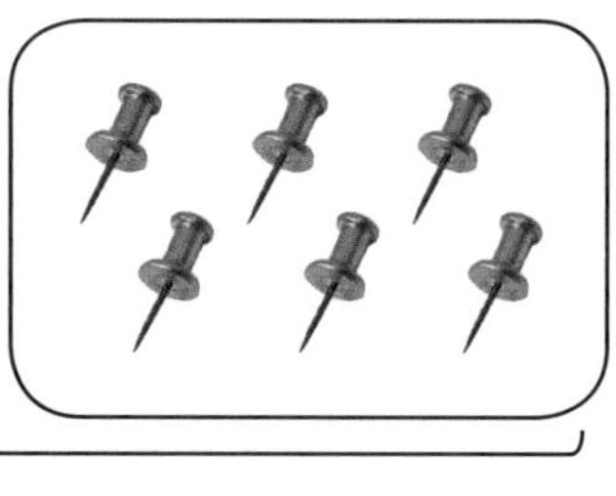

___ group of pencils ___ groups of push pins

The ratio of the number of pencils to the number of push pins is ___ : ___.

4. The equivalent ratios are ___ : , ___ : ___, and  : ___.

5. In these equivalent ratios, the ratio in its simplest form is ___ : .

6. The ratio that shows the actual numbers of pencils and push pins is ___ : .

Learn Use the greatest common factor to write ratios in simplest form.

Find the ratio 4 : 6 in simplest form.

To write a ratio in simplest form, divide the terms by their greatest common factor.

2 × 2 = 4 and 2 × 3 = 6.
2 is the greatest common factor of 4 and 6.
Divide 4 and 6 by 2.

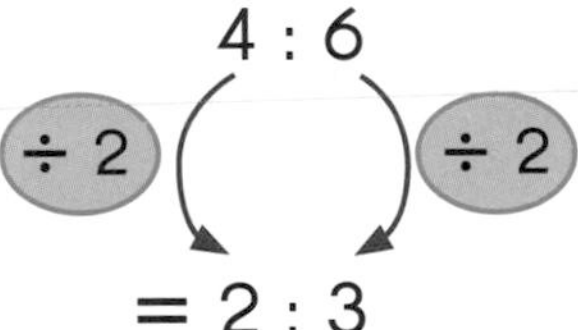

The numbers 2 and 3 cannot be divided by a common factor other than 1.
A ratio is in simplest form when its terms have only 1 as a common factor.

The ratio 4 : 6 in simplest form is 2 : 3.

Guided Learning

Complete to express each ratio in simplest form.

7 12 : 4

÷ ___ ÷ ___

= ___ : ___

The greatest common factor of 12 and 4 is ___. Divide 12 and 4 by ___.

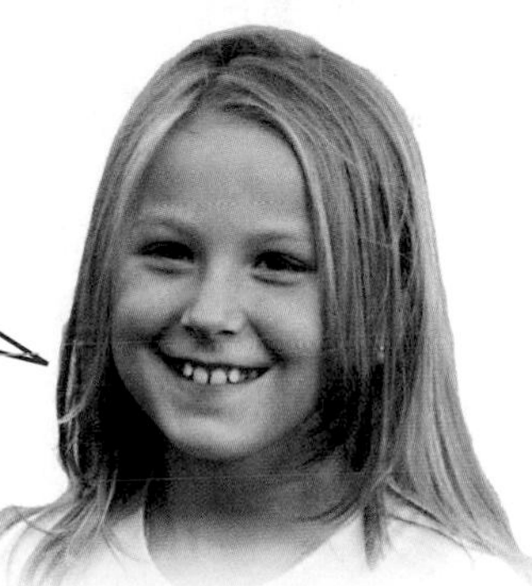

8 9 : 15

÷ ___ ÷ ___

= ___ : ___

First, find the greatest common factor of 9 and 15.

Learn Use multiplication to find missing terms in equivalent ratios.

Find the missing term in these equivalent ratios.

2 : 5 = 6 : ?

Look at the first terms of the equivalent ratios — **2** : 5 = **6** : ?.

Method 1

2 × **3** = 6

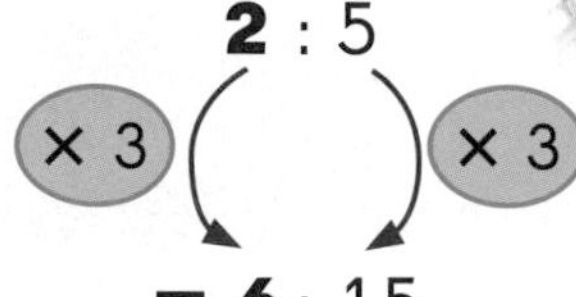

Method 2

6 ÷ 2 = **3**

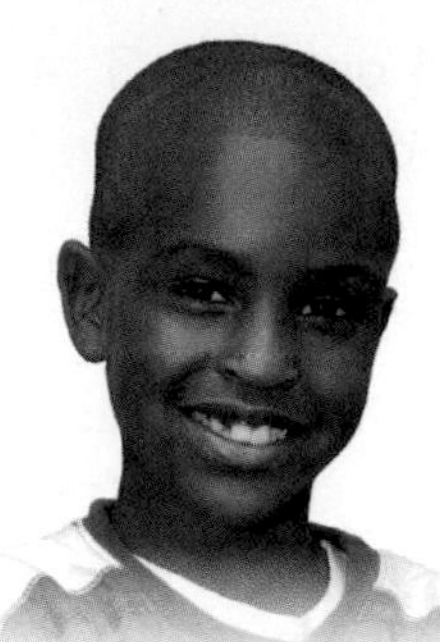

So, **3** is the multiplying factor.
3 × 5 = 15

Learn Use division to find missing terms in equivalent ratios.

Find the missing term in these equivalent ratios.

15 : 12 = ? : 4

Look at the second terms of the equivalent ratios — 15 : **12** = ? : **4**.

Method 1

12 ÷ **3** = 4
15 ÷ **3** = 5

15 : **12**
÷ 3 ÷ 3
= 5 : **4**

Method 2

12 ÷ 4 = **3**

So, **3** is the factor.
15 ÷ **3** = 5

Guided Learning

Find the missing terms in each set of equivalent ratios.

9 4 : 3 (× ___ , × ___) = 20 : ___

$20 \div 4 =$ ___

$3 \times$ ___ $=$ ___

10 7 : ___ (× ___ , × ___) = 21 : 12

$21 \div 7 =$ ___

$12 \div$ ___ $=$ ___

11 ___ : 16 (÷ ___ , ÷ ___) = 3 : 2

$16 \div 2 =$ ___

$3 \times$ ___ $=$ ___

Hands-On Activity

WORKING TOGETHER

Materials:
- 14 yellow cubes
- 28 red cubes

Work in groups of two or four.

STEP 1 Put the cubes in groups so that each group has the same number of cubes. (Do not mix yellow cubes and red cubes in a group.)

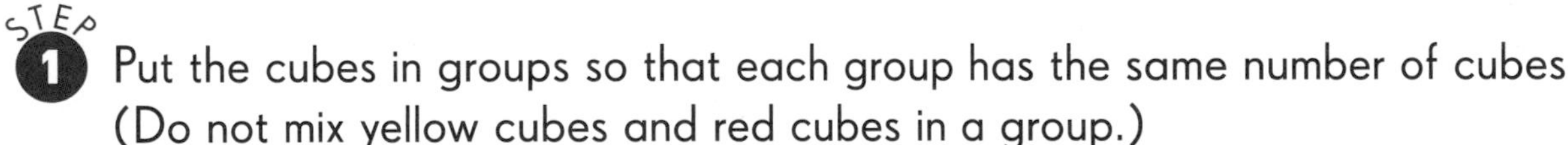

STEP 2 Write the ratio of the number of groups of yellow cubes to the number of groups of red cubes.

STEP 3 Repeat STEP 1 and STEP 2 with different numbers of cubes in each group to get another two ratios.
What can you say about these ratios?

STEP 4 Repeat the activity using 8 yellow cubes and 24 red cubes. What can you say about these ratios? Why is this so? Explain your reasoning.

Let's Practice

Solve.

Mrs. Jefferson has 3 boxes of yellow chalk and 8 boxes of white chalk. Each box contains 5 pieces of chalk.

1. Find the total number of pieces of yellow chalk. ___
2. Find the total number of pieces of white chalk. ___
3. Find the ratio of the number of pieces of yellow chalk to the number of pieces of white chalk. ___
4. Find the ratio of the number of boxes of yellow chalk to the number of boxes of white chalk. ___
5. What can you say about the ratios in 3 and 4? ___

Express each ratio in simplest form.

6. 4 : 14 = ___ : ___
7. 18 : 8 = ___ : ___
8. 8 : 32 = ___ : ___
9. 42 : 12 = ___ : ___

Find the missing term in each set of equivalent ratios.

10. 4 : 7 = 12 : ___
11. 3 : 8 = ___ : 32
12. 27 : 15 = ___ : 5
13. 6 : 42 = 2 : ___

Find the missing term in each set of equivalent ratios.

14. 3 : ___ = 48 : 80
15. ___ : 51 = 4 : 3
16. 70 : ___ = 2 : 4
17. ___ : 7 = 128 : 224

ON YOUR OWN

Go to Workbook A: Practice 2, pages 239–240

Lesson 7.3 Real-World Problems: Ratios

Lesson Objective

- Solve real-world problems involving ratios.

Learn Find simplest-form ratios to compare quantities in real-world problems.

There are 6 angelfish and 18 tetras in an aquarium. Find the ratio of the number of angelfish to the number of tetras in the aquarium.

The ratio of the number of angelfish to the number of tetras is 6 : 18.

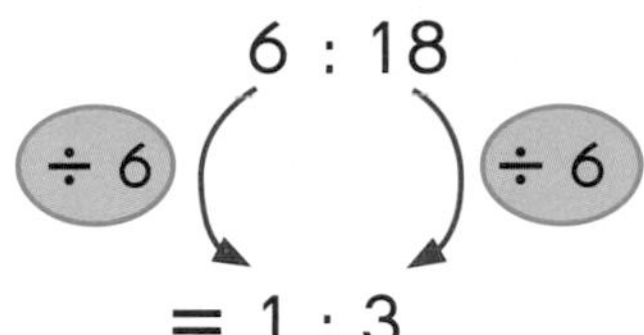
6 : 18
÷ 6
÷ 6
= 1 : 3

Write the ratio 6 : 18 in simplest form. Divide 6 and 18 by their greatest common factor 6.

The ratio of the number of angelfish to the number of tetras in the aquarium is 1 : 3.

Guided Learning

Complete.

There are 12 pink roses and 15 yellow roses in Beth's garden.

1 What is the ratio of the number of pink roses to the number of yellow roses?

12 : 15

÷ ___ ÷ ___

= ___ : ___

Write the ratio 12 : 15 in simplest form. Divide 12 and 15 by the greatest common factor 3.

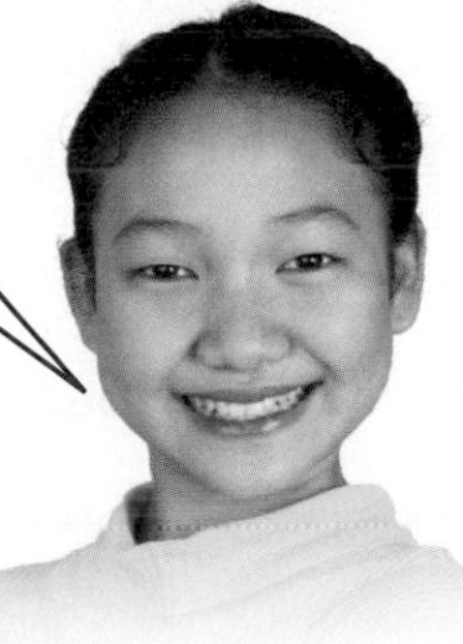

The ratio of the number of pink roses to the number of yellow roses is ___ : ___.

2 The ratio of the number of yellow roses to the number of pink roses is

: .

Learn: Use the whole to find the missing part in a ratio.

There are 48 children in a soccer program, and 16 of them are girls.
Find the ratio of the number of girls to the number of boys in the program.

48 − 16 = 32

There are 32 boys in the program.

16 : 32 = 1 : 2

16 : 32
÷ 16 ÷ 16
= 1 : 2

The ratio of the number of girls to the number of boys in the program is 1 : 2.

Give the answer in simplest form.

Guided Learning

Complete.

On a rainy day, the All-Weather Goods store sold 56 umbrellas and raincoats altogether. The number of raincoats sold was 24.

3. Find the ratio of the total number of umbrellas and raincoats sold to the number of raincoats sold.

   ___ : ___ = ___ : ___

   The ratio of the total number of umbrellas and raincoats sold to the number of raincoats sold is ___ : ___.

4. Find the ratio of the number of umbrellas sold to the number of raincoats sold.

   56 − ___ = ___
   The number of umbrellas sold was ___.

   ___ : 24 = ___ : ___

   The ratio of the number of umbrellas sold to the number of raincoats sold is ___ : ___.

Learn Find the new ratio after one term changes.

Ernesto has 25 football cards and 40 baseball cards. He gives away 5 baseball cards. What is the ratio of the number of football cards to the number of baseball cards Ernesto has now?

$40 - 5 = 35$

Ernesto has 35 baseball cards now.

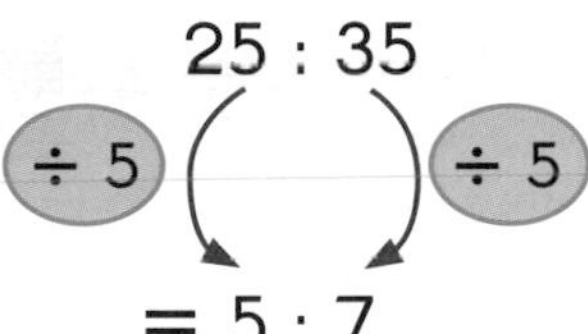

The ratio of the number of football cards to the number of baseball cards Ernesto has now is 5 : 7.

Guided Learning

Complete.

Gerald donated 30 quarters and 16 dimes to a charity collection. He then donated another 18 quarters.

5 Find the ratio of the total number of quarters to the number of dimes Gerald donated.

30 + ___ = ___

Gerald donated a total of ___ quarters.

___ : 16 = ___ : ___

The ratio of the total number of quarters Gerald donated to the number of dimes he donated is ___ : ___.

6 Find the ratio of the total number of quarters Gerald donated to the total number of coins he donated.

From **5**, the total number of quarters Gerald donated is ___.

___ + 16 = ___

Gerald donated a total of ___ coins.

___ : ___ = ___ : ___

The ratio of the total number of quarters Gerald donated to the total number of coins he donated is ___ : ___.

Learn Use models to find a ratio.

Amy has 96 comic and story books altogether. She has 60 comic books. Find the ratio of the number of comic books to the number of story books.

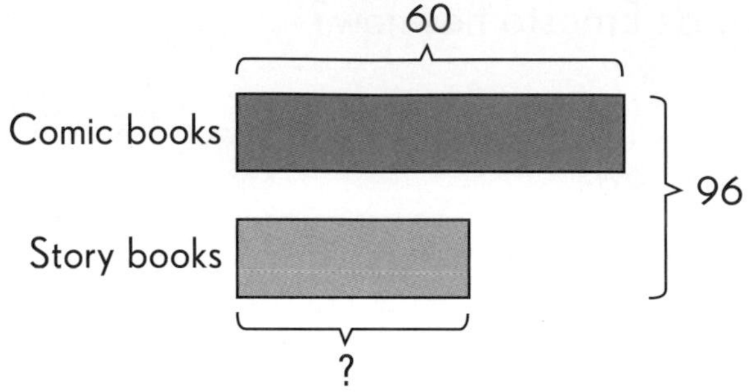

96 − 60 = 36

There are 36 story books.

60 : 36 = 5 : 3

The ratio of the number of comic books to the number of story books is 5 : 3.

Guided Learning

Complete.

Stanley collects stamps as a hobby. In his collection, he has 56 foreign and 196 U.S. stamps.

7 What is the ratio of the number of U.S. stamps to the total number of stamps he has?

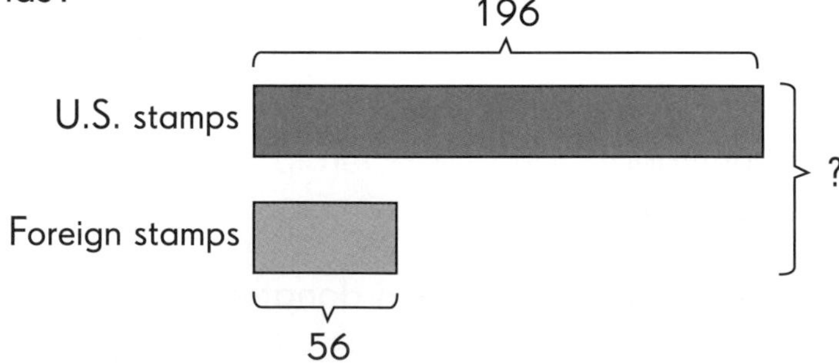

196 + 56 = ____

The total number of stamps in Stanley's collection is ____.

____ : ____ = ____ : ____

The ratio of the number of foreign stamps to the total number of stamps Stanley has is ____ : ____.

Learn Find the other term given the ratio and one term.

Harold divides a carton of tomatoes into two portions. The ratio of the mass of the bigger portion to the mass of the smaller portion is 5 : 2. The mass of the bigger portion is 15 pounds. Find the mass of the smaller portion.

Method 1

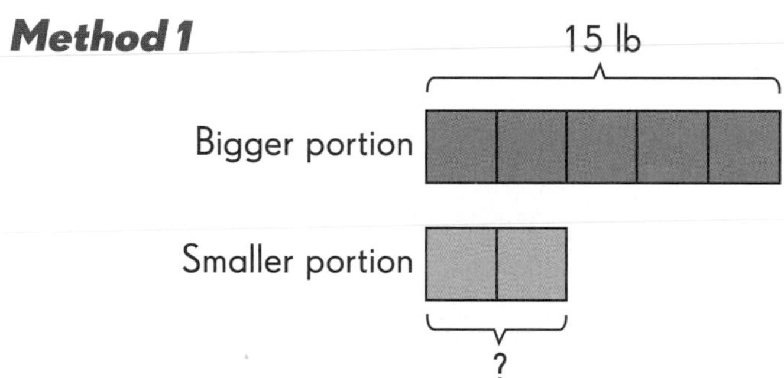

5 units ⟶ 15 lb

1 unit ⟶ $15 \div 5 = 3$ lb

2 units ⟶ $2 \times 3 = 6$ lb

The mass of the smaller portion of tomatoes is 6 pounds.

Method 2

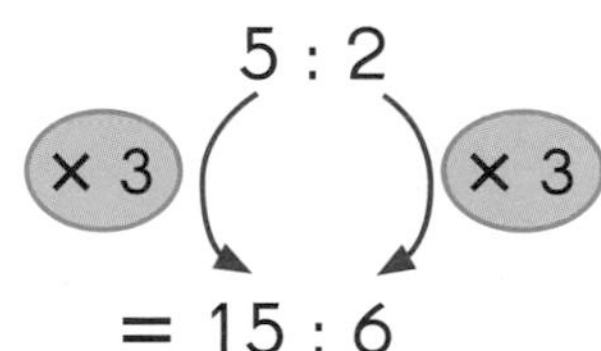

The mass of the smaller portion of tomatoes is 6 pounds.

Guided Learning

Complete.

8. Mrs. Gardner has the milk she is going to use to make a smoothie and a shortcake in two portions. The ratio of the volume of portion 1 to the volume of portion 2 is 3 : 4. The volume of portion 1 is 120 milliliters. Find the total volume of both portions.

Method 1

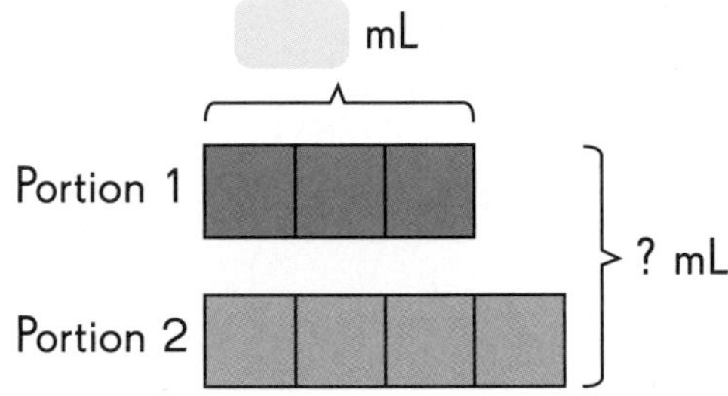

3 units → ___ mL

1 unit → ___ ÷ ___ = ___ mL

7 units → ___ × ___ = ___ mL

The total volume of both portions is ___ milliliters.

Method 2

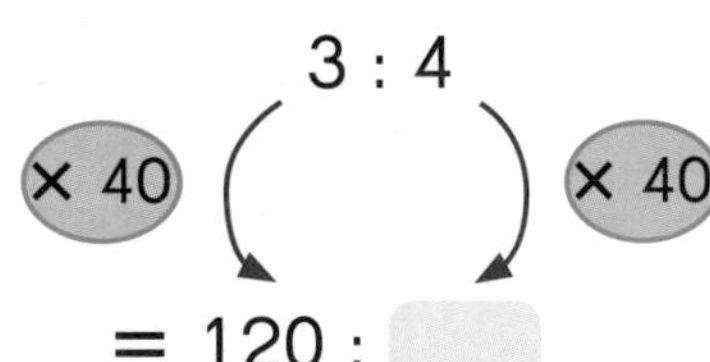

$3 \times 40 = 120$
$4 \times 40 =$ ___

The volume of portion 1 is ___ milliliters.

120 + ___ = ___

The total volume of both portions is ___ milliliters.

READING AND WRITING MATH

Math Journal

Look at the model.
Write a real-world problem that includes a ratio. Then, solve your real-world problem.

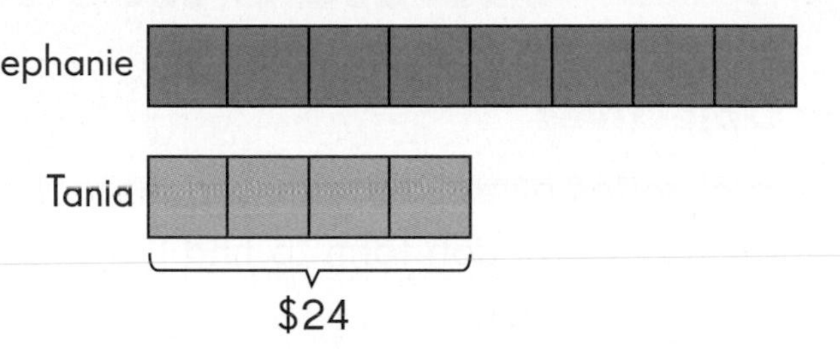

Let's Practice

Solve. Show your work.

1. Lindsay spent $24 and had $11 left. Find the ratio of the amount of money she spent to the total amount of money she had at first.
2. A box contained 42 apples and 12 of them were green. The rest of the apples were red. Find the ratio of the number of green apples to the number of red apples.
3. Stella mixed 20 milliliters of cranberry juice with 30 milliliters of blackcurrant juice. She then added another 15 milliliters of cranberry juice. Find the ratio of the amount of cranberry juice to the amount of blackcurrant juice in the end.
4. Mr. Wong cuts a coil of wire into two pieces in the ratio 3 : 4. The length of the longer piece of wire is 32 centimeters. What is the total length of the coil of wire?
5. The ratio of the number of students at the zoo in the morning to the number of students at the zoo in the afternoon was 5 : 3. There were 145 students at the zoo in the morning. What was the number of students at the zoo in the afternoon?
6. The total time that Ken and Bob worked in a week was 63 hours. Ken worked 36 hours. What is the ratio of Bob's working hours to Ken and Bob's total working hours?

ON YOUR OWN

Go to Workbook A: Practice 3, pages 241–244

Lesson 7.4 Ratios in Fraction Form

Lesson Objectives

- Interpret ratios given in fraction form.
- Write ratios in fraction form to find how many times one number or quantity is as large as another.

Learn Ratios can also be written in fraction form.

Jason has two colored pencils: one red, the other blue.

The ratio of the length of his red pencil to the length of his blue pencil is as represented in the model.

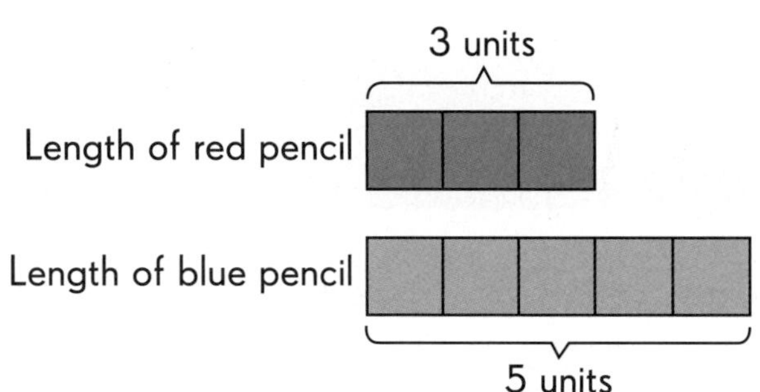

Total number of units = 3 + 5 = 8

a The ratio of the length of the red pencil to the length of the blue pencil is 3 : 5.

The same ratio can also be written in fraction form as:

$$\frac{\text{Length of the red pencil}}{\text{Length of the blue pencil}} = \frac{3}{5}$$

b The ratio of the length of the blue pencil to the length of the red pencil is 5 : 3.

The same ratio can also be written in fraction form as:

$$\frac{\text{Length of the blue pencil}}{\text{Length of the red pencil}} = \frac{5}{3}$$

c The ratio of the length of the red pencil to the total length of the two pencils is 3 : 8.

The same ratio can also be written in fraction form as:

$$\frac{\text{Length of the red pencil}}{\text{Total length of the two pencils}} = \frac{3}{8}$$

Guided Learning

Complete. You may draw models to help you.

The ratio of Sam's height to Gene's height is as represented in the model.

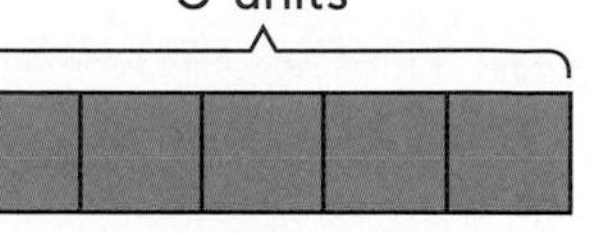

1. The ratio of Sam's height to Gene's height is ___ : ___ or $\frac{\square}{\square}$.

2. The ratio of Sam's height to the total height of the two boys is ___ : ___ or $\frac{\square}{\square}$.

Let's Explore!

In this table, you are given the ratio of a quantity to another quantity.

	Ratio form	Fraction form
A to B	3 : 8	$\frac{3}{8}$
C to D	4 : 7	$\frac{4}{7}$
E to F	5 : 9	$\frac{5}{9}$

1. Look at the fraction form of each ratio. Note the quantity in the numerator. Locate the same quantity in the corresponding ratio form. Where is its position?

2. Look at the fraction form of each ratio. Note the quantity in the denominator. Locate the same quantity in the corresponding ratio form. Where is its position?

What can you say about the relationship between the ratio form and fraction form of a ratio?

Learn

Write ratios in fraction form to find how many times one number or quantity is as large as another.

The numbers of adults and children watching a show are represented in the model.

Number of adults 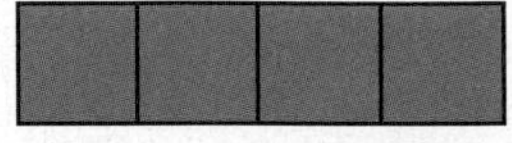

Number of children 

a How many times the number of children is the number of adults?

$$\frac{\text{Number of adults}}{\text{Number of children}} = \frac{4}{12} = \frac{1}{3}$$

The number of adults is $\frac{1}{3}$ times the number of children.

b How many times the number of adults is the number of children?

$$\frac{\text{Number of children}}{\text{Number of adults}} = \frac{3}{1}$$

The number of children is 3 times the number of adults.

Guided Learning

Complete. Give all answers in simplest form.

Felice spent \$21 and Brad spent \$42.

3 $\frac{\text{Amount of money Felice spent}}{\text{Amount of money Brad spent}} = \frac{\square}{\square}$

The amount of money Felice spent is $\frac{\square}{\square}$ times the amount of money Brad spent.

4 $\frac{\text{Amount of money Brad spent}}{\text{Amount of money Felice spent}} = \frac{\square}{\square}$

The amount of money Brad spent is $\square$ times the amount of money Felice spent.

Learn Draw a model to represent a ratio given in fraction form.

Steve saved $\frac{3}{4}$ as much money as Chyna.

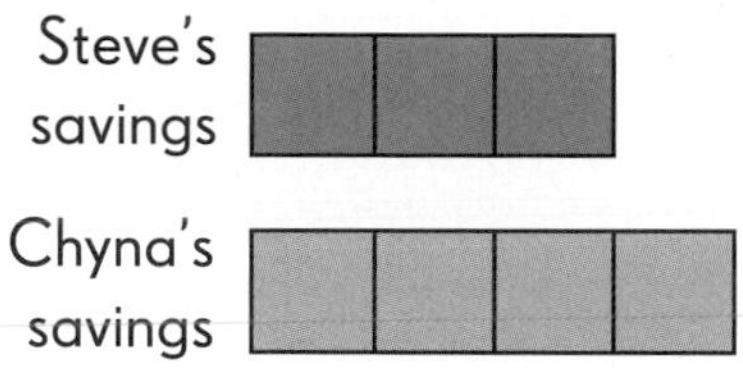

In fraction form:
Steve's savings: Chyna's savings $= \frac{3}{4}$

So, in ratio form:
Steve's savings: Chyna's savings $= 3 : 4$

I can draw a model with 3 units to represent Steve's savings and 4 units to represent Chyna's savings.

Total number of units $= 3 + 4 = 7$

From the model:

(a) The ratio of Chyna's savings to Steve's savings is $4 : 3$ or $\frac{4}{3}$.

(b) The ratio of Chyna's savings to their total savings is $4 : 7$ or $\frac{4}{7}$.

Guided Learning

Complete. Use the model to help you.

Ryan cut a rope into two pieces. The length of the first piece was $\frac{4}{7}$ of the length of the second piece.

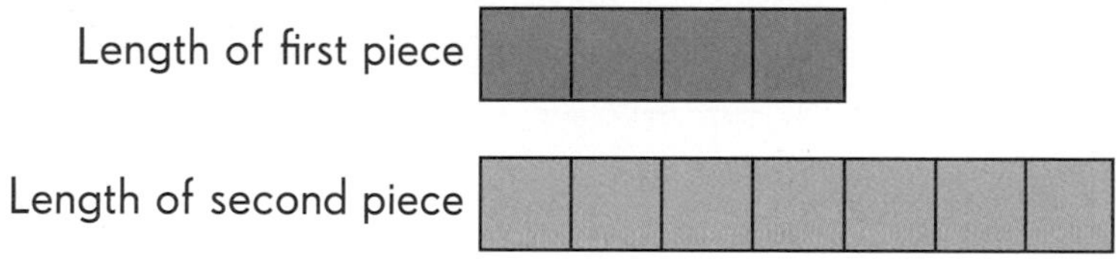

5 The ratio of the length of the second piece to the length of the first piece is ___ : ___ or $\frac{\quad}{\quad}$.

6 The ratio of the length of the second piece to the total length of the two pieces is ___ : ___ or $\frac{\quad}{\quad}$.

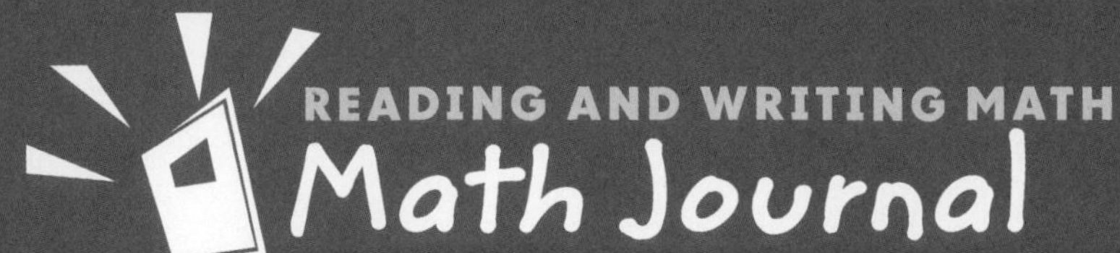

WORK IN PAIRS

Write, in fraction form, three ratios for each scenario.

1. There is $\frac{4}{7}$ times as many large eggs as there are medium eggs at Mim's grocery store.

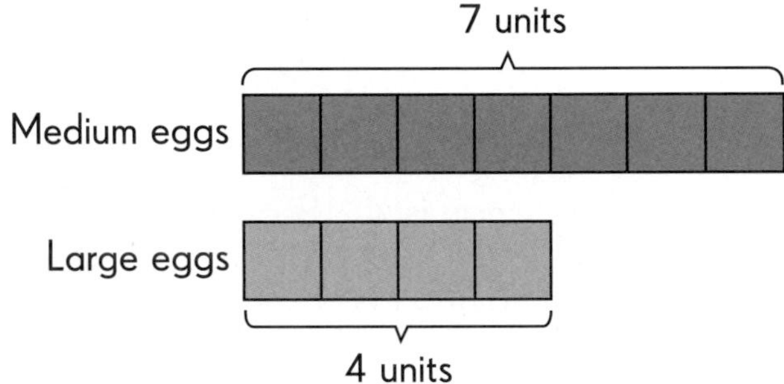

Example

Number of large eggs: number of medium eggs $= \frac{4}{7}$

2. Fran saves \$450 every month while Lily saves \$150 every month.

Let's Practice

Complete.

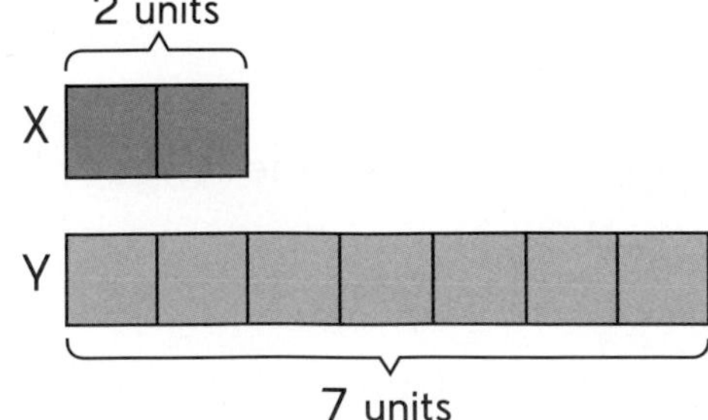

1. The ratio of X to Y is ___ : ___ or $\frac{\quad}{\quad}$.

2. X is $\frac{\quad}{\quad}$ times Y.

3. Y is $\frac{\quad}{\quad}$ times X.

Solve. Use the model to help you.

The ratio of the length of pole A to the length of pole B is as represented in the model.

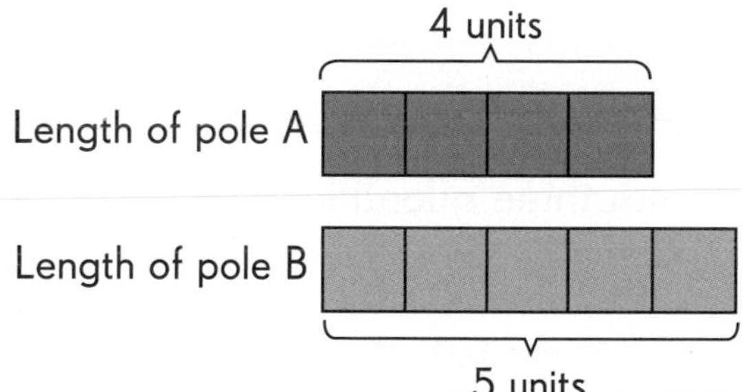

4. Find the ratio of pole A's length to the total length of the two poles. Give your answer in fraction form.
5. How many times pole A's length is pole B's length?
6. How many times pole B's length is pole A's length?
7. How many times pole A's length is the total length of both poles?
8. How many times pole B's length is the total length of both poles?

Solve. You may draw a model to help you.

Jessie has $15. Kimberley has $21.

9. Find the ratio of the amount of money Jessie has to the amount of money that Kimberley has. Give your answer in fraction form.
10. How many times the amount of money Kimberley has is the amount of money Jessie has?
11. How many times the amount of money Jessie has is the amount of money Kimberley has?
12. How many times the total amount of money they have altogether is the amount of money Jessie has?
13. How many times the amount of money Kimberley has is the total amount of money they have altogether?

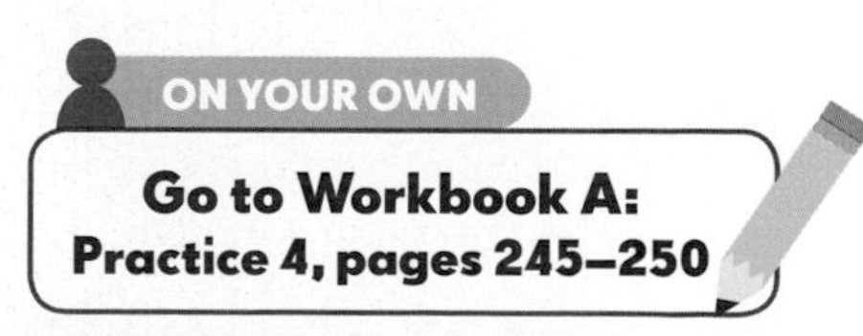

ON YOUR OWN
Go to Workbook A:
Practice 4, pages 245–250

Lesson

7.5 Comparing Three Quantities

Lesson Objectives

- Read and write ratios with three quantities.
- Express equivalent ratios with three quantities.

Learn

Use ratios to compare three quantities.

Wendy has 4 red carnations, 8 pink carnations, and 12 yellow carnations. The ratio of the number of red carnations to the number of pink carnations to the number of yellow carnations is 4 : 8 : 12.

Method 1

The greatest common factor of 4, 8, and 12 is 4.

I can take

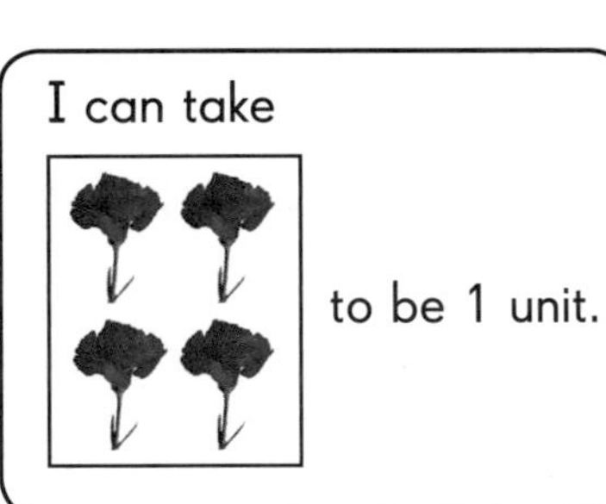

to be 1 unit.

Wendy puts 4 carnations into each box.

1 box of red carnations

2 boxes of pink carnations

3 boxes of yellow carnations

The ratio of the number of red carnations to the number of pink carnations to the number of yellow carnations is 1 : 2 : 3.

Method 2

$$4 : 8 : 12 \xrightarrow{\div 4,\ \div 4,\ \div 4} = 1 : 2 : 3$$

The greatest common factor of 4, 8, and 12 is 4.

4 : 8 : 12 is 1 : 2 : 3 in simplest form.

The ratio of the number of red carnations to the number of pink carnations to the number of yellow carnations is 1 : 2 : 3.

Guided Learning

Complete to express each ratio in simplest form.

1 15 : 12 : 18

15 : 12 : 18

÷ ___ ÷ ___ ÷ ___

= ___ : ___ : ___

The greatest common factor of 15, 12, and 18 is ___. Divide 15, 12, and 18 by ___.

2 12 : 8 : 20

12 : 8 : 20

÷ ___ ÷ ___ ÷ ___

= ___ : ___ : ___

First, find the greatest common factor of 12, 8, and 20.

Learn Use multiplication to find missing terms in equivalent ratios.

Find the missing terms in these equivalent ratios.
2 : 3 : 5 = ? : 12 : ?

Look at the second terms of the equivalent ratios.
2 : **3** : 5 = ? : **12** : ?

First, find the multiplying factor. Then, multiply the first and third terms by this multiplying factor.

Method 1

3 × **4** = 12
Multiply by **4** throughout.

Method 2

12 ÷ 3 = **4**

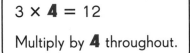

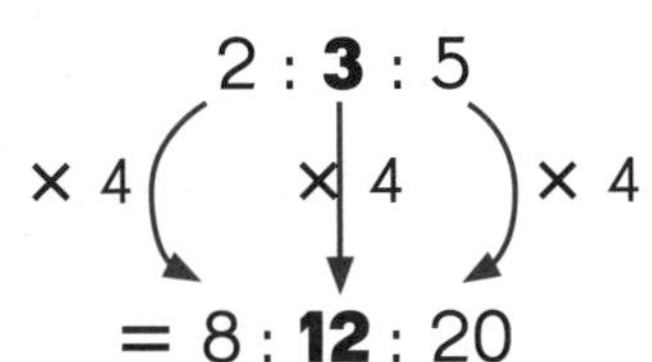

So, **4** is the multiplying factor.
4 × 2 = 8
4 × 5 = 20

Guided Learning

3 **Find the missing terms in these equivalent ratios.**

3 : 5 : 7 = 9 : ? : ?

Look at the first terms of the equivalent ratios — **3** : 5 : 7 = **9** : ? : ?.

First, find the multiplying factor. Then, multiply the second and third terms by the multiplying factor.

Method 1

3 × ___ = 9
Multiply by ___ throughout.

3 : 5 : 7
× ___ × ___ × ___
= **9** : ___ : ___

Method 2

9 ÷ 3 = ___

So, ___ is the multiplying factor.

___ × 5 = ___
___ × 7 = ___

Learn **Use division to find missing terms in equivalent ratios.**

Find the missing numbers in these equivalent ratios.

18 : 12 : 9 = ? : ? : 3

Look at the third terms of the equivalent ratios —
18 : 12 : **9** = ? : ? : **3**

First, find the greatest common factor of the third terms. Then, divide the first and second terms by the greatest common factor.

9 ÷ 3 = 3
3 is the greatest common factor.

18 : 12 : **9**
÷ 3 ÷ 3 ÷ 3
= 6 : 4 : **3**

Guided Learning

Find the missing terms in each set of equivalent ratios.

4. 15 : 5 : 20 = ___ : 1 : ___

5. 7 : 21 : 14 = ___ : ___ : 2

Hands-On Activity

Materials:
- 3 green counters
- 12 blue counters
- 18 yellow counters
- 5 ten frames

Work in groups.

STEP 1 Arrange 3 green counters, 12 blue counters, and 18 yellow counters in 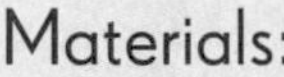s.

STEP 2 Write the ratio of the number of green counters to the number of blue counters to the number of yellow counters.

STEP 3 Take away some counters of any two colors. Find the new ratio of the number of green counters to the number of blue counters to the number of yellow counters. Give your ratio in simplest form.

Example

Take away 1 green and 2 yellow counters.

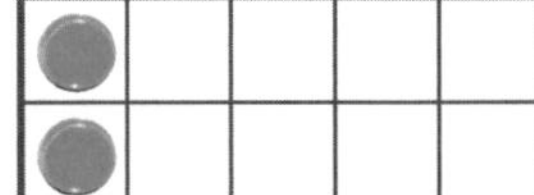
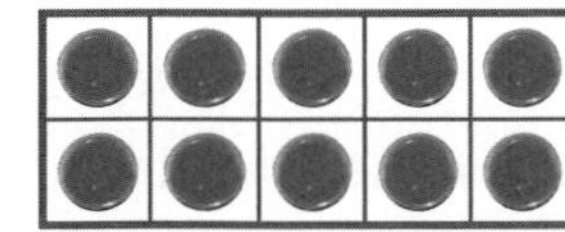
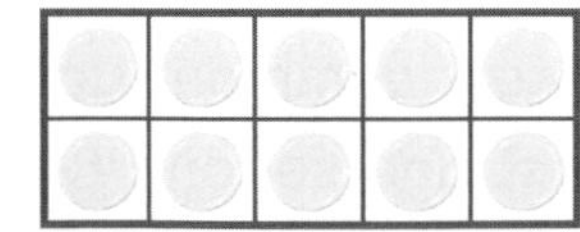
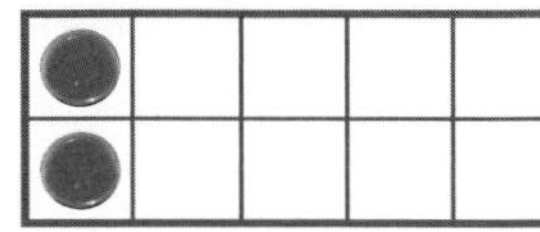
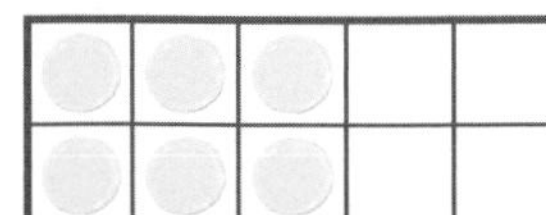

Number of  : Number of  : Number of ○ (in simplest form) = 1 : 6 : 8

Let's Practice

Complete to express each ratio in simplest form.

1. 5 : 15 : 20

   5 : 15 : 20
   ÷ ___ (÷ ___) ÷ ___
   = ___ : ___ : ___

2. 4 : 18 : 24

   4 : 18 : 24
   ÷ ___ (÷ ___) ÷ ___
   = ___ : ___ : ___

3. 12 : 16 : 28

   12 : 16 : 28
   ÷ ___ (÷ ___) ÷ ___
   = ___ : ___ : ___

4. 36 : 45 : 72

   36 : 45 : 72
   ÷ ___ (÷ ___) ÷ ___
   = ___ : ___ : ___

Find the missing terms in each set of equivalent ratios.

5. 1 : 4 : 5

   1 : 4 : 5
   × ___ (× ___) × ___
   = 3 : ___ : ___

6. 32 : 56 : 16

   32 : 56 : 16
   ÷ ___ (÷ ___) ÷ ___
   = ___ : ___ : 2

7. 2 : 3 : 8 = ___ : 18 : ___

8. 4 : 5 : 9 = ___ : ___ : 63

9. 45 : 72 : 18 = ___ : 8 : ___

10. 15 : 100 : 125 = ___ : ___ : 25

ON YOUR OWN

Go to Workbook A: Practice 5, pages 251–252

Lesson 7.6 Real-World Problems: More Ratios

Lesson Objectives

- Solve real-world problems involving ratios and fractions.
- Solve real-world problems involving ratios with three quantities.

Learn Find simplest-form ratios to compare quantities in real-world problems.

At a toy shop, Bernice bought 3 pink toy cars, 6 blue toy cars, and 9 yellow toy cars. What is the ratio of the number of pink toy cars to the number of blue toy cars to the number of yellow toy cars that Bernice bought?

Method 1

Put 3 toy cars into each box.

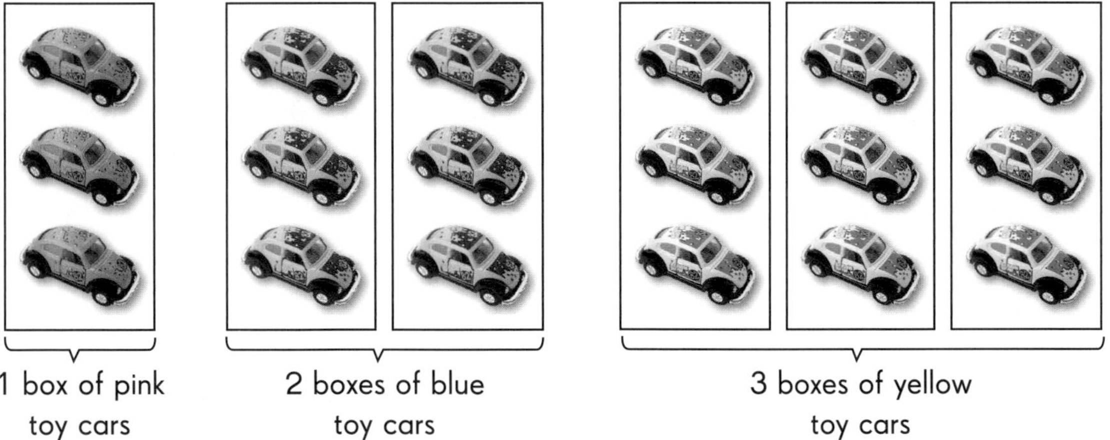

The ratio of the number of pink toy cars to the number of blue toy cars to the number of yellow toy cars that Bernice bought is 1 : 2 : 3.

Method 2

$$3 : 6 : 9 \xrightarrow{\div 3} = 1 : 2 : 3$$

The greatest common factor of 3, 6, and 9 is 3.

3 : 6 : 9 is 1 : 2 : 3 in simplest form.

The ratio of the number of pink toy cars to the number of blue toy cars to the number of yellow toy cars that Bernice bought is 1 : 2 : 3.

Guided Learning

Complete.

1 During a track event, Darren ran 200 meters, Shelby ran 800 meters, and Antonio ran 3,000 meters. What was the ratio of the distance Darren ran to the distance Shelby ran to the distance Antonio ran?

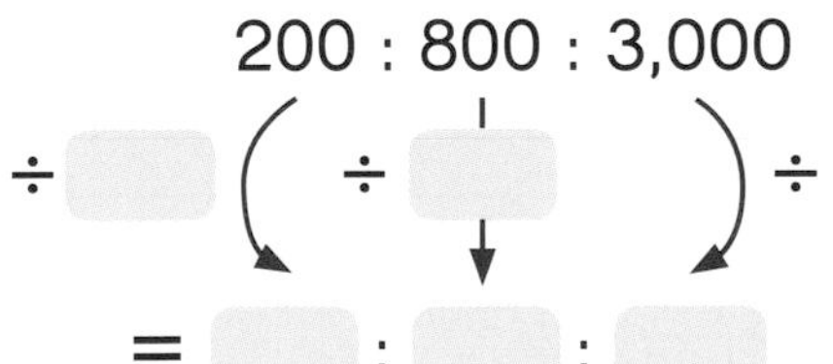

Find the common factor of 200, 800 and 3,000.

The ratio of the distance Darren ran to the distance Shelby ran to the distance Antonio ran was ___ : ___ : ___.

Learn Find equivalent ratios or use models to solve real-world problems.

Rebecca filled three containers, A, B, and C, completely with orange juice. The containers' capacities were in the ratio 2 : 3 : 4. The capacity of the largest container was 12 cups. Find the capacity of the smallest container.

Method 1

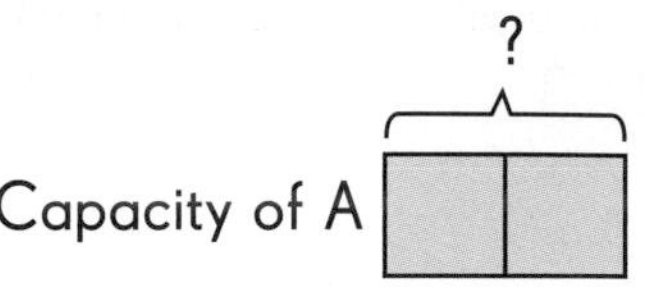

Capacity of B

Capacity of C

12 cups

4 units → 12 cups

1 unit → $12 \div 4 = 3$ cups

2 units → $2 \times 3 = 6$ cups

The capacity of the smallest container is 6 cups.

Method 2

A B C

2 : 3 : 4

× 3 × 3 × 3

= 6 : 9 : 12

The capacity of the smallest container is 6 cups.

Guided Learning

Complete.

2 Raymond cut a roll of ribbon into three pieces, X, Y, and Z, in the ratio 4 : 2 : 1. The length of the longest piece is 28 centimeters. Find the total length of the three pieces of ribbons.

28 cm

Length of X

Length of Y

Length of Z

? cm

4 units → 28 cm

1 unit → ___ ÷ ___ = ___ cm

Total number of units = $4 + 2 + 1 =$ ___

___ × ___ = ___

The total length of the three pieces of ribbon is ___ centimeters.

Guided Learning

Complete.

3. The amounts of Mrs. Caito's monthly car payment, electric bill, and grocery bill last month were in the ratio 5 : 4 : 6. The grocery bill was \$432. How much was the total amount of all three bills?

6 units → \$432

1 unit → \$____ ÷ ____ = \$____

Total number of units = 5 + 4 + 6

= 15

____ × \$____ = \$____

The total amount of all three bills was \$____.

car payment

electric bill

grocery bill

?

\$432

Learn: Draw models to solve problems involving ratios in fraction form.

Camille's salary is $\frac{2}{5}$ times Belinda's salary.

a. Find the ratio of Belinda's salary to Camille's salary. Give your answer in fraction form.

b. Belinda earned \$895. How much did they earn altogether?

Belinda's salary

Camille's salary

Total number of units = 5 + 2 = 7

From the model:

a. $\frac{\text{Belinda's salary}}{\text{Camille's salary}} = \frac{5}{2}$

The ratio of Belinda's salary to Camille's salary is $\frac{5}{2}$.

b. 5 units → \$895

1 unit → \$895 ÷ 5 = \$179

7 units → 7 × \$179 = \$1,253

They earned \$1,253 altogether.

Guided Learning

Complete.

4 The number of coins Layla has is $\frac{7}{3}$ times the number of coins Sally has.

a Find the ratio of the number of coins Sally has to the number of coins Layla has, to the total number of coins they have.

b Layla has 896 coins. How many coins do they have altogether?

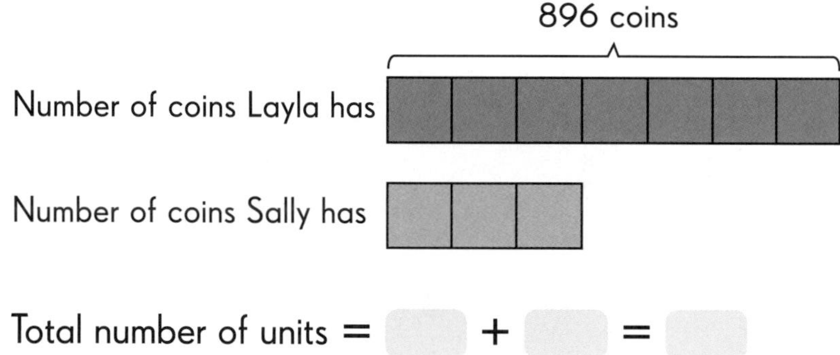

Total number of units = ___ + ___ = ___

From the model:

a The ratio of the number of coins Sally has to the number of coins Layla has to the total number of coins they have is ___ : ___ : ___.

b 7 units → ___ coins

1 unit → ___ ÷ ___ = ___ coins

___ units → $10 \times 128 =$ ___ coins

They have ___ coins altogether.

Learn Draw models to solve real-world problems.

Carla's savings is 4 times as much as Paulo's savings.

a What is the ratio of Carla's savings to Paulo's savings to their total savings?

b How many times their total savings is Carla's savings?

c How many times Carla's savings is Paulo's savings?

d They save a total of \$120. How much does Carla save?

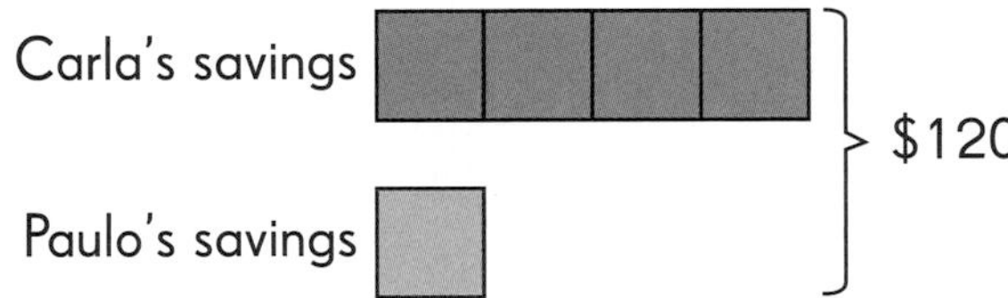

a Total number of units = 5
The ratio of Carla's savings to Paulo's savings to their total savings is 4 : 1 : 5.

b The ratio of Carla's savings to their total savings is 4 : 5 or $\frac{4}{5}$.
Carla's savings is $\frac{4}{5}$ times their total savings.

c The ratio of Paulo's savings to Carla's savings is 1 : 4 or $\frac{1}{4}$.
Paulo's savings is $\frac{1}{4}$ times Carla's savings.

d From the model:

Method 1

5 units ⟶ \$120

1 unit ⟶ \$120 ÷ 5 = \$24

4 units ⟶ 4 × \$24 = \$96

Carla saves \$96.

Method 2

The ratio of Carla's savings to their total savings is 4 : 5 or $\frac{4}{5}$.

Carla's savings is $\frac{4}{5}$ times their total savings.

So, Carla's savings $= \frac{4}{5} \times \$120$
$= \$96$

Guided Learning

Complete.

5 In a swim-and-run biathlon, Raul ran 5 times the distance that he swam.

a What is the ratio of the distance Raul ran to the distance he swam to the total distance of the biathlon?

b How many times the total distance of the biathlon is the distance Raul ran?

c Raul ran 3,200 meters more than he swam. What was the total distance of the biathlon?

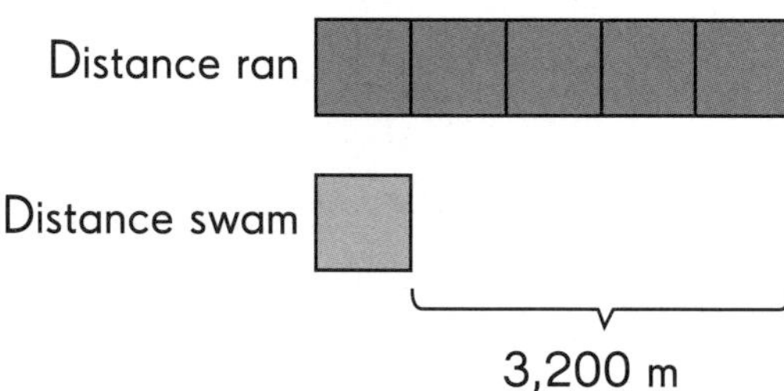

From the model:

a The ratio of the distance Raul ran to the distance he swam to the total distance of the biathlon is ___ : ___ : ___.

b $\frac{\text{Distance Raul ran}}{\text{Total distance of the biathlon}} = \frac{\square}{\square}$

The distance Raul ran is $\frac{\square}{\square}$ times the total distance of the biathlon.

Total number of units is 5 + 1 = 6

c ___ units → ___

___ unit → ___

___ units → ___

The total distance of the biathlon was ___ meters.

Let's Practice

Solve. Show your work. Give all answers in simplest form.

1. At an office supply store, Rachel bought 5 erasers, 15 pens, and 40 pencils. What is the ratio of the number of erasers to the number of pens to the number of pencils she bought?

2. Nita mixes 200 milliliters of cranberry juice, 300 milliliters of grapefruit juice, and 700 milliliters of spring water to make a fruit punch. What is the ratio of cranberry juice to grapefruit juice to spring water?

3. Ronald draws three lines in different colors — red, yellow and green. The ratio of the length of the red line to the length of the yellow line to the length of the green line is 1 : 3 : 5. The yellow line is 18 centimeters long. How long is the green line?

4. Apple, carrot and celery juices are mixed in the ratio 3 : 1 : 2. The amount of apple juice is 720 milliliters.

   a. How much more apple juice is used in the mixture than carrot juice?

   b. What is the total amount of the mixture?

5. The amount of savings that Anna, Beth and Cynthia each has is in the ratio 2 : 3 : 15. Cynthia has $1,575 in savings.

   a. Who has the least amount saved?

   b. What is the total amount that all three of them have in savings?

6. On a Saturday, La Petite Bakery sold tortillas, bagels and rolls in the ratio 12 : 5 : 7. The number of tortillas sold was 50 more than the number of rolls sold.

   a. How many tortillas did La Petite sell on that Saturday?

   b. How many tortillas, bagels and rolls in all did La Petite sell on that Saturday?

7. Lilian's present age is $\frac{2}{3}$ times May's age.

   a. Find the ratio of May's age to Lilian's age. Give your answer in fraction form.
   b. How many times the total age of the two girls is Lilian's age?
   c. How many times the total age of the two girls is May's age?
   d. Their combined age is 25 years. Find the age of each girl.

8. The weight of potatoes used by Mrs. Wilson in her cooking is $\frac{5}{2}$ times the weight of carrots used.

   a. Find the ratio of the weight of potatoes used to the weight of carrots used to the total weight of both ingredients.
   b. How many times the total weight of both ingredients was the weight of the potatoes?
   c. The weight of potatoes used was 9 pounds more than the weight of carrots used. Find the total weight of both ingredients.

9. A wall is painted yellow and brown. The area painted yellow is 3 times the area painted brown.

   a. What is the ratio of the area painted yellow to the area painted brown? Give your answer in fraction form.
   b. What is the ratio of the area painted yellow to the area of the entire wall? Give your answer in fraction form.
   c. How many times the area of the entire wall is the area painted brown?
   d. The wall has an area of 8 square meters. Find the area of the wall painted yellow.

10. Peter collects U.S. and foreign stamps. He has 5 times as many U.S. stamps as foreign stamps.

   a. What is the ratio of the number of U.S. stamps to the number of foreign stamps to the total number of stamps in his collection?
   b. How many times the total number of stamps is the number of U.S. stamps?
   c. How many times the total number of stamps is the number of foreign stamps?
   d. Peter has 140 more U.S. stamps than foreign stamps. How many stamps does he have in his collection?

ON YOUR OWN

Go to Workbook A:
Practice 6, pages 253–260

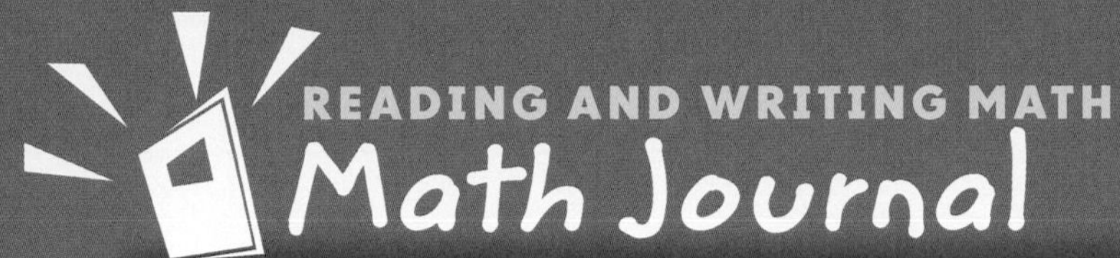

Yolanda has 6 white balloons and 15 pink balloons.
Explain how to find the ratio of the number of white balloons to the number of pink balloons.
Can the ratio be simplified?
If so, explain how to simplify the ratio.
Draw a model to help you.

1. Using these numbers, write sets of equivalent ratios in the form *a* : *b*. Use each number only once.

2	3	5	6	7	8	9	10
12	14	15	20	21	25	35	

Example 2 : 3 = 6 : 9 = 8 : 12

2. Using the same numbers in 1, write as many sets of equivalent ratios in the form *a* : *b* : *c* as you can. Use each number only once.

   How did you find the numbers for each set of equivalent ratios? Explain your answer.

CRITICAL THINKING SKILLS

Put On Your Thinking Cap!

PROBLEM SOLVING

1. The ratio of the money Chris has to the money Tina has is 5 : 2. Chris has $30.

   a. How much money does Tina have?

   b. If Tina's money consists of only quarters, how many quarters does Tina have?

2. The ratio of the number of quarters to the number of dimes in Lin's pocket is 3 : 2. Lin has 4 dimes. How much money does Lin have in all?

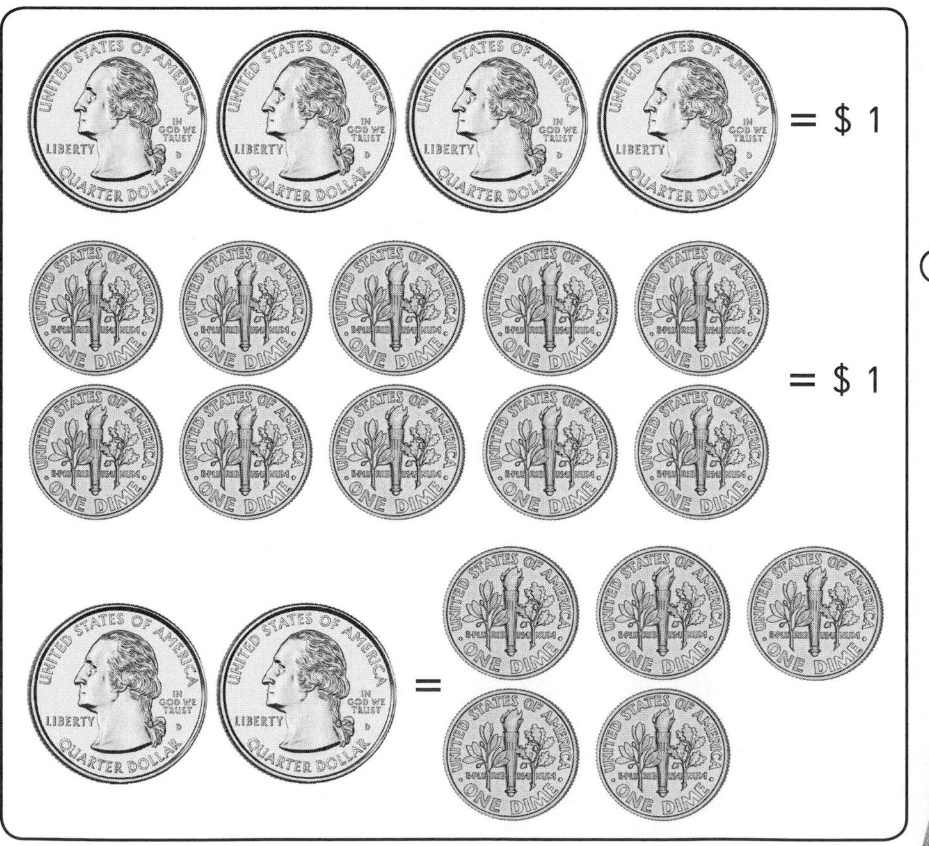

ON YOUR OWN

Go to Workbook A: Put on Your Thinking Cap! pages 261–262

Chapter Wrap Up

Study Guide

You have learned...

▶ Two numbers can be compared by subtraction. Two or more numbers or quantities can also be compared by division and the comparison expressed as a ratio.

Ratio

Comparing Numbers or Quantities

- A ratio is a comparison by division.
- Ratios can be used to compare 2 or 3 numbers or quantities.
- A ratio need not give the actual quantities compared.

Forms of a Ratio

- Ratios can be written in three forms.
  Ratio form : 1 : 5
  Fraction form : $\frac{1}{5}$
  Word form : 1 to 5
- Ratios in fraction form tell us how many times one number or quantity is as large as another.
- In $\frac{\text{Number of adults}}{\text{Number of children}} = \frac{3}{12} = \frac{1}{4}$, the number of adults is $\frac{1}{4}$ times the number of children.

Equivalent Ratios

- Divide by the greatest common factor to find the simplest form of a ratio.

  10 : 8 (÷ 2, ÷ 2) = 5 : 4

- Multiply by the same factor to find equivalent ratios.

  1 : 3 (× 3, × 3) = 3 : 9

Solve Real-World Problems

Chapter Review/Test

Vocabulary

Choose the correct word.

ratio
terms
equivalent ratios
simplest form
greatest common factor

1. A ____ is a comparison of two numbers or quantities by division. The quantities of the items you are comparing make up the ____ of the ratio.

2. Two or more different ratios that compare the same set of numbers or quantities are known as ____.

3. A ratio that cannot be simplified any further is said to be in ____.

4. The greatest number that can evenly divide two or more numbers is called the ____.

Concepts and Skills

Draw a model to show each ratio.

5. A : B = 5 : 6

6. A : B = 3 : 10

What is A : B? Write the ratio.

7. A (5 units), B (4 units) ____

8. A (3 units), B (7 units) ____

Express each ratio in simplest form.

9. 3 : 6 ____

10. 12 : 8 ____

Find the missing term in each set of equivalent ratios.

11. 1 : 5 = ____ : 10

12. 7 : 8 = 21 : ____

13. 8 : 20 = ____ : 5

14. 42 : 49 = 6 : ____

Rewrite each ratio in fraction form.

15 1 : 3

16 8 : 3

Express each ratio in simplest form.

17 2 : 6 : 14

18 8 : 20 : 16

Find the missing terms in each set of equivalent ratios.

19 1 : 5 : 3 = 3 : ___ : ___

20 4 : 3 : 7 = ___ : 15 : ___

21 18 : 20 : 12 = 9 : ___ : ___

22 40 : 55 : 15 = ___ : ___ : 3

Problem Solving

Solve. Show your work.

23 The ratio of the perimeter of a square piece of paper to the perimeter of a rectangular piece of paper is 2 : 5. Each side of the square piece of paper is 10 centimeters. Find

a. the perimeter of the square piece of paper,

b. the perimeter of the rectangular piece of paper,

c. the length of the rectangular piece of paper if its width is 15 centimeters.

24 In a packaged assortment of carpentry fasteners, the ratio of nails to screws to bolts is 10 : 8 : 3.

a. Each package contains 15 bolts. How many nails and screws does it contain?

b. How many fasteners are in each package?

c. Each carton of fasteners contains 12 packages. How many nails are in each carton?

Glossary

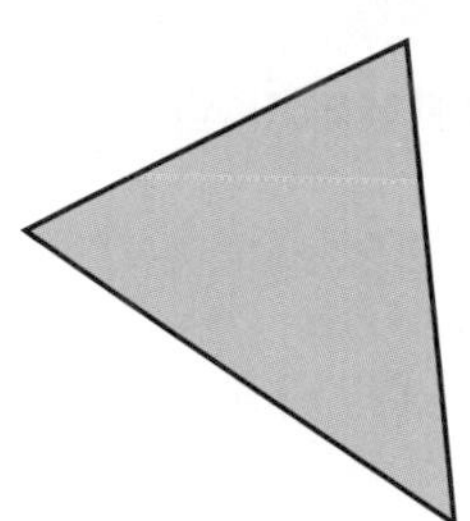

- **Acute angle**

  An angle with a measure less than 90°.

- **Acute triangle**

  A triangle with all angles measuring less than 90°.

- **Algebraic expression**

  An expression that contains at least one variable.
  $2x$, $x + 3$, $5 - x$ are algebraic expressions in terms of x.

- **Angle**

  An angle is formed by two rays with the same endpoint.

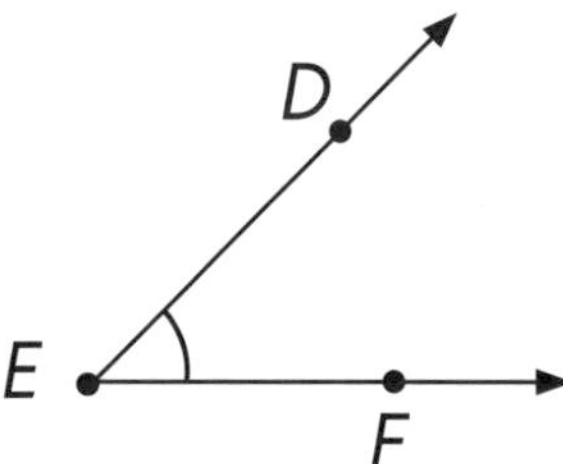

- **Area**

  The amount of surface covered; commonly measured in square units, such as square centimeters (cm^2) or square inches ($in.^2$).

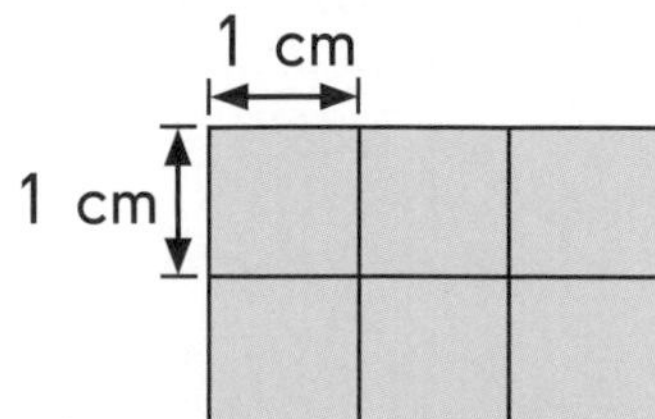

Area of the rectangle = 6 cm^2

- **Associative properties**

  When adding (or multiplying) three or more numbers, you can add (or multiply) any two of them first.
  Addition: $(1 + 3) + 6 = 1 + (3 + 6)$
  Multiplication: $(3 \times 4) \times 10 = 3 \times (4 \times 10)$

B

- **Base (of an exponent)**

  The number that is being multiplied the number of times indicated by the exponent. In 5^3, 5 is the base. The exponent indicates that 5 should be multiplied three times.

- **Base (of a triangle)**

  The face or side on which an object lies.
  In a triangle, any one side can be the base.

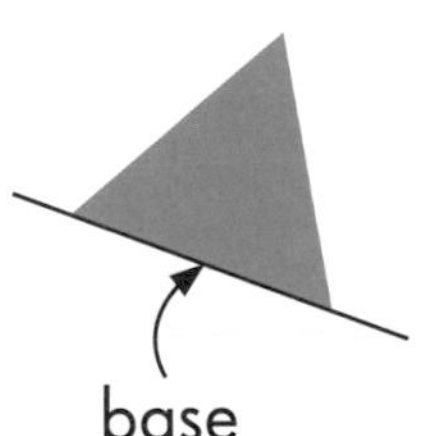

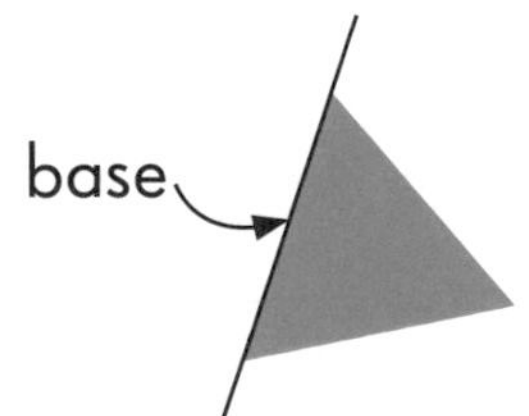

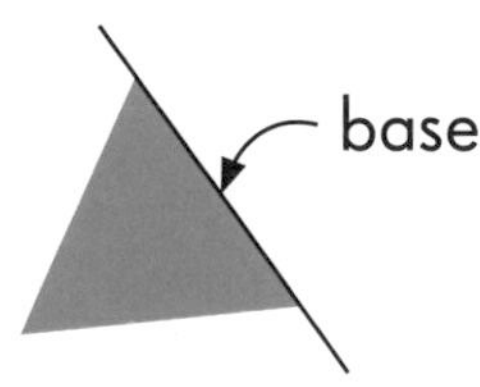

- **Benchmarks for fractions**

  Numbers which are easier to work with and to picture than others. Common benchmarks for estimating with fractions: 0, $\frac{1}{2}$ and 1.

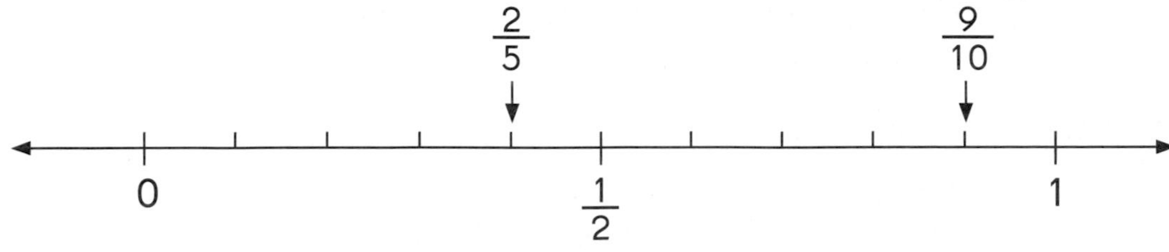

$\frac{2}{5}$ is about $\frac{1}{2}$.

$\frac{9}{10}$ is about 1.

C

- **Common factor**

  A number that is a factor of two or more numbers.
  Factors of 8: 1, 2, 4, 8
  Factors of 12: 1, 2, 3, 4, 6, 12
  1, 2, and 4 are common factors of 8 and 12.

- **Commutative properties**

  Two numbers can be added or multiplied in either order.
  Addition: $7 + 9 = 9 + 7$
  Multiplication: $7 \times 9 = 9 \times 7$

- **Compatible numbers**

  Pairs of numbers close to the original number pairs that are easy to add, subtract, multiply or divide mentally. They are used to estimate sums, differences, products and quotients.

  The numbers 240 and 6 are compatible numbers used for estimating $248 \div 6$.

- **Composite number**

  A number that has more than two factors.
  6 is a composite number, because it factors are 1, 2, 3, and 6.
  9 is a composite number because its factors are 1, 3, and 9.
  7 is not a composite number because its factors are only 1 and 7.

- **Cube (of a number)**

  A number that is the product of three equal factors.
  27 is the cube of 3, because $3 \times 3 \times 3 = 27$

- **Distributive property**

  The property of numbers that relates addition to multiplication. The product of a number and a sum is equal to the sum of the products of the number and the two addends.

  Example: $3 \times (5 + 8) = 3 \times 5 + 3 \times 8$

- **Dividend**

  The number that is being divided.

  $8\overline{)128}$

  dividend (128)

- **Division expression (in arithmetic)**

  An expression that contains only numbers and the division symbol. $2 \div 3$ is a division expression.

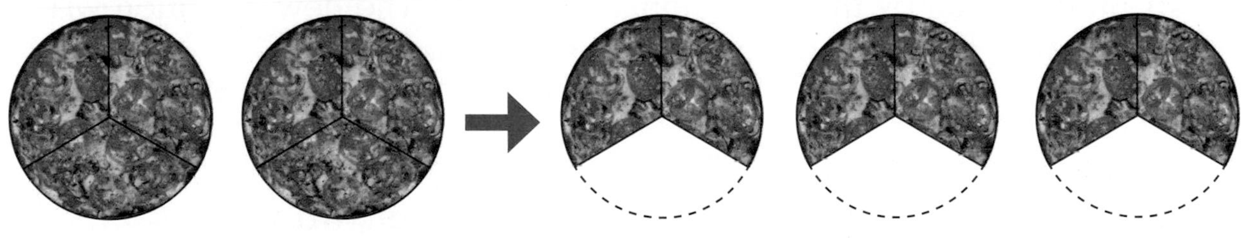

  $2 \div 3 = \frac{2}{3}$

- **Divisor**

  The number the dividend is being divided by.

  $8\overline{)128}$

  divisor (8)

E

- **Equality Properties**

  Addition and subtraction: You can add the same number to or subtract the same number from both sides of an equation. The new equation will still be true for the same value of variable.

  Look at the balance. It shows the equation $a + 4 = 5$. It is true for $a = 1$.

(counter) represents 1.

a represents a counters.

Add 2 counters to both sides of the equation.
The two sides still balance.

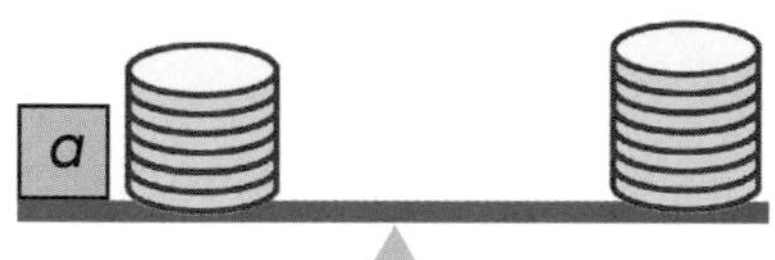

You have a new equation, $a + 6 = 7$.
It is still true for $a = 1$.

Multiplication and division : You can multiply or divide both sides of an equation by the same nonzero number. The new equation will still be true for the same value of the variable.

Look at the balance.

It shows the equation, $4a = 8$.
This equation is true for $a = 2$.

Multiply the number of counters on both sides by 2.
The two sides still balance.

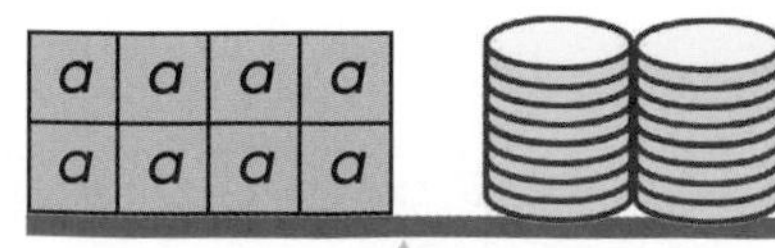

You have a new equation, $8a = 16$.
It is still true for $a = 2$.

- **Equation**

  The statement that two expressions are equal.
  $x + 5 = 10$, $x - 8 = 3$ and $2x = 4$ are equations.

- **Equivalent fractions**

  Fractions that have the same value.
  $\frac{1}{2}$, $\frac{2}{4}$, and $\frac{3}{6}$ are equivalent fractions.

- **Equivalent ratios**

  Ratios that represent the same proportional relationship.
  The ratios 1 : 4, 2 : 8, 3 : 12, and 4 : 16 are all equivalent ratios.

- **Estimate**

  To find an approximate value to a numerical expression.

- **Evaluate (an algebraic expression)**

  To substitute the value(s) given for the variable(s) of the expression and then find the value of the expression.

- **Expanded form**

  $768{,}540 = 700{,}000 + 60{,}000 + 8{,}000 + 500 + 40$
  in expanded form.

- **Exponent**

  A number that tells how many times the base is used as a factor. In 5^3, the exponent is 3. It means that this product is $5 \times 5 \times 5$.

- **Expression**

  A number or a group of numbers with operation symbols.

F

- **Factor**

  $2 \times 9 = 18$

  2 and 9 are factors of 18.

- **Front-end estimation with adjustment**

  Take the value of the front-end, or leftmost, digits.
  Then add or subtract the values.

  $$\begin{array}{r} 3{,}815 \\ 2{,}298 \\ +\,1{,}972 \\ \hline \end{array} \begin{array}{c} \rightarrow \\ \rightarrow \\ \rightarrow \\ \end{array} \begin{array}{r} 3{,}000 \\ 2{,}000 \\ +\,1{,}000 \\ \hline 6{,}000 \end{array}$$

  Estimate what is left over to the place of the leading digit of the sum or difference obtained.

  $$\begin{array}{r} 815 \\ 298 \\ +\,972 \\ \hline \end{array} \begin{array}{c} \rightarrow \\ \rightarrow \\ \rightarrow \\ \end{array} \begin{array}{r} 800 \\ 200 \\ +\,900 \\ \hline 1{,}900 \end{array} \rightarrow 2{,}000 \text{ (to the nearest thousand)}$$

  Adjust the estimate.

  $6{,}000 + 2{,}000 = 8{,}000$

- **Greater than (>)**

Hundred Thousands	Ten Thousands	Thousands	Hundreds	Tens	Ones
5	1	2	3	7	4
4	1	2	3	7	4

512,374 > 412,374
512,374 is greater than 412,374.

- **Height (of a triangle)**

The perpendicular distance from the base to the opposite vertex.

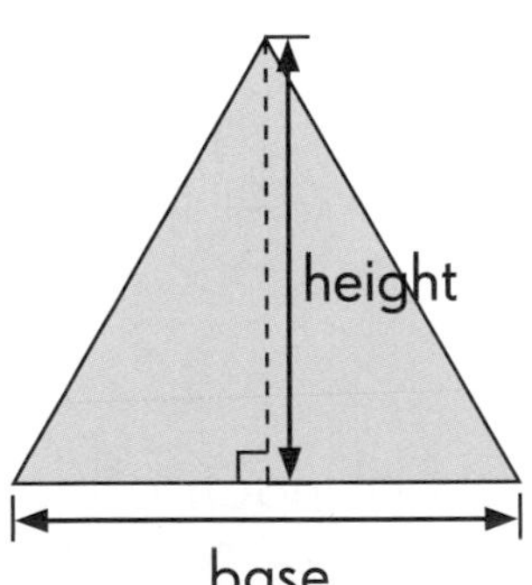

- **Hundred thousand**

10 ten thousands or 100,000

I

- **Identity properties**

  Identity property of addition: Any number plus 0 equals that number.
  $0 + 6 = 6 + 0 = 6$

  Identify property of multiplication: Any number times 1 equals that number.
  $1 \times 6 = 6 \times 1 = 6$

- **Improper fraction**

  A fraction with a numerator greater than its denominator.
  Its value is greater than 1.
  $\frac{3}{2}$, $\frac{4}{3}$, and $\frac{6}{5}$ are improper fractions.

- **Inequality**

  A statement that two expressions are not equal.
  $8 > 2$, $2x < 8$, $8 \neq 13$ and $3y \div 9 > y - 1$ are inequalities.

- **Inverse operations**

  Two operations that undo the effects of each other. Addition and subtraction are inverse operation, because $9 + 20 - 20 = 9$. Multiplication and division are inverse operations because $9 \times 20 \div 20 = 9$.

L

- **Least common denominator (LCD)**

  The least common multiple of the denominators of two or more fractions.
  The LCD of $\frac{2}{3}$ and $\frac{3}{4}$ is 12.

- **Least common multiple (LCM)**

  The least number among all the common multiples of a set of two or more numbers.
  Multiples of 4: 4, 8, 12, 16, 20, 24, ...
  Multiples of 6: 6, 12, 18, 24, 30, 36, ...
  12 is the LCM of 4 and 6.

- **Less than (<)**

Hundred Thousands	Ten Thousands	Thousands	Hundreds	Tens	Ones
5	1	2	3	7	4
4	1	2	3	7	4

  412,374 $<$ 512,374
  412,374 is less than 512,374.

- **Like fractions**

  Two or more fractions with the same denominator.
  $\frac{1}{9}$ and $\frac{5}{9}$ are like fractions.

- **Like terms**

  In the expression $a + 2a + 2$, the like terms are a and $2a$.

M

- **Million**

  10 hundred thousands or 1,000,000

- **Mixed number**

  A number made up of a whole number and a fraction.

  whole number → $4\frac{2}{3}$ ← fraction

  ↑

  mixed number

- **Multiple**

  The product of a given whole number and any other whole number.

  $2 \times 4 = 8$

  8 is a multiple of 2 and of 4.

N

- **Number pattern**

  An ordered list of numbers that usually follows a rule.
  1, 3, 5, 7, ... is a pattern whose rule is "Add 2 to a term to get the next term."

- **Numeric expression**

  An expression that contains only numbers and symbols.

O

- **Obtuse angle**

  An angle with a measure greater than 90°.

- **Obtuse triangle**

  A triangle with exactly one angle measuring greater than 90°.

- **Order of Operations**

  Set of rules stating the order in which to perform the operations, '+', '−', '×' and '÷' when simplifying any expression involving two or more operations:

  1 Work inside the parentheses, brackets, and braces.
  2 Multiply and divide from left to right.
  3 Add and subtract from left to right.

P

- **Period (of a number)**

  A group of three places commonly used for reading numbers that are 1,000 or greater.

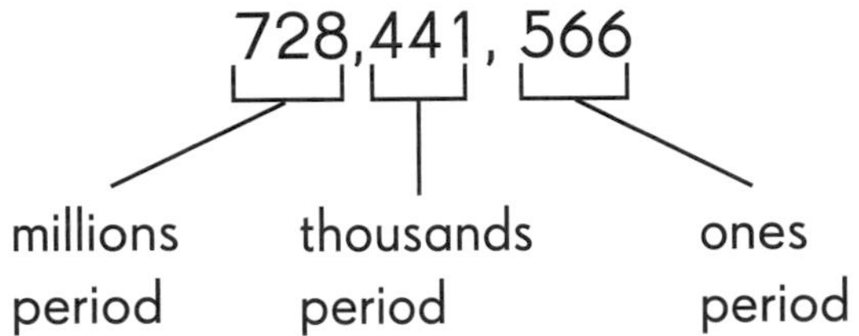

- **Perpendicular lines (⊥)**

  Lines that form right angles.

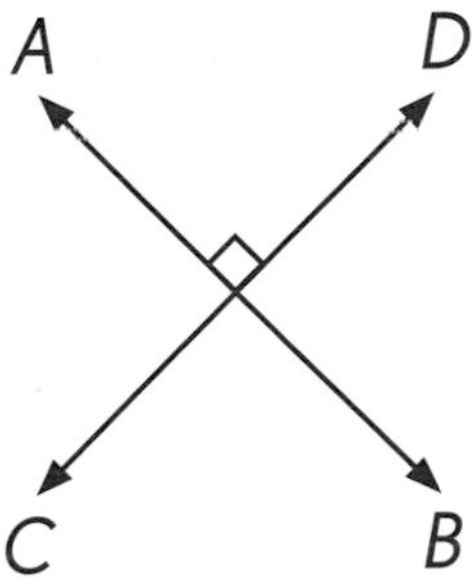

$\overleftrightarrow{AB}$ is perpendicular to $\overleftrightarrow{CD}$.

- **Place value**

  The value of a digit as determined by its place.
  In 5,873, the digit 8 is in the hundreds place, so it stands for 800.

- **Prime number**

  A whole number that has only two factors , 1 and itself. 7 is a prime number because its only factors are 1 and 7.

- **Product**

  The result of multiplication.

  $$2 \times 9 = 18$$

  factor ↗ (2), factor ↑ (9), product ↖ (18)

- **Proper fraction**

  A fraction with a numerator less than its denominator. Its value is less than 1.

  $\frac{3}{4}$, $\frac{5}{6}$, and $\frac{7}{8}$ are proper fractions.

Q

- **Quotient**

  The result of division.

  $$8\overline{)128} = 16 \leftarrow \text{quotient}$$

R

- **Ratio**

  A way of comparing two numbers using division. The ratio 1 inch : 3 inches is equivalent to 1 ÷ 3.

- **Reciprocal**

  $\frac{1}{5}$ is the reciprocal of $\frac{5}{1}$ or 5.

- **Remainder (in whole number division)**

  The number that is left over when a divisor does not divide the dividend exactly.

$$\begin{array}{r} 15 \\ 8\overline{)128} \\ \underline{80} \\ 48 \\ \underline{40} \\ 8 \end{array} \leftarrow \text{remainder}$$

- **Right angle**

  An angle with a measure of 90°.

- **Right triangle**

  A triangle with exactly one right angle.

- **Round**

  To approximate a number to the nearest ten, hundred, thousand (and so on).
  To round any number:
  Look one place to the right of the digit you want to round to.

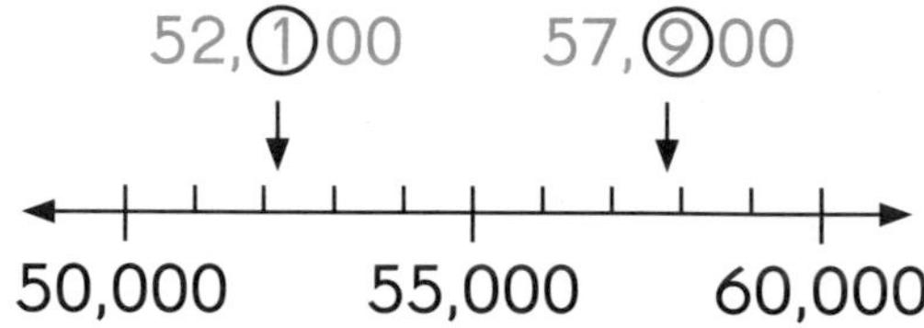

  If the digit is less than 5, do not change the number in the rounding place. 52,①00 rounded to the nearest thousand is 52,000.

  If the digit is 5 or more, add 1 to the digit in the rounding place. 57,⑨00 rounded to the nearest thousand is 58,000.

S

- **Side**

  One of the line segments that form the polygon.

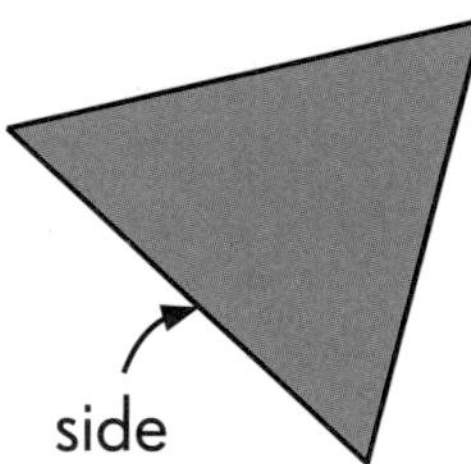

- **Simplest form (of a fraction)**

  The form in which its numerator and denominator have only 1 as a common factor.

- **Simplest form (of a ratio)**

  A ratio in which the terms have only 1 as a common factor.
  The simplest form of the ratio 4 : 12 : 8 is 1 : 3 : 2.

- **Simplify**

  Combine like terms and apply number properties to an expression.
  $9 + 5 - 4 - 1$ simplifies to 9.
  $9s + 5 - 4s - 1$ simplifies to $5s + 4$.

- **Solve**

  To find the value of the variable that will make an equation true.

- **Square (of a number)**

  A number that is the product of two equal factors.
  25 is the square of 5.

- **Standard form**

  3 million 5 hundred in standard form is 3,000,500.

T

- **Term (of an expression)**

  Any one of the numbers, variables, products or quotients which together make up the expression.
  x, 1, $3x$ and 2 are terms of the expression, $x + 1 + 3x + 2$.

- **Term (of a ratio)**

  Any one of the numbers in a ratio.
  In the ratio 4 : 5 : 8, the terms are 4, 5 and 8.

- **True**

  In $x + 5 = 9$, if $x = 4$,

  Left side:
  $x + 5 = 4 + 5$
  $= 9$ (from right side)

  $x + 5 = 9$ is said to be true for $x = 4$.

U

- **Unit fraction**

  A fraction whose numerator is 1.
  The fraction $\frac{1}{3}$ is a unit fraction.

- **Unlike fractions**

  Two fractions that have different denominators.
  $\frac{2}{3}$ and $\frac{1}{2}$ are unlike fractions.

V

- **Variable**

  A symbol, such as a letter, representing an unknown number in an algebraic expression.
  In the expression $m + 11$, m is the variable.

- **Vertex (of an angle)**

  The point at which two line segments or rays meet to form an angle.

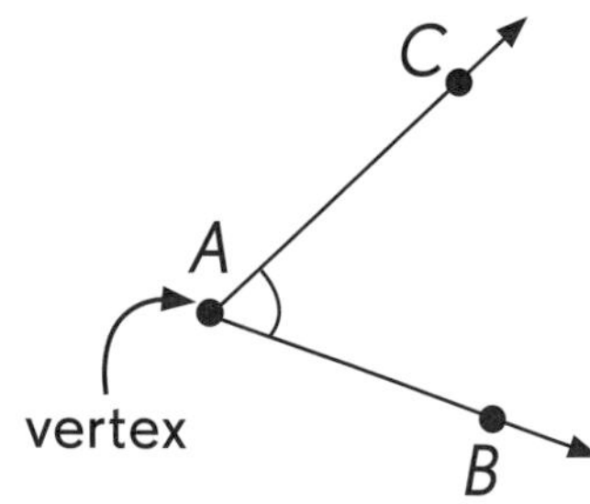

- **Vertex (of a polygon)**

  A point of a polygon where two sides meet to form an angle.

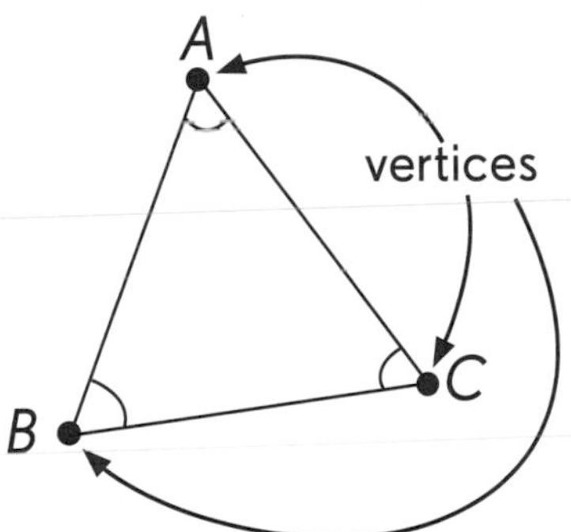

W

- **Word form**

  The word form of 7,010,000 is seven million ten thousand.

Z

- **Zero property of multiplication**

  The product of any number and 0 is 0.

Index

A

Acute triangle, *throughout, see for example,* **277**, 284

Addition
- estimating sums,
  - with fractions, **130**–132, 162, 164; *WB 106*
  - with mixed numbers, **148**–150, 162, 165; *WB 120*
  - with whole numbers, 3–4, 27–28, 30, 34–38; *WB 17, 19*
  - with decimals, 70–71, 74–76, 94–98; *WB 39, 41*
- expressions involving, *throughout, see for example,* **224**–225; *WB 189–190*
- properties, 217, 239
- sum, *throughout, see for example,* 48
- using a calculator, *throughout, see for example,* 48–49, 98–100, 110; *WB 27–28*
- with fractions,
  - like denominators, 124, 127; *WB 105*
  - unlike denominators, 124, 127–129, 131–132, 158–160, 162, 164; *WB 103–105*
  - modeling, **128**–129; *WB 103–105*
- with like terms, *throughout, see for example,* **236**
- with mixed numbers,
  - unlike denominators, 146–148, 150, 162, 165; *WB 117–119*
    - modeling, 146–148; *WB 117–119*
- with whole numbers, *throughout, see for example,* 42

Additive
- recognize volume as, 310–314, 317, 321; *WB 219–222*

Algebra
- equations, *See* Equations
- coordinate graphs of, **152**–154, 157, 181–182; *WB 111–112, 127*
- with two variables, 152–154, 181–182; *WB 111, 127–128*
- expressions, *See* Algebraic expression
- formulas, 264, 276–279, 283
- inequalities, **242**–244, 251, 254–255, 259–260; 233–238, 253–254; *WB 175–176*
- inverse operations, 218
- order of operations, **94**–99, 117–118, 218, 238; *WB 59–66*
- properties, *See* Properties
- variables, *throughout, see for example,* **225**–261

Algebraic expressions
- comparing, 243; *WB 205*
- evaluating, **227**, 229, 231–232, 234, 258, 260; *WB 194, 196, 199–200*
- forming, **224**–226, 228–234, 260; *WB 193–199*
- in inequalities and equations, **242**–257, 259, 266
- involving addition and subtraction, *throughout, see for example,* **224**–225; *WB 193–194*
- involving multiplication and division, *throughout, see for example,* **228**, 230–233, 253, 258, 265; *WB 193, 199–200*
- like terms, *throughout, see for example,* **236**
- simplifying, **235**–241, 258, 265–266; *WB 201–202*
- terms, *throughout, see for example,* **236**

Algebraic thinking
- angle sums (on a line or at a point), 189–199, 206; *WB 131–135, 137–138*
- bar models, *throughout, see for example,* 42–43, 103–106, 109, 157–158
- functions. *See* Input-output machines, Straight line graphs
- input-output machines (functions), 216
- interpret numerical expressions without evaluating them, 224, 226, 233
- inverse operations, 218
- numerical expression, *throughout, see for example,* 224
- order of operations, 218, 94–99
- patterns given two rules, 221–223
- patterns on a place-value chart, 52–53, 57–58, 75–76, 79–80, 85
- properties, *See* Properties
- parentheses, brackets, or braces, 96–101; *WB 67–68*
- variables, *throughout, see for example,* 225–232
- write simple expressions

Angle
- acute, 215, 221–222; *WB 164*
- at a point, **195**–199, 204, 206–207; *WB 135–149*
- between the parallel sides, 239–244, 246–249, 251, 253–255; *WB 179–184*
- classifying triangles by, 208–209, 214–216, 250–252; *WB 164, 167, 169, 172*
- congruent, 212, 216, 224–230, 239–244, 248, 250–255; *WB 169–173*
- degrees, 185
- equal measures, 200–207; *WB 139*
- form, 184–186, 193–194, 196
- identifying, 184, 186, 194, 198–199, 204
- intersect, 201
- measuring, 185
- measure of an, 185–186, 188–207
- naming of an, 185, 187, 196, 205, 210

obtuse, 214–216, 219–220, 229–230, 250, 252
of an acute triangle, 215–216, 218, 220, 225–230, 250–254; *WB 164*
of an equilateral triangle, 227–230, 251–252, 255; *WB 163, 171–174*
of an isosceles triangle, 224–226, 229–230, 251–255; *WB 169–170, 172–173, 186*
of an obtuse triangle, 214–216, 218–220, 230, 250, 252; *WB 164*
of a right triangle, 221–223, 226, 250–254; *WB 167–168*
of a scalene triangle, 214–216
on a line, 189–194, 205–207; *WB 131–135, 139*
opposite, 239–244, 248, 252
pairs of, 240–244, 246–249, 251–254
protractor, 185, 188–190, 193, 196, 198, 201; *WB 131–132, 135–139*
right, 263, 186
sum of angle measures
for a triangle, **217**–230; *WB 165–166*
on a line, **189**–194, 203–207, 210; *WB 131–134*
at a point, **195**–199, 203–204, 206–207; *WB 135–138, 159–160*
right, 263
unknown measure of an, 191–192, 194, 197, 199, 201–204, 206–207; *WB 131–150, 165–168, 170–173*
vertex of an, 263; 184–188
vertical, **200**–207; *WB 139–147*

Area
definition of, 264
formula,
of a rectangle, 264
fractional side lengths,
and products of fractions, 267–270
of a square, 264
of a triangle, **276**–277, 283
nets (and surface area), 277–282, 284, 316; *WB 197–199*
surface, **277**
cube, 277–278, 283, 316, 319; *WB 197*
rectangular prism, 279–280, 284, 316, 319; *WB 198*
triangular prism, 281–282, 284, 316, 319; *WB 199*

Area model
and division, 196
product of fractions, **172**, 182; *WB 139, 147*

Attributes of two-dimensional figures, 209, 212–216, 237–248

Axes of graphs, 150–151

Assessment
Chapter Review/Test, 38–40, 118–119, 164–165, 214–215, 260–261, 284–285, 334–335; 28–29, 98–99, 132–133, 180–182, 207–208, 252–254, 318–320
Cumulative Review, *WB 85–100, 173–188,* 263–276; *WB 89–100, 151–162, 229–242*
End-of-Year Review, *WB 243–266*
Mid-Year Review, *WB 277–294*
Quick Check, 4, 44–46, 125–129, 170–171, 219, 265–266, 288; 5, 35, 102, 137, 187–188, 210–211, 258

Associative properties
of Addition, 217
of Multiplication, 217; 31, 45; *WB 22, 26*

Bar graphs, 135, 137, 143, 172; *WB 107–108, 170*

Bar models, *throughout, see for example*, 42–43, 109–112, 115, 157–158; *WB 75–78*; *90–92, 116–119*
relationship to unknowns in equations, *throughout, see for example*, 45, 109–112

Base
of a solid figure, **267**, 269–271, 273–275
of a triangle, **271**–279, 282–284

Benchmark fractions,
to estimate fraction sums and differences **130**, 132, 135–136, 148–150, 153, 155, 162, 164–165; *WB 106, 109, 120, 124*

Braces (in numerical expressions), 99–101; *WB 67–68*

Brackets (in numerical expressions), 98–101; *WB 67–68*

Breaking down expressions, 247

Building up expressions, 247

Pages listed in black regular type refer to Student Book A.
Pages in blue type refer to Student Book B pages.
Pages in *italic* type refer to Workbook (WB) A.
Pages in *blue italic* type refer to Workbook (WB) B pages.
Pages in **boldface** type show where a term is introduced.

C

Calculator
- checking answers with a, 47, 49–50; *WB 28*
- computing with whole numbers, 47–50, 55, 60, 73, 82, 104–106, 108, 110, 114; *WB 27–28, 36, 69, 71–72, 78, 231*
- use to add, *throughout, see for example*, 48–49, 106, 119; *WB 27–28*
- use to divide, *throughout, see for example*, 50, 105–106, 108, 110, 114, 119; *WB 27*
- use to multiply, *throughout, see for example*, 49–50, 104–106, 108, 110, 119; *WB 27*
- use to subtract, *throughout, see for example*, 48–49, 106, 114, 119; *WB 27*

Certain outcome, 136, 138

Chapter Review/Test, *See* Assessment

Chapter Wrap Up, *See* Review

Checking
- equations, 247–249
- in problem solving, 104, 160; *WB 23–24*
- reasonableness of answers, 71–76, 96–98; *WB 39–42*
- using a calculator, 47, 49–50; *WB 28*
- using estimation, 69, 71–73, 104, 118; *WB 41–44*

Chip models for place value 52, 57, 75, 79; 18, 31–32, 43, 46–47, 62–63, 65–66; *WB 21*

Circle, *See* Geometry

Classifying
- three-dimensional figures 257, 267–276, 316, 318; *WB 193–196*
- two-dimensional shapes 209, 212–216, 229–230, 237–252; *WB 163–164, 179–184*

Collecting like terms, *throughout, see for example*, **239**

Combinations, **164**
- arranging items, 164
- meaning of, 164
- multiplication to find the number of, 166–168, 179; *WB 122*
- organized list, **164**–165, 168, 179–180; *WB 119*
- recording in systematic order, 164
- selecting items, 164
- showing, using a tree diagram, **165**–168, 170, 179–182; *WB 120–121*

Common denominator
- least, **128**, 133; *WB 102*

Common factors
- to simplify multiplication with fractions, *throughout, see for example*, **177**, 182

Common multiples
- least, **128**–129, 133–134, 162, 164, 169, 178–179, 200–202, 204; *WB 103, 107*

Communication
- Math Journal, *See* Math Journal

Commutative Property
- of Addition, 217, 239
- of Multiplication, 217

Comparing
- algebraic expressions
  - as equations, 243; *WB 205*
  - as inequalities, 243; *WB 205*
- data, 144–148, 180; *WB 107–108*
- decimals, 3, 6, 18–22, 27–28; *WB 5–6, 90*
- expressions, 184
- fractions, decimals, and percents, 103–104, 106, 108
- organized list and tree diagrams, 165; *WB 119–21, 129, 157*
- using a ratio, *throughout, see for example*, **289**–290, 316–317, 322–323, 333
- size of a product to one of its factors, 175
- volume, 285–286, 289, 291–292, 295; *WB 203–204*
- whole numbers, 2, 4, 20–21, 23, 36, 39; *WB 11–13*

Compatible numbers
- for estimating quotients, *See* Estimation

Composite numbers, 123, 127

Cones, 257

Converting measurement units
- among customary units, 153; *WB 127–128, 172*
- among metric units, 67; 34–35, 77–88; *WB 43–56*

Connections,
- analyzing points in a coordinate grid, 150–157; *WB 109–112*
- area model and the product of fractions, 182, 267–269
- connect factors and multiples and fractions, 122–123, 128–129, 133–134

connect fractions, decimals, and percents, 101, 103–110
connect place value models and numbers
for decimals, 7–15
for whole numbers, 5–13, 16–18

Coordinate plane, **150**–152, 155–157; *WB 109–112, 172, 181–182*
axes of, 150, 155
graphing points, 150–153, 155, 157; *WB 110*
graphing straight line equations, 152–154, 157, 181–182; *WB 112, 127*
locating points in, 150, 156; *WB 109*
origin, **151**
using to solve real-world problems, 152–154, 157, 181–182; *WB 111–112, 128*

Coordinates, of a point, 150–152, 155–157, 180–182

Cube
net for, 271–273, 277–278, 316; *WB 196*
surface area, 277–278, 283–284
volume, 287–290, 298–300, 316, 318–319; *WB 201, 204–205, 207–208*

Customary units of measure
converting among, 153; *WB 127–128*

Cumulative Review *See* Assessment

Cylinder, 257

Data
collecting, 171, 173–174
displaying and organizing
in a bar graph, 135, 137, 143
in a double bar graph, 143–150, 179–180
in an experiment, 171–173, 177
in a line plot, 178
in a straight line graph, 152–154, 157, 181–182
in a table, 134–135, 143, 146, 148–149, 152–153, 171–173, 175–177; *WB 108, 112, 127*
in a tally chart, 134, 147, 176
drawing conclusions from
from a bar graph, 135, 137, 143, 172
from a double bar graph, 144, 146, 148, 180; *WB 107–108*
from a straight line graph, 152–154, 157, 181–182; *WB 111–112*
from a line plot, 139–142; *WB 101–106*
from a table, 40, 107–108, 294; *WB 4, 74, 233–234*

Decimals
adding
with regrouping, 33
without regrouping, 33
comparing, 21–22, 26
greater than, 3, 6, 18–19, 21–22, 27
hundredths, 6, 19
less than, 20, 22, 27
ones, 18–19
tenths, 3, 18–19
decimal point, 36, 44, 47, 53, 65–66
denominator of 1,000, 7
digit, 13, 17, 19, 28, 31, 43, 46, 62, 65
dividend, **53**, 76
dividing
by tens, 62–64, 69, 96–98; *WB 35–37*
by hundreds, 62, 65, 69, 96–98; *WB 37–38*
by thousands, 62, 65, 67–69, 96–98; *WB 37–38*
hundredths by a whole number without regrouping, 53–54, 60; *WB 28*
tenths by a whole number without regrouping, 53, 60; *WB 27*
to three decimal places, 59–60
with one decimal place by a whole number with regrouping, *WB 29*
with two decimal places by a whole number with regrouping, 56–58, 60; *WB 31–32*
divisor, **73**
equivalent
hundredths, 9–10
thousandths, 9–10
estimate, **70**
sums, 70, 74–76, 96–98; *WB 39, 41*
differences, 71, 74–75, 96–98; *WB 39, 41*
products, 70, 72, 74–78, 96–98; *WB 40, 41*
quotients, 70, 73, 75–76, 96–98; *WB 40, 41*
expanded form, 13, 17, 26, 28; *WB 4*
expressing
fractions as, 3, 6, 11, 17, 28
mixed numbers as, 4, 6, 12
percents as, 108, 110, 131–132

Pages listed in black regular type refer to Student Book A.
Pages in blue type refer to Student Book B pages.
Pages in *italic* type refer to Workbook (WB) A.
Pages in *blue italic* type refer to Workbook (WB) B pages.
Pages in **boldface** type show where a term is introduced.

fractional form, 7
inequality, 21
multiplying
by tens, 43–45, 52, 96–98; *WB 21–23*
by hundreds, 43, 46–52, 96–98; *WB 23–26*
by thousands, 43, 46–52, 96–98; *WB 24–26*
tenths by a whole number, 36; *WB 15*
hundredths by a whole number, 39; *WB 16*
with one decimal place by a whole number, 37–38, 42; *WB 17*
with two decimal places by a whole number, 40–42; *WB 18–19*
number line, *throughout, see for example*, 2, 4, 7–8, 20–21
ordering, 18–19, 22, 27–28
greatest to least, 19, 22
least to greatest, 18–19, 22, 27–28
part of a model, 2, 5, 7–9, 15, 23–25, 29
places, *throughout, see for example*, 7–8, 19–23
place-value chart, 3, 5–6, 8–13, 16–19, 21–22, 36–39, 51, 53–55
place-value concepts, *throughout, see for example*, 13–14, 17–18, 36, 43
point, 5, 8, 15
product, 32, 35–37, 72
quotient, 33, 35, 76
real-world problems, 40, 56, 76, 80, 90–95, 99
regroup, 33–34, 37, 39–40, 53–59
rewrite
as fractions or mixed numbers, 23–25, 27, 29
in simplest form, 23–25, 29
rounding, 4, 6, 20
quotients to the nearest hundredth, 53, 58–60
quotients to the nearest tenth, 53, 58–60
to the nearest hundredth, 20–22, 27–29; *WB 32*
to the nearest tenth, 21–22, 72, 74; *WB 31*
to the nearest whole number, 4, 6, 21–22, 70–72, 76
subtracting, 34
add placeholder zeros, 33–34
with regrouping, 33–34
without regrouping, 34
understanding
hundredths, 3
tenths, 3
thousandths, 7–8
vertical form, 41

Degrees (angle measures), 185

Digit
front end, 3, 28–29
in rounding, 3, 43
leading, 3, 28–29

Decimal points,
patterns in the placement of, 36, 43–50, 62–67

Discount, 125–126, 128–133; *WB 84–85, 100*

Distance on a coordinate grid, 150–156, 181–182

Distributive Property, 217

Dividend, **83**, 118

Division
adjusting the quotient, 87–88
by multiples of ten, hundred, and thousand, 74–83, 85, 116–117, 119; *WB 47–51*
dividend, **83**, 86, 118
divisor, **83**, 84, 86, 118
estimating quotients, **33**, 34, 37, 40, 44, 46, 83–85, 87–89, 117, 119; 73, 75–76, 96–98; *WB 22, 52, 54–55*; *WB 40–41*
expressions involving, 230–233, 253, 258, 260; *WB 197–198, 200*
interpreting remainders, 102, 103, 108
mental, *throughout, see for example*, 74–83, 85; *WB 47–49, 51*
of a four-digit number by a two-digit number, *throughout, see for example*, 91–93; *WB 57–58*
of a three-digit number by a two-digit number, *throughout, see for example*, 89–90, 93; *WB 55–56, 58*
of a two-digit number by a two-digit number, *throughout, see for example*, 87–89, 93; *WB 54, 58*
quotients, 76, 80, 83, 85, 87, 118
related to decimals, 144–145; *WB 115*
related to fractions, **137**–139; *WB 111–112*
related to mixed numbers, **140**–141; *WB 113–114*
remainder, **86**–92, 102–103
to express fractions in simplest form, *throughout, see for example*, 122, 168; *WB 101, 121*
to find equivalent fractions, *throughout, see for example*, 122
to find equivalent ratios, *throughout, see for example*, 300–302, 319–321, 333–335; *WB 240, 251–252*
using a calculator, *throughout, see for example*, 50, 105–106, 108, 110, 114, 119; *WB 27–28*
with decimals, 53–70, 73, 75–76, 90–93, 96–98
with fractions, **193**–199; *WB 157–162*
modeling, **193**–198; *WB 157*
with whole numbers, *throughout, see for example*, 43

Divisor, **83**, 84, 86, 118

Double bar graph, **143**–150, 179–180; *WB 107–108*

Double line graphs, and patterns, 158–163; *WB 113–118*

Draw a diagram, *See* Problem-Solving, strategies

Edge, **268**–271

End-of-Year Review, *See* Assessment

Equal sign, 217

Equality Properties of Equations, **244**–246

Equally likely outcome, 136, 138, 169

Equations
- graphing, 150, 152–154, 157, 179, 181–182
- meaning of, 152
- modeling, **244**–246
- solving **246**–251, 254–255, 259–261; *WB 206*
  - using guess and check, **246**, 248–249
  - using inverse operations, 218–219, 247– 250, 254–255, 259
  - with two variables, 152–154, 179–182
  - with variables on both sides, **248**–251, 254–255, 259, 261
  - with variables on one side, **246**–247, 251, 261
- writing, **242**–244, 251, 254–256, 259, 261
  - to solve real-world problems, 254–257, 259, 261

Equilateral triangles, **212**–213, 215–216, 221, 227–230, 250–255; *WB 163, 171–174*

Equivalent fractions, 122, 126, 128

Equivalent ratios, **296**–309, 316–324, 331, 333–335; *WB 239–240, 251–252*

Estimate
- differences, 3–4, 27–29, 31–32, 34–37, 39, 135–136, 153–155, 162, 164–165; 71, 74–76, 96–98; *WB 18, 20–21, 109, 124*; *WB 39, 41*
- products, 32–33, 35–36, 39, 43–44, 46, 61–63, 116; 72, 74–76, 96–98; *WB 22, 35*; *WB 40–42*
- quotients, **33**, 34, 37, 40, 44, 46, 83–85, 87–89, 117, 119; 73, 75–76, 96–98; *WB 22, 52, 54–55*; *WB 40–41*
- sums, 3–4, 27–28, 30, 34–38, 130–132, 148–150, 162, 164–165; 70–71, 74–76, 96–98; *WB 17, 19, 106, 120*; *WB 39, 41*

Estimation
- front-end, 3–4, 44, 46, 116
- front-end; with adjustment,
  - to estimate differences, 29, 31–32, 35, 37; *WB 20–21*
  - to estimate sums, **28**, 30, 35, 37–38; *WB 19*
- to check answers, 69, 71–73, 106, 120; 70–75; *WB 41–44*
- using compatible numbers, to estimate quotients, *throughout, see for example*, **33,** 34, 37; 35; *WB 22*
- using rounding,
  - to estimate differences, 3, 4, 27–28, 34, 36; *WB 18*
  - to estimate products, 32–33, 35–36, 39, 43, 46, 61–63; 35; *WB 22, 35*
  - to estimate sums, 3, 4, 27–28, 34, 36; *WB 17*
- with decimals, 71–76, 96–98; *WB 39–42*
- with fractions, **130**–132, 135–136, 162, 164; *WB 106, 109*
- with mixed numbers, 148–150, 153–155, 162, 165; *WB 120, 124*

Evaluate
- algebraic expressions, **227**, 229, 231–232, 234, 258, 260; *WB 194, 196, 199–200*
- expressions with parentheses, brackets, or braces, 97–101; *WB 65–68*
- meaning of, **227**, 260

Events, likelihood of, 136, 138, 169–179

Expanded form, 2, 4, 17–19, 36, 38, 42, 44; *WB 8, 10*
- with decimals, 13, 17, 26, 28

Experimental probability, **169**–180; *WB 123–126, 130*

Experiments, 169, 171–178

Exploration
- Let's Explore! 14, 15, 85, 98–99, 131, 135, 149, 175, 187, 232, 282, 311, 331; 68, 88, 174, 229, 274–275, 283, 293

Pages listed in black regular type refer to Student Book A.
Pages in blue type refer to Student Book B pages.
Pages in *italic* type refer to Workbook (WB) A.
Pages in *blue italic* type refer to Workbook (WB) B pages.
Pages in **boldface** type show where a term is introduced.

Exponents and the powers of 10, 64–67; 48–49;
WB 37–38; *WB 24–25*

Expressions
addition, *throughout, see for example*, **224**–225; *WB 193–194*
algebraic, meaning of, **225**, 228, 230
area, 276–279, 283
breaking down, 247
building up, 247
evaluate, **227**, 229, 231–232, 234, 258, 260; *WB 194, 196, 199–200*
graph of, 152
multiplication, *throughout, see for example*, 228; *WB 195*
numerical, **224**, 228–232, 234, 258, 260; *WB 194, 196, 199–200*
simplifying, **235**–241, 258, 260–261; *WB 201–202*
subtraction, *throughout, see for example*, **224**–225; *WB 193–194*
with fractions, 230–233, 253, 258, 260; *WB 196, 199–200*

Face, **267**–271, 273–276; *WB 193–195*

Factor
common, *throughout, see for example*, **122**, 168, 287
compare to the size of product, 175
greatest common, *throughout, see for example*, **122**, 167, 287

Favorable outcome, **169**

Find a pattern, strategy, *See* Problem-Solving, strategies

Fraction form of a ratio, 310–315; *WB 245–250*

Fractional products
represent as rectangular areas 182; 267–270; *WB 211–216*

Fractional side lengths,
and the area of a rectangle, 267–270; *WB 211–216*

Fractions
adding with,
like denominators, 124, 127
unlike denominators, 124, 127–129, 131–132, 158–160, 162, 164; *WB 103–106*
modeling, **128** –129; *WB 103–106*
as decimals, 143, 145; 11–12, 102; *WB 115–116*
as percents, 105, 109, 111–112, 131–133
benchmark, **130**, 135, 148, 158, 162, 164; *WB 106, 109, 120, 124*
dividing with, **193**–199; *WB 157–162*
modeling, **193**–199; *WB 157*
equivalent, *throughout, see for example*, **128**, 133, 162
estimating differences, 135–136, 162, 164; *WB 109*
estimating sums, **130**–132, 162, 164; *WB 106*
improper, *throughout, see for example*, **182**
least common denominator, 128, 133; *WB 102*
like, *throughout, see for example*, 121, 128, 162
mixed numbers, *See* Mixed Numbers
multiplying with, **172**–175, 182–183, 212, 214; *WB 139–140, 147–150*
modeling, **172**, 174, 182; *WB 139, 140*
representing as rectangular areas, 182; 267–270; *WB 211–216*
on a number line, 128
reading, 125, 143
reciprocals, **193**, 214
simplest form, *throughout, see for example*, 287
subtracting with,
like denominators, 124, 127
unlike denominators, 124, 127, 133–134, 136, 157, 162, 164; *WB 107–108*
modeling, 133–134; *WB 107–108*
related to division, **137**–139; *WB 111–112*
unlike, *throughout, see for example*, 121, 128, 133

Front-end estimation, *See* Estimation

Functions, *See* Input-output machines, Straight line graphs

Geometric measurement, *See* Area, Volume

Geometry
angles, *See* Angles
base (of a solid figure), **267–**276
circular flat base, 257
classifying solids
by number of edges, **267**–276; *WB 193–194*
by number of faces, **267**–276; *WB 193–194*
by number of vertices, **267**–276; *WB 193–194*
classifying triangles, **212**–216; *WB 163–164*
cones, 257
congruent figures, 212, 216, 224–230, 239–244, 248, 250–255, 279–281; *WB 169–173*
cubes, 258–266, 271–273, 277–284, 287–290, 294–300

curved surfaces, 257
cylinders, 257
drawing using dot paper
cubes, 263–266; *WB 189–172*
rectangular prisms, 263–266; *WB 189–192*
edges, **268**–271
faces, **268**–271
flat surfaces, **268**–271, 276
nets, **277**–284; *WB 199*
intersecting lines, **200**, 207
line segment, 184, 186–187
perpendicular line, 186, 188, 193, 205
perpendicular line segments, 263, 186
point, 184–188
prisms, 257–258, 267–270, 272; *WB 194, 196*
hexagonal, 274
pentagonal, 269, 274
rectangular, **269**, 272, 274; *WB 193*
square, 267, 271–273; *WB 196*
triangular, **257**–258, 269, 271, 274–275; *WB 196*
pyramids, **270**–276; *WB 195–196*
hexagonal, 275; *WB 195*
pentagonal, 271, 274; *WB 195*
square, **270**, 275; *WB 195–196*
triangular, **271**–273, 275; *WB 194, 196*
rays, 247; 184–185, 187, 195; *WB 135, 150*
rectangles, area of, *throughout, see for example*, 264
special properties
parallelogram, **209**, 211, 237–243, 248, 251–254; *WB 179–180*
rhombus, **209**, 242–244, 248, 251–254; *WB 181*
trapezoid, **209**, 245–249, 251–254; *WB 183–184*
triangles, *See* Triangles
sphere, **257**
squares, *throughout, see for example*, 264
tangram, **208**
triangles, *See* Triangles
vertices, **267**–271, 273; *WB 194–195*

Glossary, 337–354; 322–334

Graphs
axes, 150, 155
bar, 144
bar graph, 135, 137, 143; *WB 107–108, 170, 235*
conversion graphs, 153; *WB 127–128, 236*
coordinates, **150**–152, 155–156, 180–182; *WB 109–110*
coordinate grid, **150**–152, 155–157; *WB 109–112*
coordinate plane, **150**
corresponding points, 153
data, 135, 143–144, 146–149, 152; *WB 107–108, 112, 127–128*
data table, 133, 135, 143, 146–149, 152–153
double bar graph, **143**–150, 179–180; *WB 107–108*
double line graph, 158–163; *WB 113–118*
equal intervals, 144
horizontal axis, 144
horizontal number line, 150
interpreting, 168, 145; *WB 107–108, 111–112, 127–128*
item, 144
line plot, 139–144, 178; *WB 101–106*
key, **144**
locate points, 150–156
location, 156
making, 143–144, 155; *WB 112, 127*
measurement, 153, 155
number line, *See* Number Line
of an equation, **150**, 152–154, 179–182; *WB 111–112, 127–128, 172, 236*
of an expression,152
ordered pair, **150**–153, 155–157; *WB 109–110*
origin, **151**
plot, 150–151, 155, 157; *WB 110*
point on a, 150–151, 155, 157; *WB 109–110*
straight line, 150, 152–155, 157; *WB 111–112, 127*
suitable scale, 144; *WB 127*
survey, 143
vertical axis, 144
vertical number line, 150
x-axis, **150**–151, 153, 155
x-coordinate, **151**–152
y-axis, **150**–151, 153, 155
y–coordinate, **151**–152

Greater than, *throughout, see for example*, 2, 20–21, 23, 36, 40, 217, 242–244; *WB 11–13*

Greatest common factor, *throughout, see for example*, 122, 168, 287
to express fractions in simplest form, *throughout, see for example*, 122, 168; *WB 101, 121*

Pages listed in black regular type refer to Student Book A.
Pages in blue type refer to Student Book B pages.
Pages in *italic* type refer to Workbook (WB) A.
Pages in *blue italic* type refer to Workbook (WB) B pages.
Pages in **boldface** type show where a term is introduced.

Grid paper, 174; 155

Guess and check, *See* Problem-Solving, strategies

Guided Practice, *See* Practice

Hands-On Activities, 11, 47, 49, 50, 53, 55, 58, 60, 76, 77, 80, 82, 84, 98, 129, 134, 139, 141, 174, 186–187, 196, 222, 232, 240–241, 277–279, 301, 320; 14, 44, 46, 51, 63, 66, 93, 114, 120, 128, 147, 155, 167, 173, 193, 198, 201, 222, 232, 238–240, 246, 272, 292

Height of a triangle, **272**–279, 282–284; *WB 221–222*

Hundredths, 2–4, 7–14, 16–22, 25–29, 33–34, 36, 39–44, 46–47, 53–60, 62–63, 65–66

Identifying patterns,
- division, 74–76; 62–65
- multiplication, 51–58; 43–46
- on a place-value chart, 51–58, 74–76; 43–46, 62–65

Identity Property
- for Addition, 217
- for Multiplication, 217

Impossible outcome, 136, 138

Improper fractions
- as decimals, *WB 116*
- as mixed numbers, 123, 127
- multiplying, **182**–183; *WB 147–150*

Inequalities
- compare lengths of sides, 231–236, 251
- form, 234–236; *WB 175–178*
- greater than, 231–236, 251
- is not equal to, **246**
- less than, 235–236
- possible lengths, 235–236, 255
- to solve problems 254–257, 259, 261
- write, **242**–244, 251, 254–256, 259, 261

Input-output machines, 216

Interpret numerical expressions without evaluating them, 224, 226, 233

Interpreting remainders 102, 103, 108

Interest, **127**–128, 130–133; *WB 83*

Intersecting lines, **200**, 207

Inverse operations
- addition and subtraction, 218
- meaning of, 218
- multiplication and division, 218
- to solve equations, 218–219, 247–250, 254–255, 259

Isosceles triangle, **212**–214, 216, 221, 223–226, 228–230, 250–255; *WB 163, 169–170, 173–174*

Is not equal to, **246**

Journal Writing, *See* Math Journal

Key, **144**

Least common denominator
- to rewrite fractions with like denominators, **128**, 133; *WB 102*

Least common multiple, **128**–129, 133–134, 162, 164, 169, 178–179, 200–201, 204; *WB 103, 107*

Lengths,
- fractional side, and area, 267–270; *WB 211–216*

Less likely, 136, 138

Less than, *throughout, see for example*, **20**, 23, 36, 40; *WB 11–13*

Let's Explore, *See* Exploration

Let's Practice, *See* Practice

Like terms
adding, *throughout, see for example,* **236**
collecting, *throughout, see for example,* 239
subtracting, *throughout, see for example,* 237

Likelihood of events (outcomes), 136, 138, 169–179

Line segments
perpendicular, 263–265; 186, 188, 205

Linear functions, *See* Straight line graphs

Line plot, 178
and a data set of fractional measurements, 139–142

Lines, 184, 186–187, 189–194, 200–207
angles on a, 189–194, 205–207; *WB 131–135, 139*
intersecting, **200**, 207
naming, 185, 187, 196, 205, 210
parallel sides, 210
perpendicular, 186

List
to find greatest common factor, 287
to find least common multiple, **128**, 133, 162
to find number of combinations, 164–165, 180
to solve problems, *See* Problem-Solving, Strategies

Manipulatives
chip models for division of decimals, 53, 55–57, 62–63, 65–66; *WB 35*
chip models for multiplication of decimals, 36–39, 43–44, 46–47; *WB 21*
chip models for place value, 52, 57, 75, 79; 63, 66
classroom objects
colored markers, 167
colored pencil, 196
crayons, 174
ruler, 279; 193, 201, 232
scissors, 277; 238, 272
connecting cubes, 260–261, 292–293
counters, 320
craft sticks, 240–241
dot paper, 263–266
drawing triangle, 274
fraction strips, 139, 141
grid paper, 174; 155
letter cards, 232
measuring tape, 155
number cards, 232
number cubes, 301
paper, 167
paper bag, 147
paper slips: blue, green, red, yellow, 147
protractor, 193, 198
straightedge, 167
tracing paper, 201

Math Journal, 93, 131, 160, 210, 233, 257, 309, 314, 311; 87, 121, 129, 168, 177, 193, 219, 229, 248, 273; *WB 23–24, 36, 45–46, 79–80, 110, 136, 170, 211–212, 225–226, 259–260*; *WB 12, 66, 86, 131, 151, 218*

Math Reasoning, *See* Reasoning

Meals tax, **124**, 130–131; *WB 80–86*

Measurement
of angles, 185, 188–190, 196, 198, 201, 189–190; *WB 131–132, 135, 139, 138, 144, 148*
of area, **276**–279, 283; *WB 223–229, 231*
of base and height, **271**–279, 282–284; *WB 221–222*
of length, 51, 153
of perimeter, 211; *WB 111*
of sides, 213, 216, 232; *WB 171, 175–176*
of surface area, 277–284, 316, 318–319; *WB 197–200*
of volume, 285–295, 296–309, 310–315, 316–317, 319–321; *WB 201–204, 205–219, 224–227*

Measurement systems,
converting units 67; 34–35, 77–88, 153; *WB 43–56; 127–128, 172*

Measurement units,
conversions, 67; 34–35, 77–88, 153; *WB 43–56; 127–128, 172*
fraction of, use to make a line plot, 139–142

Pages listed in black regular type refer to Student Book A.
Pages in blue type refer to Student Book B pages.
Pages in *italic* type refer to Workbook (WB) A.
Pages in *blue italic* type refer to Workbook (WB) B pages.
Pages in **boldface** type show where a term is introduced.

Mental Math
adding, 9, 79
decimals, 68
dividing
by multiples of 10, 77–78, 81–83, 85–86, 117, 119; *WB 47–48, 51*
by powers of 10, 74–76, 78–81, 85, 117, 119; *WB 47, 49*
multiplying,
breaking apart and putting together numbers, 109; 45, 48, 51
decimals, 36
by multiples of 10, 54–55, 59–61, 63, 116, 118; *WB 30, 32–34*
by powers of 10, **51**–54, 56–59, 63, 64–67, 116, 118; 49–50; *WB 29, 31–32, 34, 37–38*; *WB 24–25*;
with easy numbers, 115

Mid-Year Review, *See* Assessment

Millions **9**–14, 18–24, 36, 38–40, 42, 44, 58; *WB 5–6, 9 –10, 12–14*

Mixed numbers
adding, 146–148, 150, 162, 165; *WB 117–119*
modeling, 146–148; *WB 117–119*
as decimals, 144
estimating differences of, 153–155, 162, 165; *WB 124*
estimating sums of, 148–150, 162, 165; *WB 120*
multiplying, **184**–188, 213–214; *WB 151–156*
modeling, **184**–188; *WB 151*
related to division, **140**–141; *WB 113–114*
subtracting, **151**–153, 162, 165; *WB 121–123*
modeling, 151–153; *WB 121–123*

Models
addition
with fractions, 124, 129, 132; *WB 103, 104*
with mixed numbers, 146–148, 150; *WB 117–119*
area model for fractions, **172**, 182; *WB 139, 147*
bar models, *throughout, see for example*, 42–43, 109–112, 109, 151–152; 90–92, 116–119
chip models for place value, 52, 57, 75, 79; 31–32, 43, 46–47, 62–63, 65–66
division
with fractions, 193–197; *WB 157–161*
with whole numbers, 110–112,
equations, **244**–246
with decimals, 2, 5, 7–10, 15, 23–25, 29, 101–102
with fractions, 128–129, 133–134, 174, 182, 193–196; *WB 103–105, 107–108, 139, 147, 157*
with mixed numbers, 146–148, 151–153, 184–188; *WB 117–118, 121–123, 151*
with percent, 104–109, 111, 132
multiplication
with fractions, 172, 176
with mixed numbers, 182, 184–185
subtraction
with fractions, 133–134; *WB 107–108, 110*
with mixed numbers, 151–149; *WB 121–123*

More likely, 136, 138

Multiples, *throughout, see for example*, **128**, 133
least common multiple, **128**–129, 133–134, 164, 164, 169, 178–179, 200–202, 204; *WB 103, 107*

Multiplication
by a reciprocal, **193**–195, 198; *WB 157–162*
estimating products, 32–33, 35–36, 39, 43–44, 46, 61–63, 116; 72, 74–76, 96–98; *WB 22, 35*; *WB 40–42*
expressions involving, *throughout, see for example*, 228; *WB 195*
factor, *throughout, see for example*, **51**
mental, *throughout, see for example*, **51**–55, 59–61, 63, 115, 116, 118; *WB 29–32, 34*
modeling, 172, 174, 182–188; *WB 139, 147, 151*
of a four-digit number
by tens, *throughout, see for example*, 72–73; *WB 43*
by a two-digit number, *throughout, see for example*, 72–73; *WB 43–44*
of a three-digit number
by tens, *throughout, see for example*, 70, 72–73; *WB 43*
by a two-digit number, *throughout, see for example*, 69–70, 73; *WB 41–44*
of a two-digit number
by tens, *throughout, see for example*, 68–70, 73; *WB 41*
by a two-digit number, *throughout, see for example*, 71–73; *WB 42*
of decimals, *See Decimals*
of whole numbers, *throughout, see for example*, **42**
product, *throughout, see for example*, 51

properties, 217
related to volume, 298–308; *WB 206–210*
to find combinations, 166–168, 179; *WB 121–122*
to find equivalent fractions, *throughout, see for example*, 122, 128–129, 133–134, 143, 146–148, 151–153, 168, 170, 178–179, 204; *WB 101–102*
to find equivalent ratios, *throughout, see for example,* 300–302, 319–321, 333–335; *WB 240, 251–252*
using a calculator, *throughout, see for example*, 49–50, 104–106, 108, 114, 119; *WB 27*
with fractions, **172**–175, 182–183, 212, 214; *WB 139–140, 147–150*
modeling, 172, 176
with mixed numbers, **184**–188, 213–214; *WB 151–156*
modeling, 182, 184–185
with variables, **228**–229; *WB 195–196*

Negative numbers, 14, 15

Nets, **277**–284; *WB 199*

Number line
locating benchmark fractions on a, **130**, 135, 148, 153, 164; *WB 106, 109, 120, 124*
locating decimals on a, 2, 4–5, 8, 15–16, 28; *WB 2, 12*
representing decimals on a, 5, 8, 15–16, 20–21, 25, 28; *WB 2, 7, 20, 74*
representing decimals, and fractions, 101–102
representing decimals, and percents, 106, 108, 110
representing fractions on a, 116
representing fractions, and percents, 111–112
representing percents, 110; *WB 76*
rounding on a, 3, 25–27, 43; *WB 15–16*

Number properties, 217, 229, 244–246

Number theory
greatest common factor, *throughout, see for example,* 122, 168, 287
least common multiple, **128**–129, 133–134, 162, 164, 169, 178–179, 200–202, 204; *WB 99, 107*
prime and composite numbers, 123, 126–127

Numbers
compatible, **33**, 38
composite, 123,127
decimal, 143–145; *WB 115–116*; *See* Decimals
expanded form of, 2, 4, 17–19, 36, 38, 42, 44; 13, 17, 26, 28; *WB 8, 10*; *WB 4*
decimals, *See* Decimals
fractions, *See* Fractions
mixed numbers, *See* Mixed numbers
negative, 14, 15
positive, 14, 15
prime, 123, 126
standard form of, 2, 4, 6, 7, 10, 12, 14, 36, 38; 7–8, 10–12; *WB 1–3, 5–6*; *WB 1–2*
whole, 1–119; *WB 1–100*
word form of, 2, 4, 6–8, 10, 12–14, 36, 38, 40, 42, 44; *WB 1, 3–6*

Numerical expression, *throughout, see for example*, **224**
evaluate, 227–228, 231–232, 234
interpret numerical expressions without evaluating them 224–226
parentheses, brackets, or braces in, 218

Obtuse triangle, *throughout, see for example*, **277**

Operations
inverse, **218**
order of, **94**–99, 117–118, 218, 238; *WB 59–68*

Ordered pair,
from patterns, 161–163
graph in the coordinate plane, 150–153, 155–157

Ordering decimals, 18–19, 31–32, 27–28

Organized list
to find the greatest common factor, 287
to find the least common multiple, **128**, 133, 162
to find the number of combinations, 164–165, 168, 179–180; *WB 119*
to solve problems, *See* Problem-Solving, Strategies

Pages listed in black regular type refer to Student Book A.
Pages in blue type refer to Student Book B pages.
Pages in *italic* type refer to Workbook (WB) A.
Pages in *blue italic* type refer to Workbook (WB) B pages.
Pages in **boldface** type show where a term is introduced.

Origin, **151**

Outcome, 169
equally likely, 169
experiment, 173–174
favorable, 169

Parallelogram, **209**, 211, 237–243, 248, 251–254; *WB 179–180*

Parentheses, order of operations, 96, 97

Part of a whole
as a decimal, 118–119
as a fraction, 118–119
as a percent, 118–119

Pattern, find a, strategy, *See* Problem-Solving, Strategies

Patterns
division, 74–76, 78–81, 85
multiplication, **51**–54, 56–59, 63
number of zeros of the product 51, 56, 64–67; *WB 37–38*
in the placement of decimal points 43–46, 62–64

Per unit, **61**

Percents, **103**, 110, 132; *WB 71*
decimals as, 106, 109, 132; *WB 72*
denominator of, 101, 106
equivalent fraction, 107, 113; *WB 75*
expressing
as decimals, 104, 108, 110, 132; *WB 73*
as fractions, 103–104, 107, 109, 132; *WB 72*
as fractions in simplest form, 107; *WB 73*
fraction as, 94, 105, 109, 111–112, 114, 132–133; *WB 75–77*
model, 104–109
number line, 106, 108, 110–112; *WB 74, 76*
of a number, 101, 133; *WB 79–82*
parts of a whole, 88–90, 106
real-world problems, *See* real world problems as percent
involving discount, 125–126, 128–130, 133; *WB 84–85, 100*
involving interest, 127–128, 130, 133; *WB 83, 85*
involving meals tax, 124, 130; *WB 85–86*
involving sales tax, 123, 128–130, 133; *WB 83, 100*
of a number, 116–119, 121–122, 133; *WB 79–82, 98*

Perimeter, 221; *WB 111*

Period of a number, **8**, 10, 13, 38; *WB 2*

Perpendicular line segments, 263; 186, 188, 189, 193–194, 203, 205

Place value
charts,
for decimals, 3, 5–6, 8–13, 16–19, 21–22, 36–39, 48–49, 53, 55–57; *WB 1–2, 5, 21, 35*
through hundreds, 52
through thousands, 75–76, 85
through ten thousands, 2, 57, 79–80
through hundred thousands, 5–8, 16, 20–21, 53; *WB 1–3, 7, 11*
through millions 9–10, 12–13, 18, 20, 36, 38–39, 58; *WB 5–6, 9, 12*
meaning of, **16**,18

Positive numbers, 14, 15

Powers of 10,
exponents and, 64–67; 49–50; *WB 37–38*; *WB 24–25*
and patterns of placement of decimal points 49–50; *WB 24–25*
and patterns in the number of zeros of the product, 64–67; *WB 37–38*

Practice
Guided Learning, 6–8, 10, 12–13, 16–18, 21–23, 25–28, 30–34, 53–56, 59–63, 65–67, 69–73, 76, 78, 81, 83–84, 86, 88–92, 94–99, 100–104, 105–106, 110–111, 113, 129–130, 134–135, 138–139, 141–144, 147–149, 151–154, 156–158, 173, 177, 179–180, 183, 185, 189–191, 194–195, 201, 204–206, 221, 226–227, 229, 231, 236–239, 243–244, 247, 250, 252 -253, 255, 268–269, 273, 280, 290, 292–293, 298–299, 301, 303–306, 308, 311–313, 317, 319–320, 323–326, 328; 8–10, 12–14, 19, 21, 24–25, 37–38, 41, 44–45, 48–51, 54, 56, 58–60, 63–65, 67–68, 71–75, 90–92, 103–108, 112–113, 117, 119, 124, 126–127, 140 146, 151, 154, 163, 165–167, 170, 172, 190, 192, 196–197, 201–203, 213, 215, 218, 223, 226, 228, 233, 235–236, 241–245, 247, 268–269, 271–273, 260–261, 278, 280, 282, 286, 288–289, 291, 296–297, 299–300, 302–306, 311–312

Let's Practice, 14, 19, 23–24, 34–35, 63, 67, 73, 85, 93, 101, 113–114, 132, 136, 142, 145, 150, 154–155, 159, 175, 181, 183, 188, 192, 198, 208, 222, 233–234, 241, 251, 255–256, 270, 274–275, 294, 302, 309, 314–315, 321, 329–320; 15, 21, 25, 42, 52, 60, 69, 75–76, 88, 90, 109–110, 114–115, 121–122, 129–130, 141, 148–149, 155–156, 163, 168, 174–176, 194, 199, 204, 216, 220, 230, 236, 248–249, 275–276, 262, 265–266, 275–276, 283–284, 294–295, 307–309

Prerequisite skills
Quick Check, *See* Assessment
Recall Prior Knowledge, 2–3, 42–44, 121–125, 168–170, 217–218, 263–264, 287–288; 2–4, 31–34, 101, 135–138, 184–186, 209–210, 257

Prime numbers, 123, 126

Prism, 257–258, 267–270, 272; *WB 194, 196*

Probability
actual results, 171–179
displaying in a table, 171–173, 175–177
experiments, 171–177
experimental, 169, 171–180; *WB 123–126*
events, 171
favorable outcomes, **136**, 169
likelihood of an event, 136
predictions, 136, 169–170
record, 171–174, 176–178
theoretical, 169–180; *WB 123–126*
trials, 171, 179
write as a fraction, 136, 138, 170–172, 177–178

Problem Solving
Put on Your Thinking Cap!, 35, 115, 161, 211, 257, 282, 332; 25, 95, 130, 178, 205, 249, 314–315; *WB 25–26, 81–84, 137–138, 171–172, 213–214, 227–228, 261–262*; *WB 13–14, 67–68, 87–88, 127–130, 147–150, 185–186, 225–228*
real-world problems, *See* Real-World problems
strategies,
act it out, 314–315; *WB 225*
before and after concept, 111–112, 161, 304–305
draw a diagram or model, 109–114, 128–129, 157–158, 161, 165, 176–181, 184–185, 193–195, 198–206, 211, 253, 306–309, 313–315, 324–330; 25, 130, 178, 205; *WB 83, 136, 138, 171–172, 214, 260*; *WB 67–69, 87–88, 127, 130, 147–150, 168–169, 192, 220, 225, 228*
find a pattern, 35, 115, 211, 282; 314–315
guess and check, 35, 246, 248–249; 95; *WB 25–26, 82–83, 231, 284*; *WB 129*
make an organized list, 112–115, 332; 314–315; *WB 70*
restate the problem in another way, 115
simplify the problem, 249
solve part of a problem, *WB 82–83, 213, 227–230, 232, 261–262*; *WB 67–68*
work backward, *WB 25–26*
write an equation, 254–255, 261
look for patterns 35, 115, 211, 282; *WB 231, 284*
thinking skills,
analyzing parts and wholes, 161; *WB 137, 171–172, 262*; *WB 14, 67–68, 114*
comparing, 35, 332; 178; *WB 25–26, 82–83, 231, 260*; *WB 13–14, 67, 87*
deduction, 282; 205, 249; *WB 222–230*; *WB 147–150*
identifying patterns and relationships, 35, 115, 211; *WB 26, 81–83, 171–172, 213–214, 227–231, 261, 331*; *WB 68–70, 87–88,127, 185–186, 226, 228*
induction, 235
sequencing, *WB 25*
spatial visualization, 211, 282, 332; 249, 314–315; *WB 226–230, 232, 261, 332*; *WB 186, 225–227*

Problem-Solving Applications, *See* Real-World Problems

Problem-solving skills
choose the operation, 104–111, 119, 179–181, 191–192, 200–209; *WB 81–83*
solve multiple-step problems, 104–111, 113–114, 119, 179–181, 191–192, 200–209; *WB 81–83*
check whether the answer is reasonable, 104, 160; *WB 23–24*

Pages listed in black regular type refer to Student Book A.
Pages in blue type refer to Student Book B pages.
Pages in *italic* type refer to Workbook (WB) A.
Pages in *blue italic* type refer to Workbook (WB) B pages.
Pages in **boldface** type show where a term is introduced.

Products
computing, *throughout, see for example*, 49–50, 104–106, 108, 114, 119; *WB 27*
estimating, 32–33, 35–36, 39, 43–44, 46, 61–63, 116; *WB 22, 35*

Properties
angle properties, 207, 214–215, 243, 247, 224–225, 229, 250–251
associative properties, 217
commutative properties, 217, 229
distributive property, 217
equality properties, 244–246
identity properties, 217
special properties of four-sided figures, 209, 237–243, 245–247, 252
triangle properties, 212–215, 229, 250–251, 250
zero property, 217

Protractor, 185, 188–190, 193, 196, 198, 201; *WB 132, 135*

Put on Your Thinking Cap!, *See* Problem Solving

Pyramid, **267**, 270–271, 272–273, 275–276, 316; *WB 195–196*

Quick Check, *See* Assessment

Quotients
computing, *throughout, see for example*, 50, 105–106, 108, 110, 114, 119; *WB 27*
decimals, 53–69; *WB 27–38*
estimating, **33**, 34, 37, 40, 44, 46, 83–85, 87–89, 117, 119; *WB 22, 48, 54–55*
rounding to the nearest hundredth, 59–60; *WB 7–8, 13, 34*
rounding to the nearest tenth, 58, 60; *WB 7, 13, 33*

Rates, 61

Ratios
as comparison of relative size, 291
different forms of, **289**–290, 310, 333
equivalent, **296**–309, 316–324, 331, 333–335; *WB 239–240, 251–252*
in fraction form, 310–315; *WB 245–250*
part-whole models and, 293; *WB 237–238*
reading, **289**–290
simplifying, *throughout, see for example*, **299**, 316–317
terms of, **289**
using to compare,
two quantities, **289**–295; *WB 233–238*
three quantities, 316–321; *WB 251–252*
writing, 289–290, 310, 312, 333

Rays, 263; 184–185, 187, 195–196; *WB 135, 150*

Reasoning, 131, 135, 149, 175; *WB 81, 213*

Reasoning/Proof
algebraic thinking
bar models, *throughout, see for example*, 42–43, 103–106, 109, 157–158
input-output machines (functions), 216
patterns on a place-value chart, 52–53, 57–58, 75–76, 79–80, 85
checking
equations, 248–249
in problem solving, 104, 160
reasonableness of answers, 104, 160; *WB 23–24*
using a calculator, 47, 49–50; *WB 28*
using estimation, 69, 71–73, 106, 120; 70–75; *WB 41–44*
inverse operations
addition and subtraction, 218
meaning of, 218
multiplication and division, 218
to solve equations, 218–219, 247–250, 254–255, 259
order of operations, 218, 94–99
ordering decimals, 18–19, 21–22
problem-solving decisions
choose the operation, 104–111, 119, 179–181, 191–192, 200–209; *WB 81–83*
multiple-step problems, 104–111, 113–114, 119, 179–181, 191–192, 200–209; *WB 81–83*
reasonable answers, 104, 160; *WB 23–24*
proportional reasoning, *See also* Ratios
equivalent fractions, equivalent, *throughout, see for example*, **128**, 133,162

fraction and division, 310–313, 319
per unit, **61**
probability as a fraction, 136, 138, 170–172, 178–177
suitable scale, 144; *WB 127*
solving equations, **246**–251, 254–255, 259–261; *WB 206*
using guess and check, **246**, 248–249
using inverse operations, 218–219, 247–250, 254–255, 259
with two variables, 152–154, 179–182
with variables on both sides, **248**–251, 254–255, 259, 261
with variables on one side, **246**–247, 251, 261

Real-World problems
algebra, 252–256; *WB 207–210*
decimals
addition, 70, 91, 94, 99; *WB 65*
division, 53, 56, 90–92, 94, 99; *WB 57–62, 64–67*
multiplication, 39–40, 90–92, 94, 99; *WB 42, 57–65, 67–68, 70*
subtraction, 92, 94, 99; *WB 58–59, 61, 63–64, 67–68, 70*
multiplication and division with fractions, 200–209; *WB 155–156*
multiplication with fractions, 176–181; *WB 141–146*
multiplication with mixed numbers, 189–192; *WB 163–167*
percents
of a number, 116–119, 121–122, 133; *WB 79–85, 87*
involving discount, 125–126, 128–130, 133; *WB 84–85*
involving interest, 127–128, 130, 133; *WB 83*
involving meals tax, 124, 130; *WB 85–86*
involving sales tax, 123, 128–130, 133; *WB 83*
ratios and more ratios, 283–289, 302–310; *WB 217–220, 229–234*
use fractions and mixed numbers, 156–159; *WB 125–135*
use multiplication and division, 102–114; *WB 69–78*

Recall Prior Knowledge, *See* Prerequisite skills

Reciprocals
using to divide, **193**–195, 198; *WB 157–161*

Rectangles, *See* Geometry.
area of, *throughout, see for example*, 264
fractional side lengths, 267–270; *WB 211–216*
perimeter of, 221

Rectangular prism, 263–266, 267–269, 271–274; *WB 193*
volume of, 287–288, 290, 293, 296–301; *WB 199, 205–218*

Remainder
divide decimals, 55–59
whole numbers, interpreting, 102, 103, 108

Representation, *See* Models, Number lines, Variables

Resources
technology,
calculator, 47–50, 55, 60, 77, 82, 104–106, 108, 110, 114; *WB 27–28, 36, 69, 71–72, 78, 231*
computer drawing tool, 129, 134
internet, 11, 15
non-technology, *See* Manipulatives

Review
Chapter Review/Test, *See* Assessment
Chapter Wrap Up 36–37, 116–117, 162–163, 212–213, 258–259, 283, 333; 26–27, 96–97, 131, 179, 206, 250–251, 316–317

Rhombus, **209**, 211, 237, 242–244, 248; *WB 181–182, 185*

Right angle, 263

Right triangle, *throughout, see for example*, **277**

Rounding
decimals, 4, 6, 20–22, 27–29, 58–60, 70–76, 96–98; *WB 7–8, 13, 33, 34*
whole numbers, 3–4, 25–27, 34, 39, 43, 46; *WB 15–16*
to estimate 3–4, 27–28, 32–36, 39, 43, 46, 61–63; *WB 17–18, 22, 35*

Pages listed in black regular type refer to Student Book A.
Pages in blue type refer to Student Book B pages.
Pages in *italic* type refer to Workbook (WB) A.
Pages in *blue italic* type refer to Workbook (WB) B pages.
Pages in **boldface** type show where a term is introduced.

S

Sales tax, **123**, 128–131, 133; *WB 83, 85*

Sides of figures, **271**
- fractional side lengths, 267

Simplest form of fractions, *throughout, see for example*, 287

Simplest form of ratios, **296**, 298, 321

Skip counting, **5**, 6, 9, 10; *WB 1*

Sphere, **257**

Square pyramid, **270**, 275–276; *WB 195–196, 234*

Squares,
- area of, *throughout, see for example*, 264

Standard form, 2, 4, 6, 7, 10, 12, 14, 36, 38; 7–8, 10–12; *WB 1–3, 5–6*; *WB 1–2*

Straight line graph (on a coordinate grid), 152–155, 157, 181–182; *WB 111–112, 127*

Strategies, *See* Problem Solving

Subtraction
- difference, *throughout, see for example*, 48
- estimating differences
  - with fractions, 135–136, 162, 164; *WB 109*
  - with mixed numbers, 153–155, 162, 165; *WB 124*
  - with whole numbers, 3, 4, 27–29, 31–32, 34–37, 39; *WB 18, 20–21*
- expressions involving, *throughout, see for example*, **224**–225; *WB 193–194*
- using a calculator, *throughout, see for example*, 48–49, 108, 114, 119; *WB 27*
- with decimals, 71, 74–76, 96–98; *WB 39, 41*
- with fractions,
  - like denominators *throughout, see for example*, 124, 127
  - unlike denominators, *throughout, see for example*, 124, 127, 133–134, 136, 157, 162, 164; *WB 107–108*
  - modeling, 133–134; *WB 107–108*
- with like terms, *throughout, see for example*, 237
- with mixed numbers,
  - unlike denominators, **151**–155, 162, 165; *WB 121–123*
  - modeling, 151–153; *WB 121–123*
- with percents, 118–119, 122, 125–126, 130, 133; *WB 81–82, 85*
- with whole numbers, *throughout, see for example*, 42

Surface area, **277**–284, 316, 318–319; *WB 197–200, 235*

Table,
- using data from, 40, 107–108, 294; 135, 143, 146–149, 152–153; *WB 74, 233–234*

Tally chart, 135, 171–173, 175–177; *WB 126*

Tangram, 182

Terms of a ratio, **289**

Theoretical probability, **169**–170, 172–180

Three-dimensional shapes,
- cylinder, sphere, and cone, 257
- describing by its faces, edges, and vertices, 257, 267–276; *WB 194–195*
- nets, 271–273; *WB 196*
- prisms and pyramids, 267–276; *WB 193–196*; *316*

Thousandths, 7–14, 17–21, 24–26, 28, 44, 65–66

Trapezoid, **209**, 211, 237, 245–249, 251, 252–254; *WB 183–184, 186*

Tree diagram, **165**–168, 170, 179–182; *WB 120–121*

Triangles,
- acute, *throughout, see for example*, **277**, 284; 212–216; *WB 163–164*
- angles, *See* Angles
- area of, **276**–285
- base of, **271**–273, 282–284; *WB 221*
- equal, 191, 193–200, 204–205, 210–216, 240–244
- equilateral, 212–213, 221–228, 230; *WB 167, 171–172*

height of, **272**–279, 282–284; *WB 221–222*
inequalities
compare lengths of sides, 231–236; *WB 175–178*
form, 234–236; *WB 175–178*
greater than, 231–236, 251
less than, 235–236
possible lengths, 235–236
isosceles, 212–213, 216, 221–230; *WB 121,167–169*
of angles, 225; *WB 169*
of sides, 212–213, 216; *WB 163*
obtuse, *throughout, see for example,* **277**; 214–216; *WB 164*
opposite, 224–225
parts of, **271**
right, *throughout, see for example,* **277**; 214, 216; *WB 164*
scalene, 212–213, 216; *WB 163*
side, **271**
vertex, **271**

Triangular prism, **269**, 274–275; *WB 193, 196*

Triangular pyramid, **271**, 272–273, 275; *WB 194, 196*

Two-dimensional figures,
attributes, 209, 212–216, 237–248
classify, 209, 212–216, 229–230, 237–252; *WB 163–164, 179–184*
properties, 209, 237–243, 245–247, 252

Unit cube(s), **259**–265, 285–292, 294, 314–316, 318; *WB 187–188, 201–202*

Use dot paper to draw
cubes and rectangular, 263–266, 316, 318; *WB 189–192*
counting to measure volume, 287–295; *WB 201–204*

Values of digits in numbers, 2, 5–7, 9–10, 12, 16–21, 36, 39; *WB 7–10, 14*

Variables, *throughout, see for example,* **225**–261

Vertex
of angles, 263; 184–188
of cone, 257
of prisms, 267–270
of pyramids, 270–271
of a solid figure, 268–271
of triangles, **271**

Vocabulary, 5, 16, 20, 25, 38, 51, 74, 86, 94, 118, 128, 137,164,172,182, 184, 193, 214, 220, 224, 235, 242, 260, 271, 276, 284, 289, 296, 334; 7, 28, 53, 70, 98, 103, 123, 132, 143, 150, 164, 169, 180, 189, 195, 207, 212, 237, 252, 259, 263, 267, 277, 318

Volume
capacity, 257–258, 297; *WB 211–218*
centimeter cubes, 260–262, 287–295; 318; *WB 187–188, 201–204*
comparing, 295, 289, 291–292; *WB 203–204*
cube, 258–268, 287–290, 298–299; *WB 205*
cubic centimeter, 291, 293, 294, 298–299, 300, 307; *WB 202–203*
cubic feet, 291, 295, 299; *WB 204*
cubic inch, 290, 295, 299; *WB 204*
cubic meter, 290, 299, 307; *WB 203*
cubic units, 287–289, 292, 294; *WB 201*
edge lengths, 259, 266–268, 298–299
greater, 286, 289, 291, 317
height and, 290–291, 293, 295–299, 307; *WB 205–206*
length and, 290–291, 293, 295–299, 307; *WB 205–206*
lesser, 289, 295, 317
liter, 257–258, 290–293, 295–296, 300, 307, 309; *WB 211–215*
measure by counting units, 287–289, 291, 294; *WB 201–204*
measuring, 278, 284, 320; *WB 201–204*
milliliter, 257–258, 300–308, 317, 300, 320; *WB 211–215, 217*

Pages listed in black regular type refer to Student Book A.
Pages in blue type refer to Student Book B pages.
Pages in *italic* type refer to Workbook (WB) A.
Pages in *blue italic* type refer to Workbook (WB) B pages.
Pages in **boldface** type show where a term is introduced.

of liquid, 290–296, 300, 302; *WB 211–215, 217*
recognize as additive, 310–314, 317, 321; *WB 219–222*
rectangular prism, 296–299, 314, 317–319; *WB 189–192*
related to addition and multiplication and space, 285
width and, 290–291, 293, 295–299, 307; *WB 205–206*
unit cube, 259–266, 285–292, 294, 314–316, 318; *WB 187–188*

Whole numbers,
adding, *throughout, see for example,* 42
comparing, 2, 4, 20–23, 36, 39; *WB 11–14*
dividing, *throughout, see for example,* 43; 32, 35
estimating, 3–4, 27–40, 43–44, 46, 61–63, 83–85, 87–89, 116–119; *WB 17–22, 35, 52, 54–55*
expanded form of, 2, 4, 17–19, 36, 38, 42, 44; *WB 8, 10*
multiplying, *throughout, see for example,* 42; 31, 35
place value of, 16–21, 36, 39; *WB 7–10*
reading, **8**, 13
rounding, 3–4, 25–27, 34, 39, 43, 46; *WB 15–16*
standard form of, 2, 4, 6, 7, 10, 12, 14, 36, 38; *WB 1–3, 5–6*
subtracting, *throughout, see for example,* 42
word form of, 2, 4, 6–8, 10, 12–14, 36, 38, 40, 42, 44; *WB 1, 3–6*
writing, 2, 4–10, 12–14, 36, 42, 44; *WB 1–3, 5–6*

Write
algebraic expressions, **224**–226, 228–234, 260; *WB 193–199*
equations, *throughout, see for example,* **226**–228, 235, 238–240, 243, 245 226–228, 235; 152–154, 181–182
inequalities, **242**–244, 251, 254–256, 259, 261; 231–236; *WB 175–178*
ratios, **289**–290, 310, 312, 313
story problems for equations, 254–256, 261

x-axis, **150**–151, 153, 155

x-coordinate, **151**–152

y-axis, **150**–151, 153, 155

y-coordinate, **151**–152

Zero Property,
of multiplication, 217

Zeros (in decimals)
as a place holder, 42–52, 53–61; 96; *WB 21–28*
patterns in the number of, 42–52, 53–61; 96; *WB 21–28*

Photo Credits

cover: ©Houghton Mifflin Harcourt, *5:* ©iStockphoto.com/Thomas Perkins, *6:* ©iStockphoto.com/Jennifer Conner, *9l:* ©iStockphoto.com/Ana Abejon, *9r:* ©iStockphoto.com/Irina Shoyhet, *10:* ©iStockphoto.com/Quavondo, *11l:* ©Dreamstime.com/Erdosain, *11r:* ©iStockphoto.com/Jacom Stephens, *17:* ©iStockphoto.com/Pathathai Chungyam, *20:* ©iStockphoto.com/Jose Manuel Gelpi Diaz, *22t:* ©iStockphoto.com/Jani Bryson, *22b:* ©iStockphoto.com/Ana Abejon, *28:* ©iStockphoto.com/Andrey Shadrin, *33t:* ©iStockphoto.com/Eileen Hart, *33b:* ©iStockphoto.com/Tracy Whiteside, *34:* ©iStockphoto.com/Ana Abejon, *48t:* ©iStockphoto.com/Ana Abejon, *48b:* ©iStockphoto.com/Jennifer Conner, *49:* ©iStockphoto.com/Ana Abejon, *50:* ©iStockphoto.com/Jani Bryson, *51:* ©iStockphoto.com/Andrey Shadrin, *52t:* ©iStockphoto.com/Lisa Howard, *52b:* ©iStockphoto.com/Tracy Whiteside, *53:* ©iStockphoto.com/Quavondo, *54:* ©iStockphoto.com/Jose Manuel Gelpi Diaz, *56t:* ©iStockphoto.com/Pathathai Chungyam, *56b:* ©iStockphoto.com/Andrey Shadrin, *57:* ©iStockphoto.com/Tracy Whiteside, *58l:* ©iStockphoto.com/Ana Abejon, *58r:* ©iStockphoto.com/Lisa Howard, *59:* ©iStockphoto.com/Irina Shoyhet, *61:* ©iStockphoto.com/Tracy Whiteside, *64:* ©iStockphoto.com/Jani Bryson, *65:* ©iStockphoto.com/Tracy Whiteside, *68t:* ©iStockphoto.com/Irina Shoyhet, *68b:* ©iStockphoto.com/Jose Manuel Gelpi Diaz, *69:* ©iStockphoto.com/Jani Bryson, *70:* ©iStockphoto.com/Tracy Whiteside, *71l:* ©iStockphoto.com/Ana Abejon, *71m:* ©iStockphoto.com/Jani Bryson, *71r:* ©iStockphoto.com/Andrey Shadrin, *72:* ©iStockphoto.com/Jennifer Conner, *74t:* ©iStockphoto.com/caracterdesign, *74b:* ©iStockphoto.com/Jose Manuel Gelpi Diaz, *75t:* ©iStockphoto.com/Lisa Howard, *75b:* ©iStockphoto.com/Ana Abejon, *76:* ©iStockphoto.com/Jennifer Conner, *77:* ©iStockphoto.com/Ana Abejon, *79t:* ©iStockphoto.com/Irina Shoyhet, *79b:* ©iStockphoto.com/Andrey Shadrin, *80l:* ©iStockphoto.com/caracterdesign, *80r:* ©iStockphoto.com/Jose Manuel Gelpi Diaz, *81:* ©iStockphoto.com/Eileen Hart, *83:* ©iStockphoto.com/Pathathai Chungyam, *84:* ©iStockphoto.com/Tracy Whiteside, *86:* ©iStockphoto.com/Jacom Stephens, *87t:* ©iStockphoto.com/Jani Bryson, *87m:* ©iStockphoto.com/Tracy Whiteside, *87m:* ©iStockphoto.com/Ana Abejon, *87b:* ©iStockphoto.com/Irina Shoyhet, *88t:* ©iStockphoto.com/Jacom Stephens, *88m:* ©iStockphoto.com/Eileen Hart, *88m:* ©iStockphoto.com/caracterdesign, *88b:* ©iStockphoto.com/Ana Abejon, *89t:* ©iStockphoto.com/Pathathai Chungyam, *89b:* ©iStockphoto.com/Ana Abejon, *90:* ©iStockphoto.com/Jose Manuel Gelpi Diaz, *91:* ©iStockphoto.com/Jani Bryson, *92:* ©iStockphoto.com/Jennifer Conner, *95:* ©iStockphoto.com/caracterdesign, *96:* ©iStockphoto.com/Jani Bryson, *98:* ©iStockphoto.com/Ana Abejon, *104t:* ©iStockphoto.com/Ana Abejon, *104b:* ©iStockphoto.com/Lisa Howard, *105:* ©iStockphoto.com/Ana Abejon, *106t:* ©iStockphoto.com/Jennifer Conner, *106b:* ©Wikimedia Commons/Rudolf Stricker, *107t:* ©iStockphoto.com/Jose Manuel Gelpi Diaz, *107b:* ©iStockphoto.com/caracterdesign, *110t:* ©iStockphoto.com/Jacom Stephens, *110b:* ©iStockphoto.com/Jacom Stephens, *111:* ©iStockphoto.com/Jani Bryson, *112t:* ©iStockphoto.com/Ana Abejon, *112b:* ©iStockphoto.com/Jennifer Conner, *113:* ©iStockphoto.com/Tracy Whiteside, *115:* ©iStockphoto.com/Irina Shoyhet, *121t:* ©Wikimedia Commons/MECU, *121b:* ©Marshall Cavendish Education, *122:* ©Marshall Cavendish Education, *128t:* ©iStockphoto.com/Ana Abejon, *128b:* ©iStockphoto.com/Pathathai Chungyam, *129:* ©iStockphoto.com/caracterdesign, *130:* ©iStockphoto.com/Thomas Perkins, *133t:* ©iStockphoto.com/Jennifer Conner, *133b:* ©iStockphoto.com/Ana Abejon, *134:* ©iStockphoto.com/Pathathai Chungyam, *137ml:* ©Marshall Cavendish Education, *137mr:* ©iStockphoto.com/Andrey Shadrin, *137b:* ©iStockphoto.com/Eileen Hart, *138t:* ©iStockphoto.com/Tracy Whiteside, *138b:* ©iStockphoto.com/Jennifer Conner, *140t:* ©iStockphoto.com/Tracy Whiteside, *140b:* ©iStockphoto.com/Lisa Howard, *146:* ©iStockphoto.com/Eileen Hart, *147:* ©iStockphoto.com/Jennifer Conner, *151:* ©iStockphoto.com/Jani Bryson, *152:* ©iStockphoto.com/Ana Abejon, *156:* ©Wikimedia Commons/Przykuta, *157:* ©Marshall Cavendish Education, *158t:* ©iStockphoto.com/Pathathai

Chungyam, *158b:* ©iStockphoto.com/Ana Abejon, *160:* ©iStockphoto.com/caracterdesign, *161:* ©iStockphoto.com/Tracy Whiteside, *173:* ©iStockphoto.com/Jani Bryson, *177:* ©Marshall Cavendish Education, *178:* ©iStockphoto.com/Jacom Stephens, *179:* ©iStockphoto.com/Pathathai Chungyam, *180:* ©Comstock Klips Photo CD, *181:* ©Comstock Klips Photo CD, *182:* ©iStockphoto.com/Tracy Whiteside, *184:* ©iStockphoto.com/Lisa Howard, *185:* ©iStockphoto.com/Ana Abejon, *187:* ©iStockphoto.com/Jacom Stephens, *190:* ©Marshall Cavendish Education, *192:* ©Marshall Cavendish Education, *193:* ©iStockphoto.com/Jose Manuel Gelpi Diaz, *197:* ©iStockphoto.com/Pathathai Chungyam, *200:* ©iStockphoto.com/Pathathai Chungyam, *201:* ©iStockphoto.com/Lisa Howard, *202:* ©iStockphoto.com/Jacom Stephens, *204:* ©iStockphoto.com/Jani Bryson, *209:* ©Marshall Cavendish Education, *210:* ©iStockphoto.com/Jani Bryson, *211:* ©Marshall Cavendish Education, *220:* ©iStockphoto.com/Irina Shoyhet, *225l:* ©iStockphoto.com/Irina Shoyhet, *225r:* ©iStockphoto.com/Ana Abejon, *227:* ©iStockphoto.com/Lisa Howard, *228l:* ©iStockphoto.com/Jacom Stephens, *228m:* ©iStockphoto.com/Lisa Howard, *228r:* ©iStockphoto.com/Tracy Whiteside, *229:* ©iStockphoto.com/Tracy Whiteside, *230l:* ©iStockphoto.com/Jennifer Conner, *230r:* ©iStockphoto.com/Ana Abejon, *235:* ©Marshall Cavendish Education, *237t:* ©iStockphoto.com/Lisa Howard, *237b:* ©iStockphoto.com/Jennifer Conner, *239:* ©iStockphoto.com/Irina Shoyhet, *244:* ©iStockphoto.com/caracterdesign, *246l:* ©iStockphoto.com/Jacom Stephens, *246r:* ©iStockphoto.com/Lisa Howard, *247:* ©iStockphoto.com/Tracy Whiteside, *248:* ©iStockphoto.com/Ana Abejon, *249t:* ©iStockphoto.com/Pathathai Chungyam, *249b:* ©iStockphoto.com/Tracy Whiteside, *250:* ©iStockphoto.com/Jose Manuel Gelpi Diaz, *251:* ©iStockphoto.com/Ana Abejon, *269:* ©iStockphoto.com/Jose Manuel Gelpi Diaz, *271l:* ©Dreamstime.com/Ivonne Wierink, *271m:* ©Dreamstime.com/Photoeuphoria, *272:* ©iStockphoto.com/Irina Shoyhet, *276:* ©iStockphoto.com/Tracy Whiteside, *277:* ©iStockphoto.com/Jose Manuel Gelpi Diaz, *278:* ©iStockphoto.com/Ana Abejon, *289tl:* ©Comstock Klips Photo CD, *289tr:* ©Wikimedia Commons/17Drew, *289bl:* ©iStockphoto.com/Jose Manuel Gelpi Diaz, *289br:* ©iStockphoto.com/Pathathai Chungyam, *290t:* ©iStockphoto.com/Andrey Shadrin, *290b:* ©iStockphoto.com/Thomas Perkins, *291t:* ©iStockphoto.com/Ana Abejon, *291m:* ©iStockphoto.com/Jani Bryson, *291bl:* ©Marshall Cavendish Education, *291br:* ©iStockphoto.com/Ana Abejon, *292t:* ©iStockphoto.com/Irina Shoyhet, *292b:* ©iStockphoto.com/Tracy Whiteside, *293:* ©iStockphoto.com/Jani Bryson, *294:* ©Marshall Cavendish Education, *295:* ©Marshall Cavendish Education, *296t:* ©Comstock Klips Photo CD, *296t:* ©Marshall Cavendish Education, *296m:* ©Marshall Cavendish Education, *296b:* ©iStockphoto.com/Jacom Stephens, *297t:* ©Marshall Cavendish Education, *297ml:* ©Marshall Cavendish Education, *297mr:* ©iStockphoto.com/Tracy Whiteside, *298:* ©Marshall Cavendish Education, *299t:* ©iStockphoto.com/Quavondo, *299m:* ©iStockphoto.com/Andrey Shadrin, *299m:* ©iStockphoto.com/Irina Shoyhet, *299b:* ©iStockphoto.com/Ana Abejon, *300tl:* ©iStockphoto.com/Lisa Howard, *300tr:* ©iStockphoto.com/Ana Abejon, *300bl:* ©iStockphoto.com/caracterdesign, *300br:* ©iStockphoto.com/Tracy Whiteside, *303t:* ©iStockphoto.com/Jani Bryson, *303b:* ©iStockphoto.com/Pathathai Chungyam, *304:* ©iStockphoto.com/Lisa Howard, *307:* ©iStockphoto.com/Andrey Shadrin, *308:* ©iStockphoto.com/Jennifer Conner, *313:* ©iStockphoto.com/Jani Bryson, *316t:* ©iStockphoto.com/Jennifer Conner, *316b:* ©Marshall Cavendish Education, *317t:* ©iStockphoto.com/Jose Manuel Gelpi Diaz, *317m:* ©iStockphoto.com/Ana Abejon, *317b:* ©iStockphoto.com/caracterdesign, *318:* ©iStockphoto.com/Jacom Stephens, *319t:* ©iStockphoto.com/Irina Shoyhet, *319b:* ©iStockphoto.com/Jani Bryson, *322:* ©Marshall Cavendish Education, *323t:* ©iStockphoto.com/Quavondo, *323b:* ©iStockphoto.com/Ana Abejon, *327:* ©morgueFile.com/mconnors, *328:* ©iStockphoto.com/Ana Abejon, *329:* ©Marshall Cavendish Education, *331:* ©Marshall Cavendish Education, *332l:* ©Houghton Mifflin Harcourt, *332r:* ©iStockphoto.com/Tracy Whiteside, *340:* ©Marshall Cavendish Education

COMMON CORE STATE STANDARDS FOR MATHEMATICAL CONTENT		
STANDARD	**DESCRIPTOR**	**PAGE CITATIONS**
5.OA OPERATIONS AND ALGEBRAIC THINKING		
Write and interpret numerical expressions.		
5.OA.1	Use parentheses, brackets, or braces in numerical expressions, and evaluate expressions with these symbols.	SE-5A: 68–72, 86–93, 94–101, 102–114, 115, 216–219, 224–234, 242–251, 252–257
5.OA.2	Write simple expressions that record calculations with numbers, and interpret numerical expressions without evaluating them.	SE-5A: 94–101, 102–114, 115, 224–234, 257
Analyze patterns and relationships.		
5.OA.3	Generate two numerical patterns using two given rules. Identify apparent relationships between corresponding terms. Form ordered pairs consisting of corresponding terms from the two patterns, and graph the ordered pairs on a coordinate plane.	SE-5A: 216–219 SE-5B: 158–163
5.NBT NUMBER AND OPERATIONS IN BASE TEN		
Understand the place value system.		
5.NBT.1	Recognize that in a multi-digit number, a digit in one place represents 10 times as much as it represents in the place to its right and 1/10 of what it represents in the place to its left.	SE-5A: 5–15, 16–19, 20–24, 51–63, 74–85 SE-5B: 7–17, 18–22, 23–25, 36–42, 43–52, 53–61, 62–69
5.NBT.2	Explain patterns in the number of zeros of the product when multiplying a number by powers of 10, and explain patterns in the placement of the decimal point when a decimal is multiplied or divided by a power of 10. Use whole-number exponents to denote powers of 10.	SE-5A: 51–63, 64–67, 68–73 SE-5B: 30–35, 43–52, 62–69
5.NBT.3	Read, write, and compare decimals to thousandths.	
5.NBT.3.a	Read and write decimals to thousandths using base-ten numerals, number names, and expanded form, e.g., 347.392 = 3 × 100 + 4 × 10 + 7 × 1 + 3 × (1/10) + 9 × (1/100) + 2 × (1/1000).	SE-5B: 7–17, 23–25

COMMON CORE STATE STANDARDS FOR MATHEMATICAL CONTENT		
STANDARD	**DESCRIPTOR**	**PAGE CITATIONS**
5.NBT.3.b	Compare two decimals to thousandths based on meanings of the digits in each place, using >, =, and < symbols to record the results of comparisons.	SE-5B: 18–22
5.NBT.4	Use place value understanding to round decimals to any place.	SE-5B: 1–6, 18–22, 53–61, 70–76, 89–94
Perform operations with multi-digit whole numbers and with decimals to hundredths.		
5.NBT.5	Fluently multiply multi-digit whole numbers using the standard algorithm.	SE-5A: 47–50, 51–63, 68–72, 102–114, 115 SE-5B: 277–284
5.NBT.6	Find whole-number quotients of whole numbers with up to four-digit dividends and two-digit divisors, using strategies based on place value, the properties of operations, and/or the relationship between multiplication and division. Illustrate and explain the calculation by using equations, rectangular arrays, and/or area models.	SE-5A: 47–50, 74–85, 86–93, 102–114
5.NBT.7	Add, subtract, multiply, and divide decimals to hundredths, using concrete models or drawings and strategies based on place value, properties of operations, and/or the relationship between addition and subtraction; relate the strategy to a written method and explain the reasoning used.	SE-5B: 7–17, 30–35, 36–42, 43–52, 53–61, 62–69, 70–76, 89–94
5.NF NUMBER AND OPERATIONS – FRACTIONS		
Use equivalent fractions as a strategy to add and subtract fractions.		
5.NF.1	Add and subtract fractions with unlike denominators (including mixed numbers) by replacing given fractions with equivalent fractions in such a way as to produce an equivalent sum or difference of fractions with like denominators.	SE-5A: 120–127, 128–132, 133–136, 146–150, 151–155, 156–160

COMMON CORE STATE STANDARDS FOR MATHEMATICAL CONTENT		
STANDARD	**DESCRIPTOR**	**PAGE CITATIONS**
5.NF.2	Solve word problems involving addition and subtraction of fractions referring to the same whole, including cases of unlike denominators, e.g., by using visual fraction models or equations to represent the problem. Use benchmark fractions and number sense of fractions to estimate mentally and assess the reasonableness of answers.	SE-5A: 128–132, 133–136, 156–160
Apply and extend previous understandings of multiplication and division to multiply and divide fractions.		
5.NF.3	Interpret a fraction as division of the numerator by the denominator (a/b = a ÷ b). Solve word problems involving division of whole numbers leading to answers in the form of fractions or mixed numbers, e.g., by using visual fraction models or equations to represent the problem.	SE-5A: 137–142, 143–145
5.NF.4	Apply and extend previous understandings of multiplication to multiply a fraction or whole number by a fraction.	
5.NF.4.a	Interpret the product (a/b) × q as a parts of a partition of q into b equal parts; equivalently, as the result of a sequence of operations a × q ÷ b.	SE-5A: 172–175, 176–181, 182–183, 189–192
5.NF.4.b	Find the area of a rectangle with fractional side lengths by tiling it with unit squares of the appropriate unit fraction side lengths, and show that the area is the same as would be found by multiplying the side lengths. Multiply fractional side lengths to find areas of rectangles, and represent fraction products as rectangular areas.	SE-5A: 172–175, 182–183, 267–270
Perform operations with multi-digit whole numbers and with decimals to hundredths.		
5.NF.5	Interpret multiplication as scaling (resizing), by:	
5.NF.5.a	Comparing the size of a product to the size of one factor on the basis of the size of the other factor, without performing the indicated multiplication.	SE-5A: 184–188, 296–302, 316–321, 322–331
5.NF.5.b	Explaining why multiplying a given number by a fraction greater than 1 results in a product greater than the given number (recognizing multiplication by whole numbers greater than 1 as a familiar case); explaining why multiplying a given number by a fraction less than 1 results in a product smaller than the given number; and relating the principle of fraction equivalence a/b = (n×a)/(n×b) to the effect of multiplying a/b by 1.	SE-5A: 184–188

COMMON CORE STATE STANDARDS FOR MATHEMATICAL CONTENT		
STANDARD	**DESCRIPTOR**	**PAGE CITATIONS**
5.NF.6	Solve real world problems involving multiplication of fractions and mixed numbers, e.g., by using visual fraction models or equations to represent the problem.	SE-5A: 176–181, 184–188, 189–192, 200–210, 211
5.NF.7	Apply and extend previous understandings of division to divide unit fractions by whole numbers and whole numbers by unit fractions.	
5.NF.7.a	Interpret division of a unit fraction by a non-zero whole number, and compute such quotients.	SE-5A: 193–199, 200–210
5.NF.7.b	Interpret division of a whole number by a unit fraction, and compute such quotients.	SE-5A: 193–199
5.NF.7.c	Solve real world problems involving division of unit fractions by non-zero whole numbers and division of whole numbers by unit fractions, e.g., by using visual fraction models and equations to represent the problem.	SE-5A: 193–199, 200–210
4.MD MEASUREMENT AND DATA		
Convert like measurement units within a given measurement system.		
5.MD.1	Convert among different-sized standard measurement units within a given measurement system (e.g., convert 5 cm to 0.05 m), and use these conversions in solving multi-step, real world problems.	SE-5B: 77–88, 150–157, 256–258, 296–309
Represent and interpret data.		
5.MD.2	Make a line plot to display a data set of measurements in fractions of a unit (1/2, 1/4, 1/8). Use operations on fractions for this grade to solve problems involving information presented in line plots.	SE-5B: 139–142, 169–177
Geometric measurement: understand concepts of volume and relate volume to multiplication and to addition.		
5.MD.3	Recognize volume as an attribute of solid figures and understand concepts of volume measurement.	SE-5B: 285–295, 296–309
5.MD.3.a	A cube with side length 1 unit, called a "unit cube," is said to have "one cubic unit" of volume, and can be used to measure volume.	SE-5B: 285–295, 296–309
5.MD.3.b	A solid figure which can be packed without gaps or overlaps using n unit cubes is said to have a volume of n cubic units.	SE-5B: 285–295, 296–309
5.MD.4	Measure volumes by counting unit cubes, using cubic cm, cubic in, cubic ft, and improvised units.	SE-5B: 285–295, 296–309
5.MD.5	Relate volume to the operations of multiplication and addition and solve real world and mathematical problems involving volume.	

COMMON CORE STATE STANDARDS FOR MATHEMATICAL CONTENT		
STANDARD	**DESCRIPTOR**	**PAGE CITATIONS**
5.MD.5.a	Find the volume of a right rectangular prism with whole-number side lengths by packing it with unit cubes, and show that the volume is the same as would be found by multiplying the edge lengths, equivalently by multiplying the height by the area of the base. Represent threefold whole-number products as volumes, e.g., to represent the associative property of multiplication.	SE-5B: 285–295, 296–309
5.MD.5.b	Apply the formulas V = l × w × h and V = b × h for rectangular prisms to find volumes of right rectangular prisms with whole-number edge lengths in the context of solving real world and mathematical problems.	SE-5B: 296–309
5.MD.5.c	Recognize volume as additive. Find volumes of solid figures composed of two non-overlapping right rectangular prisms by adding the volumes of the non-overlapping parts, applying this technique to solve real world problems.	SE-5B: 310–314
5.G GEOMETRY		
Graph points on the coordinate plane to solve real-world and mathematical problems.		
5.G.1	Use a pair of perpendicular number lines, called axes, to define a coordinate system, with the intersection of the lines (the origin) arranged to coincide with the 0 on each line and a given point in the plane located by using an ordered pair of numbers, called its coordinates. Understand that the first number indicates how far to travel from the origin in the direction of one axis, and the second number indicates how far to travel in the direction of the second axis, with the convention that the names of the two axes and the coordinates correspond (e.g., x-axis and x-coordinate, y-axis and y-coordinate).	SE-5B: 150–157
5.G.2	Represent real world and mathematical problems by graphing points in the first quadrant of the coordinate plane, and interpret coordinate values of points in the context of the situation.	SE-5B: 150–157
Classify two-dimensional figures into categories based on their properties.		
5.G.3	Understand that attributes belonging to a category of two-dimensional figures also belong to all subcategories of that category.	SE-5A: 276–282 SE-5B: 212–216, 221–230, 237–249
5.G.4	Classify two-dimensional figures in a hierarchy based on properties.	SE-5A: 276–282 SE-5B: 212–216, 221–230, 237–249

COMMON CORE STATE STANDARDS FOR MATHEMATICAL PRACTICE

STANDARDS	PAGE CITATIONS
1. MAKE SENSE OF PROBLEMS AND PERSEVERE IN SOLVING THEM.	
How *Math in Focus*® Aligns: ***Math in Focus*®** is built around the Singapore Ministry of Education's mathematics framework pentagon, which places mathematical problem solving at the core of the curriculum. Encircling the pentagon are the skills and knowledge needed to develop successful problem solvers, with concepts, skills, and processes building a foundation for attitudes and metacognition. ***Math in Focus*®** is based on the premise that in order for students to persevere and solve both routine and non-routine problems, they need to be given tools that they can use consistently and successfully. They need to understand both the how and the why of math so that they can self-monitor and become empowered problem solvers. This in turn spurs positive attitudes that allow students to solidify their learning and enjoy mathematics. ***Math in Focus*®** teaches content through a problem solving perspective. Strong emphasis is placed on the concrete-to-pictorial-to-abstract progress to solve and master problems. This leads to strong conceptual understanding. Problem solving is embedded throughout the program.	*For example:* SE-5A: 5–15, 25–35, 74–85, 94–101, 102–114, 115, 128–132, 133–136, 156–160, 161, 176–181, 189–192, 193–199, 200–210, 224–234, 242–251, 252–257, 276–282, 303–309, 310–315, 322–331 SE-5B: 23–25, 53–61, 62–69, 70–76, 89–94, 95, 123–130, 169–177, 178, 189–194, 200–204, 221–230, 237–249, 259–262, 277–284, 296–309
2. REASON ABSTRACTLY AND QUANTITATIVELY.	
How *Math in Focus*® Aligns: ***Math in Focus*®** concrete-pictorial-abstract progression helps students effectively contextualize and decontextualize situations by developing a deep mastery of concepts. Each topic is approached with the expectation that students will understand both how it works, and also why. Students start by experiencing the concept through hands-on manipulative use. Then, they must translate what they learned in the concrete stage into a visual representation of the concept. Finally, once they have gained astrong understanding, they are able to represent the concept abstractly. Once students reach the abstract stage, they have had enough exposure to the concept and they are able to manipulate it and apply it in multiple contexts. They are also able to extend and make inferences; this prepares them for success in more advanced levels of mathematics. They are able to both use the symbols and also understand why they work, which allows students to relate them to other situations and apply them effectively.	*For example:* SE-5A: 25–35, 68–72, 102–114, 115, 128–132, 133–136, 137–142, 143–145, 151–155, 161, 176–181, 182–183, 200–210, 242–251, 252–257, 276–282, 332 SE-5B: 70–76, 95, 139–142, 143–149, 150–157, 158–163, 169–177, 178, 189–194, 195–199, 200–204, 217–220, 221–230, 237–249
3. CONSTRUCT VIABLE ARGUMENTS AND CRITIQUE THE REASONING OF OTHERS.	
How *Math in Focus*® Aligns: As seen on the Singapore Mathematics Framework pentagon, metacognition is a foundational part of the Singapore curriculum. Students are taught to self-monitor, so they can determine whether or not their solutions make sense. Journal questions and other opportunities to explain their thinking are found throughout the program. Students are systematically taught to use visual diagrams to represent mathematical relationships in such a way as to not only accurately solve problems, but also to justify their answers. Chapters conclude with a Put on Your Thinking Cap! problem. This is a comprehensive opportunity for students to apply concepts and present viable arguments. Games, explorations, and hands-on activities are also strategically placed in chapters when students are learning concepts. During these collaborative experiences, students interact with one another to construct viable arguments and critique the reasoning of others in a constructive manner. In addition, thought bubbles provide tutorial guidance throughout the entire Student Book. These scaffolded dialogues help students articulate concepts, check for understanding, analyze, justify conclusions, and self-regulate if necessary.	*For example:* SE-5A: 5–15, 74–85, 94–101, 115, 128–132, 133–136, 146–150, 172–175, 184–188, 224–234, 276–282, 310–315, 322–331 SE-5B: 62–69, 169–177, 221–230, 259–262, 277–284

COMMON CORE STATE STANDARDS FOR MATHEMATICAL PRACTICE

STANDARDS	PAGE CITATIONS
4. MODEL WITH MATHEMATICS.	
How *Math in Focus*® Aligns: ***Math in Focus*®** follows a concrete-pictorial-abstract progression, introducing concepts first with physical manipulatives or objects, then moving to pictorial representation, and finally on to abstract symbols. A number of models are found throughout the program that support the pictorial stage of learning. ***Math in Focus*®** places a strong emphasis on number and number relationships, using place-value manipulatives and place-value charts to model concepts consistently throughout the program. In all grades, operations are modeled with place-value materials so students understand how the standard algorithms work. Even the mental math instruction uses understanding of place value to model how mental arithmetic can be understood and done. These place-value models build throughout the program to cover increasingly complex concepts. Singapore Math® is also known for its use of model drawing, often called "bar modeling" in the U.S. Model drawing is a systematic method of representing word problems and number relationships that is explicitly taught beginning in Grade 2 and extends all the way to secondary school. Students are taught to use rectangular "bars" to represent the relationship between known and unknown numerical quantities and to solve problems related to these quantities. This gives students the tools to develop mastery and tackle problems as they become increasingly more complex.	*For example:* SE-5A: 47–50, 51–63, 74–85, 102–114, 137–142, 143–145, 146–150, 151–155, 161, 172–175, 182–183, 193–199, 200–210, 224–234, 235–241, 267–270, 271–275, 276–282, 296–302, 316–321, 332 SE–5B: 36–42, 43–52, 53–61, 62–69, 77–88, 139–142, 143–149, 150–157, 158–163, 164–168, 178, 189–194, 195–199, 200–204, 231–236, 237–249, 259–262, 263–266, 285–295, 310–314
5. USE APPROPRIATE TOOLS STRATEGICALLY.	
How *Math in Focus*® Aligns: ***Math in Focus*®** helps students explore the different mathematical tools that are available to them. New concepts are introduced using concrete objects, which help students break down concepts to develop mastery. They learn how to use these manipulatives to attain a better understanding of the problem and solve it appropriately. ***Math in Focus*®** includes representative pictures and icons as well as thought bubbles that model the thought processes students should use with the tools. Several examples are listed below. Additional tools referenced and used in the program include clocks, money, dot paper, place-value charts, geometric tools, and figures.	*For example:* SE-5A: 47–50, 51–63, 74–85, 102–114 SE–5B: 95, 189–194, 195–199, 200–204
6. ATTEND TO PRECISION.	
How *Math in Focus*® Aligns: As seen in the Singapore Mathematics Framework, metacognition, or the ability to monitor one's own thinking, is key in Singapore Math®. This is modeled for students throughout ***Math in Focus*®** through the use of thought bubbles, journal writing, and prompts to explain reasoning. When students are taught to monitor their own thinking, they are better able to attend to precision, as they consistently ask themselves, "does this make sense?" This questioning requires students to be able to understand and explain their reasoning to others, as well as catch mistakes early on and identify when incorrect labels or units have been used. Additionally, precise language is an important aspect of ***Math in Focus*®**. Students attend to the precision of language with terms like factor, quotient, difference, and capacity.	*For example:* SE-5A: 5–15, 47–50, 51–63, 74–85, 94–101, 128–132, 133–136, 137–142, 143–145, 146–150, 151–155, 161, 172–175, 184–188, 193–199, 224–234, 235–241, 271–275, 276–282, 296–302, 310–315, 316–321, 322–331, 332 SE-5B: 7–17, 36–42, 43–52, 62–69, 77–88, 89–94, 111–115, 116–122, 123–130, 143–149, 150–157, 164–168, 169–177, 189–194, 195–199, 200–204, 221–230, 231–236, 237–249, 259–262, 277–284, 285–295, 310–314

COMMON CORE STATE STANDARDS FOR MATHEMATICAL PRACTICE

STANDARDS	PAGE CITATIONS
7. LOOK FOR AND MAKE USE OF STRUCTURE.	
How *Math in Focus*® Aligns: The inherent pedagogy of Singapore Math® allows students to look for, and make use of, structure. Place value is one of the underlying principles in ***Math in Focus***®. Concepts in the program start simple and grow in complexity throughout the chapter, year, and grade. This helps students master the structure of a given skill, see its utility, and advance to higher levels. Many of the models in the program, particularly number bonds and bar models, allow students to easily see patterns within concepts and make inferences. As students progress through grade levels, this level of structure becomes more advanced.	*For example:* SE-5A: 94–101, 102–114, 115, 156–160, 184–188, 189–192, 193–199, 235–241, 267–270 SE-5B: 77–88, 89–94
8. LOOK FOR AND EXPRESS REGULARITY IN REPEATED REASONING.	
How *Math in Focus*® Aligns: A strong foundation in place value, combined with modeling tools such as bar modeling and number bonds, gives students the foundation they need to look for and express regularity in repeated reasoning. Operations are taught with place value materials so students understand how the standard algorithms work in all grades. Even the mental math instruction uses understanding of place value to model how mental arithmetic can be understood and done. This allows students to learn shortcuts for solving problems and understand why they work. Additionally, because students are given consistent tools for solving problems, they have the opportunity to see the similarities in how different problems are solved and understand efficient means for solving them. Throughout the program, students see regularity with the reasoning and patterns between the four key operations. Students continually evaluate the reasonableness of solutions throughout the program; the consistent models for solving, checking, and self-regulation help them validate their answers.	*For example:* SE-5A: 25–35, 51–63, 64–67, 74–85, 94–101, 102–114, 184–188, 200–210, 216–219, 267–270, 276–282 SE-5B: 18–22, 43–52, 158–163, 310–314